Itō Hirobumi – Japan's First Prime Minister and Father of the Meiji Constitution

A brilliant and influential statesman and the first Prime Minister of Japan's modern state, Itō Hirobumi (1841–1909) has been poorly understood. This biography attempts to set the record straight about his thought and vision for Japan's modernization based on research in primary sources. It outlines Itō's life: the son of a poor farmer, he showed exceptional talent as a boy and was sent to study in Europe and the United States. He returned home convinced that Western civilization was the only viable path for Japan. Following the Meiji Restoration of 1868, Itō became a powerful intellectual and political force behind the reform of Japanese laws and institutions aimed at shaping a modern government based on informed leadership and a knowledgeable populace. Among his many achievements were the establishment of Japan's first constitution—the Meiji Constitution of 1889—and the founding in 1900 of a new type of constitutional party, the Rikken Seiyūkai (Friends of Constitutional Government), which, reformulated after 1945, became the Liberal Democratic Party that has dominated Japanese politics in the postwar period. Concerning Itō's role as Japanese Resident-General in Korea from 1905, the author argues that Itō's aim, not understood by either the Japanese home government or the Koreans themselves, was not to colonize Korea. He was determined to modernize Korea and consolidate further constitutional reforms in Japan. This aim was not shared by others, and Itō resigned in 1909. He was assassinated the same year in Manchuria by a Korean nationalist. The Japanese language edition of this book is a bestseller in Japan and it has received the Suntory Prize for Social Sciences and Humanities, one of Japan's most prestigious publishing awards.

Takii Kazuhiro is a Professor at the International Research Center for Japanese Studies, Kyoto, Japan.

Routledge Studies in the Modern History of Asia

1 **The Police in Occupation Japan**
Control, corruption and resistance to reform
Christopher Aldous

2 **Chinese Workers**
A new history
Jackie Sheehan

3 **The Aftermath of Partition in South Asia**
Tai Yong Tan and Gyanesh Kudaisya

4 **The Australia–Japan Political Alignment**
1952 to the present
Alan Rix

5 **Japan and Singapore in the World Economy**
Japan's economic advance into Singapore, 1870–1965
Shimizu Hiroshi and Hirakawa Hitoshi

6 **The Triads as Business**
Yiu Kong Chu

7 **Contemporary Taiwanese Cultural Nationalism**
A-chin Hsiau

8 **Religion and Nationalism in India**
The case of the Punjab
Harnik Deol

9 **Japanese Industrialisation**
Historical and cultural perspectives
Ian Inkster

10 **War and Nationalism in China**
1925–1945
Hans J. van de Ven

11 **Hong Kong in Transition**
One country, two systems
Edited by Robert Ash, Peter Ferdinand, Brian Hook and Robin Porter

12 **Japan's Postwar Economic Recovery and Anglo-Japanese Relations, 1948–1962**
Noriko Yokoi

13 **Japanese Army Stragglers and Memories of the War in Japan, 1950–1975**
Beatrice Trefalt

14 **Ending the Vietnam War**
The Vietnamese communists' perspective
Ang Cheng Guan

15 **The Development of the Japanese Nursing Profession**
Adopting and adapting Western influences
Aya Takahashi

16 **Women's Suffrage in Asia**
Gender nationalism and democracy
Louise Edwards and Mina Roces

17 **The Anglo-Japanese Alliance, 1902–1922**
Phillips Payson O'Brien

18 **The United States and Cambodia, 1870–1969**
From curiosity to confrontation
Kenton Clymer

19 **Capitalist Restructuring and the Pacific Rim**
Ravi Arvind Palat

20 **The United States and Cambodia, 1969–2000**
A troubled relationship
Kenton Clymer

21 **British Business in Post-Colonial Malaysia, 1957–70**
'Neo-colonialism' or 'disengagement'?
Nicholas J. White

22 **The Rise and Decline of Thai Absolutism**
Kullada Kesboonchoo Mead

23 **Russian Views of Japan, 1792–1913**
An anthology of travel writing
David N. Wells

24 **The Internment of Western Civilians under the Japanese, 1941–1945**
A patchwork of internment
Bernice Archer

25 **The British Empire and Tibet**
1900–1922
Wendy Palace

26 **Nationalism in Southeast Asia**
If the people are with us
Nicholas Tarling

27 **Women, Work and the Japanese Economic Miracle**
The case of the cotton textile industry, 1945–1975
Helen Macnaughtan

28 **A Colonial Economy in Crisis**
Burma's rice cultivators and the world depression of the 1930s
Ian Brown

29 **A Vietnamese Royal Exile in Japan**
Prince Cuong De (1882–1951)
Tran My-Van

30 **Corruption and Good Governance in Asia**
Nicholas Tarling

31 **US–China Cold War Collaboration, 1971–1989**
S. Mahmud Ali

32 **Rural Economic Development in Japan**
From the nineteenth century to the Pacific War
Penelope Francks

33 **Colonial Armies in Southeast Asia**
Edited by Karl Hack and Tobias Rettig

34 **Intra Asian Trade and the World Market**
A. J. H. Latham and Heita Kawakatsu

35 **Japanese–German Relations, 1895–1945**
War, diplomacy and public opinion
Edited by Christian W. Spang and Rolf-Harald Wippich

36 **Britain's Imperial Cornerstone in China**
The Chinese maritime customs service, 1854–1949
Donna Brunero

37 **Colonial Cambodia's 'Bad Frenchmen'**
The rise of French rule and the life of Thomas Caraman, 1840–1887
Gregor Muller

38 **Japanese–American Civilian Prisoner Exchanges and Detention Camps, 1941–45**
Bruce Elleman

39 **Regionalism in Southeast Asia**
Nicholas Tarling

40 **Changing Visions of East Asia, 1943–93**
Transformations and continuities
R. B. Smith, edited by Chad J. Mitcham

41 **Christian Heretics in Late Imperial China**
Christian inculturation and state control, 1720–1850
Lars P. Laamann

42 **Beijing – A Concise History**
Stephen G. Haw

43 **The Impact of the Russo-Japanese War**
Edited by Rotem Kowner

44 **Business–Government Relations in Prewar Japan**
Peter von Staden

45 **India's Princely States**
People, princes and colonialism
Edited by Waltraud Ernst and Biswamoy Pati

46 **Rethinking Gandhi and Nonviolent Relationality**
Global perspectives
Edited by Debjani Ganguly and John Docker

47 **The Quest for Gentility in China**
Negotiations beyond gender and class
Edited by Daria Berg and Chloë Starr

48 **Forgotten Captives in Japanese Occupied Asia**
Edited by Kevin Blackburn and Karl Hack

49 **Japanese Diplomacy in the 1950s**
From isolation to integration
Edited by Iokibe Makoto, Caroline Rose, Tomaru Junko and John Weste

50 **The Limits of British Colonial Control in South Asia**
Spaces of disorder in the Indian Ocean region
Edited by Ashwini Tambe and Harald Fischer-Tiné

51 **On The Borders of State Power**
Frontiers in the greater Mekong sub-region
Edited by Martin Gainsborough

52 **Pre-Communist Indochina**
R. B. Smith, edited by Beryl Williams

53 **Port Cities in Asia and Europe**
Edited by Arndt Graf and Chua Beng Huat

54 **Moscow and the Emergence of Communist Power in China, 1925–30**
The Nanchang Rising and the birth of the Red Army
Bruce A. Elleman

55 **Colonialism, Violence and Muslims in Southeast Asia**
The Maria Hertogh controversy and its aftermath
Syed Muhd Khairudin Aljunied

56 **Japanese and Hong Kong Film Industries**
Understanding the origins of East Asian film networks
Kinnia Shuk-ting

57 **Provincial Life and the Military in Imperial Japan**
The phantom samurai
Stewart Lone

58 **Southeast Asia and the Vietnam War**
Ang Cheng Guan

59 **Southeast Asia and the Great Powers**
Nicholas Tarling

60 **The Cold War and National Assertion in Southeast Asia**
Britain, the United States and Burma, 1948–1962
Matthew Foley

61 **The International History of East Asia, 1900–1968**
Trade, ideology and the quest for order
Edited by Antony Best

62 **Journalism and Politics in Indonesia**
A critical biography of Mochtar Lubis (1922–2004) as editor and author
David T. Hill

63 **Atrocity and American Military Justice in Southeast Asia**
Trial by army
Louise Barnett

64 **The Japanese Occupation of Borneo, 1941–1945**
Ooi Keat Gin

65 **National Pasts in Europe and East Asia**
P. W. Preston

66 **Modern China's Ethnic Frontiers**
A journey to the West
Hsiao-ting Lin

67 **New Perspectives on the History and Historiography of Southeast Asia**
Continuing explorations
Michael Aung-Thwin and Kenneth R. Hall

68 **Food Culture in Colonial Asia**
A taste of empire
Cecilia Leong-Salobir

69 **China's Political Economy in Modern Times**
Changes and economic consequences, 1800–2000
Kent Deng

70 **Science, Public Health and the State in Modern Asia**
Edited by Liping Bu, Darwin Stapleton and Ka-che Yip

71 **Russo-Japanese Relations, 1905–1917**
From enemies to allies
Peter Berton

72 **Reforming Public Health in Occupied Japan, 1945–52**
Alien prescriptions?
Christopher Aldous and Akihito Suzuki

73 **Trans-Colonial Modernities in South Asia**
Edited by Michael S. Dodson and Brian A. Hatcher

74 **The Evolution of the Japanese Developmental State**
Institutions locked in by ideas
Hironori Sasada

75 **Status and Security in Southeast Asian States**
Nicholas Tarling

76 **Lee Kuan Yew's Strategic Thought**
Ang Cheng Guan

77 **Government, Imperialism and Nationalism in China**
The Maritime Customs Service and its Chinese staff
Chihyun Chang

78 **China and Japan in the Russian Imagination, 1685–1922**
To the Ends of the Orient
Susanna Soojung Lim

79 **Chinese Complaint Systems**
Natural resistance
Qiang Fang

80 **Martial Arts and the Body Politic in Meiji Japan**
Denis Gainty

81 **Gambling, the State and Society in Thailand, c.1800–1945**
James A. Warren

82 **Post-war Borneo, 1945–50**
Nationalism, empire and state-building
Ooi Keat Gin

83 **China and the First Vietnam War, 1947–54**
Laura M. Calkins

84 **The Jesuit Missions to China and Peru, 1570–1610**
Ana Carolina Hosne

85 **Macao – Cultural Interaction and Literary Representations**
Edited by Katrine K. Wong and C. X. George Wei

86 **Macao – The Formation of a Global City**
Edited by C. X. George Wei

87 **Women in Modern Burma**
Tharaphi Than

88 **Museums in China**
Materialized power and objectified identities
Tracey L.-D. Lu

89 **Transcultural Encounters between Germany and India**
Kindred spirits in the 19th and 20th centuries
Edited by Joanne Miyang Cho, Eric Kurlander and Douglas T. McGetchin

90 **The Philosophy of Japanese Wartime Resistance**
A reading, with commentary, of the complete texts of the Kyoto School discussions of "The Standpoint of World History and Japan"
David Williams

91 **A History of Alcohol and Drugs in Modern South Asia**
Intoxicating affairs
Edited by Harald Fischer-Tiné and Jana Tschurenev

92 **Military Force and Elite Power in the Formation of Modern China**
Edward A. McCord

93 **Japan's Household Registration System and Citizenship**
Koseki, identification and documentation
Edited by David Chapman and Karl Jakob Krogness

94 **Itō Hirobumi – Japan's First Prime Minister and Father of the Meiji Constitution**
Kazuhiro Takii

Nichibunken Monograph Series No. 16

Itō Hirobumi – Japan's First Prime Minister and Father of the Meiji Constitution

Takii Kazuhiro

Translated by Takechi Manabu
Edited by Patricia Murray

International Research Center
for Japanese Studies
Kyoto

LONDON AND NEW YORK

First edition published as *Itō Hirobumi: Chi no seijika* © 2010 Takii Kazuhiro
by Chūō Kōron Shinsha

This English translation published 2014
by Routledge
2 Park Square, Milton Park, Abingdon, Oxon, OX14 4RN

and by Routledge
711 Third Avenue, New York, NY 10017

In association with
International Research Center for Japanese Studies (Nichibunken)
3-2 Oeyama-cho, Goryo
Nishikyo-ku, Kyoto 610-1192
Japan

Routledge is an imprint of the Taylor & Francis Group, an informa business

© 2014 Takii Kazuhiro
The right of Takii Kazuhiro to be identified as author of this work has been asserted by him in accordance with the Copyright, Designs and Patents Act 1988.

All rights reserved. No part of this book may be reprinted or reproduced or utilised in any form or by any electronic, mechanical, or other means, now known or hereafter invented, including photocopying and recording, or in any information storage or retrieval system, without permission in writing from the publishers.

Trademark notice: Product or corporate names may be trademarks or registered trademarks, and are used only for identification and explanation without intent to infringe.

British Library Cataloguing in Publication Data
A catalogue record for this book is available from the British Library

Library of Congress Cataloging in Publication Data
A catalog record has been requested for this book

ISBN: 978-0-415-83886-3 (hbk)
ISBN: 978-1-315-81897-9 (ebk)

Typeset in Times New Roman
by Sunrise Setting Ltd, Paignton, UK

Routledge Studies in the Modern History of Asia Series
and
Nichibunken Monograph Series No. 16, Series Editor: Patricia Fister

Printed and bound in the United States of America by Publishers Graphics, LLC on sustainably sourced paper.

Contents

List of illustrations — xi
Preface to the English edition — xiii

Introduction — 1
Previous scholarship on Itō Hirobumi 2
Itō in Shiba's historical fiction 4
Reconsideration based on the latest research 5

1 **Encounter with Western civilization** — 7
   Early years 7
   Institutions and the West 16
   The Iwakura Mission and shift to gradualism 23

2 **A constitution for Japan: building the foundation** — 37
   Moving toward constitutional government: 1873–80 37
   The Political Crisis of 1881 43
   Constitutional study tour in Europe 47
   Education and knowledge in constitutional government 51
   Enactment of the Constitution and party government:
      Itō's speeches 61
   Constitutional government as popular government:
      Itō's address to royalty and peers 66

3 **Itō the constitutional evangelist** — 75
   All things change: Itō's worldview 75
   Nationwide campaign: stumping for the Constitution 81
   Treaty revision and a new status in the world 89
   Implanting the idea of popular government 93
   Educating the people in practical science 95
   Personal experience 97

4 Creating a society for knowledge: the Seiyūkai — 101
From oligarch to party politician 101
Constitutional government and party-led government 106
Forming the Seiyūkai 110
From "faction" to "society" 116
The party as think-tank 122

5 Consolidating the national structure: the Constitutional Reforms of 1907 — 127
Seiyūkai setback 127
The Imperial Household Research Committee and constitutional reform 135
Constitutional reforms of 1907 (1): integrating the emperor into the state 138
Constitutional reforms of 1907 (2): responsible government and control over the military 143
Itō Hirobumi's idea of the nation 152

6 Itō and China — 158
Two months in Korea and China 158
Lessons of the 1898 coup in China 163
Meeting with Zhang Zhidong 166
Views on China and plans for Japan 173
Hands off political change in China 178

7 Fostering governance in two countries — 183
Itō's dual role and the resident-generalship 183
The showdown with Confucian tradition 190
Governing Korea and military reforms in Japan: extension of constitutional reform 201
The breakdown of Korean rule 208

Afterword — 217

References 222
Chronology 236
Index 245

Illustrations

1.1	Yoshida Shōin (1830–59)	9
1.2	The "Chōshū Five" smuggled out of Japan to study in Britain. From left: Inoue Kaoru, Endō Kinsuke, Nomura Yakichi, Yamao Yōzō, and Itō Hirobumi	12
1.3	Inoue Kaoru (1836–1915)	13
1.4	Members of the Iwakura Mission in San Francisco. From left: Kido Takayoshi, Yamaguchi Naoyoshi, Iwakura Tomomi, Itō Hirobumi, and Ōkubo Toshimichi	23
1.5	Iwakura Tomomi (1825–83)	25
1.6	Ōkubo Toshimichi (1830–78)	27
1.7	Kido Takayoshi (1833–77)	29
2.1	Ōkuma Shigenobu (1838–1922)	44
2.2	Inoue Kowashi (1844–95)	45
2.3	Itō Hirobumi in Europe in 1883	47
2.4	Kuroda Kiyotaka (1840–1900)	63
3.1	Itō Miyoji (1857–1934)	79
3.2	Yamagata Aritomo (1838–1922)	83
3.3	Itinerary for the tour of western Japan	85
3.4	Itinerary for the tour of Hokuriku region	87
4.1	Caricature of political figures on nationwide electoral campaign. From right: Itagaki, Itō, and Ōkuma. *Jiji shinpō*, May 24, 1899	103
4.2	Hoshi Tōru (1850–1901)	105
4.3	Shibusawa Eiichi (1840–1931)	112
4.4	Iwasaki Yanosuke (1851–1908)	113
4.5	Group celebrates the new Seiyūkai (1900). Itō (front row, tenth from right) with main party members	116
5.1	Hara Takashi (1856–1921)	130
5.2	Katsura Tarō (1848–1913)	133
5.3	Ariga Nagao (1860–1921)	139
5.4	Itō (left) with Yamagata Aritomo	151
6.1	Emperor Gojong (1852–1919)	159

xii *Illustrations*

6.2	Zhang Zhidong (1837–1909)	169
7.1	Saionji Kinmochi (1849–1940)	203
7.2	Terauchi Masatake (1852–1919)	204
7.3	Itō Hirobumi with Korean Crown Prince Yi Un, 1908	212
8.1	Fukuzawa Yukichi (1835–1901)	218

Preface to the English edition

This book is an English translation of my third monograph *Itō Hirobumi: Chi no seijika* (Chūō Kōron Shinsha, 2010), and is the second one to be published in English after *Meiji Constitution* (International House of Japan, 2007). The Japanese version of *Itō Hirobumi* was awarded the Suntory Prize for Social Sciences and Humanities and it was also selected as one of the top paperback books in the 2011 Shinsho Prize competition.[1] It is my great pleasure to present this volume to anglophonic readers who are interested not only in modern Japanese history, but also in themes such as "what is politics?" or "what is a constitution?"

Itō Hirobumi (1841–1909) was the first prime minister of Japan's modern state and without question one of the most famous political figures in Japanese history. Noteworthy among Itō's achievements are the establishment of the Constitution of the Empire of Japan (Meiji Constitution; promulgated in 1889) and the founding in 1900 of the political party Rikken Seiyūkai (Friends of Constitutional Government).[2] Under Itō's strong leadership, these two accomplishments represented two critical milestones in the establishment of parliamentary democracy in Japan, and yet his contributions have not been adequately recognized. Drawing on primary historical sources that so far have been given little attention, I have boldly attempted to rewrite the conventional image of Itō Hirobumi, presenting a new image of Itō as a principle-driven, thoroughly professional statesman.

It is my hope that the English version of my book will enable readers in many countries to reconsider the historical significance of Itō Hirobumi as a pioneering constitutional leader in East Asia, and to take a fresh look at the significance in Asia of Japan's strides in modernization. Amid the turmoil of political change in the world today, the debate about political leadership will greatly benefit from this account of the challenges Itō faced and the vision he hoped would triumph in his own era. For nations seeking to develop a future order for East Asia and further the course of their own state-building, as well as for the people and organizations supporting such endeavors, the story of how Itō, with his cosmopolitan perspective and ideal of a modern state, set about to modernize his own developing country (Japan) and foster stability in the East Asian region offers many valuable lessons.

I have received a great deal of assistance and advice from many colleagues in bringing the English version of my book to fruition. Among them, I would like to thank Dr. Antony Best, Senior Lecturer in International History at the London School of Economics, for recommending my book to Routledge. I am grateful to Peter Sowden, editor of Asian books at Routledge, for recognizing the merits of my research and for overseeing the negotiations to co-publish it with the International Research Center for Japanese Studies (Nichibunken).

I would especially like to thank veteran translator, Takechi Manabu, of the Center for Intercultural Communication (CIC) for his careful and well-researched translation, Patricia Murray for her editing of the translation, and Lynne E. Riggs who provided editorial suggestions that helped to shape the final manuscript. Finally I owe a special debt to my colleague Patricia Fister, Professor and Editor of the Nichibunken Monograph Series, for without her dedicated supervision this publication could not have been realized. She was assisted in many ways by Shiraishi Eri, managing editor of publications at Nichibunken. With their help, I am hopeful that my work will contribute to international research on Itō Hirobumi.

Takii Kazuhiro
Nishinomiya
May 2013

Editorial note: Japanese names in this book are given in customary order, surname first. Japanese publishers are located in Tokyo unless otherwise stated.

Notes

1 For this competition, professionals in the publishing industry select, by vote, the twenty best books from among all the new *shinsho* paperbacks published during the previous year.
2 The Rikken Seiyūkai is the forerunner of today's Liberal Democratic party, which became Japan's largest political party after World War II and has held a nearly continuous grip on power since 1955.

Introduction

> Anyone who dares to institute a people must feel capable of, so to speak, changing human nature.
>
> Rousseau[1]

Japan's National Diet building has three statues of Itō Hirobumi. One is located in a corner of the Diet building's central hall inside the main entrance. There, the bronze statue of Itō overlooks the hall along with those of two other leaders of Meiji (1868–1912) era Japan, Ōkuma Shigenobu and Itagaki Taisuke. They occupy three of the pedestals standing at the four corners of the hall.

One pedestal is empty, and there are a number of theories as to why. Some say it turned out to be impossible to agree on a fourth figure, others believe the vacant pedestal represents the incompleteness of government. Still others propose that it is a message encouraging Diet members to work hard, in the hope that their own image might one day be placed in the hall in the company of their distinguished predecessors.

A second statue of Itō stands immediately outside the Diet building, in the front courtyard of the House of Councilors. An impressive eleven-meter-tall work, it was erected in 1936 by the Shunpo-kō Tsuishōkai, a society organized in 1933 to honor the achievements of Itō, whose alias was Prince Shunpo (Spring Field). Initially the statue stood in the outer garden of the Diet building, and the area around it was known as Prince Itō Memorial Park. Later donated to the then House of Peers, it was moved to the area within its grounds.

Where is the third statue? Actually it is something of a phantom. It must be imagined, atop the tower of the Diet building. The tower, explains architectural historian Suzuki Hiroyuki, is modeled after the large podium that once supported a bronze statue of Itō placed in Ōkurayama Park in Kobe in 1911, soon after Itō's death.[2] The statue itself was later removed and added to the obligatory supply of metal donated to the government during World War II, but the podium, designed by architect Takeda Goichi, the first professor in the Department of Architecture, College of Engineering at Kyoto Imperial University, remains in the park. Among Takeda's students was Yoshitake Tōri, one of the designers of the Diet building completed in 1936. When Yoshitake set about studying the history of the Imperial

Diet, he undoubtedly grasped the major role that Itō Hirobumi had played in Japan's decision in the late nineteenth century to institute a parliamentary system. During research on historic sites related to Itō, Yoshitake learned about the statue in Ōkurayama Park and realized that its podium had been designed by none other than his own teacher—Takeda. A replica of that podium, he thought, would be the perfect crown for the new Diet building. And that is how the design of the tower atop the Diet building came into being. In Yoshitake's imagination, writes Suzuki, the figure of Itō Hirobumi stands atop the tower. So Yoshitake must have thought of the Diet building as a memorial to Itō. The imagined statue of Itō, writes Suzuki, "must have been meant to remind the representatives gathered in the Diet of the way their great forefather devoted his life to running the national government—a *memento mori* on a national scale."[3]

So the Diet has three Itō statues, including one that must be imagined. There may not be many buildings housing a nation's legislative body that have more than one statue of the same individual. Also noteworthy is the fact that Prince Itō Memorial Park and the statue erected there were officially unveiled on the day celebrating the completion of the Diet building we see today.[4] It is as though the statue had been built as part of a set with the Diet building.

Whatever the case, it is true that parliamentary government in modern Japan and the name of Itō Hirobumi are inseparable. As he pursued the history of the Diet, Yoshitake must have encountered the presence of Itō at every turn. It is quite possible that his design was intentionally contrived so as to crown the Diet building with the imaginary figure, that is to say the spirit, of Itō Hirobumi.

Previous scholarship on Itō Hirobumi

No discussion of the birth of Japan's modern government can proceed without taking into account the statesman Itō Hirobumi, father of the Meiji Constitution and Japan's parliament, and the nation's first prime minister. In his final years he served as the first resident-general (1905–1909) in Korea, then a Japanese protectorate, and to many he symbolizes imperialist Japan's annexation of Korea (1910). Representing the new generation that came after the three great leaders of the Meiji Restoration of 1868—Kido Takayoshi (Kōin), Ōkubo Toshimichi, and Saigō Takamori—he is among the best known figures of the Meiji era.

Japanese scholars, for the most part, have tended to dismiss Itō's achievements in building Japan's modern state. Nagao Ryūichi, a scholar of the philosophy of law with deep insight into history, writes as follows:

> In the popular historical mind, the figure that looms largest in establishing the Meiji Constitution is Itō Hirobumi, political groundbreaker who studied constitutional law in Germany in 1882–83 and went on to draft Japan's first constitution. Scholars of history, however, regard that view as uninformed amateurism misled by Itō's dashing but superficial performance. The real architect of the Meiji Constitution, they argue, is Inoue Kowashi. They credit Inoue with working behind the scenes to engineer the so-called political

change of 1881, when advocates of a British-style constitution were overcome and the adoption of a constitution on the German [Prussian] model was assured. Thereupon, they point out, Inoue prepared the constitution draft and after its enactment wrote the authoritative commentary on it (*Kenpō gikai*, published under the name of Itō Hirobumi).⁵

There is often a large gap between how widely known a person is and the significance accorded to him or her by scholars. Itō Hirobumi is such a person—he is a popular figure, much more highly esteemed by the general public than by historians. Scholars may regard the "great man" view of Itō with professional scorn, but many historians seem at a loss as to decide just how they should indeed regard him. The following exchange between Banno Junji, a leading authority on modern Japanese history, and historical novelist and essayist Shiba Ryōtarō, illustrates this puzzlement and lack of agreement:

BANNO: When I write about Meiji history, I can never get a clear image of Itō Hirobumi; with his constant shifting between starkly opposing positions, I just don't understand him.
SHIBA: That's exactly why he was a great statesman. He was flexibility itself.⁶

Even the expert Banno, one of the most knowledgeable scholars of the period, openly admits that a clear grasp of Itō eludes him. A few years after this dialogue with Shiba, in a conversation with Nagao Ryūichi, Banno observed:

> The man Itō Hirobumi was like a white canvas. He was very good at spotting trends and would side with whoever represented a major trend. At one time it was Ōkubo Toshimichi, at another Inoue Kowashi, and so on; he moved freely to align himself with the person of the moment. He even joined hands with the Liberal party. That's why I can't write about him. I could if it were Inoue [Kaoru]. He was consistent, sticking to his pursuit of a moderate British-style parliamentary cabinet system, "democratization from above," and so forth. Ōkuma Shigenobu underwent an ideological conversion, and that was because he had something to say. Itō was incapable of making an ideological change like that.⁷

Here too, Banno admits how perplexing he found Itō. Let me briefly explain what Banno saw when he considered Itō's career. After the Satsuma Rebellion of 1877, Itō was ready and willing to support Ōkubo Toshimichi in the latter's attempt to consolidate his control of government and to establish "development dictatorship." Then, facing the rising momentum of a political movement for constitutional government after Ōkubo's assassination, Itō sided with Inoue Kowashi in his drive to institute a Prussian-style monarchical constitution and non-party cabinet, and later Itō garnered credit as the central figure in establishing the Meiji Constitution. After the opening of the first parliament, furthermore,

Itō refashioned himself into a strong supporter of party government. He aligned himself with his erstwhile enemy, the popular rights-championing and then largest opposition party—the Liberal party. He ended up organizing the Rikken Seiyūkai (Friends of Constitutional Government) as the successor to the Liberal party. It is that lack of consistency—the chameleon-like changes made with the shifting trends of the times—that so irritate and frustrate Banno.

Itō in Shiba's historical fiction

The world of historical fiction treats Itō little better than does the academic community. In his dialogue with Banno, Shiba Ryōtarō described Itō as "flexibility itself." How, then, does he present Itō in his fiction? In *Tobu ga gotoku*, the widely read historical novel about Saigō Takamori (the model for the main character in the film *Last Samurai*), Shiba says,

> Itō lacked the statesman's philosophy that Saigō or Kido [Takayoshi] had, which gave him that much less appeal both to the people of his time and to subsequent generations. But, in politics, that fearsome battleground of clashing powers, Itō's very lack of a philosophy only served to make him a more skilled strategist than either Saigō or Kido.[8]

Shiba is saying loud and clear that here is a political tactician without a philosophy, a realist without guiding ideas, and, he goes on, "A dedicated realist in politics can never be more than a second- or third-rate politician." Moreover, "The quality of a statesman is determined by the ideals he has." But then Shiba confounds us by writing, "Itō always reconciled his ideals with reality," a statement that seems to undercut what he said in the excerpt above. What did Shiba mean by "reconciling his ideals with reality"? What were Itō's "ideals"? Shiba's pen went silent on that subject. Obviously Itō was as enigmatic to Shiba as he was to Banno. At least Banno's, "I just don't understand him" must have struck a chord with Shiba.

Itō turns out to be an elusive figure in the eyes of both the professional historian and the writer of serious historical fiction, yet his was an image that appears to have been ambiguous to many even when he was alive. Numerous contemporary accounts relate how dumbfounded or indignant people would become in watching Itō maneuver in politics—not blinking an eye as he moved from oligarch in the *hanbatsu* government (political control by former Chōshū and Satsuma domain members) to involvement in party politics, to a seat on the Privy Council, and also to advisor to the imperial court. He showed little apparent hesitation in aligning himself with people like Ōkuma Shigenobu, Mutsu Munemitsu, Hoshi Tōru, all of them yesterday's foes. Emperor Meiji (1852–1912) reportedly saw through Itō's capricious behavior, saying, "Itō has wit and intelligence but frequently changes his mind. He won't stick to anything long."[9]

Contemporary witnesses to Itō's indecisiveness, and a please-all approach that sometimes extended even to his foes, are legion. Among them was Shinagawa

Yajirō (1843–1900), the home minister known for his suppression of popular rights groups during the early years of the parliamentary system, most notably the harsh police action he employed to intervene in the second House of Representatives election of 1892. At the 5th Diet session, then roiling over the issue of unequal treaties, Shinagawa, discontented with Itō's flexible opportunism, urged the latter to take a firm, non-conciliatory approach like his own and move decisively against the opposition. "Count Itō is obsessed with having things go smoothly," Shinagawa complained. "He refuses to set a firm policy in advance; instead he insists on always going with the tide."[10]

Reconsideration based on the latest research

The driving force behind the recent reconsideration of Itō Hirobumi is a series of studies by historian and Kyoto University professor Itō Yukio. These studies (Itō Yukio 1999, 2000, 2009) persuasively show that within Itō Hirobumi's actions and words, which may have seemed unanchored and constantly fluctuating amid the political turmoil going on around him, there was a farsighted plan for state management rooted in strong, consistent convictions and aiming at the establishment of an enduring constitutional state. Professor Itō takes an empirical approach to political and diplomatic history, making extensive use of primary sources.

Anglophile scholarship on Itō Hirobumi got a head start with University of Hawai'i professor George Akita's 1967 work, *Foundations of Constitutional Government in Modern Japan 1868–1900* (Harvard University Press), which described how Japan's parliamentary system was established under Itō Hirobumi's political leadership. In the four decades since the appearance of Akita's pioneering work, many new primary sources have naturally come to light and conditions for research have greatly improved, making the time now ripe for a fresh portrayal of this important historical figure. The strength of the focus on Itō in *Foundations of Constitutional Government* is on Itō mainly as a pioneer of party government, and the book does not attempt to examine Itō's political and constitutional thought or reassess his rule in Korea from 1905 to 1909.

My own study pays close attention to Itō Hirobumi's grand design in building a constitutional state (as suggested by Professor Itō) in order to elucidate the ideas behind it. As Itō Yukio's research indicates, a clear and consistent idea of what Japan's constitutional state should be was embedded in Itō Hirobumi's mind and it informed his activities in public life.

Encouraged by a surge of interest today among scholars in re-examining Itō's thinking and career, I set out here to interpret him in a fresh light, drawing on the achievements of recent research. To present his thinking as a statesman, a dimension that has received comparatively less attention so far, I have taken as themes the three core principles that guided Itō: civilization, the constitutional state, and popular government. Observing Western society and civilization firsthand when he was young, Itō became committed early on to building Japan into a nation modeled after the West. The "civilized" state he envisioned was categorically a constitutional state, one that would provide the vehicle for popular government and would ultimately be a political system centered on the people. In Itō's vision, the "people" were educated and civilized citizens, bearers of knowledge. In establishing the Meiji Constitution, and through the subsequent working of constitutional government, he attempted to shape the Meiji state around these core principles. The ultimate form of the state, in his view, was what could be called the "knowledge-based state," one that is governed by laws deriving from knowledge and experience and by leaders conversant in the knowledge required for good governance. This is why I have described Itō as a "statesman of knowledge."

Believing that it is high time that the entrenched image among scholars of Itō as an unprincipled opportunist was re-examined, I have focused on the philosophical dimension of his life as a statesman. With the hope that I have convincingly presented this image of Itō in the pages that follow, I will begin by looking at his activities during the last years of the Tokugawa shogunate (founded in 1615 and abolished in 1868) and the beginning of the Meiji era. Then we will go on to examine the budding ideas informing those three principles that governed Itō's political career.

Notes

1 From Jean Jacques Rousseau, *The Social Contract and Other Later Political Writings*, Victor Gourevitch, trans. (Cambridge University Press, 1997), p. 69.
2 Suzuki 1999.
3 Ibid., p. 26.
4 Three short-lived Diet buildings were built prior to 1936. The first was completed in 1890 but burned down the following year. The second was quickly erected within the year, but it also burned to ashes in 1925. The third was hastily finished to open in time for a regular session of the Diet late the same year.
5 Nagao 2000, p. 91.
6 Shiba and Banno 1995, pp. 35–6.
7 Ōishi *et al.* 1998.
8 Shiba 2002, vol. 2, p. 278.
9 Tsuda 1970, p. 745.
10 Takahashi 1976, vol. 2, p. 43.

1 Encounter with Western civilization

Early years

On October 16, 1841 (2nd day of the 9th month, Tenpō 12), Itō Hirobumi was born to Hayashi Jōzō and his wife Kotoko in the village of Tsukari in Kumage county, Suō province (now Hikari city, Yamaguchi prefecture). His childhood name was Risuke. They were a farming family, but to support the household his father served a man named Itō in the castle town of Hagi. When Hirobumi was still very young, his whole family was adopted into and given the name of the Itō family. After the adoption, Hayashi Risuke's name was changed to Itō Risuke, and later to Itō Shunsuke (1858) and then to Hirobumi (around 1869). Becoming part of the Itō family brought them into the samurai class, albeit at the bottom level. The head of the adoptive Itō family was Naoemon, a low-ranking retainer (*chūgen*) of the Chōshū domain. The categorization of families immediately following the 1868 Meiji Restoration identified low-ranking families like the Itōs as "sotsuzoku" as distinct from other former samurai houses known as "shizoku."

Yoshida Shōin and Shōka Sonjuku

In 1856 (Ansei 3), Itō Hirobumi was sent by the Chōshū domain to Sagami province on guard duty at Edo Bay (now Tokyo Bay). There, in the second month of 1857 (Ansei 4), Kuruhara Ryōzō (1829–62) was assigned to head the guard at Sagami. A younger brother-in-law of Kido Takayoshi (Kōin; 1833–77), one of the leading figures in the Meiji Restoration, Kuruhara liked Itō and took good care of him, and the encounter was to greatly influence Itō's career.

A letter home affords a glimpse into Itō as a knowledge-hungry teenager with high aspirations. He wrote, "Kuruhara Ryōzō-sama, my superior, has been introducing me to some reading matter and I have been working particularly hard these days."[1] A smile-provoking passage at the end of the letter reads:

> This is a personal thing, but I am embarrassed that my clothes have become too small. Please tell this to Grandma [Itō's adoptive grandmother] and Mother. I am also a big eater, another embarrassment. I'm afraid both of these make me a laughing stock.[2]

In the ninth month of the same year, Itō was released from his assignment and he returned to Chōshū carrying a letter of introduction to the scholar, political reformer, and activist Yoshida Torajirō (1830–59; widely known as Shōin, one of his literary names), written by Kuruhara. In Hagi, Itō visited Shōin and requested that he be allowed to study under the great teacher at his private academy, Shōka Sonjuku ("village school under the pines"). Some time after he was admitted, Itō wrote to a friend with whom he probably became acquainted while on guard duty in Sagami province. The two apparently had trained together under Kuruhara. Vividly expressing the intellectual excitement he felt about his studies and all around him at the academy during his early days there, Itō wrote,

> Literature is flourishing here. There is no one who is not always reading something. All of Matsumoto village is alive with our academy Shōka Sonjuku. We students read day and night. I urge you, too, to keep reading and studying. I don't for a moment think you are neglecting your studies, but I do believe it is very important.[3]

Shōka Sonjuku was a tiny private academy far from Kyoto or Edo, but it produced many of the determined and capable activists (later known as *shishi*) who became major players in the last days of the Tokugawa shogunate and the restoration of the emperor to the center of government. Among them were Kusaka Genzui (1840–64), Takasugi Shinsaku (1839–67), Maebara Issei (1834–76), Yamagata Aritomo (1838–1922), and also Itō Hirobumi. What kind of relationship did Itō have with his teacher Shōin? We can begin to formulate an answer by considering the death of Shōin, who was eventually imprisoned for treason, taken to Edo, and executed in the Ansei Purge of 1858. Itō happened to be in Edo as an attendant to Kido Takayoshi. It was Itō, Kido, and a few others who retrieved Yoshida Shōin's body and gave him a proper funeral.

One can imagine the shock experienced by the young and sensitive Itō upon learning of the execution and seeing the dead and cold headless body of the teacher he had respected so deeply. From that point, working behind the scenes, he became deeply involved in the movement fired by Chōshū activists to forcibly rid Japan of the presence of Western powers and overthrow the shogunate. He had a part in an abortive attempt in 1862 to assassinate Nagai Uta (1819–63), a high-ranking Chōshū official.[4] Late that year a band of activists organized by Takasugi Shinsaku burned the British legation then under construction at Goten'yama in Shinagawa, Edo. Itō took part in that act of arson, and a few days later, together with Yamao Yōzō (1837–1917),[5] he assassinated Japanese classics scholar Hanawa Jirō Tadatomi (1808–62), son of the eminent scholar Hanawa Hokiichi, believing a false report that Hanawa was seeking ancient precedents for dethroning an emperor. Among all the prime ministers of Japan, Itō is the only one known to have killed a person outside the battlefield (except Kuroda Kiyotaka [1840–1900], who was rumored to have beaten his wife while drunk, resulting in her death).

Figure 1.1 Yoshida Shōin (1830–59).
Source: Photograph courtesy of the National Diet Library of Japan.

Teacher and student: mutual admiration

For a period following Shōin's death, Itō was unmistakably a terrorist. Fueling his acts of violence was the *sonnō jōi* ideology—"Revere the emperor, expel the barbarians [Westerners]"—preached by Shōin during the years prior to his early death. This was an exhortation to overthrow the shogunate by force. The leaders of the Chōshū domain would have none of it, and so Shōin turned to dissident, out-of-power sympathizers to build a movement that he believed would rise like a flood tide for revolution. This, Shōin eagerly hoped, would be the grassroots uprising ("sōmō kukki") that would turn the tide. Itō was right there in the thick of the movement. Yet, there was a vast difference in temperament between teacher and student. Even while he sympathized with Shōin's ideology, Itō kept a discreet distance from his teacher while the latter was alive.

Shōin described Itō as a "shūsenka," a negotiator.[6] He also said about Itō, "He is of a petty official rank but enjoys himself with his colleagues. He is not very talented and is slow in learning. But he is serious-minded and modest. I like this very much."[7] Shōin saw Itō as a diligent and cheerful student and an untalented, simple, and honest son of a low-ranking foot soldier. As suggested by this appraisal, Shōin might have thought Itō able to become a competent bureaucrat skilled at negotiating. He most likely did not consider Itō capable of leading the management of the state.

How did Itō remember his teacher? In his later years he described Shōin as being "in no way an advocate either of expelling Western influences or overthrowing the shogunate," but, Itō said, "He was extreme. He sometimes did things at his own discretion without realizing the real intentions of the Chōshū government, thus getting the government into trouble." Shōin was like "the head of a political party today," Itō observed, and added that the anti-Western "expel-the-barbarians ideology of those days was entirely emotional; it had nothing to do with thoughtful political calculations."[8]

In the same account Itō commended Nagai Uta (in whose abortive assassination plot he himself had taken part all those years before) for his sharp insights:

> Nagai believed Japan should be unified at all costs. Regardless of whether it opened its doors or kept them closed, the nation first needed to unite the imperial court and the shogunate and then decide which way to go. Otherwise Japan would never be either a genuinely open or genuinely closed country. In any case, Nagai's primary objective was to bring together all of Japan as a nation."

Itō concluded that Nagai "saw through things very clearly for a man of those days.[9] Itō saw in Nagai a man whose "political strategy" was decisively informed by level-headed deliberation on the future of Japan, and he found more sympathy with this than with the radical idealism of Shōin. These recollections are clear testimony to the character of Itō as a statesman. It is safe to say that, as in his commendation of Nagai, what Itō meant by "political strategy" was not clever tactical maneuvering but thoughtful consideration of policy. Itō was a thinker who, while keeping to his political ideals, worked tirelessly to reconcile the competing interests of the various forces in play in his time and took pains to ensure that nothing he ever did or said could be construed as coming from irrational idealism. In that sense, Itō and Shōin were of two entirely different minds that could not possibly understand each other. Itō began to truly find himself only after he had broken free of Shōin's influence.

Smuggled out to Britain

Having been introduced to the world of learning by Kuruhara and Shōin, Itō was eager for more. His next big step was to somehow get to Britain, but anti-Western feeling in Japan was at a peak and the official policy of seclusion was still in effect, so leaving the country involved subterfuge. One such project underway in the Chōshū domain was a secret plan to send retainers to study in the West. Sufu Masanosuke (1823–64), a high official in the domain government, believed their objective was to prepare the country:

> I think Chōshū needs tools. By "tools" I mean human tools. Considering all that is happening in our country today, many domains are actively

supporting the movement to restore the emperor to the seat of government and exclude Westerners from the land, but much of that activity is just a show of the valor of Japan. The day is sure to come when there will be active interaction among countries. When that time comes, if we still know little of things Western then our country will be at a serious disadvantage. In order to prepare the tools we need to use on that day, I want to send Nomura Yakichi and Yamao Yōzō to Britain.[10]

Ordered by the domain leaders to become human "tools," prepared to absorb and understand Western civilization, a total of five young men from Chōshū were selected and sent to Britain in violation of the national isolationist laws, which made their journey illegal. The other three, besides Nomura and Yamao mentioned above, were Inoue Kaoru (1836–1915), Endō Kinsuke (1836–93), and Itō Hirobumi. At one time Yoshida Shōin himself boarded one of Commodore Perry's ships anchored at Uraga in Edo Bay in an unsuccessful attempt to persuade the commodore to take him to America. Like Shōin, Sufu and many others who spouted anti-Western ideology were not interested so much in routing Western influence out of Japan as they were in searching for ways to enable the country to take its place in the world by learning and mastering as much as they could about the West. For those who made it abroad in those days, the excitement of seeing more of the world was just as exhilarating as the fiery drive to get the better of the Westerners and push them out of Japan. From early on, Itō had expressed a wish to study abroad. In a letter to Kuruhara, written in early 1861, Itō said he had nursed "the ambition to study in Britain since last year," and in another letter written to a friend the following year he wrote, "I am determined to go to Britain."[11]

Itō's long-cherished ambition materialized when, on June 27, 1863 (12th day of the 5th month, Bunkyū 3) he and Inoue quietly left the country. In a letter to his father just before he left, Itō tried to explain why he was going abroad:

> Today there is a pressing need to learn about everything in that country [Britain] and to master naval technology; otherwise there is no hope for us. It is with those thoughts that I go to carry out my tasks, for three years only, before returning home.[12]

After more than four months of travel by ship, Itō and Inoue arrived in London on November 4 (23rd day of the 9th month). They were reunited with Nomura, Endō, and Yamao, who had arrived earlier, and the five young retainers of the Chōshū domain launched Japan's very first study-abroad program in the West. They are now known as the Chōshū Five, and their story is a popular subject in the history of the last years of the shogunate. A stone monument honoring their legacy stands in the courtyard of University College London, where the Chōshū Five began their studies.

Endō, Yamao, and Nomura stayed on in Britain to receive full-fledged training in technology for several more years. Each one in his own distinctive way contributed greatly to transforming Japan into a modern state. Yamao promoted

Figure 1.2 The "Chōshū Five" smuggled out of Japan to study in Britain. From left: Inoue Kaoru, Endō Kinsuke, Nomura Yakichi, Yamao Yōzō, and Itō Hirobumi.

Source: Chūō Kōron Shinsha, p. 9.

education in engineering as the minister of public works and laid the foundations for the education of children with disabilities. Endō became a finance ministry official, and as director of the Imperial Mint played the leading role in establishing a modern monetary system. Nomura Masaru (previously Yakichi; 1843–1910) served as director general of the Railway Agency, heading the construction of the country's rail network beginning with the first line that ran from Shimbashi in Tokyo

Figure 1.3 Inoue Kaoru (1836–1915).
Source: Photograph courtesy of the National Diet Library of Japan.

to Yokohama and including the Kyoto–Ōtsu line, the latter built entirely by Japanese without any Western participation.

The other two, Inoue and Itō, made far greater contributions to the country's modernization as *genrō* (elder statesmen). One day in Britain, both were shocked to read in *The Times* that Chōshū domain cannons had fired on Western vessels in the Shimonoseki strait in late June, as well as about the exchange of cannon fire between the Satsuma domain and a British naval squadron in mid-August. The two men decided to return home to persuade the domain leaders that any attempt to expel the foreigners was totally useless. Instead of the three years Itō had mentioned in the letter to his father, he stayed in Britain only half a year.

Itō's advent as a negotiator

Itō's study abroad was thus suddenly cut very short. The lack of records on his activities during that brief stay makes it difficult to determine the significance of his first overseas sojourn. Nonetheless, it is clear that his trip abroad was a major turning point in Itō's life in several regards.

First of all, coming home when they did (July 13, 1864) turned out to be very fortunate. Itō and Inoue returned "from the West" in the midst of a national crisis, and their experience abroad made them valuable. They were allowed to offer their opinions directly not only to high-ranking domain officials but to the lord of their Chōshū domain himself, urging that the exclusion policy be abandoned. Such special treatment was extraordinary for a person of lowly birth like Itō. He and Inoue failed to persuade the domain to change policy, but subsequent events proved how badly new expertise was needed. The domain was defeated when the joint naval forces of Britain, France, the Netherlands, and the United States occupied its Shimonoseki battery, and it became painfully clear to its leaders how vital was the knowledge that Itō and Inoue had acquired. Within the domain, Itō used his personal experience of the West to advocate opening the country, and in dealings with the four Western powers, he was directly involved in peace negotiations. His reputation soared within the domain government. If he had not come home at that point, but had stayed on studying in Britain, he most likely would have ended up being a mere, if competent, technocrat. His sudden and fortuitous return led to the flowering of his talent as a negotiator, as Yoshida Shōin had foreseen.

Learning English

Another outcome of Itō's sojourn in Britain was more predictable—his acquisition of English language skills. He had been interested in the language and the country of Britain from early on, and as a young man trying to rise above the social class of his birth by mastering new knowledge, he burned with the desire to know more about the wide world and its peoples lying out there before his eyes, even as the anti-Western storm swirled around him. Once Kuruhara and Shōin had lit the spark in Itō, it was inevitable that one day he would go to the West and learn all he possibly could. After their arrival in London, the Chōshū Five obtained lodgings at the house of Alexander Williamson (1824–1904), professor of chemistry at University College, through the good offices of Hugh Matheson (1796–1878), president of Jardine Matheson & Co., which held a monopoly on Britain's Far Eastern trade. Under Williamson they studied English and learned Western manners.

In the end, Itō and Inoue remained only six months, so it is not clear how much English they learned during such a short time. Yet Itō must have gotten somewhat used to communicating in English, for, upon returning home, he acted as the chief intermediary in peace negotiations between his domain and the Western powers after the battles of Shimonoseki.

In the winter of 1871, when Itō revisited the West as deputy ambassador of the Iwakura Mission, he made a speech in English on behalf of mission leader Iwakura Tomomi (1825–83) at a welcome party in San Francisco. It is also recorded that he took advantage of his linguistic ability to enjoy American nightlife while in the United States.[13] Perhaps this came from his inborn fearlessness, but, more to the point, he was not excessively impressed or awed by the civilization and people of the West. He had a sangfroid that presumably resulted from his first trip to Britain.

Itō's English in practice

How good was Itō's actual command of English? One account is found in the papers of the above-mentioned Alexander Williamson, including excerpts from Mrs. Williamson's diary, which contains this passage: "Ito wrote to me from Provost Rd where he, Nomura and Endo were left for Xmas with my eldest brother Tom."[14]

That Itō sent a letter to Mrs. Williamson on this occasion suggests not only friendly relations between Itō and the Williamsons, but also an ability to actively use English. There are accounts by his Japanese contemporaries that make fun of his broken English, but many Europeans and Americans who met him praised his use of the language. Prior to the Iwakura Mission's departure from Japan, a banquet was held at the British legation attended by members of the mission. Later, in a report sent to London, Francis Ottiwell Adams (1825–89), secretary of the British legation in Tokyo, wrote that Itō's English was fluent, and added that Itō was thought to be "a clever useful fellow, but easily got hold of by foreigners not always of the best class." Adams must have been a keen observer.[15]

Itō himself seemed proud of his English. A regular customer at Maruzen, one of Japan's first enterprises to import Western books and magazines, he always looked forward to purchasing the latest English publications. In a horse-drawn carriage, on his way to work, he would read the English books and newspapers he had just bought. To some people it came across as pompous posing and others thought he was showing off and found it embarrassing, but Itō was, it seems, not just showing off. While riding with him in a carriage one day, Tokutomi Sohō (1863–1957), a well-known journalist, learned from Itō about the publication of *Resurrection* by Leo Tolstoy, Sohō's favorite author. It is also said that Itō lent Tsuda Umeko (1864–1929), who became a leader of education for women and founder of Tsuda College, a copy of the English edition of Alexis de Tocqueville's (1805–59) *De la démocratie en Amérique* (Democracy in America). "This book is one of the best accounts of the United States," he said as he gave it to her.

Itō often gave exclusive interviews with representatives of the Western media. As his reputation grew in Europe and the United States he became the best-known Japanese statesman at that time. By the 1880s they had dubbed him (somewhat misleadingly) the "Bismarck of Japan."[16] That reputation grew out of Itō's frequent interaction with reporters, when, it seems, he often answered questions without an interpreter. He not only spoke English, but also wrote it well enough, as in the letter to Mrs. Williamson. Judging from the letters Itō wrote, which are found today in archives in Europe and the United States, he wrote numerous letters in English throughout his adult life to scholars, statesmen, and many others in several countries. Some of them I have discovered myself.[17] He expresses himself honestly and clearly in an easy-to-read style without complex turns of phrase, giving the impression that his English skills were quite solid.

Impact of Britain on Itō's character

Beginning with his first trip to Britain in 1863, Itō became a rarity in his time—a Japanese statesman competent in English. There he learned basic English reading, writing, and speaking, but more importantly, he became able to see Westerners as people—no different from those around him back in Japan. In these and other ways, his time in England built on his Chōshū upbringing and education and helped him build character and grow into the person he would become. His education at Yoshida Shōin's academy, in particular, taught him that social class was relative—no matter what class one is born into, a person can always acquire more knowledge. Going to London and learning English, moreover, helped Itō to see beyond the chauvinistic nationalism of the "expel-the-barbarians" movement. As he learned more about Britain and the world, Itō was able to reach beyond the narrow, fixed political and social order of domain, and class, and family, to achieve a broader perspective. In a very real way, he exemplified the truth of the words "knowledge is power."

Itō's name, "Hirobumi," comes from *The Analects of Confucius* and literally means "extensive learning."[18] Itō began calling himself Hirobumi—a name reportedly suggested by Takasugi Shinsaku—around the time he began working in the finance ministry in 1869. His independent spirit, grounded in "extensive learning," was given room to grow by that first trip abroad in 1863.

Institutions and the West

The ability to communicate with Westerners acquired through that first visit to Britain soon proved invaluable to Itō. Back in his native Chōshū domain, he was quickly recognized as a much-needed negotiator and go-between, and despite his low social rank he found himself working on the front lines of domain government operations. His familiarity with the civilization of the West gave Itō powerful leverage that propelled him into the success that marked his career.

Itō's view of civilization

When, in his last years, he became resident-general of Korea, Itō said with the earnestness of a missionary, "I have assumed this post here because I want to bring Korea into the ranks of the civilized countries of the world."[19] We cannot dismiss those words as mere hypocrisy. Ever since his first direct encounter with the West as a young man, Itō had never stopped trying to bring in what he thought were the best elements of that new civilization and give them palpable, viable reality in Japan. After he became involved in national government, the principle that guided him was his vision of a truly independent, civilized Japan whose people all shared in the benefits of its progressive culture. He had the same vision for Korea when, many years later, he became resident-general there.

The passage below offers a glimpse of the fascination the West—the "new" civilization—held for Itō when he was young. It is from a letter to Kido Takayoshi, dated August 6, 1871 (20th day of the 6th month, Meiji 4). Earlier, Itō had outlined to Kido his proposal for reform involving the separation of the legislative and administrative functions of government. Since then, they had been engaged in a heated argument over the issue of reform. In the letter Itō explained his views, writing:

> People have their own opinions. Discussion can become heated, and that is only natural. Today, I believe, civilized countries do not try to coerce people into changing their opinions. Nonetheless, if everyone were freely able to say whatever they wanted, discussion would get out of control and would be destabilizing. Thus there is a need for restraint through moral education and laws.[20]

This passage gives a fairly straightforward picture of Itō's view of civilization. It boils down to two points. He believed, first, in freedom of individual thought and belief and the freedom to express such ideas and beliefs, and second, in the establishment of institutions to regulate them. Here, we will focus on Itō's ideas on institutions. Central to his thinking was that civilization was itself only as good as its institutions. Nearly three decades later, he remarked:

> Only when the state has institutions does it function. This is the case in the European countries. They are full of vigor. Their influence has spread throughout the world and their ideas have become the world's ideas. Asia, on the other hand, is half dead. This is because Asian countries do not have institutions. How can a country survive without institutions?[21]

Here, the indicator he uses to distinguish between the West and Asia is "institutions." Taken together, the two statements by Itō (quoted above) express the view that institutions, while they place checks on individual freedoms, also help assure harmony in society and raise the work of the state to a higher level. Itō's faith in the beneficial power of institutions was the driving force in his career from the early days of the Meiji era. Immediately following the Restoration of 1868, Itō proposed several institutional reforms to the government. No longer was he simply a negotiator or intermediary; with the establishment of the new Meiji government, he became what Jean-Jacques Rousseau called a "legislator." Itō was to become one of the main architects of Japan's institutions during the first years of the Meiji era.

Adulation of the United States

In February 1868 (the first month of Keiō 4) Itō was put in charge of foreign affairs in the new Meiji regime. Reputed to be an authority on the West in the Chōshū domain, he began to secure a foothold in the field of foreign affairs in the national government as well. His appointment as the first governor of Hyōgo prefecture in the same year was part of that vector in his career. Hyōgo, where the newly opened port of Kōbe was located, was the nation's diplomatic frontline, providing customs services and supervising the foreign settlement.

As he carried out his duties as governor, Itō's mind was on plans for the new government's institutions. In February 1869 (the first month of Meiji 2) he drafted a set of "principles for national policy" ("Kokuze kōmoku") that became known as the Hyōgo-ron, or "Hyōgo Proposal." Submitted with four others, the "Proposal" consists of six items: first, it advocates monarchy; second, it argues the necessity to draw together the dispersed "political and military prerogatives" in the country in the name of imperial rule; third, it calls for interaction with the countries of the world; fourth, it recommends eliminating the class differences created by the traditional stratification of society and granting people the right to freedom; fifth, it argues for promoting scientific learning from around the world; and sixth, it calls for international cooperation and the end of anti-foreignism (*jōi*).

Especially interesting in the context of this volume is the fifth item, which stresses the necessity "to let people throughout Japan learn the science behind the scientific achievements of the world, thereby spreading knowledge of the natural sciences." It hints at the emphasis on education and study that would characterize him as what I call a "statesman of knowledge." Itō was insistent that the government must be behind efforts to encourage the Japanese to undertake "useful studies of the world" and should govern the people in a "civilized and enlightened" way. Our government must, he declared, "remedy the long-standing abuses that have continued over the last several centuries in this country and encourage people to broaden their outlook and thinking." He also proposed establishing universities in Tokyo and Kyoto.

The strongest emphasis was on the second item, however. There, Itō insisted that the prerogatives of domain government be relinquished to the imperial court. "Unless all orders and laws are issued by the imperial court alone," it would be difficult to "civilize" all of Japan's people. Before he issued the Hyōgo Proposal, Itō planned to give his backing to a memorial submitted to the government in December 1868 (on the eleventh month of the previous year) by Sakai Tadakuni, lord of Himeji domain. The memorial called for the "return" to the emperor of the lands and people of all the domains (*hanseki hōkan*). As soon as he learned about Sakai's memorial, Itō offered his support by presenting his view to the government:

> If Japan hopes to have a civilized government like those of the Western countries and wishes all its people to receive the blessings of the emperor, then there is no other way than to integrate all the governing entities throughout the country into one.[22]

What occupied Itō's mind at that time was not just the integration of government but also how to unite the hearts and minds of the people of Japan; how to create a unified nation. There were rumors that Tokugawa Yoshinobu (1837–1913), the erstwhile shogun, planned a rally after the formal relinquishing of power to the emperor a few months before. Amid the flurry of talk, Itō wrote to Kido Takayoshi on January 29, 1868 (fifth day of the first month, Keiō 4) and spoke of how he envisioned a new form of government:

> When they sought their independence, in a situation different from that in Japan, the American people had no military to speak of but they came together in unity and destroyed a powerful adversary. Each of them had unswerving loyalty to their country, and they created the greatly prosperous America we see today. In Japan, our people have been oblivious to the great favor they have received from the Imperial Throne, whose line is unbroken over several thousand years. They cringe before the Emperor but do not really follow Him. It is truly disgraceful.[23]

In bringing up the case of American independence, Itō wanted to show that the driving force behind a nation's prosperity is the "united hearts and minds of the people," when every member supports the country. But in the Chōshū domain, he said, the bizarre idea is circulating that "a man born in Chōshū who does not consider the Tokugawa his enemy is not a member of the domain." With such narrow regional allegiances, Itō lamented, how dare we look in the face of Americans, whom we call "barbarians"? He urged fairness in judgment and an end to self-centered attitudes that prioritized "Chōshū or Tokugawa." Just as the separate states were able to form the larger political community that is the United States, so Japanese should shake themselves free of the narrow domain- or shogun-centered thinking they had become used to, and start to see Japan broadly, as a country where the people are one. The most pressing need, he said, was to unite the minds of the people and create a single Japanese people, a nation of Japan.

In the years just after the Meiji Restoration, Itō was deeply interested in the history of the founding of the United States. He thought and talked about building a nation-state for Japan modeled on the United States. In 1870 he had the opportunity to visit the United States and observe its political and economic institutions. At that time, as Japan's deputy vice-minister of finance, he requested and received permission to make an inspection tour of American financial and monetary agencies. What he observed there broadened his perspectives on institutions in general, as we will see in the following section.

Radical reformist bureaucrat

Itō spent the months from December 1870 until June 1871 in the United States. What he saw and learned there led to the establishment in 1871 of modern Japan's first monetary law, the New Currency Regulation (Shinka Jōrei).[24] This law put Japan on the gold standard and in line with Western countries. It was considered a "great feat" for Japan, a country in the East Asian economic sphere where silver was king among currencies. It was Itō who most vociferously championed the conversion to the gold standard. On February 18, 1871 (29th day of the 12th month, Meiji 3) soon after his arrival in the United States, he sent a memorandum to the Japanese government regarding coinage legislation. He wrote:

> Eminent specialists in civilized Western countries with many years of research and experience are adamant that only the gold standard makes sense. . . . Any country that is creating a new monetary system should definitely go on the gold standard. When our country mints new currency, we should proceed in the most intelligent way we can, based on the experience of [Western] countries and in consideration of expert opinion. If trial and error shows that our nation would suffer severe harm unless we keep to silver, then we have no choice. Otherwise, it would be best to adopt the gold standard.[25]

Itō was clearly enamored of the ways of Europe and America. His feelings were so strong that he sent the memorandum and also had his attendant, Yoshida Jirō, go back to Japan and make the case for the gold standard to the government. Itō's effort bore fruit. The government issued the New Currency Regulation, putting Japan on gold.

How is adoption of the gold standard at that time regarded today? Scholars often point out that it was radical and sudden. Economic historian Yamamoto Yūzō describes it as a product of the combination of two things: Itō's idealistic aspiration to lay "eternal foundations for the country by ensuring parity of standard prices with international common currencies" and the young nationalism of the monetary agencies in Japan, which considered it "exciting" to be in the vanguard of other countries by adopting the gold standard.[26]

There can be no doubt that in those days Itō, almost delirious with "civilization" fever, was tinged with the impetuousness of the "young military officers" who would loudly advocate radical reforms in the early part of the Shōwa era (1926–89). Earlier, I cited a letter to Kido in which he elaborated on his view of civilization. Watching Itō demanding immediate separation of the administrative and legislative functions of government soon after his return from the United States, Kido upbraided him for being too hasty: "You may know a lot about a faraway place but you do not know our own country all that well. Your logic sounds good, but you are not paying attention to the real situation around you in Japan."[27] It was in the middle of this exchange that Itō wrote Kido on August 6, 1871, to defend his position.

Germination of Itō's gradualism

In the early years of Meiji, Itō was a young and energetic bureaucrat intent on radical reform, with all the hallmarks of a former samurai and political activist. On the other hand he had a capacity for realistic judgment. Even the New Currency Regulation, radical as it was, embodied an element of continuity between external and internal monetary conditions. For one thing, the monetary system in the late years of the Edo period (1603–1867), especially after the

Man'en monetary reforms that took place in 1860–61, showed signs of moving toward the gold standard. For another, if the gold standard was adopted as Itō proposed, then one dollar would equal one yen, which, by a coincidence of history, was one *ryō*, a unit used in the Edo period. So, the decision to move to gold most likely involved the political judgment that moving from the *ryō* to the yen would be a very smooth transition. Indeed, Yamamoto points out that in the apparently hasty, nationalism-propelled move to the gold standard dictated by the New Currency Regulation, there is an element of continuity from the premodern system.[28]

Itō's concern for continuity, which arose from his understanding of current realities, would be a fundamental characteristic of the statesman he became. Later on, his attitude as a legislator impelled him to implement reforms in gradual, step-by-step measures and always to consider the political and social circumstances while holding fast to his ideal of civilized government. His zeal to adopt the gold standard might seem to have been an expression of radical idealism, but in reality it represented the germination of a brand of gradualism that would later become one of Itō's distinctive qualities.

Early signs of his gradualism can be found in his proposal to found a bank of issue—a bank authorized to issue bank notes—something Itō had been zealously campaigning for. In December 1872, the National Bank Regulation (Kokuritsu Ginkō Jōrei) was inaugurated, marking the start of a modern banking system in Japan. The regulation was modeled after America's National Bank Act, reflecting Itō's deep involvement in development of the banking system, as he had been in the adoption of the gold standard.

The main idea of his proposal was as follows: The United States had instituted several national banks—commercial banks authorized to issue notes. Itō proposed that, following the American model, Japan should establish banks that would be licensed to issue bank notes by depositing government bonds issued to them in the government treasury as security. Itō hoped that in that way commercial banks would deal in currency transactions in a free financial market, withdrawing inconvertible paper currency currently issued by the government and circulating banknotes convertible into specie. "If measures are taken to gradually replace paper currency with government bonds," Itō wrote,

> then in several years one-half of new paper money will be replaced by specie and the other half will be converted into government bonds. All the paper money that remains in circulation, then, will be only bank-issued notes. Paper money in circulation will be no different from genuine coin.[29]

One of the interesting aspects of this argument in favor of the step-by-step establishment of a new monetary system is that it represents an early sign of the gradualism for which Itō came to be known.

Itō's idea ended in failure, however. The bank notes that were issued were immediately converted into specie and few of them were circulated—a typical case of Gresham's law that "bad money drives out good." But, aside from that hard fact of economic history, let me call your attention to Itō's argument for the gradual formation of an institution at that time.

Farsighted vision

Itō's formative ideas about institutional gradualism can also be seen in what he envisioned for changing the form of government. In September 1871 (Meiji 4), after he came back from the United States, Itō wrote up his disagreements with some of the changes in government organization that had been hurriedly made during that time. One major change in the central governing structure made a month earlier related to the abolition of feudal domains and establishment of prefectures (*haihan chiken*). A Central Chamber (Sei-in) was set up as a cabinet for supervising all affairs of state in the presence of the emperor; a Left Chamber (Sa-in) was put in charge of actual administration, and the Right Chamber (U-in) was intended for deliberation on legislation. That, essentially, put in place a governing system in which legislative and administrative functions were separate, just as Itō had outlined to Kido.

But Itō was not happy with the reorganization of the finance ministry that took place at the same time. In early July 1871 he had presented a draft reform for the finance ministry modeled after the U.S. Department of the Treasury, which he said was "reputed to be an excellent system of national accounting"[30] He was indignant that his proposal was not reflected in what emerged as the new structure of the finance ministry. He expressed disagreement on a number of points, but what he says below is of special interest:

> All money coming from the Ministry of Finance is government or public revenue, that is, taxes collected from all parts of Japan. Even one sen [1/100 of the yen] is of value. . . . Today, important accounts and papers are left piled up in paper cases in every section of the ministry, and no one pays any notice when some of them are lost. The only records of accounts from the prefectures in the country are kept in small insignificant books. If those records are lost, there will be no way to recover or calculate the accounts. If things remain this way for the next several decades, how can we possibly know anything about the fiscal records of today? When, in the future, we have made great progress toward enlightened ways, and the representatives of the people gather in a parliament to deliberate on our nation's finances, how can the minister of finance reply to the queries of the people if he has no records of the accounts of the past?[31]

That passage contains the earliest discussion I have found by Itō concerning the establishment of a parliamentary system. He argues that, "When, in the future, we have made great progress toward enlightened ways," the people's representatives will gather in a parliament and discuss the financial conditions of the nation. They will need access to the accounts of the past, and in preparation for that day, he says, government expenditures and revenues of public money must be recorded, starting as soon as possible.

Encounter with Western civilization 23

The real significance in this statement is not just Itō's call for change in the structure of government. It also gives us a preview of his farsighted vision of a parliamentary system and reveals his understanding that efforts to establish it would take time, but they had to begin immediately. In short, while he was fully behind radical reforms in government, he had a broad perspective and understood that it would take gradual, step-by-step efforts to build the civilized nation that he saw in Japan's future. It was a nation-state where free individuals gather to form a nation and work together to support a state built on institutions.

It is this kind of gradualism that marked Itō Hirobumi as a statesman. It developed partly as a result of his 1870–71 trip to the United States. He had an idea of what the ideal state could be, and he believed in a gradual approach to change, but his grand plan for the state was modeled after the United States.

The Iwakura Mission and shift to gradualism

Until 1871, Itō had been enthralled by what he had learned about Western civilization and impatient to absorb and apply its lessons; he had argued for radical change in Japan. He understood the folly, certainly, of trying simply to transplant

Figure 1.4 Members of the Iwakura Mission in San Francisco. From left: Kido Takayoshi, Yamaguchi Naoyoshi, Iwakura Tomomi, Itō Hirobumi, and Ōkubo Toshimichi.

Source: Chūō Kōron Shinsha, p. 30.

Western ideals and institutions; from his research on the American banking system, for example, he had become sensitive to the need for a gradual approach in the formation of a national monetary system. During that period he was overall a radical reformist bureaucrat, somewhat carried away by the ideals of the West. After 1871, however, his thinking changed and he became committed to gradual reform.

Euphoria

The occasion of Itō's transformation was the Iwakura Mission, an ambitious eighteen-month embassy to the United States and Europe made in 1871–3. Itō was a member of the mission, as one of four deputy ambassadors,[32] sent by the Meiji government to make preliminary negotiations for the revision of the unequal treaties and observe Western civilization firsthand. That is how, only six months after returning from his first tour of the United States, Itō once more left Japan on this wide-ranging voyage around the world.

Itō had been instrumental, at least indirectly, in initiating the mission. A month after his February 1871 (12th month, Meiji 3) memo, sent from Washington to his government concerning a new monetary system, he had sent another missive, this time about the negotiations for revising the unequal treaties with fifteen Western countries that were to begin in 1872. Therein he advised that the negotiations be "based on consideration of the principles of humanity and lawful government as practiced in the advanced countries of the world," and that "various treaties observed between and among the countries of East and West be held up for comparison."[33] Itō suggested selecting some capable government officials and sending them to Europe and the United States to study treaty revision and related matters, thus using treaty revision as an opportunity to set Japan on a course that would put it "on the same level as the advanced countries, in both its human principles and public law, sweep away bad practices of the past, and lay a firm foundation for independence, self-defense, and self-reliance."[34] This dramatic and extremely bold proposal was perhaps not the direct impetus for the Iwakura Mission, but, as its author, Itō was made one of its primary members. It is easy to imagine his elation at the recognition his ideas had received.

Itō's personal behavior during the Iwakura Mission tour continues to be a subject of considerable interest.[35] No sooner had their ship left Yokohama for the United States in December 1871, than he began boasting of his English-speaking abilities and posing as an authority on the ways of the West. He lectured on the etiquette of using a Western-style toilet. Fighting the boredom of the long ocean voyage, he held a mock trial to chasten a mission attendant who had made advances to a young woman, one of the students on board who were going to study in the United States. This was the first trip abroad for virtually all the members of the mission, including Iwakura Tomomi, the head of the mission. Out of necessity, they had to rely for many things on Itō, who had already been to the West twice and had been actively involved in talks with

Figure 1.5 Iwakura Tomomi (1825–83).

Source: Photograph courtesy of the National Diet Library of Japan.

Westerners since before the fall of the shogunate. But Itō's behavior was both offensive and irritating to many members of the mission. One of them, Sasaki Takayuki (1830–1910; later a privy councilor) set down bitter words in his diary:

> Itō is all very clever, to be sure, yet it quite astounds me that such a person should be made a deputy ambassador. With everything that is happening nowadays, however, men like him will no doubt be useful and will become more and more influential.[36]

Itō's spirits remained irrepressible even after the mission arrived in the United States. On January 10, 1872, he delivered a speech brimming with confidence at a welcoming event held in San Francisco. Describing Japan's "civilizing" policy in effect since the Meiji Restoration, he boasted:

> Through accounts they have read and heard and some firsthand observation overseas, our people have acquired a general knowledge of the political systems and manners and customs of most foreign [Western] countries. Today, foreign ways are understood throughout Japan. The most earnest

wish of our country's government and people now is to achieve the high level of civilization shared by the advanced countries. To that end we have incorporated [Western] institutions into our army and navy and into our educational system, and the growth of foreign trade has brought with it a free inflow of new knowledge and information. Our country has seen rapid improvement in the material level of society, but the rising and hopeful spirit of our people is even more impressive.

Itō concluded the speech by saying:

No longer should the red disk at the center of our national flag be seen as a blob of sealing wax keeping our imperial state confined within its borders. No, as it originally was meant to do, it symbolizes the rising sun, moving upward and onward as Japan rises to take its place among the civilized countries of the world.[37]

This ebullient declamation became known as the "rising sun speech" (*hinomaru enzetsu*). Takahashi Hidenao, a scholar of Japanese history, notes "a kind of euphoria" pervading the mission. Only four months before the mission's departure from Yokohama, the Meiji government had implemented the major administrative measure that replaced the feudal domains with prefectures, and its leaders were exulting in the success of the reform. They were overflowing with confidence and optimism about the prospects of reform in their country, and the Itō speech gave full voice to that mood.[38]

In Itō's case, the euphoria seems to have been amplified by his inherently cheerful disposition, self-confidence, and open personality. As noted earlier, he is said to have had no qualms about indulging in "after-work" pleasures. His son recounted that he "spent money lavishly and took advantage of the local nightlife and entertainments."[39]

"Letters of Credence Incident"

Itō's know-it-all attitude tended toward the cavalier, in one case leading to an egregious blunder. Arriving in Washington in February 1872, the party was met by Secretary of State Hamilton Fish (1808–93), who suggested that they set about negotiating a new treaty with the United States then and there, instead of keeping to the plan and working out revisions through a joint conference later on with the Western powers as a group. On the Japanese side it was Itō who prodded the mission members to go along with that idea. Having confidently assured them that they now had "excellent prospects for revising the treaty"[40] with the United States, he left Washington together with Ōkubo Toshimichi (1830–78), going all the way back to Japan to obtain the appropriate Letters of Credence necessary for the negotiations with the American officials.

Awaiting the two when they hurried back to Washington, however, was the indignant glare of their colleagues, who had decided to go back to the original

Figure 1.6 Ōkubo Toshimichi (1830–78).

Source: Photograph courtesy of the National Diet Library of Japan.

plan and negotiate with the powers as a group. In Itō and Ōkubo's absence, Iwakura and others had learned from British and German diplomats in Washington about what they could expect from unilateral most-favored-nation treatment in separate treaties with the Western powers. They had been shocked to learn about the tricky trade-off they would have to make: If a new bilateral treaty was made with Washington and, as would happen, Japan gave most-favored-nation status to the United States, the same status would automatically be accorded to the other European powers having treaties with Japan, and the status would not be reciprocal. On July 22, 1872 (17th day of the 6th month, Meiji 5), the same day Itō and Ōkubo returned to Washington, Iwakura wrote to Grand Minister of State Sanjō Sanetomi (1837–91) in Japan, saying, "Our discussions led to the conclusion that a joint treaty is the best policy and a separate treaty is unacceptable."[41] In other words, they had decided that the original plan to hold a joint conference at another time for treaty revision negotiations with the Western powers as a group was most advantageous, and that it was not acceptable to negotiate a separate treaty with each country as they made the rounds of America and Europe. Terashima Munenori (later serving as foreign minister, 1873–79), whom Itō and Ōkubo had brought to Washington with them, wrote home to Foreign Minister Soejima Taneomi (1828–1905) about what Iwakura and the others were doing:

> They have returned to the original plan, and the official credentials that were carried from Japan will be presented neither to the United States nor to the European countries. They have decided to respect the original diplomatic advisory they brought with them last year. All the mission members greatly regret having stayed here in the capital for such an extended period of time.[42]

It had been a long four months for the mission group, and, some of them felt, a tremendous waste of time and energy.

That is a thumbnail sketch of the infamous "Letters of Credence Incident." It was a colossal loss of face for Itō. Since the launch of the Meiji regime, he had been fascinated with the history of the founding of the United States and American institutions. Fascinated by what he knew of the dreams and successes of the young America, it is possible that he was fired to achieve something similar for Japan, thus explaining his over-enthusiasm for a diplomatic coup for his country.

Kido's wrath

No one was angrier about Itō's gaffe than Kido Takayoshi, who, like Itō, had joined the mission as a deputy ambassador. As Itō himself said much later, "His [Kido's] attitude toward me had completely changed" after his return to Washington.[43] But the two had to go on traveling together, despite considerable ill will between them. While the mission was in Germany, Aoki Shūzō (1844–1914) and Shinagawa Yajirō went to Itō with an offer to help patch things up: "You and Kido seem to have bad feelings toward each other, so let us mediate," they proposed. However, Itō wrote, "I refused their offer, and told them not to take the trouble of doing anything for me and Mr. Kido."[44]

These recollections tell us two things. One, the strained relations between Itō and Kido were still not resolved as of May 1873 when they were in Germany. Two, Itō was probably too proud to let a third party mediate between himself and Kido. He seemed to think their relationship was a special one. He had often engaged in heated debates with Kido, as we saw in his letter to Kido cited earlier, and had aroused the latter's anger on many occasions. For Itō, Kido was a big brother figure with whom he felt he could speak without reserve. Confident of such a relationship up to that point, Itō probably considered the latest incident an extension of their usual disagreements and was certain that their underlying bond had not been affected.

He may also have been bluffing, knowing full well the gravity of the rupture. In any case, what is noteworthy is that, while it was serious enough to have threatened his political survival in other circumstances, Itō's huge miscalculation during the mission did not bring about his downfall. After the dust settled, Itō managed to restrain himself for some time, and he made a gradual comeback. We can identify several factors behind his fortuitous situation.

Figure 1.7 Kido Takayoshi (1833–77).

Source: Photograph courtesy of the National Diet Library of Japan.

First, he had gotten Ōkubo involved, and Ōkubo's presence loomed very large among the mission members. If it had been Itō alone, he would have been penalized in some way or other. But Ōkubo was with him when they returned to Japan to fetch the Letters of Credence, making him an "accomplice," and this made it difficult to penalize Itō alone. Ōkubo was so influential that any kind of sanctions might have frustrated the outcome of the mission itself.

Second, Kido's prestige was not very high within the mission group. During the journey he suffered from hemorrhoids and toothache, as well as homesickness. Not being in good physical or emotional shape, he was easily irritated and angered, often intimidating those around him. This rather diminished their sympathy with his ire regarding Itō's transgressions.

Third, Itō underwent an inner change. Given his characteristic optimism, after the Washington debacle he might predictably have resolved to redouble his efforts to restore his honor and make a comeback. It might have been a case of Itō the radical simply deciding to lie low until the storm blew over. But that is not at all what happened. The blunder prodded him into developing a new political acumen—the birth of Itō the gradualist. This internal change led to the mending of strained relations with Kido. Let us look at how the thaw between them unfolded.

The "conversion to Christianity" issue

On August 17, 1872 (14th day of the 7th month, Meiji 5), Iwakura and his party reached London. It was less than a month after Itō and Ōkubo's reunion with their colleagues in Washington, and Kido's indignation with Itō had not yet abated. Around that time Aoki Shūzō came from Germany, where he had been studying, to visit Kido. An admirer of Germany, Aoki contacted Kido a number of times during the latter's stay in Europe in an eager attempt to establish a German connection with Japan.

Aoki's autobiography describes an episode in London involving Kido, Itō, and himself. One day, in the presence of Itō, Kido told Aoki that influential persons in the United States had advised them that the entire Japanese population should convert to Christianity. Kido added,

> Some of our group suggest we present this advice to His Majesty the Emperor and petition him to be the first to convert to Christianity; that if enough high-ranking officials then became Christians, the general public would follow suit, and if that happened it would be very beneficial politically as well as in relations with the Western countries. What is your opinion about this?

In response, Aoki recalled the war-ravaged history of religious sectarianism in Europe, and then he continued, "Attempts to petition the Emperor to convert and urge the general public to become Christians for political reasons would set off disturbances everywhere in our country." Thereupon Kido turned to Itō and, with considerable sarcasm, spat out:

> Well, it seems that [Japanese] students studying in Europe are a good deal more extensive and profound in their learning and more logically consistent than those studying in the United States. Even worse is someone who has never studied even in the United States, but seizes upon something he hears from missionaries and frivolous politicians in that country and immediately begins to fantasize and make reckless suggestions that would throw the country into a total mess—intolerable! Absolutely dreadful!

Kido shouted at Itō, "Aoki's argument is the complete opposite of your blithe pronouncements. I can't trust anything you say!" According to Aoki's account, Itō grew pale and left the scene.[45]

The story of Itō's call for Japan's conversion to Christianity is a well-known episode among history buffs, but is it really true? The Aoki autobiography is a fairly transparent endeavor by the author to make a favorable mark on history, and the passage cited is an undisguised attempt to show off the results of his study in Germany. Aoki, too, had difficulty getting along with Itō, so it is possible that he used his autobiography to vent his discomfort with the other man. Without checking against other sources, the authenticity of this episode should probably be doubted.

The allegation made in this story, however, prompts the question: What were Itō's ideas about religion? We get a glimpse of his attitude toward Christianity in his January 2, 1873[46] letter to Ōkuma Shigenobu (1838–1922) and Soejima Taneomi, two of the men left in charge of the government in Tokyo.[47] In every country he visited, Itō wrote, people voiced concerns about Japan's persistent antipathy toward Christianity following the old pattern in East Asia, and about continued Japanese government discrimination against Christianity rooted in outdated practices and regardless of the law. Western countries were now trying to bring discussion of such general sentiments to the diplomatic table. Itō recommended that Christianity be tacitly permitted and that discrimination be legally discouraged.

Yet informal, tacit tolerance of Christianity might not truly address international concerns, Itō continued. The Western countries, he said, appeared very well informed about Japan; they knew, for example, that bulletins (*kōsatsu*) publicizing the continued ban on Christianity were still in place around the country. He argued that Westerners would hardly be satisfied to be told simply that the ban on Christianity would not be actively enforced. Furthermore he asked, if Japan keeps in place a ban that is not observed, "What does that do for our national prestige? Also, such a practice would be a disgraceful subversion of the old teaching that the ruled should be protected with sincerity." He went on, "The law in an independent sovereign nation does not discriminate between its own and foreign citizens within its territory. It is only that the legal rights of its citizens are more closely protected than those of foreign citizens." Underlying his argument was the recognition of the contradiction in Japan whereby the prohibition of Christianity remained but it was enforced only among Japanese; foreigners were given tacit permission to exercise freedom of faith. Itō thus argued that the ban on Christianity should be abolished and the inconsistency resolved.

In that letter of 1873, Itō's stance toward Christianity indicates that he favored freedom of religion, and he presents his argument in terms of state sovereignty. We will recall Itō's letter to Kido in which he declared, "People have their own opinions. Discussion can become heated, and that is only natural." He regarded the guarantee of freedom of conscience as a hallmark of a civilized country. Consistent with that line of argument, Itō considered religious faith to be a matter of freedom of conscience that should be left up to the individual. Even if Aoki's account of the encounter between Itō and Kido were true, Itō nonetheless persisted in advocating freedom of faith.[48]

Around the time Itō wrote to Ōkuma and Soejima, Aoki, too, wrote back to Japan of his thoughts on Japan's policy toward Christianity.[49] He proposed that faith in Christianity be unofficially tolerated but the ban on Christianity be left in place. This position clearly contrasted with Itō's thinking and offers a glimpse into how the two differed.

Change of attitude

With the faux pas in the United States behind him, Itō remained an open-minded and eager observer of Western ways. His close, firsthand observation of European politics gave him a new view of civilization. One thing he was quick to observe was the political instability in Europe. In the above-mentioned letter to Ōkuma and Soejima, he wrote,

> In France, concord among those in government is not yet established, and order seems to be maintained through the power of the president alone. [In Germany], when Prime Minister Bismarck differed in opinion from his cabinet ministers, he resigned as prime minister.[50]

Prior to that letter, he wrote to Inoue Kaoru:

> The French government these days is having great difficulty. The president may not be able to stay in his post. Will another person be selected to replace him? Or will there be a return to monarchy? Opinion is fragmented and there could be another civil war.[51]

The job of president was not stable and Bismarck's political charisma was not lasting. Itō saw firsthand the unexpected vulnerability of "civilized" government. We can say with certainty that it was on the Iwakura Mission tour that he realized for the first time the key importance of institutions. As soon as they got to Germany in March, Itō embarked on an investigation of its system of government. The Japanese National Diet Library's Kensei Shiryōshitsu (Modern Japanese Political History Documents Room) has a diary Itō kept during his stay in Germany. The diary includes a memo entitled "Polity and Government," concerning his findings on Prussia's parliamentary system.[52] This memo is evidence of Itō's thorough and painstaking study. His earlier ebullience and overconfidence seem to have been put aside as he settled down to serious efforts to learn about Western institutions.

This was a change for Itō, and perhaps it was inspired by his observation of Kido, who methodically assessed the system of government of each country they visited on the tour. In a letter to Inoue Kaoru dated July 7, 1873, Itō wrote:

> Kido has been laboriously studying during the tour and is now familiar with many aspects of the countries we have visited. I believe he has gained some insights into how Japan should proceed in the future. The changes that have been made in Japan so far undoubtedly leave much to be desired. So, when [Kido] arrives you should meet and talk directly with him about the developments over the months [in Japan].[53]

Itō's suggestion to Inoue that he consult Kido, who was soon to leave Europe for Japan, was a salute to Kido and his assiduous study. Indeed, Kido's diary confirms how deeply engaged he was in his inquiry into the laws and constitutions of the countries he visited, beginning with the United States, then Britain, France, Germany, and elsewhere. In his January 22, 1873 entry Kido wrote:

> At the busiest time among the events of the Restoration [1868], following my proposal, daimyo, nobility, and government officials swore the Oath of Five

Articles, thereby finally setting the direction of the nation.[54] Today, it is incumbent on us to firmly establish a fundamental legal code. In hopes of deliberating the laws, government systems, and so forth that form the foundations of the countries we are visiting, I have notified Ga[55] of what we should do.[56]

From this entry onward, the term "seitaisho torishirabe" (investigation of constitutions and laws) begins to appear frequently in Kido's diary. He ordered his aides to translate the American Constitution, for example, and major British laws and regulations and so forth, to report on deliberations in the British parliament, and to research Maurice Block (1816–1901) and Rudolf von Gneist (1816–95) eminent scholars in France and Germany respectively.

Watching Kido's activities as a fellow member of the mission, perhaps Itō was impressed and moved to renew his own efforts. If we recall Itō's own investigations about the parliamentary system in Germany and how he commended Kido in his letter to Inoue, it is possible that because of Kido, Itō turned his focus back to the political infrastructure and once again became what I call a "statesman of institutions." In the same letter to Inoue, he vehemently opposed radical reforms by the home government, saying, "I earnestly entreat you to take great care not to make hasty changes. . . . My deepest wish is that the progress of reform be as slow and steady as we can make it."[57] This part of the letter can be read as a declaration of Itō's shift to gradualism, in name and in reality.

Itō's evolving thought led to the repair of his relations with Kido. On April 14, 1873, Kido had left the mission in St. Petersburg to make his way home. An imperial order had been issued the previous month for Kido as well as Ōkubo to return to Japan. On his way he visited several European cities. Reaching Rome, Kido felt a deep inner excitement at seeing for himself sites that celebrated the wellspring of Western civilization.[58] He wrote about how he felt at that time in a private letter to Itō. Reading it and later setting foot in Rome himself, Itō wrote back:

> Italy, the fount of enlightenment, teems with amazing wonders, including its architectural creations. I can well imagine how thoroughly you studied this place and how widely you roamed in viewing its sights.[59]

Itō was as captivated by the civilization of Rome as Kido was. He conveyed that admiration in another letter written a week later, this time addressed to Ōkubo Toshimichi, who had left Europe for Japan earlier:

> How very regrettable it is that you did not visit Italy during your stay in Europe. Here one sees 2,000-year-old ruins, palaces, temples, all of astounding grandeur and in countless numbers.[60]

Rome was not built in a day. That much Itō appreciated. He was less attracted by the outward magnificence of a civilization as it appeared at a certain time than by the idea of civilization being built over long, long epochs. Kido had no reason to avoid Itō, so just before he left Europe, he went back to Rome, where he met up with Itō. In his diary Kido wrote that in Rome "I heard from Itō about recent developments back home." They must have talked at length about reforms needed in Japan while ruminating about Western civilization in ancient times. At Marseilles on June 7, one day before his departure for Japan, Kido received another letter from Itō. "A letter from Itō arrived, and so did a letter from Aoki."[61] Everything seemed once more in place and the close relationship between Kido and Itō back on track.

Now in Europe with his earlier blunder behind him, Itō regained the trust of Kido, but not because of his charm or diplomacy. It evolved out of something deeper: an internal change that had been taking place in his thinking. Going out to see the sights of Rome, following Kido's suggestion, Itō recognized a feeling that Kido had described in an earlier letter: "Putting aside the outer trappings—the skin—for now," Kido had written, thinking of Japan, "if progress does not take place within—in the bones—what looks like enlightened civilization today might all be lost tomorrow."[62]

This strong and perceptive sentiment—which Itō clearly shared—came not of despair in sensing some essential, impossible gap between Japan and the civilization of the West. An exchange with Iwakura indicates that this was not the case at all. When the party was in Rome, mission leader Iwakura said to Itō:

> We have observed much in several countries. Not only the powerful countries like Britain, the United States, Germany, and France, but even second- and third-rank countries have culturally prospered so greatly that Japan couldn't possibly catch up. No matter how hard we study the elements of their civilization, there is no hope that we can ever put them to practical use in our country. I fear that our mission to observe and learn from Europe and the United States might be a disgraceful failure.

Itō replied,

> Your Excellency, such worry is unnecessary. Your task is to report faithfully what you have seen firsthand. As for which cultural elements [of the West] might be selected or rejected, please leave that to us and we will do our best. You need not worry at all, sir.[63]

Itō was determined that nothing in the West should overwhelm or daunt them. Why was he so confident? Partly because Japan's post-Restoration modernization program had become well established. The reform line adopted when the Meiji state came into being had equipped Japan with the institutional framework of a modern country. For Japan to modernize sufficiently to rank among the Western powers was not an impossible dream, even though the process that would take it there would require great care and prudence. Just as Western civilization had been nurtured through the rise and fall of powers over the centuries since the flowering of ancient Rome, so Japan, too, had its own accumulation of history. That history and tradition would not hinder modernization had been proven by the changes achieved over the last few years. The next stage was to push the "enlightenment" (modernization) policy forward and ensure that it took root at the core, in the "bone" of Japanese culture and society. And so it was that Itō returned to Japan more convinced than ever of the possibility of successful modernization; he was now certain that gradualism, not radical change, was the best way to achieve it.

Notes

1 *Itō den*, vol. 1, p. 19.
2 *Itō-kō zenshū*, vol. 1, "Shokan" [Letters], p. 117. This passage is shortened in *Itō den*.
3 Ibid., p. 118.
4 In his *Kōkai enryaku saku*, a proposal offered to the lord of Chōshū, Nagai advocated trade with the Western countries and proposed a policy of reconciliation between the imperial court and the Tokugawa shogunate.
5 Yamao later founded the Imperial College of Engineering, predecessor of the Department of Technology at Tokyo Imperial University.
6 *Yoshida Shōin zenshū*, vol. 6, p. 43; letter to Kusaka Genzui dated 6/19/Ansei 5 (1858).
7 Ibid., vol. 4, p. 61.
8 *Itō-kō zenshū*, vol. 3, "Jikiwa" [Itō's Personal Accounts], pp. 43–4.
9 Ibid., p. 44.
10 Sufu 1977, vol. 2, pp. 722–3.
11 *Itō den*, vol. 1, pp. 84–5.
12 Ibid., p. 97.
13 Itō Shin'ichi 1979, p. 41.
14 The documents in the UCL Library Special Collections; see December 30, 1863 entry, Ms.ADD356, A484.
15 Beasley 1995, p. 161.
16 Erwin von Bälz (1849–1913), German internist who lived in Japan for many years and introduced modern European medicine to Japan, was one of the Europeans who dubbed Itō the "Bismarck of Japan" (*Itō den* 1970, vol. 3, p. 919). Others include Alexander von Siebold (1846–1911), German Japanologist and Philipp Franz von Siebold's son who made valuable contributions to Japan's foreign policy, and Ludwig Riess (1861–1928), German historian who, as professor of history at Tokyo Imperial University, introduced Ranke's research methods of historical research to Japan. Pro-Japanese intellectuals in Germany, and German doctors, engineers, and others hired by the Meiji government were inclined, as a group, to compare Itō with Bismarck.
17 Takii 1998a, Takii 1998b, and Takii 1998c.
18 The Master said, "The superior man, extensively studying all learning, and keeping himself under the restraint of the rules of propriety, may thus likewise not overstep what is right." (Book 6-27). Available at: www.wright-house.com/religions/confucius/Analects.html (accessed October 4, 2013).
19 Kim 1966, vol. 6–1, p. 247.
20 *Kido monjo*, vol. 1, p. 243.
21 Speech at Taiwan-kai social gathering, April 1897; *Itō-kō zenshū*, vol. 1, "Bunshū," p. 213.
22 *Itō den*, vol. 1, p. 416.
23 Ibid., p. 332.
24 The discussion on the establishment and historical significance of the New Currency Regulation is based on Yamamoto 1994, pp. 27 ff.

25 *Itō den*, vol. 1, p. 537.
26 Yamamoto 1994, p. 79.
27 *Kido nikki*, vol. 2, p. 52.
28 Yamamoto 1994, pp. 27–8.
29 *Itō den*, vol. 1, pp. 527–88.
30 Ibid., vol. 1, p. 577.
31 Ibid., p. 580.
32 The other three were Kido Takayoshi, Ōkubo Toshimichi, and Yamaguchi Masuka.
33 *Iwakura monjo*, vol. 7, p. 332.
34 Ibid., p. 336.
35 Takii 2003.
36 *Hogohiroi*, vol. 5, p. 245.
37 *Itō den*, vol. 1, pp. 625 ff.
38 Takahashi Hidenao 1992, p. 91.
39 Itō Shin'ichi 1979, p. 41.
40 *Hogohiroi*, vol. 5, p. 291.
41 *Gaikō*, vol. 5, p. 64.
42 Ibid., pp. 67–8.
43 *Itō den*, vol. 1, pp. 709–10.
44 Ibid., p. 711.
45 Aoki 1970, pp. 41 ff.
46 The solar calendar went into effect on January 1, 1873 (3rd day of the 12th month of Meiji 5).
47 *Itō den*, vol. 1, pp. 684 ff.; *Ōkuma monjo* 2004, vol. 1, pp. 204 ff.
48 Yamazaki 2006, pp. 128 and 143.
49 *Kido monjo*, vol. 1, pp. 44–5.
50 Ibid.
51 Letter dated 1872/12/6, *Inoue Kaoru Monjo Kōdokukai* 2008, no. 628–8.
52 "Itō Hirobumi shuki gaiyū nikki."
53 *Itō den*, vol. 1, p. 725.
54 Kido's understanding that the Oath of Five Articles was sworn by "daimyo, nobility, and government officials" is noteworthy. For a study that illustrates the political significance of the oath from the point of view of political propriety, see Breen 1996.
55 Ga Noriyuki (1840–1923), translator and one of Kido's aides on the mission.
56 *Kido nikki*, vol. 2, p. 142.
57 Letter dated June 2, 1873, *Itō den*, vol. 1, p. 725.
58 *Kido nikki*, vol. 2, pp. 362 ff.
59 Letter to Kido dated May 12, *Itō den*, vol. 1, pp. 718–19.
60 Ibid., p. 721, letter to Ōkubo dated May 19.
61 *Kido nikki*, vol. 2, p. 391.
62 Kido letter to Watanabe Hiromoto (Kōki) dated 1872/11/27, *Kido monjo*, vol. 4, p. 424.
63 *Itō den*, vol. 1, p. 724.

2 A constitution for Japan
Building the foundation

Moving toward constitutional government: 1873–80

Itō Hirobumi, Iwakura Tomomi, and the other members of the Iwakura Mission returned to Japan on September 12, 1873. Awaiting them were initiatives for radical reform and modernization being pressed forward by the caretaker government under Saigō Takamori (1828–77), Itagaki Taisuke (1837–1919), and others who had been left in charge while the Meiji government's leading members (Iwakura was minister of the right cum foreign minister, Kido councilor [*sangi*], Ōkubo finance minister) were away.

News of those policy moves, in addition to other developments in Tokyo, was the main reason Ōkubo and Kido had hurried home in advance of the others. Ōkubo arrived in Yokohama on May 26 and Kido on July 23. The two men were not on good terms, but they were united in their disapproval of the turn toward rapid modernization being pushed by members of the caretaker government and in their commitment to gradualism. Through their many months of travel, all the mission members had come to appreciate how different the paths to modernization were among the more advanced countries of the West. The process of modernization and the development of institutions, they saw clearly, were in part products of their respective histories and cultures. Thus Itō Hirobumi was not the only member of the Iwakura Mission who had become convinced that their country's modernization, too, should be a gradual process, adapted to its own conditions, culture, and history.

Divide over the "Korea expedition"

The strain between the mission participants and the officials of the interim government—in many respects between belief in gradualism and the impulse to quick action—festered and finally erupted openly in the form of a clash of opinions over Japan's stance toward Korea. Since its inception, the Meiji government had repeatedly approached Korea to establish diplomatic relations, and Korea continued to rebuff Japan. Many officials in the caretaker government had grown impatient and were demanding that Japan force Korea to open its doors by military means (a stance referred to as *seikanron*, "Korea expedition" policy), rejecting arguments to proceed slowly and with caution. On August 17, 1873, Japan's interim government had informally decided to dispatch one of its leading figures, Saigō Takamori, to Korea, and that decision had been sanctioned by the emperor. But, since everyone knew that sending Saigō to Korea would almost certainly lead to hostilities between the countries, they put off implementing the decision until it could be deliberated again when Iwakura, who was serving as foreign minister, was back to Japan.[1]

Immediately upon his return to Japan in September, Itō found himself embroiled in political turmoil. Going back and forth among Iwakura, Kido, and Ōkubo, he plunged into the effort to unite those who opposed punitive action against Korea. His negotiating skills proved to be formidable. Particularly interesting about Itō's activities at that time was how consistently they reflected his determination to establish modern institutions for Japan; he was like a crusading "statesman of institutions." Bearing that point in mind, let us look at what he was thinking and what he was doing in the 1870s.

With foreign minister and Minister of the Right, Iwakura, back home, the cabinet (in 1873, it was the Central Chamber, made up of the grand minister of state, ministers of the left and right, and *sangi* councilors) was convened on October 14 and 15. It approved sending Saigō to Korea, largely because Grand Minister of State Sanjō Sanetomi changed his mind and agreed, fearing that Saigō would resign in protest if he were not sent, which would provoke an uprising by the pro-Saigō militia.[2] That was a defeat for Iwakura and the mission group, but they wasted no time in launching new efforts to get the decision reversed. As Iwakura wrote to Itō, "We will be undaunted and will do everything humanly possible."[3] The government was split, and Sanjō, pressed hard from both sides, suffered a nervous breakdown and fell into a coma.

Because it was Iwakura who took the place of the ailing Sanjō, the latter's illness worked to the advantage of those opposed to sending Saigō to Korea. Iwakura proposed that the issue be submitted to the emperor for a decision and then worked his connections in the court to ensure that the emperor would be persuaded to support his position. An imperial order to desist came out on October 24. The disgruntled Saigō and other councilors who had championed the military expedition against Korea resigned their positions and left the government, an action later called the "Political Crisis" of 1873 (Meiji 6-nen Seihen).

Itō's promotion

While Itō busied himself behind the scenes with containing the forces advocating the Korea expedition, he took great pains to bring Kido and Ōkubo together. Both were widely expected to assume leadership in the government once the crisis had been settled, but there was some discord between them. By improving their relations, Itō presumably sought to lay the foundations for a new regime that would emerge after the pro-Korea expedition councilors were all out of the government. On October 20, 1873, in the midst of the furor over the expedition, Itō visited Kido and told him about how Iwakura and Ōkubo had been working to prevent military action against Korea. Kido wrote in his diary, "Heard in detail about the furor in the cabinet. Also heard about the determination of Iwa[kura] and Ōku[bo], and this has assuaged my concerns."[4]

Itō's powers of persuasion aroused in Kido a patriotic sense of solidarity with Ōkubo and inspired deeper trust in Itō. That day Kido wrote to Iwakura recommending Itō as a councilor. "Itō Hirobumi has been a friend of mine since ten-odd years ago," he wrote. "As you know, he is disciplined and honest in character, and has lately been particularly reasoned and thoughtful as well as attentive to detail. In that respect he is a rarity among my friends."[5] Gone was any trace of the rancor between them during the Iwakura Mission tour. On the contrary, Kido communicated only high regard for Itō.

The next day, October 21, Itō saw Kido again to warn him that the pro-Korea expedition faction was once more on the rise and had pressured Iwakura into agreeing to consider sending Saigō to Korea again. Having relayed this news, Kido wrote, Itō "groaned for a long moment, complaining that any reconsideration was going to be tough. He is outraged and profoundly depressed out of worry for our country."[6] Finding Itō in such a state over the fate of the nation, Kido must have been impressed, thinking that here was a real patriot qualified to help govern the state. On October 25, in the aftermath of these events, Itō was appointed councilor-cum-public-works minister. The appointment signified recognition of Itō as a central figure in the Meiji government.

Kido and Ōkubo memorials on the Constitution

The positions of councilor and state minister were, in a sense, a reward to Itō for his difficult and committed work as a mediator. It was from that time onward that Itō would increasingly display his unique talents as a "statesman of institutions." On November 19, 1873, the councilors met and selected Itō and Terashima Munenori (1832–93) as the two in charge of "investigating constitutional government" (*seitai torishirabe*),[7] that is, working out how constitutional government would be instituted in Japan. The Iwakura Mission group had returned from their long trip abroad convinced that Japan could become an independent, modern, and strong nation on a par with Western countries only if it adopted a constitutional government. This conviction comes out clearly in two memorials, or formal position papers, on constitutional government prepared separately by Kido and Ōkubo. Kido had been an avid student during the tour of the workings of the constitutional systems he had encountered in Europe and the United States, and soon after returning home he wrote his paper and submitted it to the emperor. Ōkubo, on the other hand, wrote his in November and sent it to Itō, who was now heading the project to study constitutional government.

The two papers differed markedly in several respects. Above all else, as Kido told Itō, he advocated a "despotic" monarchy: "Our country should be founded on a 'desupochikku' [despotic] system; it could not be run otherwise."[8]

Ōkubo's proposal called for government by the monarch and the people together (*kunmin kyōchi*):

> The basis of the constitution is joint governance by the monarch and the people. The constitution will stipulate imperial prerogatives above and define popular rights below. It will provide for perfect fairness between the monarch and the people. Neither side may arrogate powers to themselves.[9]

It might be surprising that Kido, who considered himself—and is generally recognized—as an enlightenment thinker, upheld a level of despotism while Ōkubo, whose image generally is that of a dictatorial politician, supported popular participation in government.

Yet the differences are less important than what the two papers shared: both advocated the same basic principles—democracy and gradualism. They both sought a system with, eventually, some degree of popular participation in government, a system that would allow the Japanese people to learn and adapt and participate in the advancement of their country. Kido called for a "despotic monarch" only as the first step in a gradual approach to that end, while Ōkubo believed government by the people and the emperor together could best be achieved gradually, taking into account Japan's history and the progress its people made in adopting new forms of social and political activity.

Having observed Western societies firsthand, both Kido and Ōkubo believed that it was inevitable that Japan would have to adopt a constitutional government. Neither of them, however, would tackle the challenge directly themselves. Ōkubo chose to dedicate himself to promoting industry rather than building systems and institutions. Kido was so debilitated by mental and physical health problems that it was difficult for him to concentrate on work for long hours. It was under these circumstances, and in accordance with both men's wishes, that Itō came onto center stage as the expert on constitutional government in October 1873.

Gradualist approach to institution-building

As soon as he was appointed to the office of investigating constitutional government, Itō turned to Kido for advice. Kido told him,

> You might be able to install a new system of government and make it look quite impressive in form, but if our people have not advanced enough to understand it, it will be difficult to turn it into a government that works like those of the Western countries. So my only wish is to prevent rash action, make sure rules and regulations are followed, and to proceed steadily and surely.[10]

He stressed the need for a gradual approach: "We should proceed slowly as we gain new learning and achieve a more advanced society. Never be hasty and so miss the essential part."[11]

Itō received the same advice from Ōkubo, who presented his views in the position paper mentioned above. Later in his life, Itō recalled the paper Ōkubo had written at that time. According to Itō, Ōkubo had said in effect, "Radical change, of course, would be detrimental to the state. What needs to be done is to base the constitution on our nation's customs and manners and prevailing circumstances." In other words, Ōkubo also called for a gradual approach to constitutional government. Itō added that Ōkubo had been one of the leading proponents of constitutional government from early on.[12]

The central task for Itō and Terashima, charged with investigating ways to introduce constitutional government, was monumental; they were to design specific institutions on the basis of Kido and Ōkubo's principle of gradualism. On November 29, 1873, only ten days after his appointment, Itō had already come up with a plan. On that day he wrote to Kido:

> Terashima and I are fully engaged in our study of constitutional government. We are considering convening local governors to form a lower assembly and somewhat expanding the Jakō-no-ma[13] body to make it into an upper assembly without increasing its membership by very much.[14]

That plan was to bear fruit about a year later, in April 1875, when, after the "Osaka Conference,"[15] an edict was issued stipulating the establishment of constitutional government in gradual stages. That led to the convening of an Assembly of Prefectural Governors in June and a Genrōin (Chamber of Elders) in July 1875. The achievement of these two assemblies adorned the last days of Kido's political career, but they originated in Itō's constitutional government investigation office.

Protest to Sanjō Sanetomi

Itō himself was fully confident about his governmental reform plan. But in the months after he made it public in late November 1873, there ensued a series of difficult developments—a rebellion by Saga prefecture loyalists against the Meiji government; Japan's 1874 punitive military expedition to Taiwan; and Kido's resignation as councilor—causing serious political turmoil. To deal with it all, in 1875 Itō held the Osaka Conference to rebuild the Kido-Ōkubo system of leadership, and in the meantime he concentrated on his program of gradual reform.

In June 1874 an institution known as the Kazoku Kaikan (Peers Club) was opened as an organization for the peerage to study and conduct research and other activities. Earlier, Itō apparently had assumed it would play a role in the expansion of the Jakō-no-ma into a slightly larger assembly. But when a clause about holding conferences was removed from its founding regulations, it seemed to Itō that the Kazoku Kaikan was being turned into nothing more than a "study society" and he lodged an indignant protest with Grand Minister of State, Sanjō Sanetomi:

> Removing the conference clause seems to have been your idea, and it will make the [Kaikan] more like a school or a library. That completely goes

against what I had expected. Perhaps it was discussed and decided not to make the Kaikan a national institution, but even so, the government need only give tacit approval, and if you set your mind to making it into an upper legislative assembly in the future, that tacit approval will, I believe, be enough to make it possible.[16]

To paraphrase Itō's idea, it was decided that the Kaikan would be a non-national institution, but, once it was established, if the will were rallied to make it an "upper legislative assembly," the government would go along with this, giving it the leeway to become such a body eventually. Here we see Itō's stance in favor of gradualism and the emergence of a "spontaneous order." The passage is a vivid reflection of Itō's attitude toward institutions.

A few months later the Meiji leaders put in place the Assembly of Prefectural Governors and the Genrōin, in accordance with the edict issued in April. This was the first cautious step in instituting a constitutional government. The actual creation of a constitution was put off for the time being; largely because of the Satsuma Rebellion (February–September 1877) led by Saigō Takamori against the Meiji regime, Kido's death from illness (May 1877), and Ōkubo's assassination (May 1878). Momentum to draw up a constitution had grown strong enough by early 1880 that the emperor that year ordered each councilor to prepare an opinion paper on bringing a constitutional system into Japanese government. Itō's paper is summed up below.[17]

Itō paper on the Constitution

In the paper he submitted to the emperor, Itō's first point concerns the enlargement of the existing Genrōin. "We must not rush into establishing a parliament," he asserts. Instituting joint governance by monarch and people through the agency of a newly created Diet (parliament) would necessitate an unsettling "change in national polity," and, "Such an unprecedented, grave matter should never be pursued with too much haste." So Itō, always keeping to the gradualist path, proposed increasing the numbers of the Genrōin, whose members came from the nobility and gentry. This was Itō's way of sustaining the spirit of the Osaka Conference and "pursuing a gradual approach as my teachers [Kido and Ōkubo] wished."

His second point relates to auditors to be selected from candidates from the public at large. His idea was to recruit auditors from among the people and make sure they became well versed in the national government's fiscal and administrative matters:

> Their authority will be confined to auditing accounts, and they will not be allowed to interfere in the government's budgetary policy. In addition to encouraging public deliberation on public finance, this will also create a group of ordinary citizens who are knowledgeable about and experienced in fiscal and budgetary practices.

Itō most likely attempted to set up positions for such auditors within the Assembly of Prefectural Governors, in the hope of stimulating popular participation in public finance transactions and then gradually moving toward democratic control of public finance.

Itō concluded his paper with a third point, a proposal to "ask for the emperor's thoughts on the course that the nation should take." Just then, when the movement for people's rights (*jiyū minken undō*) was growing increasingly more strident in its demands for a parliamentary system, Itō considered it vital for the emperor to demonstrate the "principle of gradualism."

Itō's position paper has been regarded as a lukewarm conservative statement of policy aimed at preserving the status quo, in contrast with Ōkuma Shigenobu's proposals for a constitution, which are taken up in the next section. Still, however else it might be read, Itō's paper is one more expression of the philosophy of gradualism that had taken hold and had grown in him since his life-changing experience during the Iwakura Mission tour. He remained stoutly behind the plan for gradual introduction of a parliamentary system that had been worked out in the aftermath of the wrangling over the Korea expedition.

The political situation was seething, however, and was about to boil up in ways that Itō had not anticipated. The following year, 1881, a major event occurred, triggered by a position paper submitted that year by Ōkuma Shigenobu. Soon to be known as the Political Crisis of 1881, it marked a major change in the history of the Meiji Constitution.

The Political Crisis of 1881

In January 1874, Itagaki Taisuke and some associates had submitted an opinion paper to the government calling for a popularly elected assembly. Itagaki was no longer in office then—he had already left the government in protest over the defeat of the Korea expedition plan—but a movement for a popular assembly was born. It continued to gain momentum. Demands to convene a Diet had become much louder as more Japanese in the intervening years became familiar with the idea and practice of constitutionalism in government. It seemed to many that the time was ripe. No longer was it possible to turn a deaf ear to their voices and just keep on urging patience and "gradualism."

The Ōkuma opinion paper sensation

Of those who were then councilors, it was Ōkuma Shigenobu who was most perceptive of the political mood. Those who held the post of councilor were required to personally write and submit proposals on the establishment of a constitution, and when the way Ōkuma had submitted his and its content became known, a brouhaha ensued that it is known as the Political Crisis of 1881.

Ōkuma's paper, which he presented—apparently by quietly handing it to the Minister of the Left, Prince Arisugawa Taruhito (1835–95), who was in charge of the proposals—in March 1881, called for a British-style parliamentary cabinet

Figure 2.1 Ōkuma Shigenobu (1838–1922).

Source: Photograph courtesy of the National Diet Library of Japan.

system, in which the party winning a majority in the election would form the cabinet. His secretive method of delivering it (which others suspected he had used in hopes it would be given to the emperor directly), and the proposal to adopt the British system, aroused much consternation among his colleagues. Itō, in particular, was incensed. In January that year, Ōkuma and Itō had met in Atami, joined by Inoue Kaoru, and had thoroughly discussed points relating to a constitution for Japan. At the time, Itō had been confident that he and Ōkuma were allies in full agreement on the matter. To Itō, it was an outrageous breach of faith that Ōkuma had tried to present his opinion to the emperor without telling him.[18]

More important from the perspective of constitutional history was the content of the Ōkuma paper. In June, Prince Arisugawa showed the paper privately to Iwakura Tomomi, minister of the right. Iwakura was shocked to find that, on top of advocating the British-model parliamentary cabinet system, Ōkuma had put forth the completely radical proposal of holding a national election the following year and convening a Diet two years later.

Also, privately, Iwakura showed the document to Inoue Kowashi (1844–95) and asked for his advice. A leading expert on constitutional law in the bureaucracy,

A constitution for Japan 45

Inoue was to become the de facto drafter of the Constitution. He did some rapid research, and replied to Iwakura:

> I looked into this, and, after my informal reading of the secret document [the Ōkuma paper], I must report that among the leading European nations, the parliament in Germany in particular still does not have the full powers that Britain's parliament has. In Britain, the parliament has not only legislative but also administrative powers.[19]

Learning that, Iwakura instructed Inoue to write up an opinion on constitution that could be used to counter Ōkuma. The result was the "Iwakura paper on constitution," which contained several theses, including "Daikōryō" (General Principles) and "Kōryō" (Principles). Iwakura submitted his work to the government on July 5. In striking contrast to the Ōkuma paper, Iwakura proposed that Japan adopt a constitution granted by the emperor (following the Prussian model) and also provide for broad imperial prerogatives and a system whereby the previous year's budget would come automatically into force if a budget bill did not pass in parliament. These items would later be incorporated into the Meiji

Figure 2.2 Inoue Kowashi (1844–95).

Source: Photograph courtesy of the National Diet Library of Japan.

Constitution. All this activity over the Ōkuma paper constituted Act One of the Political Crisis of 1881.

The Hokkaido Colonization Office scandal

Act Two was the so-called Hokkaido Colonization Office scandal. It was revealed that the Colonization Office, a government agency set up to develop Hokkaido, had tried to sell facilities built with government funds to a private company for an inflated price. Because of the close ties the company had with an influential politician (Kuroda Kiyotaka), and the government's inept handling of the scandal, a large-scale anti-government campaign ensued.

In the government's eyes, the really serious problem was not the sale itself, which had been proceeding nicely in a very surreptitious manner, but how and why it had been leaked to the public. In their eager search for the culprit, they lit upon Ōkuma as the most likely suspect. That was not surprising; he was, after all, the one who was pushing for a British-style party government, an idea originally put forward by the hardened critics of the government who led the people's rights movement. The leak smacked of treachery, of pressuring for regime change from outside the government.

As soon as he had read Ōkuma's opinion paper, shown to him by Iwakura, Itō wrote, "I suspect Ōkuma's paper probably does not come out of his own ideas."[20] Ōkuma had brought into government young intellectuals from the people's rights movement—Ono Azusa (1852–86), Yano Fumio (1851–1931), and Inukai Tsuyoshi (1855–1932)—and he and this group of subordinates had formed a policy research group. A plausible rumor had circulated that, through this network of personal connections, Ōkuma had been conspiring with people's rights activists to overthrow the government.

The Ōkuma opinion paper became the fuse that, when lit by the Colonization Office scandal, set off the 1881 crisis. Under the mounting pressure of accusations, the government decided on October 11 to cancel the sale of assets of the Colonization Office. At the same time it announced Ōkuma Shigenobu's dismissal from the cabinet as well as his expulsion from government. That is what is called the Crisis of 1881, but the important point is that on the very next day, an imperial edict was issued promising the establishment of a national Diet. Under the name of the emperor it was made public that a national assembly, or Diet, was scheduled to open in 1890. That meant, of course, that a constitution would have to be drawn up and approved by then.

The Political Crisis of 1881 was pivotal in the history of constitution-building in Japan for two reasons: first, as a result, the government imposed upon itself a definite time limit to enact the Constitution and establish a Diet; and second, it was agreed that the content would be modeled on that of Germany (Prussia). Some may question whether the Prussian Constitution was really the model for the Meiji Constitution. At least, was it the *only* model? In explaining the relevance of these questions, let us examine Itō Hirobumi's tour of constitutional study in Europe, which began soon after the Crisis of 1881 was resolved.

Constitutional study tour in Europe

Motivated, or pressured, by the imperial edict the previous year promising a Diet for Japan, Itō and a small delegation left on another trip to Europe in March 1882, one purpose being to learn more about constitutions and constitutional government. For Itō, it was a chance to study Europe's constitutions more deeply in preparation for the day that one would be written for Japan. Sending him to Europe was partly intended to give him a chance to recuperate, since, after the Political Crisis, Itō suffered from debilitating psychological problems. Inoue Kaoru wrote in a letter to Sasaki Takayuki (1830–1910) and others, dated November 23, 1881:

> Lately Itō has been in deep anguish. He suffers nervous collapses and sleeps very badly every night. He drinks a 1-sho [1.8 liter] bottle of sake before he can finally get to sleep. Left as is, his condition will worsen. So if he can take a year-long trip to Europe, this will be a good thing for him, don't you agree?[21]

From the vantage point of the present, it does not seem strange that Itō Hirobumi, known to us now as the "father of the Meiji Constitution," should

Figure 2.3 Itō Hirobumi in Europe in 1883.
Source: Chūō Kōron Shinsha, p. 61.

make another difficult, expensive, and time-consuming trip to Europe. In hindsight the whole venture seems heroic and grandly justified. But his contemporaries both in and out of government looked upon this European tour with skeptical bewilderment. Why, went the general reaction, should a top government leader absent himself from Japan for many months in Europe, when the situation at home was unsettled, merely to study constitutional texts and systems? Investigation and research of that kind, argued the press and some in government, should be entrusted to the bureaucrats in charge of such things and to the diplomats stationed in Europe.

But besides studying constitutional documents, there was another objective. By the order he received from the emperor before he left, Itō was also to "meet important people in government and eminent scholars in the constitutional states of Europe and to observe the way society is organized in these countries and the concrete conditions of life there."[22] His ultimate goal, in other words, was not just to study the framework that guided these states—their constitutions—but also to learn more about how to give living substance to that framework. To get a sense of what Itō actually did, and how, let us follow him through Europe on that tour of study in 1882.

To Berlin

Since one result of the Political Crisis of 1881 had been the decision to use the German constitution as a model for Japan's, Itō's first destination was Berlin, capital of the German empire. There he arranged for personal study with Rudolf von Gneist, professor of law at the University of Berlin.

Itō did not have an easy time learning from Gneist, however, who was very negative about his project from the outset. According to a member of Itō's study group, at their first meeting Gneist asserted that a constitution was the expression of the spirit of a people and evolved out of the history of that people, and that he, being ignorant of Japanese history, was not in the least confident that he would be of any help. That line of thinking was at the heart of the school of historical jurisprudence that rose to predominance in mid-nineteenth century Germany. Gneist had succeeded Friedrich Carl von Savigny (1779–1861), founder of the school, as a lecturer at the University of Berlin. Now Gneist, having assumed the mantle of leader of the school, tried to convince Itō that law, like language, manners, and customs, was a product of history and was rooted in the "spirit" of a people.

Itō had not crossed half the world to just learn interesting academic theories. He met with Gneist several more times in the hope of gaining a basis for productive constitutional study, and he also heard lectures giving clause-for-clause commentary on the text of the Prussian Constitution from Gneist's student Albert Mosse (1846–1925). But Itō was not satisfied, as he wrote in letters to Japan at that time. He lamented his inability to communicate in German and anguished over his lack of progress. He requested an extension to his stay in Europe.[23] Perhaps his greatest fear at this time was that his European tour would end in failure.

Between Gneist and Stein

In August 1882, Itō went to Vienna, where he met Lorenz von Stein (1815–90), legal scholar and professor of *Staatswissenschaft*, political economy or theory of the state, at the University of Vienna. Deriving valuable suggestions from Stein's ideas on administration as the core principle of action by the state, Itō began to breathe easier as prospects for constructive, practical results of his trip brightened. In a letter sent home, Itō wrote that he had met Stein and found him to be a "good teacher," and "I secretly felt as though if I died now, I could die happy."[24]

What made the difference between his study in Vienna and that in Berlin? For one thing, the orientation of Stein's discussions was quite different from the lectures of Gneist (and Mosse). What Itō wanted was not an understanding of specific clauses to be written into a constitution, but a holistic grasp of a constitutional state and a guideline for running the state after the Constitution came into force. Itō found Stein's science of the state to be more practical and relevant to what he had been seeking.

In Berlin, Itō had frequently encountered anti-parliamentarian attitudes and comments. After his first meeting with Gneist, he wrote home that the professor's thesis was "extremely despotic." He reported that Gneist had said, "It will be a calamity if a parliament is established and allowed to interfere in military authority, national accounting, and so forth; the best policy is to make sure at the outset that parliament is very weak."[25]

Kaiser Wilhelm I (1797–1888) expressed a similar view. On August 28, during a short trip back to Berlin, Itō dined with the Kaiser. According to Itō, Wilhelm I made an "unexpected remark" in the course of the meal, saying that, "For the sake of the Japanese emperor I do not want to send congratulations on the forthcoming creation of a national assembly." The Kaiser went on:

> If things come to such a pass that Japan cannot avoid bringing in a parliament, you will have to be extremely attentive in the way you govern. Whatever else happens, never take the disastrous step of making tax collection impossible without parliamentary approval.[26]

Kaiser Wilhelm's comment probably stemmed not so much from doubts about Japan's political, social, or economic advancement as from Germany's own bitter experiences with parliamentary government. Germans had been wrangling over the Prussian Constitution since 1862, when Bismarck famously used extra-legal means to force through an expansion of military spending without parliamentary approval. Itō's arrival in Germany happened to coincide with another maddening battle over a tobacco monopoly bill that was being deliberated in the German Reichstag. The Reichstag looked upon the bill "very unfavorably," and it was "extremely difficult to reach agreement." Itō wrote of reports that Bismarck, in a cranky huff, shut himself up at home.[27]

In their advice and comments to Itō, Kaiser Wilhelm I and Gneist communicated at least some of the grim realities of parliamentary government in Germany.

Doubtless the Germans believed that if they themselves found a parliamentary system so hard to manage, how could the untutored, neophyte Japanese possibly handle it?

Despite the advice he received in Germany, and having seen firsthand what Bismarck was up against in dealing with the tobacco monopoly bill, Itō never betrayed any sign of hesitation about running Japan's government in collaboration with a parliament. His primary concern was not whether, but how to effect the transplant of such an institution from foreign origins without the risk of its rejection by the nation into which it was placed.

Itō's admiration for Stein's theory of the state

In that regard, Stein's lectures were compatible with Itō's aims. Stein's "political realist" theory of the state holds that constitutional government (*Verfassung*), or the parliamentary system, by its nature, has no impact without administrative action, and that administration by itself is powerless without constitutional government. His thesis can be taken as an attempt to reconcile parliamentary government and state administration. According to Stein, a parliamentary system is a necessary means of effecting popular participation in government, but by itself only creates unstable government susceptible to conflicts of interest. Parliamentary systems need to be complemented by effective administration (*Verwaltung*) to secure the public interest of the state. This was a theory of the state that Itō could admire. Back in Japan, he enthusiastically recommended Stein to everyone he met, encouraging what literally turned into a "Stein pilgrimage" to Austria by Japanese eager to learn more. An endless stream of statesmen, bureaucrats, scholars, and students began visiting Stein in Vienna, seeking his instruction and guidance.

Back in Vienna, in September, after his brief visit to Berlin, Itō continued to attend Stein's lectures until November 5. "I have done enough study of constitutions now," he commented in a letter dated October 22.[28]

"It is of little use to study constitutions by themselves," he wrote on another occasion. "No matter how impeccably the constitution may be designed, and no matter how solid a parliament you may have," he went on, "if governance is not good, then obviously you cannot expect good results. It is essential for good, effective governance to establish high standards of both government organization and administration."[29]

The encounter with Stein jolted Itō into a broad reconsideration of constitutional systems, this time in relation to their institutional base—administration. Itō took pride in being a "statesman of institutions" within the oligarchic form of government.[30] Stein's theory of the state provided exactly what he had sought, but Stein's influence went further, helping Itō to gain a perspective on institutions as founded in knowledge and made workable by educated people with the necessary knowledge, a point that will be discussed in the next section.

Itō went back to Berlin and studied with Mosse again until February 19, 1883. On March 3, he went to London and spent about two months doing further research. A letter to Inoue Kaoru gives a taste of the energy he put into it: "I've been in London for almost two months, engaging in study every day. I've exerted myself to the utmost in an effort to understand. But the more I learn about constitutional government, the more difficult I find it."[31] Other than a few letters, there is not much record of how Itō spent his time in London. Therefore later scholars researching that period in Itō's life when he was avidly trying to learn about constitutions, myself included, have tended to focus on the influence of the European scholars he encountered, notably Gneist in Germany and Stein in Austria.[32] In the conclusion to this chapter I venture to speculate on the results of Itō's research in England.

Leaving England, Itō went on to Russia and, as Japan's ambassador plenipotentiary, attended the coronation of Emperor Alexander III on May 9. On June 26, he departed from Naples for Japan. His ship arrived at Yokohama on August 3, 1883, bringing to a close a year and a half of study in Europe. Before he left Japan, there had been a great deal of opposition to his tour both within and outside the government, but Itō returned home with great confidence in the prospects of establishing a constitution for Japan.

Education and knowledge in constitutional government

What was the historical significance of this first ever constitution in Japan, on which the country was staking its national prestige? The Meiji Constitution has long been labeled the product of "sham constitutionalism (*Scheinkonstitutionalismus*)" that codified strong imperial prerogatives and weak powers of the parliament. As such, it has been seen as having a more reactionary than modernizing character. In fact, however, it was under this constitution that parliamentary government first took root and developed in Japan and with it the English-style two-party system and party cabinet that were maintained until the 1920s. Was this development something that Itō, "father of the Constitution," had not anticipated or planned for? With that question in mind, we will focus in this section on Itō's thinking at the time when the Constitution was enacted. In so doing, we will pay particular attention to "constitution" not only in the sense of a code of law or set of principles for governing, but also broadly in terms of the structure of the nation and its governing system.

Structure of the state

Let us first look at the Meiji Constitution as a code of law. The text marks it as a set of principles affirming and codifying the divine rights and absolute power of the emperor by stating that Japan "is governed by a line of emperors unbroken for ages eternal" (Article 1) and the emperor "is sacred and inviolable" (Article 3). Apart from the "divine rights" references,[33] in other respects the Prussian Constitution (1850) furnished the model for provisions in the Meiji Constitution. The Prussian model might not have been adopted had it not been for the Political Crisis of 1881, which purged Ōkuma Shigenobu and his associates from the government. With Ōkuma gone, the English model was rejected. The way was cleared for the German alternative, the one that Iwakura and Inoue Kowashi had been pushing. With that, the principles guiding the draft were settled, which meant that the basic principles of the Constitution itself were established at that time.

Itō Hirobumi's constitutional research in Europe in 1882–3, however, added a new dimension to the meaning of the Japanese word for constitution. It seems that by the time Itō was sent back to Europe for further study, the Japanese *kenpō* had been officially selected as the rendering of the English and French *constitution* and German *Verfassung*. *Kenpō* is the Japanese reading of an ancient Chinese word meaning "rules or laws of state" and was adopted with that meaning early in the Meiji era. That is the only meaning of the term. In contrast, both *constitution* and *Verfassung* have multiple meanings. Prior to "code of law" they denote the structure or composition of something, the way something is put together, or, by extension, national structure.[34] Therefore, the Japanese gloss for the European terms is both more specific to its meaning and more deeply embedded in its cultural roots.

What Itō's research in Europe accomplished was to go beyond the study of constitutions as codes of law to include the overall structure of the state. Stein helped him to gain the more sophisticated understanding that Japan's *kenpō* would be no more than a document; what was important was an administration able to act on its own through a capable bureaucracy. Wiser, more realistic, and intent on practical outcomes, Itō embarked upon the administrative and structural reform of government not long after he returned to Japan.

Reforming the state structure

Back in Japan, Itō first set out to make changes in the political powers of the imperial court, going by the principle of separation of court and national government. Emperor Meiji, now in his thirties, had a dignity and regal mien befitting a young monarch. The Japanese people liked and respected him and they had formed a movement calling for the emperor to directly administer the affairs of state. Itō was staunchly opposed. To put control of national politics into the hands of one monarch would not be desirable for the type of state he envisioned for Japan. He was able to get the support needed to block the movement for direct imperial rule and to put into effect reforms that removed the court's direct influence from national government.[35]

In December 1885, Itō set about restructuring administration by establishing a cabinet system. That year he became the nation's first prime minister. Until then, those eligible to serve as state ministers (grand minister of state and ministers of the left and right) had been confined to members of the imperial family and the hereditary peerage (families like the Arisugawa, Sanjō, and Iwakura), but from then onward, it became possible, at least in theory, for any Japanese citizen of any social class to be appointed a cabinet minister.

Itō then launched a project to reform higher education. He began by establishing, in 1886, what was then called the Imperial University (renamed Tokyo

Imperial University in 1897) and is today's University of Tokyo. He characterized the new university as an institution designed to recruit and train Japan's bureaucratic elite, the men who would be involved in administering the state. The following year, a research association, Kokka Gakkai (the Society for *Staatswissenschaft*), was set up within the university's College of Law (present-day Law Faculty of the University of Tokyo). Created with the support of Itō Hirobumi, it was Japan's first policy think-tank.

In 1888, the Privy Council was founded, initially to deliberate on the drafts of the Constitution and the Imperial Household Law. As its first president, Itō gave it the additional role of advisory body concerning the emperor's political activity, following his intention to keep the emperor away from political affairs by separating court and government. Since the Meiji Constitution stipulated that the emperor was head of state and held the rights of sovereignty, Itō needed a way to institutionalize and impose order on political activities by the emperor. His idea therefore, was to use the Privy Council; whenever the emperor as sovereign engaged in political decision-making, he would attend the Privy Council in person and make no decisions except through deliberations at the council.

Itō's last vital touch to the series of reforms was the promulgation of the Meiji Constitution in 1889. With that, for the first time, the nation became a constitutional state.

Challenge from Ōkuma

Itō saw that an essential prerequisite to the institution of a constitutional system was a different perspective on knowledge and a system of acquiring knowledge that would support the new state. One of the great legacies of Lorenz von Stein to Japan was what he had helped Itō to understand during his time studying with the professor in Vienna. Because of Stein, Itō had come to believe that a state was founded on knowledge. At this point, therefore, let us reflect further upon the significance of Stein's theory of the state.

Itō had always been hungry for knowledge. From his own experience beginning in boyhood, he came to believe that knowledge was the key to success in one's career and recognition in society. Itō himself rose in the world spurred by a passionate yearning for knowledge and the courage to throw off social shackles in his determination to learn. For a person with such a personality and background, the Political Crisis of 1881 must have given Itō a serious jolt. Ōkuma had been successfully rallying intellectuals and preparing proposals for institutional reforms, threatening to outdo Itō on his home ground. When Ōkuma laid out his vision for a constitution and for the nation at that time, Itō could see how far it outshone his own; his sense of himself as a "statesman of institutions" must have been shaken to the core, and for his determination to be a "statesman-advocate of knowledge," it created a crisis.

While still in government, Ōkuma had brought in brilliant intellectuals in an effort to expand his influence. To name some of them, we can start with Agriculture and Commerce Minister Kōno Togama (1844–95) and Postmaster-General

Maejima Hisoka (1835–1919). Up-and-coming bureaucrats included Yano Fumio (holding concurrent posts as Statistics Bureau secretary and Dajōkan senior secretary), Inukai Tsuyoshi (Statistics Bureau vice junior secretary), Ozaki Yukio (1858–1954; Statistics Bureau vice junior secretary), and Ono Azusa (Board of Audit first auditor).[36] Almost all of these young talented bureaucrats had studied at Fukuzawa Yukichi's Keiō Gijuku school and, through the good offices of Ōkuma, had found employment in government service. This was all part of Ōkuma's plan to introduce a system of English party government into Japan, and for that, he had counted on alumni of Keiō Gijuku to serve as his staff when the plan came to fruition.

Ozaki Yukio, while working with the Statistics Bureau, wrote that Yano Fumio, Ōkuma's right-hand man, had told him:

> Caught up in the current movement, people in the cabinet, also, are calling for a Diet in our government. Councilor Ōkuma hopes for a Diet to be established in 1883 and has already begun preparing for it. When the Diet is convened, there will be a need for many executive branch officials who can and will be called upon to explain state affairs. He therefore set to work finding talented people from the private sector to serve as interns, as it were, to get practice in government matters for two years to prepare them for that day.[37]

It is not surprising that the government, shocked by Ōkuma's radical constitutional proposal, became suspicious of the gathering of intellectual bureaucrats around him. Sanjō Sanetomi, then grand minister of state, wrote, "It seems like everyone is outraged that since making his proposals, Ōkuma has managed to infiltrate the government with Fukuzawa faction members."[38] The only way to block Ōkuma's radical move was to remove not just Ōkuma but the Fukuzawa faction elements en masse from the government.

Political versus scientific intellectuals

The purge of the Ōkuma faction merely diverted their energies into other channels. Almost as soon as they were ejected from government, Ōkuma and his associates launched a vigorous anti-government campaign by establishing a political party, the Rikken Kaishintō (Constitutional Reform party, often called simply Kaishintō), and founding the Tōkyō Senmon Gakkō (later Waseda University) in 1882. With "a political party in one hand and a school in the other," they set out to train political experts at that private school and recruit them into a political party. Ōkuma's confidant, Ono Azusa, is reported to have said in a lecture at Tōkyō Senmon Gakkō:

> Mr. Ono's lectures were much like political speechmaking. Instead of teaching the principles of finance, he spent the time in impassioned political talk. Talking to us that way he was able to get all of us students excited by political

debate. Extraordinary indeed. . . . The whole school's two hundred students were all spirited young politicians.[39]

This anti-government force had hit upon a brilliant formula for regenerating itself, and it posed a great threat to the ruling oligarchy. At the same time, those in government no doubt realized that they should have known better than to let private schools take the initiative in training people for the political elite. One of those most painfully aware of that fact was certainly Itō himself. Tsuchiya Tadao, scholar of Meiji education policy, writes,

> The primary and unwavering concern of Itō Hirobumi since his 1869 paper "Principles of National Policy" ("Kokuze kōmoku"; also known as the "Hyōgo Proposal") was how to establish the structure and organization of a modern unified state governed by law; how should education be administered and what kind of school system should be adopted by the state; and what kind of education is needed to produce people who are proud and competent modern Japanese.[40]

The idea of establishing a university as an institution to provide for that kind of learning had been on Itō's mind for a long time. The "Principles of National Policy" that he and four others submitted in 1869, when he was governor of Hyōgo prefecture, called for an immediate start to providing "scientific learning from around the world" for Japanese people. It proposed the founding of a "new university devoted to that purpose so that the traditional way of learning might be completely changed." Itō believed that a new state must be run by a new breed of people who had mastered the latest in scientific and practical learning.

Ōkuma's program of higher education, therefore, was daunting for Itō. First was the bare fact of Ōkuma's college, but there was also the difference in their ideas about the "qualities" of the intellectuals they hoped to nurture. As the above recollection of Ono's talk at Tōkyō Senmon Gakkō suggests, Ōkuma envisioned being surrounded by "political intellectuals" trained and practiced in political debate and speech-making. What Itō had in mind were more rigorously analytic "scientific intellectuals." That "science" should be the means to overwhelm those who practiced "political debate" was a matter of serious concern for Itō.

In a 1879 proposal called "Kyōiku-gi" [On Education], Itō had argued that in the post-Restoration era, an overhaul of higher education was inevitable in order to deal with new conditions, among them the significant numbers of dissatisfied and under-employed former samurai, and the rise of radical Western ideas. In this passage from "Kyōiku-gi" he discusses the importance of stressing "science" over "political debate" in education:

> Higher school students should be encouraged to pursue science; don't induce them into political debate. Too many versed in political debate would hinder the well-being of the people. If the present trend is allowed to continue, we will soon find gentlemen and youth of some intelligence

vying to best each other in political speech and debate. . . . To counter this ominous development it is essential to promote a wide range of subjects in engineering and technology. Those who receive higher education should commit themselves wholeheartedly to the pursuit of practical learning, examining and observing things in fine detail and becoming more and more proficient year after year. That way we can get rid of the frivolous, over-passionate currents of the moment. Science is to political debate as rising is to falling.[41]

Misgivings about Inoue Kowashi

Contrary to what Itō urged in his proposal on education, the situation just got worse. Political gadflies were "all over town and country" and they began making their way into the government in early 1881, partly through Ōkuma's good offices. A frustrated Itō remarked acidly, "Nowadays some of these insolent government secretaries try to press on us their exceedingly radical ideas."[42]

Naturally, Itō was more sensitive and concerned about the movement of Ōkuma's Tōkyō Senmon Gakkō than any other leader in the government. That was a problem coming from outside the government, but there was another cause of worry for Itō, which came from inside. The Political Crisis of 1881 can be characterized as a power struggle over different visions of the state, but, as has been recognized for a long time, the real players in the struggle were not Itō or Ōkuma but Inoue Kowashi and Ono Azusa.[43] Facing the rise of intellectuals like Ono who were familiar with Western theories of the state and politics, Itō no doubt felt it urgent to have a better grasp of constitutional government than this new breed of intellectuals, partly to secure his influence and boost his leadership.

As for Inoue Kowashi, certainly he was a man of great talent—well versed in the Prussian constitutional monarchy and a strong advocate of introducing its principles into Japan. He was the government-side ideologue who had destroyed Ōkuma's radical proposal and who had persuaded Itō to take on the task of drafting a constitution. Inoue's presence, however, was becoming a threat, for his actions often bypassed Itō, and he came close to bossing Iwakura and Inoue Kaoru around as if they were his juniors. All this was part of Inoue's attempt to shift the whole government toward adopting the Prussian-style constitution that he envisioned.

Inoue Kowashi also curried the favor of Inoue Kaoru so that he could persuade him to be the one to criticize Itō's thinking on the Constitution, particularly proposals regarding reform of the Genrōin (Chamber of Elders). He wanted Inoue Kaoru to urge Itō to "take the model of the Prussian constitution."[44] Inoue Kowashi's behind-the-scenes maneuvering promised to put Itō in the position of spearheading the move to realize Inoue's Prussian-style constitution plan. It is easy to imagine that Inoue's manipulations seemed to Itō to go beyond the duty of a government official. Itō was thus keenly concerned not just about non-government ideologues like Ono Azusa, but also the "beyond the call of duty" political activities of intellectuals within the Establishment like Inoue Kowashi. One of the foremost questions facing Itō when he left Japan on his constitutional study tour to Europe was how to "tame" the manipulators like Ono and Inoue Kowashi and establish a "system of knowledge" to support his power base.

Stein's theory becomes Itō's strength

So it was that Itō had to rise against and prevail over both the Ōkuma-Ono and the Iwakura-Inoue lines of constitutional thinking if he hoped to pursue his own, third path to constitutional government. The situation he found himself in was undoubtedly at work in his decision to make the European trip, despite the considerable cost and possible political risk. Staying in Japan would get him nowhere, and he would end up unable to move ahead of Ono and Inoue. If he hoped to develop a distinctive vision for constitutional government in Japan, one of sufficient magnitude to confront the emerging political intellectuals, it was imperative for Itō to leave Japan as soon as possible, and pursue a new theory of state in Germany and Austria.

Itō's research in Europe, therefore, was not aimed simply at gaining added prestige as a drafter of the Constitution; it had a supremely practical purpose, and Stein's theory of state gave Itō what he was looking for. When he left Japan he was filled with anxiety about the kind of political intellectuals that were emerging inside and outside government, but, having encountered Stein, he declared he had found a whole new way of seeing and approaching constitutional government; he had found the "logic and means" to outdo them in pushing his agenda. Now calling these intellectuals [the Ōkuma protégés] "still-green students" (*hebokure shosei*),[45] he showed steadily increasing confidence in his new understanding of constitutional systems.

> Today the tendency in Japan to blindly believe only the writings of liberal radicals in Britain, America, and France has grown so strong that it threatens to ruin the country. That is the situation, but I have found a way, a logic and the means, to turn the situation around.[46]

What lay behind Itō's supreme confidence? Most important was his realization that the arguments for constitutional government cited by the popular rights advocates in Japan were already a thing of the past in Europe. In Japan, anti-government ideologues continued to rely heavily on already outmoded ideas of Rousseau and other eighteenth-century theories of state and society. Accordingly, as is frequently the case with anti-Establishment intellectuals, they often seized on an abstract idea or natural law and used that law or concept as the conduit for expression of uncritical faith in radical parliamentarian ideas, and they also used it to justify their cause. By the time Itō got to Europe, new ideas had come to the fore, and Rousseau's abstract natural law approach to government and society had been superseded by historicism, a perspective that focused on specific cultures and histories. He wrote on September 6, 1882 in a letter to Matsukata Masayoshi:

> Young people and students struggle to read Western works and draw meaning from them, and using only the logic they can get from the surface meaning of the text, they take that to be some eternal, unchanging truth. Trying to apply such dicta to the real world, I think, is shallow and superficial. That way of thinking ignores the specific polity and history of one's own nation. It is a narrow-minded approach, no more relevant than trying to set up a new government in a place where no one lives.[47]

Indeed, by that time in Europe hypothetical, abstract, idealistic social theories like the social contract doctrine had receded, and were being, or had been, replaced by concrete, place-specific historicism and positivism as the guiding principles of learning. The primary object of understanding was no longer the abstract "individual" but real social factors that affect individuals in diverse ways. In Germany, as elsewhere, idealism had relinquished its paramount place in learning to more research- and data-oriented fields such as history, economics, and sociology. This was the context in which Stein was able to proclaim the emergence of a view of society as a system of class antagonisms with its own laws. Stein's thinking exerted significant influence on Karl Marx and other socialist thinkers and thus occupies a distinctive place in the history of socialist thought and sociology in Germany.[48]

Now confident that he had absorbed the latest political thought and the latest theories of society in Europe, Itō was in high spirits. He was finally able to declare, "How very poor and backward Mr. Progressive [Ōkuma]'s doings are!"[49] Itō appears to have made a complete mental recovery.

Stein and higher education in Japan

There was one more reason for Itō's confidence: through Stein he vividly understood the need for a system of education that would support the goal of securing public peace and order in the nation. This idea comes through in his vision of reorganizing higher education, creating national institutes of learning, and disseminating knowledge in preparation for a constitutional state. These institutes would turn out new generations of political elites, who would then be equipped to manage and support a political system. With that in mind, Itō decided to invite Stein to spearhead changes in the education system in Japan. Writing to Inoue Kaoru on August 23, when he first proposed the invitation, Itō said, "Given Japan's situation, what we need to discuss is establishing a foundation for higher education and redirecting the course of learning."[50]

Itō subsequently stressed this point again and again in his correspondence to persons in Japan. He wrote, for example, to Yamada Akiyoshi, councilor and home minister:

> In my letter to Foreign Minister Inoue I recommended that Mr. Stein, Austrian scholar, be invited to Japan. I believe that if the Cabinet Council

decides to hire this scholar, having him supervise the university and set the direction of learning will be truly effective in doing away with irrelevant educational practices and will yield great benefits for the future.[51]

In another letter to Inoue, he wrote:

> In the previous letter I proposed employing Dr. Stein. What do you think? Having seen the solid basis of German scholarship, I have become more and more convinced that Japan today needs men like him. If he were to come to Japan, mainly to help plan the practical directions for the establishment, organization, and curriculum of the university, and if he could also serve as an advisor to the government on our country's legal system, we would not only reap benefits right now but would be able to lay solid foundations to last for the next one hundred years.[52]

These letters make it clear that Itō's idea of inviting Stein to Japan was closely connected to his plans for higher education reform. They also underline how entirely consistent his thinking was. Urging approval of the invitation, Itō added in a subsequent letter:

> When Dr. Stein's employment is approved, I would like to have him engage in the additional task of school curriculum reform as a government advisor. To reshape the mindset of the people, there is no way but to start with reform of school education.[53]

That last sentence, "reform of school education" as a way to "reshape the mindset of the people," shows the extraordinary ambitions Itō had. Ultimately, Stein did not accept the offer to go to Japan and get fully involved with educational reform, but said that he would be happy to assist in higher education reform indirectly from Vienna, presenting an alternative proposition as follows:

> From the sidelines, I will help your country's youth and students who come to Vienna to study, and on their behalf I will not only exercise my good offices for their entrance into university but will also encourage their studies as a devoted friend. For Japanese students to master European courses of study, I will act as an intermediary to contribute to the founding of a university in your country some day. There is nothing more important in the advancement of knowledge than to establish a university. If university education flourishes in your country its benefits will surely be extended to the rest of Asia. I have long believed this, but I have not yet had a chance to actually pursue it.[54]

Here, Stein presupposes the inevitability of a modern university founded in Japan, and he expresses his willingness to serve as a facilitator. He even declared a long-cherished dream to spread university education in Asia. He was clearly an enthusiastic supporter of Itō's vision for a new, modern university in Japan, which is what made the two men find in each other kindred spirits.[55]

The encounter with Stein in Europe brought home to Itō the importance of state structure and administration, as well as of knowledge as the essential supporting element. It was a turning point, as we have seen, and from then on he worked tirelessly to establish a sound administrative system.

Charisma of a constitutional expert

For Itō, Stein's encouragement and interest validated his determination to reform higher education and make it into a national institution that would be central to the successful management of the modern Japanese state. In Japan, surrounded by the stormy proliferation of political intellectuals in government and outside it, he had found it difficult to seize the initiative in the drive to make Japan into a constitutional government. But returning to Japan after studying with Stein, Itō was filled with confidence that he was way ahead of the thinking of his countrymen. He had written earlier from Vienna with a comment on Hermann Roesler (1834–94), the German advisor who had long served as advisor to the Japanese cabinet: "I have all too often found Roesler's ideas to be overly inclined toward liberalism."[56] It is not hard to detect a note of self-satisfaction here; Itō had found a great German scholar he believed worthy of their full attention—suggesting that Japan needed to move beyond Roesler. With the help of Stein, he was now equipped with the "logic and means," the theoretical and practical punch, that would arm him to counter what had been the first wave of German political thought that was circulating in Japan.

Itō's time in Europe studying constitutionalism and constitutions was an irreplaceable experience that gave him not only a vastly greater understanding of constitutional government, but also lent him a kind of charisma when he returned home. Now Japan's undisputed authority in the field, he was ready to take leadership in all constitutional matters.

Knowledge as the foundation for the state

Among the notes he took on Stein's lectures on the state, found in "Itō monjo" (Itō papers) in the collection of the Japanese National Diet Library, one contains this passage:

> Training bureaucrats to form a solid foundation for constitutional government is one of the paramount missions of the university. The university, therefore, serves a crucial purpose in public administration. Simply teaching academic subjects goes only halfway toward its real purpose, and a university that stops there cannot be said to be complete as a university.[57]

Stein saw the university as a state organ that provides the "solid foundation for constitutional government." Only when knowledge and knowledgeable people are produced at university can the state be administered well. In other words, when the structure of a state is changed, it is essential to create an apparatus to impart and disseminate knowledge, and those who learn—the "educated class" will lead in making and administering the restructuring process. Stein was a fervent believer in knowledge gained and imparted in response to the needs of the state—"state knowledge" as it were. Itō, absorbing from Stein the same conviction that such knowledge was absolutely essential in building and administering constitutional government, returned to Japan with a new dimension to his image that boosted his spectacular comeback in political life: he was not just a "statesman of institutions" but had become a "statesman-advocate of knowledge" as well.

Enactment of the Constitution and party government: Itō's speeches

The Constitution of the Empire of Japan, commonly called the Meiji Constitution, was promulgated on February 11, 1889. On that day the streets of Tokyo were transformed with the mood of a national celebration. The way the festive atmosphere swept up people high and low has been documented in numerous accounts, including those of foreign advisors hired by the Meiji government. But the events of the day were also recorded by many others as well. Here is part of a recollection by a Japanese artisan:

> I saw the Constitution promulgated with my very eyes. There was such huge excitement. Well, I think I was nine then, and at shops everywhere they were breaking open big *shitodaru* barrels of sake, passing it out to everyone for free, like at a festival. People were getting tipsy all over the place. The same thing was going on everywhere in Japan, I heard. Even when the soldiers came back triumphant after the Russo-Japanese War [of 1904–5], it paled compared to the hoopla on Constitution Day.[58]

Everybody, people in government and ordinary folk, were intoxicated on that day, certain that they finally had the ticket to becoming a first-rank country.

There were other matters, however, that also concerned Itō in those days, and to which he gave hard, thoughtful attention. One of them was to work out what kind of constitutional state was best for Japan, that is, what political substance should fill out the constitutional framework. What was the "substance" Itō was thinking of? It was popular government. He envisioned redesigning and improving the structure of the state to center it on the administrative sector. Itō believed the spirit of popular government could be infused into that new form. This is Itō's distinctive idea, going beyond what he learned from Stein. He discussed that point clearly in speeches made immediately following the promulgation of the Meiji Constitution, so let us examine what he said in those talks to get an idea of the spirit of constitutional government he hoped for, as well as to demonstrate the full extent of his thinking at the time of the establishment of the Constitution.

Emperor-granted Constitution

After the promulgation, Itō delivered several speeches aimed at promoting a better understanding of the Constitution among the people. The best known is a speech he gave to the heads of the prefectural assemblies on February 15, 1889. This, together with the address made by the then Prime Minister Kuroda Kiyotaka three days before, has often been cited as a declaration of *chōzen-shugi*, or "transcendental" policy under which the government keeps a distance from political parties. What Itō actually said on that occasion had deeper implications, however. This speech has been widely cited and exhaustively studied, but let us take a fresh look at it here.[59]

At the beginning Itō says "The Constitution recently promulgated is, it is needless to say, a constitution granted by the Emperor." His first emphasis, then, was the point that the emperor himself established the Constitution and gave it to the Japanese people. "The Constitution was granted to the subjects by the grace and benevolence of His Majesty the Emperor" (p. 651).

Being granted by the emperor is the most notable feature of the Meiji Constitution. Itō went on to explain:

> A comparison of our Constitution and those of other constitutional states shows a vast difference between them. The Imperial prerogatives, or monarchical sovereignty, are spelled out in Chapter I [of the Meiji Constitution] and this is something of which we find no examples in the other countries. Give it just a little thought and you will immediately understand the reason why this is so. Ever since the founding of our country aeons ago, the Emperor, its creator, has directly ruled it. Placing the provision at the beginning of the Constitution, therefore, is perfectly suited to our national polity (*kokutai*). That is what makes our Constitution so eminently different in text and composition from the other countries' constitutions. (p. 652)

Here Itō explains why the confirmation of imperial sovereignty comes first, giving the Meiji Constitution its distinct tone, and, in the way he speaks, he seems to equate the emperor with the state. And in fact he states:

> Judging from the history and realities of our country since its founding, its sovereignty resides in the monarch, that is, the Royal Household. There is no precedent [in Japanese history] of sovereignty ever having been transferred somewhere else, and there is now no reason for such transfer. (p. 654)

He continues:

> Sovereignty should be vested in a single individual, not divisible. As long as it lies with the monarch, everything that government officials do is done on

A constitution for Japan 63

Figure 2.4 Kuroda Kiyotaka (1840–1900).

Source: Photograph courtesy of the National Diet Library of Japan.

his behalf, at his behest. The activities of each administrative agency of the government are never inherent to that agency but are merely delegated to it by the sovereign. The action of each official, therefore, is no more than the exercise of the power of attorney. Although each administrative agency is divided into various sections, each of which has a distinct role to play and is accordingly operated independently, the monarch superintends them all. Even though a parliament may be convened as a place of public opinion and deliberation, we should not forget that sovereignty rests only in a single monarch. (pp. 655–6)

Itō explained further that this idea of sovereignty was currently accepted in Europe as greatly preferable to the once widely espoused views of Montesquieu on the need for the separation of powers. Itō reinforced his own argument by citing the "organic thinking" that had taken deep hold among Western intellectuals. This was at the root of theories that compared the state and its agencies to the unity of the human body and its organs; just as human thought and mind had their source in the brain, Itō went on, "as virtually every scholar who lectures on sovereignty affirms, sovereignty must come from a single, not divided, source" (p. 655). Itō saw in that idea a perfect parallel with Japan's national polity, and it was for that reason that the Meiji Constitution specified the indivisibility of sovereign power right in Article 1.

Itō took great pride in having developed a constitution that was the first to actually incorporate the latest theory of the state. The person in whom that single and indivisible sovereignty should reside was, in the case of Japan, the emperor. Stressing the immobility of sovereignty, Itō said:

> In Japan, on the basis of its national polity in force since the very founding of the country, the Emperor has held the status of head of state, and I sincerely hope sovereignty will never be transferred to the people. (p. 656)

As for governance of the state, he espoused direct imperial rule, stating, "The Emperor superintends all state affairs," and the government is "the Emperor's government" from the start, and "our government shall be ruled and operated by the sovereign" (p. 653).

Inevitability of party government

A close study of this speech by Itō, which is included in the *Itō den*, may lead one to conclude that here he is simply trying to vindicate a despotic state with the emperor as sovereign. There is an extension of Itō's argument, however, which we find by looking at a *Tōkyō nichinichi* newspaper article that contains the whole text of the Itō speech that day. It is this extended part of the speech, not included in the *Itō den*, that shows how far his thinking goes beyond the notion of "transcendental government" (keeping aloof from political parties), an idea that he himself had advocated but that had been popularly interpreted somewhat differently from what he actually meant.

"When a constitution is established and a parliament convened," Itō writes, "given the propensity for humans to congregate, it is inevitable for political parties to arise."[60] What clearer statement could there be of a belief that party-based government that is bound to arise once a constitution goes into force?[61] Underlying this thinking is his observation that constitutional government involves reconciling different interests. That is, constitutional government, which by definition ensures popular participation, by definition guarantees that people can advocate for their own interests and engage in political activities based on those interests.

What is important, then, is in what direction a government based on the management of various interests should be guided. Itō continues from the observation quoted above:

> In the future, when representatives of the subjects gather and make resolutions concerning national affairs, the interests they consider should be not

the interests of one prefecture but the interests of the whole nation. Each member of the Imperial Diet does not represent only that segment of Japan's subjects who elected him. Diet members represent all subjects across the country and do not cater to the narrow interests of their home regions. Thus Diet members should make judgments based on their conscientious and full consideration of the interests of the whole nation.

Many years later Itō would often refer to Edmund Burke's (1729–97) "Speech to the Electors of Bristol," and not quite quoting him, would repeat, in his own words, "I go to parliament as a representative of you, residents of my electoral district. Upon arriving at the parliament, however, I act not as your representative but as a representative of the whole nation."[62] The groundwork for such thinking was already laid by the time of the 1889 speech. Itō hoped that each and every parliamentary statesman, while burdened with the specific interests of his constituency, would act as the spokesman for the entire nation.

Leaving that responsibility to the individual discretion and moral principles of each government representative would have been overly idealistic. And so Itō sought to separate parliamentary government from governance of the nation, saying:

> Differences in opinion naturally lead to formation of different parties. We have to accept the fact that parties or factions will arise within a parliament or society, but the government must never allow itself to be identified with one party or another.

Denial of radicalism

What Itō had in mind here is undoubtedly what he had learned in Vienna about Stein's theory of state. Stein's theory is strongly characterized by a dualism of state and society. In this view, society (*Gesellschaft*) is made up of profit-oriented individual special interests, whereas the state (*Staat*) is the embodiment of the universal interests of the whole national community. State activities, being neutral and free from involvement with private interests, are essential in order to extract from society, which is basically a system for organizing human desires, what are public values and then act on them. Perhaps trying to be consistent with that idea, Itō stated that struggles over interests among parties were inevitable in society, but no such wrangling should occur in national government. "The national government should not protect and benefit particular parties," he added.

Itō thus recognized free competition among individual interests in the private sector and supported the principle of keeping national government out of the fray—completely away from all that competition. It is a declaration par excellence of his "transcendental" policy, but we should note the following passage:

> It would be precipitous to seek immediately to install a parliamentary government, with a cabinet formed by a political party. Many people are

talking of the merits and advantages of parties, but parties have to have acquired the necessary skills if they are to be able to establish basic national policies and function effectively in a deliberative assembly. If they lack such abilities and carelessly undermine the foundations of the state, this will have a terrible impact on the future of our country!

This is an unambiguous expression of Itō's opposition to introducing a party cabinet system right away, which he saw as radical and too risky at that juncture. In his view, it was still too soon for political parties to be able to fully function as they should in parliamentary government, but he did not reject parliamentary government itself. In other words, he was not ruling out the possibility of a party cabinet being formed in the future. That could happen, he believed, but not until parties had acquired the experience and know-how to "establish basic national policies and function effectively in a deliberative assembly." A party cabinet government was, in fact, precisely the type of constitutional government he envisioned for Japan someday. For Itō, constitutional government meant popular government. Let us consider some of the remarks Itō made around that time, which give ample testimony to his thinking on that point.

Constitutional government as popular government: Itō's address to royalty and peers

On February 17, 1889, two days after he spoke to the prefectural assembly heads, Itō gave another speech before a group of judges on the relation between judicial and executive powers under the Meiji Constitution. Stressing the independence of the two from each other, Itō warned that judicial power should never interfere with executive power.[63] He also took great pains to make sure that the peers had a solid understanding of the Constitution. Three times he delivered lectures for members of the Kazoku Dōhō Kai (Peers Research Association) and others, on December 8, 1888, and February 26 and 27, 1889.[64] Itō addressed other groups as well. Drafts of speeches he made in Ōtsu and Kyoto during a lecture tour in the Kansai region can be found among the "Itō Miyoji kankei monjo" [Itō Miyoji Papers] in the collection of the Japanese National Diet Library's Kensei Shiryōshitsu (Modern Japanese Political History Documents Room).

The February 27, 1889 speech noted above, titled "Kaku shinnō denka oyobi kizoku ni taishi" [To the Imperial Princes and the Peers][65] is noteworthy for his forthright discussion, while addressing royalty and peers—many of whom were former daimyo—about what should be expected of constitutional government. Itō worked hard around the time of the promulgation to promote an understanding of the Constitution among the peers. These people, being the elite of the emperor's circle, would have an influential place in the constitutional government, and it is easy to imagine that Itō made efforts to exalt their political responsibility. Until recently we have had only the accounts published in the press to go by, but they do not report the speech accurately in its entirety, or convey the heart of his message. The speech as reported in the press argues that the Constitution allowed the executive branch to act independently without restraint from the judicial or legislative branches. Actually, Itō's real emphasis in that February 27 speech is on democratic government centering on the people. Since no light has ever been cast on this document, let us look at it in detail.[66]

Itō begins by speaking highly of the unique character of Japan's national polity (*kokutai*):

> History tells us that ever since its founding Japan has been ruled by an unbroken line of emperors, and, in like manner, our people too have continued to be the same people. A perusal of ancient history does show that some people from Korea came here, but we have to say that the overwhelming majority of Japanese have descended from those who lived here at the time of the founding of our country.

Itō is saying that Japan, with its homogeneous people governed by "an unbroken line of emperors" since the country's beginnings, is unique throughout the world. Besides Japan, no country in the entire world has experienced no change in royal family, no change in its people.

This passage echoes the belief about Japan's national polity that was typical in those days, but what Itō says next is very interesting. He does something unusual, and that is to relativize the national polity by placing it in context of contemporary history, and using the term *kunigara* (more akin to "national character" than "national polity"), he conveys a subtle difference in connotation:

> In the past when there was no intercourse with other countries as there is today, scholars in Japan would talk as if Japan alone was noble and all other countries barbarian. Instead of thinking of Japan as noble because it is cultured while all the rest are savage, we should think of our country as having continued since its birth to be the same nation and people. This, I think, is something of which we can take pride in the world.

What we see here is a slight reformulation whereby Itō upholds the national polity based on the unbroken imperial line of emperors while cautioning against overdependence on its infallibility and encouraging reconsideration of its categorical authority by placing it in the broader context of relationships with the international community. He draws a clear distinction between international realities and the "expel the barbarians"/"Japan as a divinely appointed land" ideology prevailing at the end of the Tokugawa period, and he indicates a distancing from the Confucian conservatism that still held sway in the Meiji period. His thinking is premised on his vision of Japan as a modern, independent state capable of building open, constructive relationships with other countries. It is no leap to suspect that Itō's use of "national polity" (*kokutai*) is an expedient to advocate an independent state capable of becoming an active and cooperative actor in international society. Such an interpretation might be feasible in light of a passage of the speech by Itō:

> Japan's *kunigara* [national polity, or national character] is thus unique in the world. The country with this unique *kunigara* has just begun to open relations with other countries of the world. We must derive benefits from such relations and use those relations for the sake of our own protection and advancement.

Evolutionist approach

However it was handled ideologically, Itō was interested in pursuing Japan's national interests by forging relationships with countries throughout the international community. To those who fretted about how the national polity might be transformed by broad openness to relationships with the outside world, Itō had this to say:

> Even if change is brought [to the national polity], it will be only limited change. Interacting with the outside will help to protect us, help us advance, prevent outside interference, and enable us to compete with others and maintain our independent status. It won't change our "body" itself, although some improvements in it as well as "internal" improvement and advancement can occur as necessity dictates.

Here we get a glimpse of Itō's evolutionist approach. His position is that, through contact with the outside, the "body" of the state won't change into something completely different, but rather it will—and ought to—improve of its own accord; a gradual evolutionism. We can also say that here Itō is concerned not so much with external aspects of the state as with the internal mindset of the Japanese people. In his view, guiding the people to become more cultured and educated was a crucial factor that would determine the advancement of the state. As he explains:

> In order [for Japan] to be able to compete with other countries and thereby maintain its independent status and keep its national prestige from harm, it is imperative to enhance the learning and advance the knowledge of its people. The natural result will be tremendous growth of its national power.

Already Japan's doors had been opened wide to the world, and Itō believed that international competitiveness depended on the cultural standards of its people. "Leaving the people ignorant would prevent the country from growing in national power, and therefore," says Itō, "it is crucial to advance knowledge and virtue and raise the standard of their learning, thus providing the base on which to build up national power." By increasing the intellectual ability of the population, the nation would improve and advance of its own accord.

A constitution for Japan 69

What political system did Itō envision as the country continued to move ahead? Let us hear what he had to say:

> As the country fosters its people's knowledge and intellect and guides them to become more cultured, the people will get to know more and more about their country, their government, other countries' governments, other countries' national strengths, and other countries' military might. The more the people know the more necessary it will become to supervise them. If they are supervised in erroneous ways, governing this country will be impossible. When the people have become able to tell right from wrong and good from bad, simply to silence them will not be workable.

For a ruler, as history shows, creating a better-educated population can be a double-edged sword. An enlightened people can contribute to the strength of the nation, but can also develop critical attitudes toward government that are hard to deal with. Itō knew that all too well, but he nevertheless remained committed to building a government founded in a people enlightened in the ways of modernity; education of the populace, he had come to understand, was the rule in the advanced countries of the West and he believed Japan could achieve the same.

How to rule

The question was, what methods and principles or rule should be changed in preparation for the emergence of a people equipped with enlightened attitudes and critical minds? "Ambiguity is no good," says Itō:

> The monarch in his capacity as sovereign should govern the country by exercising the rights of sovereignty. The duties his subjects are to fulfill must also be made clear. All this is necessary in constitutional government.

It thus becomes necessary to clearly define the rights and powers of the ruler and the duties of the ruled. That is precisely what a constitution should do. Itō continues:

> He who rules a country is a monarch, or the sovereign of that country. Through what is his power exercised? The power should be exercised through various agencies of government. The beauty of a constitution is that it defines how far and in what ways those agencies are to exercise the sovereign's power, each according to the way it is set up and operated.

Under a constitution the ruler must never govern arbitrarily, and the exercise and application of his power are limited by the provisions laid down in it. That is how Itō explains a system of rule that is clear and unambiguous; sovereign power is limited by the constitution and the exercise of that power is regulated by it.

Toward a people-centered government

The underlying logic of Itō's February 1889 speech to the princes and nobility is that in order for the state to enhance its competitive power in the world, it is essential that the people reach a certain level of "cultural maturity"; that achieved, constitutional government will inevitably follow. Itō talked about noblesse oblige and responsibilities of the politically privileged class—his audience that day—but he also argued in support of giving the imperial subjects, those who are ruled, a stronger standing in politics, urging his listeners to be willing to yield in this matter.

This speech shows no trace of Itō's reputed attachment to transcendental government. Instead, presenting it as natural, even preferable, that an educated people should increase their political awareness and become interested in how the state is governed, he veers directly toward a people-centered government. In the view expressed here, a constitutional system is a framework for drawing political vitality from the people and integrating it into the state's overall governing structure.

But, one might argue, in that speech wasn't he really pushing for a kind of enlightened despotism for Japan? Wasn't Itō planning a state where, while allowing some degree of popular participation in government, a constitutional system would in fact be used as a legal divider, a shield as it were, to guarantee the emperor and oligarchy the political right to rule? Even if one tried to understand it in such a way, it is impossible to gloss over what he sees in "the people." It is the same theme we encountered before—a vision of how an enlightened, educated Japanese people will become the bulwark of national power, and as they become more educated, more modern, it is only natural that the ways of ruling the country will change. Certainly, therefore, in his vision of the new Japanese state, there is the possibility that "government for the people" will eventually develop into "government of the people and by the people." At very least, nothing in what he said to the royalty suggests that it might be necessary or desirable to block the progress toward government by the people.

What kind of nation?

When the Meiji Constitution was established, Itō understood the concept of constitution in multiple ways. He saw that it was not just a legal document but that it embodied the elemental structure of the state, and on that understanding he sought to mobilize a spirit of popular government that could be incorporated into the constitutional state. The result of this pursuit, as shall be discussed in the following chapters, was the Rikken Seiyūkai (Friends of Constitutional Government; Seiyūkai for short), the political party he founded in 1900. Its creation marked the birth of a responsible party capable of holding the reins of government and the party expanded to hold a pivotal role in the two-party system until 1940. That Itō had "turned" to found the Seiyūkai—a political party—has long been seen as a defection from his principle of transcendental government. But evidence from the February 27 speech to the royalty and nobility of Japan strongly suggests that the intent to facilitate popular participation in government and establish a political system centering around parliament had been part of Itō's vision since he began working on preparations for the Constitution.

Evidence indicating such thinking can be found in what Itō said and did during his time in Europe studying constitutionalism. For one, he made known his opposition to the anti-parliamentarian attitudes of Gneist and the German emperor Kaiser Wilhelm I. Also, his April 1883 letter to Inoue Kaoru from London indicates he was concerned about a parliamentary system in Japan's future constitutional government. What he was studying during his two-month stay in England was "constitutional government," he wrote. That is what Stein taught him about— *Verfassung* (constitution). *Verfassung* in Stein's theory of state can be relativized by *Verwaltung* (administration). When Itō went to England, we may surmise that he was searching for approaches and practices that would go beyond Stein's thesis. With his new perspective on administration, through Stein, he was able to see national structure as a second meaning of constitution, and now in England, where he observed parliamentary politics firsthand, he quite likely recognized a third meaning of constitution, that is, "constitutional government" in the form of popular participation in government. Itō's own theory of state bridges "national structure" and "constitutional government."

Since his return from the Iwakura Mission tour, Itō had viewed changes in Japan's government in terms of the gradual evolution of new institutions. After the political changes in the wake of the power plays over the Korean expedition, Itō was charged with investigating constitutional government. Itō advocated a policy of gradual adoption of a constitutional system, and echoing the thinking of Kido and Ōkubo, he advocated gradual adoption of a constitutional system. Via the Osaka Conference, that policy was translated into practice under Kido's leadership, resulting in the creation of the Genrōin and the Assembly of Prefectural Governors. At that time, Itō intended that these two would eventually develop into the upper and lower assemblies respectively, and a parliament would thereby spontaneously come into being.

His plan for indigenous constitutionalism was temporarily frustrated by the radical proposals in Ōkuma's paper on constitutional government. But because of the Political Crisis of 1881, which was triggered by the Ōkuma paper, clear deadlines were set forth to convene a parliament and establish a constitution, and constitutional government became the government's top policy priority.

As these new developments unfolded, Itō left for Europe to study under Stein and Gneist, and he came back with a new and broader understanding of constitution as the embodiment of national structure or "shape of the nation." His conviction was renewed that Japan would be best served by constitutional government in the form of "popular government" with a parliament at the center.

Consequently, his gradualism was revived. The establishment of a constitutional system, he knew, did not mean that a party government or parliamentary cabinet would come into being overnight. Institutional reform to adapt a constitutional system to popular government would require careful political maneuvering that considered both the level of the people's political awareness and major changes in the external environment. In that sense, for Itō Hirobumi, the establishment of the Meiji Constitution was not the ending point but the starting point for building the best possible national structure for Meiji Japan. It took a decade after the promulgation of the Constitution to build the structure, but at that point Itō took the lead in a full-fledged effort to do just that.

Notes

1. The advocates of sending a punitive expedition to Korea and the opponents of such action differed in their views of what "deliberate again" signified. The former saw it as an opportunity to obtain *ex post facto* sanction for their action, and the latter saw it as a chance for the officials who had been abroad on the Iwakura Mission to regain control of the government. For details on this point and the *seikanron* issue, see Takahashi 1993.
2. For more detail see Takahashi 1993.
3. Letter from Iwakura to Ōkuma and Itō dated October 15, 1873, *Itō den*, vol. 1, p. 755.
4. *Kido nikki*, vol. 2, p. 435.
5. *Itō den*, vol. 1, p. 762.
6. *Kido nikki*, vol. 2, p. 435.
7. *Ōkubo nikki*, vol. 2, p. 214.
8. *Kido nikki*, vol. 2, p. 453.
9. *Ōkubo monjo*, vol. 5, p. 186.
10. *Kido nikki*, vol. 2, p. 452.
11. Ibid., p. 454.
12. *Ōkubo monjo*, vol. 5, pp. 203 ff.
13. The "Jakō-no-ma" was a high-ranking advisory body to the emperor, made up of members of the imperial family and nobility.
14. *Kido nikki*, vol. 1, p. 258.
15. In February 1875, Ōkubo, Kido, and Itagaki Taisuke, the last two having left government—Kido in protest against the Taiwan expedition and Itagaki in protest of the government's refusal to proceed with the Korea expedition—gathered in Osaka, with Inoue Kaoru and Itō as mediators, to discuss establishment of constitutional government and national and regional assemblies.
16. Itō's letter to Sanjō dated April 23, 1874, *Iwakura monjo*, vol. 6, p. 76.
17. *Itō den*, vol. 2, pp. 192 ff.
18. Sakamoto 1991.
19. Letter from Inoue Kowashi to Iwakura dated June 14, 1881, *Inoue Kowashi den*, vol. 4, p. 338.
20. Letter from Itō to Sanjō Sanetomi dated July 1, "Sanjō-ke monjo," no. 188–12.
21. *Hogohiroi*, vol. 11, pp. 22–3. In a letter to Itō, dated January 11, 1882, right before he left for Europe, Inoue advised him to "be sure to refrain from drinking." (*Itō monjo* [Hanawa], vol. 1, p. 169) In his April 6 letter to Itō, the first after the latter left Yokohama, Inoue revealed how worried he was about his colleague's health: "I hope you're feeling better and refreshed, and your trip is going smoothly. I trust you're drinking less and breathing the clean, fresh air of the vast ocean, and so perhaps you have regained your health."
22. *Itō den*, vol. 2, p. 253.
23. Letter to Inoue Kowashi dated July 1, *Hiroku*, vol. 2, p. 40; letter to Inoue Kaoru dated July 5, Inoue Kaoru Monjo Kōdokukai 2008, pp. 628–9; letters to Yamagata Aritomo, Inoue Kaoru, and Yamada Akiyoshi dated August 4, *Itō den*, vol. 2, pp. 282 ff.
24. Ibid., p. 303, letter to Yamada Akiyoshi dated August 27, and p. 297, letter to Iwakura dated August 11.

25 Ibid., p. 271, letter to Matsukata Masayoshi dated May 24.
26 Ibid., p. 314, letter to Matsukata dated September 6.
27 Ibid., pp. 271–2, letter to Matsukata dated May 24.
28 Ibid., p. 320, letter to Inoue Kaoru dated October 22.
29 *Hiroku*, vol. 2, pp. 46–7.
30 Japan's oligarchs at the time were leaders of the Chōshū and Satsuma domains who led the overthrow of the Tokugawa shogunate.
31 Letter dated April 27, 1883, "Inoue Kaoru monjo," no. 628–7.
32 For a work that helps to highlight the importance of Itō's study in England, see Toriumi 2005.
33 Hermann Roesler, a German legal advisor to the Meiji government whose thinking had a profound influence on the drafting of the Constitution, "was critical of the wording in Article I that states, 'The Empire of Japan shall be reigned over and governed by a line of emperors unbroken for ages eternal.'" (Siemmes 1970, pp. 129 ff.) Yet the European and American experts who were consulted about the Meiji Constitution soon after its promulgation generally expressed approval of the emperor's position as defined in Chapter I. (Kaneko 2001) Their perspective was affected by the rise of nationalist thinking in Europe. The combination of nationalism and historicism produced the thesis that a constitution has an organic relation to and evolves out of the history, culture, and spirit of the nation. Many Western specialists argued that a constitution unmarked by traditional national culture was spurious. What they were saying, in other words, along lines articulated by Gneist, was that a constitution had to demonstrate the incorporation of national culture and tradition in order to be recognized internationally. In that sense, Chapter I of the Meiji Constitution, reflecting some degree of Westerners' views of what Japan should be, can be understood as a product of late nineteenth-century "Orientalism" in the sense proposed by Edward Said.
34 Takii 2005.
35 Sakamoto 1991.
36 Others are: Ushiba Takuzō, Statistics Bureau junior secretary; Nakamigawa Hikojirō (1854–1901), Foreign Ministry vice senior secretary; Mutaguchi Gengaku, Agriculture and Commerce Ministry vice junior secretary; Komatsubara Eitarō (1852–1919), Foreign Ministry vice junior secretary; Nakano Takenaka, Agriculture and Commerce Ministry vice junior secretary; Shimada Saburō (1852–1923), Education Ministry vice senior secretary; Tanaka Kōzō, Education Ministry junior secretary; and Morishita Iwakusu, Finance Ministry vice junior secretary.
37 Ozaki 1962, p. 74.
38 Letter from Sanjō to Iwakura dated September 6, 1881, *Jikki*, vol. 3, p. 753.
39 *Waseda Daigaku hyakunen-shi*, vol. 1, p. 474.
40 Tsuchiya 1962, p. 274.
41 *Itō den*, vol. 2, pp. 153–4.
42 *Hogohiroi*, vol. 10, March 4, 1881 entry, p. 105.
43 Yamamuro 1984.
44 Letter from Inoue Kaoru to Itō dated July 27, 1881, *Itō monjo* (Hanawa), vol. 1, p. 165.
45 "Here it's completely different from Japan, where the still-green students say nothing of substance but just translate words in the text, and tell you that this is the constitution of such-and-such a country, this is how its government is organized, and so on, and thus misinform the ignorant public. Here I very much enjoy listening to lectures presented very clearly, based on thorough knowledge of the history of a given country and of the issues in question, and the sound judgment achieved by weighing the pros and cons of each issue." (*Hiroku*, vol. 1, p. 307)
46 Letter from Itō to Iwakura dated August 11, 1882, *Itō den*, vol. 2, p. 296.
47 Ibid., p. 310.
48 Stein 1991.
49 Letter to Matsukata Masayoshi dated September 6, *Itō den*, vol. 2, p. 310.

74 A constitution for Japan

50 "Sutain-shi Yatoiire" [Hiring of Mr. Stein], proposal by Yamagata Aritomo submitted to Grand Minister of State Sanjō Sanetomi, dated October 24, 1882.
51 Letter to Yamada Akiyoshi dated August 27, 1882, *Itō den*, vol. 2, pp. 305–6.
52 Ibid., p. 318, letter to Inoue Kaoru dated September 23, 1882.
53 Ibid., pp. 320–1, letter to Inoue Kaoru dated October 22, 1882.
54 Ibid., pp. 329–30, letter from Stein to Itō dated November 15, 1882.
55 The central role of the university in Stein's theory of the state is discussed in detail in Takii 1999.
56 Letter to Yamada Akiyoshi dated August 27, 1882, *Itō den*, vol. 2, p. 305.
57 "Sutain-shi kōgi hikki" [Notes from Dr. Stein's Lectures] (2 parts), "Itō monjo," nos. 234–1 and –2.
58 Saitō 1967.
59 Translation of passages here and to end of the following three sections based on *Itō den*, vol. 2, pp. 651–6.
60 *Tōkyō nichinichi shinbun*, February 19, 1889. Quotes hereafter are from the same newspaper article.
61 In 1882, at the time of his constitutional study tour in Europe, Itō had already declared in his August 27 letter to Yamada Akiyoshi, "Where there is a parliament there naturally are political parties. The situation over here [in Europe] is unlike that in Japan, where people form not political parties but factions whose covert intention is to use the power of the people to weaken or destroy the power of the monarch. To put it clearly, they are no more than rebel mobs." *Itō den*, vol. 2, pp. 304–5.
62 Burke's own words are: . . . parliament is a *deliberative* assembly of *one* nation, with *one* interest, that of the whole; where, not local purposes, not local prejudices, ought to guide, but the general good, resulting from the general reason of the whole. You choose a member indeed; but when you have chosen him, he is not member of Bristol, but he is a member of *parliament*. (Edmund Burke, "Speech to the Electors of Bristol," *The Founders' Constitution*, Volume 1, Chapter 13, Document 7, http://press-pubs. uchicago.edu/founders/documents/v1ch13s7.html, University of Chicago Press, accessed October 4, 2013).
63 *Tōkyō nichinichi shinbun*, February 21, 1889.
64 *Kazoku Dōhō Kai enzetsushū*, vol. 4, pp. 1–28 ("Shuken oyobi jōin no soshiki" [Sovereignty and the Organization of the Upper Assembly], December 8, 1888) and vol. 5, pp. 1–16 ("Kenpō ni kansuru enzetsu" [Speech on the Constitution], February 26, 1889).
65 "Itō monjo," Shorui-no-bu 104.
66 Handwritten draft of speech made in Tokyo at the Kazoku Dōhō Kai on February 27, 1889. Collection of National Diet Library, Kensei Shiryōshitsu.

3 Itō the constitutional evangelist

All things change: Itō's worldview

For Itō Hirobumi, the late 1880s was a transitional period teeming with diverse and often conflicting positions. Writing in his later years, he grouped Japan of the time into four main persuasions: the Kokugaku (National Learning) scholars, who made the emperor's divinity their core premise, the Manchester school liberalists, the bureaucrats and others who had studied under German mentors, and the people's rights champions of French Enlightenment thinking:

> On one side there was the old guard, people who clung to the idea of the emperor as divinely ordained to rule, who looked on anyone who sought to limit the Emperor's prerogatives as guilty of treason. On the other side were young leaders who, having received their education when the Manchester school was at the peak of its influence, embraced radical liberal thought, as well as government officials who were drawn to the doctrines of German scholars during that reactionary period. Quite in contrast to them were the opposition politicians who, still knowing little of what real political responsibility was, were intoxicated by the exhilarating theories and unconventional arguments of Montesquieu, Rousseau, and other French thinkers.[1]

Itō himself kept a safe distance from all of them—proponents of imperial divinity, extreme liberalism, German school reactionaries, and radical French ideology. He had an instinctive aversion to making any specific doctrine into dogma. To the contrary, he adhered to a spirit of tolerance as essential to a functioning parliamentary system. That inclination might have colored his recollections of the times when the Meiji Constitution was born; in his view, it was an era of such rampant self-centeredness and intolerance in the various schools of thought that a shared belief in freedom of speech and common dedication to orderly open parliamentary proceedings seemed a very long way off.

"Only after gaining a great deal of experience," Itō continued, "is one able to acquire the capacities and attitudes necessary for smoothly working constitutionalism. These include belief in freedom of speech, belief in open parliamentary proceedings, and a spirit of tolerance toward opinions contrary to your own."[2]

Of course, recollections penned in the latter years of a life should be read with caution. Did Itō really think that way in the late 1880s? Considering the discussion of the Meiji Constitution in his February 1889 speech to the nobility, we have good reason to believe that such convictions were at least germinating in Itō's mind at the time. To the assembled imperial princes and nobles, Itō pressed the thesis that the people should be at the heart of government and the way the nation was governed should change as the people became more knowledgeable and better educated. That is the way government has progressed, he told them, in all the advanced countries of the West. His argument was also a product of his view that politics, like everything else in the world, was part of the constant process of change.

Mindful of the forces moving toward popular government, Itō worked hard to persuade the ruling class to make concessions and to respond with circumspection. The speech cited above is a case in point: he recommended prudence and a broadminded attitude toward people participating in the country's first venture into constitutional government. This determination to prepare the country for the practice of popular government based on the spirit of tolerance was behind Itō's founding in 1900 of the Seiyūkai political party, predecessor of the Liberal Democratic party, which (with the exception of a few years) has been at the helm of Japanese government almost continuously since 1955.

This chapter and the next examine the founding of the Seiyūkai and its significance in the building of the Meiji state. It has been widely held that when Itō established the party, he was abandoning the "transcendental government" policy of keeping aloof from political parties. As confirmed in his February 1889 address to the nobility, however, already before 1900 he was speaking unambiguously about the prospect of popular government. In Itō's vision, while administrative reforms in the structure of the state were necessary, the new structure must provide a framework within which movements encouraging popular participation in government could develop. His championing of the Seiyūkai, as we will see below, was not a product of an about-face in his thinking, but grew out of convictions that he had consistently held since the establishment of the constitution.

Itō's worldview

Before examining the founding of the Seiyūkai, let us first look at Itō's broader worldview. That Itō, a leading member of the oligarchy, should spearhead the creation of a political party, has long been misunderstood as signaling his defection from the transcendental government position that he and his fellow architects of the Meiji regime had stood by—a change of mind brought on as he yielded to the upsurge of popular and partisan activism that burgeoned after the opening of the Diet (1890). It is more accurate, however, to regard Itō's actions as consistent with his own political philosophy and view of the world, which was that, since all things in this world are in a constant state of flux, government, too, must continually change accordingly. The direction of that change, he believed, was toward popular government. The idea that action had to be taken, sooner or later, to break away from the oligarchy-centered policy of transcendental government must already have been in Itō's mind when the Meiji Constitution went into effect (1889).

Itō's thoughts on the natural order of humanity and nature are expressed in large strokes in a letter he wrote to Inoue Kaoru on August 4, 1889, about half a year after the promulgation of the Constitution:

> As things stand, our dream of constitutional government might end up being just that—only a dream; [cabinet ministers] say that they'll stand firm and stick it out no matter what happens; those bluffers have no intention whatsoever of preparing the people to become a civilized nation. They seem completely unaware to the fact that everything in the universe is in perpetual motion, always changing in a certain order. Just as a seed needs to be tended and cultivated to grow into a healthy flower or tree, it takes many years to cultivate and nurture people who have long known only despotic rule so that they can thrive as participants in constitutional government.[3]

This letter was a direct criticism of the Kuroda Kiyotaka cabinet for its inept handling of diplomatic negotiations to revise the unequal treaties that Japan had signed with the Western powers toward the end of the Tokugawa shogunate. Under the previous cabinet, which Itō Hirobumi had headed himself as Japan's first prime minister, the negotiations led by Foreign Minister Inoue Kaoru had ended in failure.[4] Ōkuma Shigenobu succeeded Inoue as foreign minister in February 1888 and took over the task of treaty revision. At the end of April, Itō resigned as prime minister to become the first president of the Privy Council, and Kuroda was made the new prime minister. Remaining as foreign minister in the Kuroda cabinet, Ōkuma continued his efforts for treaty revision, but his proposals sparked a public outcry that was explosive enough to split the cabinet.

It was against the backdrop of those strained political circumstances that Itō wrote to Inoue, making jabs at the rigid position of the group of treaty revision advocates led by Ōkuma and Kuroda. The letter criticizes Ōkuma and his associates for refusing to budge from their treaty revision plan. They would be totally useless, he wrote, in guiding their countrymen—most of whom had never known anything but despotism—to an understanding of the constitutional system and their role in it, helping them to become a "civilized" people. Then, perhaps venting his indignation and frustration, he expressed his view of the world: "Everything in the universe is in perpetual motion." Everything happens in a certain order but nothing stops changing, not even for a moment.

The order of political developments was no exception. What is required of political leadership is not to resist the flow of change but guide it so it runs smoothly in its natural direction—that is, keep it under control so it does not become a raging current, and steer it along as it becomes a large river flowing placidly out into a vast ocean. For Itō, the "vast ocean" into which the political current of that time would be guided was constitutional government. It would take many years of fostering a sense of popular participation in and responsibility for government, Itō believed, before the people were ready to take the leading role in constitutionalism, just as it takes many years to nurture a small seed into a strong tree. They had to be prepared to believe in freedom of speech, open parliamentary proceedings, and be tolerant of opinions contrary to their own.

Given those assumptions, it is easy to understand why Itō saw the enactment of the Constitution in 1889 not as the destination but as the starting point of a long journey toward participatory constitutional government. It gave Meiji Japan the framework within which to begin the journey. "A state is not built in a day," he remarked in a letter written less than a year after the Constitution was promulgated.[5] Before him lay the task of fleshing out the structure of the state in accordance with the Constitution, and through education and nurture, nudging the people living through the change to become the protagonists in their own constitutional state.

Misinterpretation of Itō's speech

Another incident serves to highlight Itō Hirobumi's view of constitutional government around the time when the Constitution was enacted. On September 21, 1891 he gave a talk in Yamaguchi, his home prefecture, on the way constitutional government should work. A summary of the lecture was published in *Jiji shinpō* on September 26. It stirred anger among people's rights activists in Tokyo. What happened was conveyed to Itō, who was away from Tokyo at the time, by his right-hand man Itō Miyoji (1857–1934) and by Prime Minister Matsukata Masayoshi. In a letter dated October 4 Itō Miyoji reported to Itō:

> From your recent letter I imagine Your Excellency's speech in Yamaguchi was frank and honest. I don't think the summary carried in *Jiji shinpō* contains any particular problem or was written with any ill will. It communicates your point very well, but the Kaishintō, probably having nothing else to do, may have seen it as a good target and directed their offensives at Your Excellency, leveling groundless accusations with abandon. I could not leave the issue as it was and so I immediately refuted the Kaishintō's allegations by sending out the gist of your speech to the [*Tōkyō*] *nichinichi shinbun* and *Tōkyō shinpō*.[6]

As Itō Miyoji saw it, the summary of Itō's speech published in *Jiji shinpō*, a newspaper founded and edited by Fukuzawa Yukichi, raised no particular problems, but the Rikken Kaishintō (Constitutional Reform party, Kaishintō for short) strenuously objected, which Itō Miyoji tried to refute by publishing the gist of the speech in the two Tokyo newspapers.

What, then, did the *Jiji shinpō* article say? The September 26, 1891 article, titled "Itō-haku no seidan enzetsu" (Count Itō's Speech on Politics), reported that Itō Hirobumi had spoken on the theme, "The People of Our Country Should Be Prepared for the Future," to some 300 local government officials and members of the general public. As illustrated in the summary that follows, Itō had talked

Figure 3.1 Itō Miyoji (1857–1934).

Source: Photograph courtesy of the National Diet Library of Japan.

about how, since the Restoration, Japan had opened its doors wide, imported Western things, and built a civilized country; constitutional government had been established as a result. He had deplored, however, how politicians (infatuated with the party-based cabinets known to exist in Europe and the United States) now advocated toppling the present cabinet. The summary notes Itō's statement that, "A party-based cabinet is not acceptable for Japan, as is obvious by comparing Japan's case to the history of Britain." That is, a statesman with integrity would never support a party-led cabinet. He said quite clearly that political parties in Japan were as yet immature and their discourse was irresponsible. In the final analysis, what is essential, he is reported as saying, is that "the people work together to strengthen the nation step by step and restore Japan's sovereign rights." The article concludes by mentioning Itō's lament that government officials are looked upon as mere clerks and misunderstood as the "hired hands" of the people.

After this article appeared, the *Yūbin hōchi shinbun* and *Yomiuri shinbun*, newspapers on the side of the Kaishintō, roared in protest at Itō's explicit opposition to the concept of party-led government. Itō Miyoji had expected and even hoped for such a reaction. He had probably helped draft the speech and may have wanted the chance to come out against the people's rights forces and keep them in check. He therefore reported in his letter that the *Jiji shinpō* article had "no particular problem" and "is exactly as we anticipated."

Real message

What about Itō Hirobumi? Was he satisfied with the *Jiji shinpō* article? The truth is that there were significant discrepancies between what he said in his address and the *Jiji shinpō* summary, and therefore between his view of constitutional government and Itō Miyoji's. In his reply to the younger Itō, the older Itō thanked him for sending the article and then observed that it "differs considerably from the actual message of my speech."[7]

What did Itō Hirobumi's speech actually say? Let him explain in his own words as he wrote in his letter to the younger Itō:

> I explained that political parties and party-led cabinets, which Japanese increasingly have been advocating in recent years, originate in Britain and I gave a rough idea of their history. Then I discussed the distinction between unwritten and written constitutions, that is, between *idō* (movable, or flexible) and *fudō* (immovable, or rigid) constitutions, and pointed out that constitutions vary from country to country. Next I explained that although our constitution is founded on our national polity, in academic terms it can be classified in such and such a category. I explained about how constitutional monarchy differs from a parliamentary system. In concluding I said that a constitution must accord with and embody the founding polity of the country, stressing that our constitution is so closely related to the national polity that the prerogatives of the monarch cannot be passed down [to another agency]. It takes few words, therefore, to point out what is so evident: that the calls to put a party-led cabinet in place immediately go against our country's constitution and national polity.

Itō Hirobumi did say that party-led cabinets were first instituted in Britain, but he did not say "a party-based cabinet is not acceptable for Japan, as is obvious by comparing Japan's case to the history of Britain," as stated in the *Jiji shinpō* summary. Instead he moved on to a general discussion that included the differences between unwritten and written constitutions and between a constitutional monarchy and a parliamentary system of government. He declared that a constitution must conform to the national polity and that the emperor's prerogatives, therefore, cannot be given to anyone else. Thus it becomes obvious whether or not a party-led cabinet would suit Japan's constitution and national polity.

Itō's words up to this point might give the impression that he wanted to suppress party government by upholding the emperor-centered national polity. But, he continued in his letter:

> I then said that I am not foretelling what changes might come in the future, however. Just as the hegemonic seat of government was established in

Kamakura,[8] a general trend toward change cannot just be turned back. I stated in addition that because our constitution has written provisions that prevent officials in the executive branch of government from becoming despotic and guarantee the rights of the subjects, our country will be unimpeded in enjoying the fruits of constitutional government even without party-led cabinets.

In saying "I am not foretelling what changes might come in the future," he meant that despite the foregoing, he had not been talking about developments that might lie ahead. A "general trend toward change" is something that will happen, regardless; that is, the course of history is irrevocable. That brings in a new note. Itō now seems to be saying that the argument that party cabinets are unacceptable because they do not conform with the idea of *kokutai* (national polity) is no more than theory and that if the "general trend" is toward party cabinets, then they will prevail—party cabinets will come into being in any case.

That argument, which turns the first part on its head, is the real message in Itō's speech, I would say. And that line of thinking is perfectly consistent with his 1889 speech given to the nobility. They both display his conviction that the dominant trend of the times is toward people-centered government and the rise of party government is inevitable.

Despite such an assessment of current developments, however, Itō was ambivalent toward party government per se. His concept of "constitutional government" relativized party-led government; it allowed him to argue that because of constitutional provisions to prevent "despotic" practices by executive branch officials and protect the rights of the people, the benefits of constitutional government would be felt by everyone even without party cabinets. There, in the letter, he was referring to executive branch officials alone, but as he noted in the 1889 speech, an intriguing part of a constitutional system was that it achieved a balance among all the branches of government to prevent any one of them from monopolizing power.

In Itō's opinion, the essence of constitutional government was harmony and unity among the branches of government, or organs of the state, including the monarch, the Diet, and the administration. He saw constitutional government as essentially different, in a separate category, from party-led cabinets. That was why he said that "our country will be unimpeded in enjoying the fruits of constitutional government even without party-led cabinets."

Party-led government, in Itō's mind, was a current bound to history. It follows that a major task he saw for himself was to promote popular participation in government through the step-by-step development of party government, and to bring popular government and constitutionalism together into a unity with which to build a political system—a nation-state—of conciliation and cooperation. He found the means to perform that task in the creation of the Seiyūkai in 1900.

Nationwide campaign: stumping for the Constitution

The Meiji Constitution promulgated the previous year came into effect on November 29, 1890 and the first Imperial Diet session opened. For a long time after World War II, Japan's academic community generally did not question the view that the parliamentary system formed in the Meiji era was seriously hampered by constrictions placed on it by the Meiji Constitution. It was widely accepted that because of its heavily monarchist character, the Constitution was little more than a showpiece. However, this thesis is not supported by a close study of how Japan's parliamentary government developed in the early days.

Advent of party cabinets

In fact, parliamentary government made steady progress under the Meiji Constitution right through the early 1930s. As early as 1918 a politician affiliated with a political party, Seiyūkai leader Hara Takashi (1856–1921), was made prime minister and formed a party cabinet. In 1924, a coalition cabinet was formed of three pro-constitution parties under Katō Takaaki (1860–1926), head of the Kenseikai (Constitutional Association), ushering in eight years of British-style parliamentary government characterized by frequent changes of power among the leading parties.[9] This era, known as a time when Japanese politics followed the "normal course of constitutional government" (*kensei no jōdō*), lasted until the May 15 Incident[10] in 1932.

Behind the growth of party government are a number of factors, one of the most important being the design of the Meiji Constitution. Following the model of Prussia, various restraints on parliamentary government were built into the Constitution, but, importantly, it made explicit provision for Diet control over the budget. Of course some of the constraints had significant consequences, including provisions in Article 71 that obliged the government to use the previous year's budget if a budget bill did not pass in the Diet, and Article 67, which required the Diet to get government approval in order to reject or reduce any expenditures that were fixed by imperial prerogative. On the other hand, the government could not increase the budget without approval of the Diet. The Satsuma-Chōshū oligarchy, which had been able to pursue the policy of "enrich the country and strengthen the military" only by constantly increasing taxes and spending, often had no choice but to beg the ruling party to get the budget passed.[11] Parliamentary government thus began to find its footing as a logical consequence of mechanisms inherent in the design of the Meiji Constitution.

The parliamentary system had become somewhat seasoned by the time a party cabinet emerged eight years after the opening of the Diet. On June 22, 1898, Ōkuma Shigenobu merged his Shinpotō (Progressive) party with Itagaki Taisuke's Jiyūtō (Liberal) party to create the Kenseitō (Constitutional) party; on June 30, with Ōkuma as prime minister, they formed Japan's first party cabinet. Almost all the ministerial posts in the Ōkuma-Itagaki cabinet were filled by members of the Kenseitō, except for the foreign minister and army and navy ministers. (Itagaki served concurrently as deputy prime minister and home minister.)

Interestingly, this cabinet came into being almost by accident. Itō Hirobumi, who had put together his third cabinet in January of that year, had been having great difficulties running the government, sandwiched as he was between a

Yamagata Aritomo-led group of government bureaucrats on the one hand and the opposition forces of the Jiyūtō and Shinpotō parties from the parliament on the other. As soon as the new Kenseitō was born out of the merger of the opposition parties, Itō gave up and dissolved the cabinet, leaving the next move in the hands of the leaders of these two pro-constitution parties. The unexpected chance to form a cabinet was a windfall for them. For the Satsuma-Chōshū oligarchy, it meant surrendering control of the Meiji government.[12]

That epochal cabinet, however, was short-lived. Politicians of the ruling party were so busy trying to get preferential posts for themselves that the cabinet collapsed after only four months. Yamagata was appointed the next prime minister and a "transcendental" cabinet—one that distanced itself from the political parties—returned. Even so, the fact that party forces came to power at that point, if only for a short time, is of great significance. The formation of the Ōkuma-Itagaki cabinet proved that party-led political power was not an impossible dream. Immediately after the Sino-Japanese War of 1894–5, the nation's finances were badly stretched and needed an infusion coming from an increase in the land tax, which would have been impossible under the Meiji Constitution without the cooperation of the opposition parties in the Diet. Even Yamagata,

Figure 3.2 Yamagata Aritomo (1838–1922).

Source: Photograph courtesy of the National Diet Library of Japan.

who loathed political parties, found himself having to declare his alliance with the Kenseitō, which had by then emerged as the largest opposition party.[13]

Abortive attempts to found a party

In January 1892, Itō tried to form a party based on the existing government party (Taiseikai), but the effort failed because he could not win support from the emperor. His second try in June 1898, during his third term as prime minister, was also frustrated when Yamagata came out firmly against the idea. At a conference in the presence of the emperor on June 24, Yamagata challenged Itō:

> Your creation of a political party would open the way to party-based cabinets, but a party cabinet system runs counter to our national polity, goes against the spirit of the constitution granted by the emperor, and will degenerate into popular government. Is that not so?

Itō countered, "Whether a party cabinet system is good or bad is only a minor detail; what's important is whether or not it will contribute to the advancement of the empire."[14] Seeing that he was not getting any general endorsement, Itō reported to the emperor forthwith that he was resigning as prime minister and recommended party leaders Ōkuma and Itagaki to form the next cabinet.

Later, in 1898, after giving up on his third cabinet, Itō Hirobumi left the government for a time. A plausible rumor began to circulate that he was planning to create a major political party. People watched closely, suspecting that he was laying the groundwork for collaboration with a faction led by Hoshi Tōru (1850–1901) within the ruling Kenseitō and Hoshi's followers in government officialdom. Hoshi was a prominent member of the former Liberal party.

Pushing aside all the rumors and speculation, Itō traveled to China and Korea from August to October 1898, and, beginning in April in 1899, he went out on a series of several tours to various parts of Japan to give public speeches about politics and the constitution that extended over six months until October. His itineraries show that he covered wide swaths of the country, including areas remote from major cities. In that year, 1899, considered a major turning point in the history of the Meiji Constitution, how did he decide where to go, and what was he trying to say to his countrymen? We will look first at the routes he traveled.

To Nagano and western Japan

On April 9, 1899 Itō traveled north of Tokyo to the Nagano prefecture summer resort town of Karuizawa. On that trip he had a total of eighteen people in his entourage, including Ozaki Saburō (1842–1918; former director of the Bureau of Legislation) and Ōoka Ikuzō (1856–1928; a member of the House of Representatives), as well as a *Tōkyō nichinichi* newspaper reporter and an employee of Hakubunkan, the publisher of *Taiyō*, an influential general-interest magazine.[15]

May 8	Departs on a speaking tour of Kansai and Kyushu regions
10	Visits Shijō Nawate shrine (Osaka) and gives speech at welcome party held by interested persons group from Kawachi area
11	Arrives in Kobe
12	Arrives in Bakan (Shimonoseki)
13	Gives speech at reception held by Bakan businessmen's group
14	Arrives in Beppu (Oita prefecture)
15	Gives speeches at Oita-prefecture joint official-private reception and at Oita Toyokuni Brotherhood Club inaugural ceremony
16	Gives speech at Beppu welcome party
17	Arrives in Nakatsu and gives speech at town of Nakatsu welcome party
18	Arrives at Yukuhashi via Ushima (Fukuoka prefecture); gives speeches at welcome parties in Ushima and Yukuhashi
19	Arrives in Kurume and gives speech at welcome party
20	Arrives in city of Fukuoka and gives speech at welcome party
21	Gives speech at welcome parties in Kokura and Moji; returns to Bakan
22	Arrives in Chōfu and gives speech at Kōzanji temple[17]
25	Inspects Wakamatsu harbor improvement construction from boat; returns to Bakan; physical condition undermined by demanding schedule
29	Despite poor health, leaves Bakan and arrives in Mitajiri via Tokuyama
30	Gives speech at welcome party in Mitajiri; arrives in Yamaguchi town and gives speech at Yamaguchi prefecture joint official-private reception
31	Gives speeches at Yamaguchi Middle School and at Yamaguchi welcome party
June 1	Arrives in town of Hagi
2	Gives speech at Hagi welcome party
4	Departs Hagi
5	Returns to town of Yamaguchi; comes down with a cold
9	Health recovering, leaves town of Yamaguchi; gives speeches in Tokuyama and birthplace Yanaitsu; arrives in Itsukushima (Hiroshima prefecture)
10	Gives speech at Itsukushima welcome party
11	Arrives in Hiroshima city and gives speech at welcome party
12	Arrives in Kobe
16	Gives speech at Aichi prefecture joint official-private reception in Nagoya on his way back to Ōiso

Figure 3.3 Itinerary for the tour of western Japan.

The next day, April 10, Itō and his entourage arrived in the city of Nagano and stayed there until April 12. They returned to Tokyo the following day. During this short five-day tour, Itō delivered three speeches, which were very well attended. Ozaki described their welcome in his diary:

> At each station that Itō's train passed through, the county mayor, village heads, and other local people had gathered and bowed as the train went by. On the platform of the station where he got off, prominent local figures were lined up smartly to welcome him. National flags and lanterns were displayed in front of houses, and once in a while there was a display of fireworks. Row upon row of people crowded along the streets to get a glimpse of Itō.[16]

The response to this brief Nagano tour was very favorable for Itō, which in hindsight came to be seen as his testing of the waters before plunging into a series of what appeared to be full-fledged political stumping tours. Less than a month after returning to Tokyo, he was off again on a forty-day tour in western Japan. His schedule was extremely ambitious.

The pace of this tour was punishing, often allowing him barely one night between stops, and Itō kept it up for forty days, moving from place to place and giving speeches almost everywhere he went. A few times he got off the train at a stop en route, spoke to the people there, and then hurried on. All together, he managed to give twenty-two speeches. Not surprisingly, the strain took a toll on his physical health during the latter half of the tour.

Speech-making and media strategy

Itō got back to Tokyo in the middle of June 1899, and right away began thinking about opportunities to make another speaking tour. On July 16, he went to Utsunomiya, 100 kilometers north of Tokyo, to speak at the invitation of a group of local businessmen. For the following month, August, he planned a campaign in the Hokuriku region on the Sea of Japan side, but it was not until October that he actually left for the region. The itinerary gave him just under two weeks.

This tour, too, was hectic; during the twelve-day period Itō gave a total of ten speeches in eight different places. During this year, before he formed the Seiyūkai, he was like a man obsessed, busily getting himself here and there across the country to speak as widely as possible in the attempt to bring his messages to the Japanese public.

Itō's eagerness to optimize the chance to reach a lot of people shows up in his media strategy. Members of the media, including a *Tōkyō nichinichi* newspaper reporter, accompanied his entourage on the five-day Nagano tour in April and a *Tōkyō nichinichi* reporter was also allowed to come along on all of his subsequent tours. Some politicians frowned on the way Itō traveled, happy to have reporters close around him and not particularly worried about making indiscreet remarks.[18] But Itō was unperturbed and continued around the country with the reporters in tow.

Naturally, with his media-feeders traveling with him, Itō's movements during the campaigns were reported quickly and efficiently in Tokyo; they were printed in articles and reached the public in no time. Newspaper readers were informed every day of where Itō was, what he did, and what he said. In the past, the *Tōkyō nichinichi* had reported on his campaigns and published excerpts of his speeches made at regional locations, but this time was different. Now the paper made special efforts to give detailed accounts of traveling with Itō on tour, and it published eye-catching reports that were serialized under the titles "Record of Marquis Itō's Tour of the West" and "Account: Marquis Itō Goes North." The newspaper was clearly trying to do all it could to relay to its readers the complete record of Itō's words and full accounts of his activities. The *Tōkyō nichinichi* daily paper also provided the public with the content of each of his speeches so that the latter

October 14	Departs for Hokuriku region
15	Arrives in city of Fukui from Nagoya
16	Visits *habutae* silk-weaving factory and gives speech at city of Fukui welcome party
17	Arrives in Mikuni from Fukui and gives speech at welcome party
18	Leaves Mikuni for Kanazawa; disembarks train at Komatsu en route and gives speech at Hongakuji temple; arrives in Kanazawa
19	Gives speech at Ishikawa prefectural assembly hall in Kanazawa
20	Visits *habutae* silk-weaving factory; gives speeches at Fourth Higher School and Kinjō Kōyūkai; leaves for Nanao
21	Gives speech at Nanao and inspects the harbor; from there, arrives in Takaoka and gives speech at welcome party held by local Kenseitō members
22	Inspects Toyama prefectural polytechnic school; inspects harbor at Fushiki town: returns to Takaoka and gives speech at Seianji temple
23	Departs Takaoka; gives speech in Toyama; goes on to Fukui
24	Visits Eiheiji Zen temple
25	Leaves Fukui for return to Tokyo

Figure 3.4 Itinerary for the tour of Hokuriku region.

could have access to them. In a letter he wrote to Yamagata Aritomo after returning from Kyushu in June, Itō stated:

> The everyday opinions I've expressed and statements I've made before large audiences at the many places I've visited on my tour in the last month have been carried in the newspapers, so I presume you have read some of them.[19]

In this letter, there is a hint of Itō's resolve to get the content of his speeches out across the country. His stumping tours of 1899 were aimed not so much at winning the support of or currying favor with regional voters as making his views known, directly or indirectly, to as many segments of the population as he could. He also wanted to make sure that all those talks did not just fade away in people's minds, and so, after they had appeared in the newspapers, Itō's speeches were gathered into a book and published as *Itō-kō enzetsushū* [Collected Speeches by Marquis Itō], which was distributed to *Tōkyō nichinichi* subscribers.

Purpose of the tours

So we come to the question of just what it was that Itō wanted to get across to the public in his speeches and through the media. Previous studies have concluded that the tours were part of his preparation to form the Seiyūkai party the following year. In that line of reasoning, in order to create a responsible political party capable of leading the government, he traveled far and wide around the country to win popular favor and pave the way for the party.

A careful reading of the speeches he made on these tours, however, indicates that his original motivation was a sense of the need to enlighten the people of his country and help equip them to become members of a constitutional state. The year was 1899, the tenth anniversary of the promulgation of the Meiji Constitution. At a meeting to celebrate the anniversary, Itō commented that the past decade had been an experimental period for the Constitution and that the result was "remarkably good."[20] As proof of this good result, he explains:

> ... the condition of the state today has changed vastly from the days when the Meiji Constitution was promulgated in 1889. The tax burden of the people at the time of the promulgation was hardly 80 million yen. It is double that today, and the people now have that much more political power and are participating that much more in government. What about their duties to the state? Some might say that now, since people are wealthier, it is only natural that their financial contributions should expand. But people also fulfill their duties by sending out representatives who help to run the country. They differ greatly from people living under tyranny. This alone is enough to assert that these years of experiment have been successful.[21]

Itō expressed pride and admiration at the degree of popular participation in government since the constitution was established and at how it was continuing to grow.

That decade was not a smooth one. Japan's parliamentary system, still in its infancy and the first of its kind in the non-Western world, was shaken by crises resulting from repeated dissolution of parliament and the concomitant possibility that the Constitution would be suspended. But it survived. Without question, the parliamentary system was set firmly in place during that decade. Especially significant was the expansion of political party forces into the arena of parliament, where they came to stay permanently. The experimental period over, Japan moved on to confront the next major task, which was to put a constitutional government into full motion. That challenge was what occupied Itō's mind at the time. His main purpose in giving speeches across the country was to reach out directly to the people and make them aware that they were members of a constitutional state. He was like a missionary, a constitutional evangelist, setting out across the country to propagate the message of a constitutional state. His own words convey his dogged enthusiasm for the task:

> As for the constitution, I have followed the wishes of my mentors and, sent by His Majesty the Emperor, went to Europe for constitutional research; after returning home I prepared and presented the draft of the constitution to His Majesty and it was promulgated as the Imperial Constitution. I believe, therefore, that I have the unlimited responsibility to live and die for this constitution. That is why, no matter what scholar may confront me and no matter what political party may confront me, I will never yield where I should not.[22]

Treaty revision and a new status in the world

As noted earlier, 1898 marks an important juncture in the history of the Meiji Constitution, for in that year the oligarchic government "surrendered" and a party cabinet was formed for the first time. Itō was keenly aware that the event was an epochal turning point. As he considered it, his anxious attention was directed not just toward domestic politics, but outwardly, as well.

Opening the land to strengthen Japan

In its international relations, too, Japan was facing a major turning point around that time. In 1894 Foreign Minister Mutsu Munemitsu (1844–97) had succeeded in negotiating the abolition of the unequal treaties and replacing them with treaties similar to those contracted among European countries. Japan's new treaties with the Western countries came into effect in July–August 1899, ending extraterritoriality and partially recovering tariff autonomy. The foreign settlements were abolished, allowing foreign residents to live wherever they wanted in Japan—the start of "mixed residence" of foreigners and Japanese (*naichi zakkyo*). This completed in name and reality the process of opening the country that had started in 1854, before the end of the Tokugawa shogunate (1867).

During his 1899 speaking tours Itō stressed that point, repeatedly telling his audiences of the need to adjust to the new era after the new treaties had gone into effect. According to Itō, the new treaties brought Japan into "an encounter with a situation that has never before arisen since the dawn of our country's history." Opening relations with foreign countries meant that for the first time "we [the Japanese] will begin to associate with people from all over the world."[23] Itō saw the enactment of the new treaties as a historical feat that allowed Japan to emerge from its long isolation and enter on its own accord into the dynamism of the world outside.

There were two implications. First, with its doors now open wide, Japan was fully incorporated into the world market, and the exchange of people, goods, money, and knowledge with other countries would begin to expand on a large scale. In some quarters there was fierce opposition to the new treaties arising from the fear that such exchanges would cause an economic invasion of Japan by the Western powers. In response, Itō expressed his belief that the opening of the land would, on the contrary, facilitate Japan's economic growth:

> European countries and the United States not only have abundant capital but they are rich in knowledge and experience. Some of their people may come to Japan and start enterprises together with Japanese, and others by themselves, and if they start businesses by themselves our people should observe how they do it so that they will be able to compete with them. I believe the competition will advance Japan's commerce and industry and that [Japanese] will benefit greatly from observing the experiences of [Westerners].[24]

Itō had been studying Western affairs for four decades; he had faith in the civilization of Europe and the United States, and he was also confident of the national power Japan had built since the Meiji Restoration. With that outlook he was able to stress the positive aspect of opening the country further, namely, to encourage the inflow of advanced technology and knowledge from other countries and thereby boost Japan's economic growth.

What worried him was something else. Completing the process of opening the country meant that Japan would be exposed to the world far more than ever before. There were deep fears among the Japanese that liberalization of economic activities by foreigners within Japan, and the presence of foreign residents in their midst, might lead to the exploitation by outsiders of Japanese real estate and capital assets. Anti-foreign speeches and demonstrations flared up in many places. Itō reminded his audiences that Japan now ranked among the civilized countries, and that it must face the world "with the magnanimity of a great nation."[25] In other words, as a new member of the community of nations, Japan's civilization would be constantly watched and measured by established members of that community. So, another purpose of his speaking tours was to calm the fears and anxieties that people were feeling at the prospect of having foreigners live among them. With regard to this subject, let us consider Itō's ideas on patriotism.

What is patriotism?

Around that time, with anti-foreign fever mounting, the word "aikokushin," meaning love of one's nation or patriotism, was on everyone's lips. Warning against the dangers of this trend, Itō said, "Scholars especially go too far, always talking about patriotism, on and on. Indulging in arousing patriotic emotions, they forget their duties."[26] As Itō saw it, excessive patriotism was fanned by politically-oriented "scholars," who became followers of "false" learning without paying attention to the facts. "Genuine patriotism and courage are not something anyone should talk about with boastful swagger or with eyes glaring angrily. . ."[27] Genuine patriotism is a practical wish or desire to gain prosperity for the country, as suggested by his comment:

> Without wealth the culture of the people cannot advance. For patriotism to grow, it should serve the creation of wealth. People say we have to protect the land, but what is the use of protecting it if it remains just barren soil?[28]

Itō called for economic activities rooted in daily life, not ideological patriotism or nationalism. As ever, at the back of his mind was the imperative that Japan become "civilized," a country as advanced and as cultured as the West. For example, he said:

> If we cannot implement the revised treaties smoothly, that will be proof that Japan's civilization is not advanced enough to have cultivated what is called

social sense. If we cannot keep up with these things and the implementation is not smooth, Japan must prepare itself to being once again pushed to the outside of the community of civilization.[29]

Itō's fervent hope was to see Japan as a country among equals in the international community, a truly "civilized" country able to keep pace with the West, commanding its respect. Above all, he wanted to see the political system change and the people's attitudes and thinking advance in ways that matched and supported the kind of Japan he envisioned. And what was it like, that civilized country he saw in his mind's eye?

> A civilized government is obligated to develop the people's intellect and wisdom and let them enjoy their rights within certain limits of order, as well as unify them into one people. A civilized nation must have that kind of government.[30]

In this vision of a civilized country the people are knowledgeable and well educated, and certain rights are guaranteed them. True to form, Itō's first prerequisite is an intellectually awakened people. Even back in his speech to the nobility in February 1889, he expressed his concern with the advancement of people's knowledge and virtue as the basis of national power. In short, government must always keep the nation's people at its center. Itō was steadfast in this view.

Parliamentary system: a full-fledged civilized nation

On the other hand, says Itō, the government must find ways to unify that population of highly knowledgeable people and maintain order in the land. This is totally different from the job of controlling an ignorant people, as government had done in the past. A country becomes advanced only when its people can learn and be able to express their opinions, not by "keeping them in the dark" as in former times. These are some of the ideas Itō had already been trying to convey to the nation's upper stratum in the February 1889 speech to the nobility. At that time, he was speaking in private. Now he was speaking openly to the public.

Giving freedom of expression to educated people who are awakened to knowledge may not be expedient from the viewpoint of control, says Itō, as that gives them the freedom to criticize their own government. But the government of a civilized country must let them speak and cannot quiet them in a high-handed, domineering way. Indeed it benefits from their speaking. To maintain order, it, too, must govern in an orderly manner. How? It must "present to the people the great law of the land, based on the constitution and national laws, and require them to act within that framework," says Itō. The point is that an advanced country must inevitably be governed by the rule of law:

> There is a certain system or method of ruling a country. What is called civilized government follows laws and regulations to govern the people,

thereby letting them enjoy all those rights that they should enjoy and requiring of them the duties they should perform. This is what is called a constitutional state. Only by following the rule of law can government be called civilized.[31]

Here he points out that another requirement for a civilized country is to be a constitutional state that governs by laws and regulations; a state guarantees the people certain rights by law and at the same time limits their rights. One might suspect that Itō is doing little more than using the guarantee of individual rights to a certain amount of political activity in order to justify the current ruling power. In other words, that he is only expressing the oligarchy's logic of controlling the people by taming them. But Itō goes further in arguing the need for an educated people as the foundation of government:

> The power of education is remarkable. . . . Through education people learn myriad things about the world. If people are knowledgeable, they can tell good government from bad. Enabling people to make that distinction, in fact, is the purpose of education. As a natural result of the ability to make such distinctions, they will start advocating what they believe is good. Completely unlike the era of despotic rule, when the rulers sought to keep the people in the dark and force them to obey, government leadership should let people acquire knowledge and let them speak. But those things must take place within an established public order. How should that order be established? The best way is to open what is called a parliament and discuss there the merits and demerits of the government in power, as the history and development of the advanced countries of Europe and the United States show so clearly. If it is sluggish and dull, discussion of merits and demerits, good and bad things, will go nowhere. And if it is heated with many clashing arguments, there must be certain rules. That is, the wishes and ideas, and opinions of the people should be expressed through one agency, or parliament, and that is an element in constitutional government. We can safely say that constitutional government means civilized government.[32]

In Itō's view, civilized government is always people-centered government premised on the parliamentary system. That is, government proceeds properly when the political will of the people is expressed in parliament and, as public opinion, it is expressed within the bounds of public order, and then it is reflected in the national administration. Since a system of rule centered on parliament is "an element of constitutional government," therefore, "constitutional government means civilized government." Itō understood a civilized country, a parliamentary system, and a constitution as a trinity, with the constitution at its crown:

> Only when constitutional government was adopted did the Japanese people attain the status of a true nation. This is what is called in modern times civilized

government. Civilized government can be run only by civilized people, and therefore Japanese have reached the status of a civilized nation.[33]

The promulgation of the Meiji Constitution in 1889 meant that the people of Japan were now qualified to participate in government as citizens of a civilized nation. Only when civilized people participated in government in an orderly way, by sending representatives to parliament, would their country become a truly civilized country. In a sense, in Itō's formulation of a civilized country, the constitutional system was the hardware and popular government was the software.

Implanting the idea of popular government

Itō's nationwide speaking campaign of 1899 was much more than just preparation for forming a political party, as will be discussed more closely in Chapter 4. Here, I propose that a close study of Itō's speeches that year reveals that the campaign was motivated not so much by plans to start a new political party, as by his determination to reconsider constitutional government as the lodestone in a more fundamental vision of the state.[34]

Toward people-led government

The "civilized" nation Itō envisioned was equipped with a constitutional system and to make it work, he encouraged an ethos of popular participation in government. What he had said to the nobility behind closed doors ten years earlier, he now said openly to the Japanese public:

> People of the feudal era took no part in government. They were simply ruled. If they wanted to know how government was run they could learn nothing except matters directly related to them. Today, however, the people need to know even those things that do not directly affect them. They have the right to do so. Now that they have the right to know about government, they have the right to get involved in national government. This kind of system is the only way to sustain a civilized government and a civilized people.[35]

After the enactment of the constitution Itō had spoken repeatedly of government being *for* the people and *centered around* the people, but now he was beginning to talk about government *by* the people. Going directly to the people, he delivered his political creed that "the people themselves must lead government."[36]

"Is there anyone in any occupation who is not related to government?" asked Itō.[37] In the civilized world, he believed, government permeates every aspect of people's activities in society. That is to say, the state is in the backdrop of every activity people engage in, and the state is expected to support and promote such activities whenever necessary. Thinking that way, Itō was eager to see Japanese become people not only *for* whom but *by* whom government was run. He had been trying at that time to expand the electorate by revising the House of

Representatives election law. At the time, voting rights were held by high taxpayers—chiefly landowners. If the law were changed to require those with lower incomes to also pay annual tax at a lower rate, that would convert a broad segment of the population into taxpayers who were eligible to vote and it would also increase the proportion of income tax contribution to the national revenue.[38] That reflects, some argue, a policy of mobilizing urban merchants and industrialists as participants in the political process and transforming Japan into a bourgeois state.

The people's power

We must note, however, that any effort Itō made to muster political participation by the urban bourgeoisie was probably not intended as an end in itself; rather he saw government *by* the people—including the middle classes—as a stepping-stone to "civilized government." Holding up the ideal of civilization, he would discuss his political philosophy in broad terms, but its premise was the need for the people to take a leading role in making government work:

> Civilized people must be familiar not only with private matters but with government matters as well. Aware of government matters, they must also know for what purposes the government collects taxes and how it uses the money it collects.[39]

Itō thought of the nation-state as a constituency in which the people—who pay taxes to the state—check and direct the way the state is governed. Of course "the people" must be equipped to do this. They need financial power and they must have the power of knowledge. These two capacities, Itō says, form the foundation of national strength. In 1889, speaking to the nobility, he had outlined a view of an enlightened, educated people as the source of national strength. Along the same lines when speaking to the public in 1899, he stated:

> What is this power of the people that underlies national power? It is the people's financial power and their knowledge power, both of which must continue to grow. The one is tangible progress and the other is intangible progress. By combining growth in tangible and intangible strengths, we will support the progress of our nation. Intangible progress means development of education and tangible progress means improvement and expansion of business and industry.[40]

Itō cites business/industry and education as the main factors needed to strengthen the power of the people. The basic requirement is education, which is behind the growth of business and industry and the development of constitutional government. Probably an even greater objective of Itō's nationwide speaking campaign was to arouse awareness of the importance of education. Beneath his message about the need for and role of education lay his ideals for governing.

Educating the people in practical science

"For a country to prosper requires education for its people," said Itō. Behind his emphasis on the need for education there lay a wish to raise popular political awareness.

Apolitical education

As Itō observed in one of his 1899 speeches, despotic government keeps things secret. The Confucian approach was to keep the masses in the dark and force them to obey without question. And he went on to say:

> Constitutional government, however, is an approach that lets the people know as much about the merits and demerits of a government as possible. How much they can learn about their government has much to do with education. It is not easy to improve education overnight, of course, but gradually, as you send children to school, as their education is improved, as times change, and as experience accumulates in interpreting the ways and approaches of constitutional government, little by little it becomes easier to understand government and everything else.[41]

That passage also echoes part of his February 1889 speech to the nobles and peers, in which he said that the people, as they became better educated and more enlightened, would "get to know more and more about their country, their government, other countries' governments, other countries' national strengths, and other countries' military might." He had observed that when people were educated and informed, it would not be enough just to try and silence them. He highlights the importance of informing educated people about the strengths and shortcomings in a government and allowing them to air opinions and carry on political debate. The forum for such discussion was, of course, the parliament.

What did Itō think should be taught, and what kind of people should education try to produce? Education in ancient Greece had fostered citizens of the polis who were adept at and committed to politics: was that a good model? The answer for Itō was, no.

Given his political goals, it might sound paradoxical, but Itō believed that education must be apolitical. It should, above all, produce professionals in business and industry. "Learning today has to be practical science," he says.[42] In Itō's mind practical science was first and foremost apolitical. He thought that science was a large part of learning and that it excluded any political discussion or debate. He stated as much twenty years earlier in his 1879 proposal, "On Education," introduced in the previous chapter. There he argued for wider education in "practical science" that would quell excessively passionate political debate. Because it is important, let's take another look at the quotation:

> ... it is essential to promote a wide range of subjects in engineering and technology. Those who receive higher education should commit themselves

wholeheartedly to the pursuit of practical learning, examining and observing things in fine detail and becoming more and more proficient year after year. That way we can get rid of the frivolous, over-passionate currents of the moment. Science is to political wrangling as rising is to falling.[43]

Chinese classics vs. practical science

Itō would reiterate this proposition in 1899, the difference being what he wanted to get rid of. In "On Education," the kind of ideas Itō wanted to dispense with were those he saw in activists coming out of private academies who were involved in the movement for people's rights. But two decades later, his target was the ideas of nationalists brandishing excessive patriotism—ideas fanned by national polity (*kokutai*) ideologues using mainly the Chinese classics to justify their position.

According to Itō, Chinese classics scholars "seem to believe that only despotism is suitable for Japan's national polity," and this "mistaken" view arises from "their narrow perspective and their inability to understand government ancient or modern and its reality." They fail to have a real grasp of the old saying, "In this vast world there is no land or people not subject to the monarch," he asserted, and continued:

> It is all right to regard all land and people as subject to the monarch, but under constitutional government, unlike despotism, someone's belongings are his own; what happens when someone's belongings are stolen by another? Such barbaric acts are prohibited. Everyone's life and property are protected by law. To be otherwise would be despotism; or worse, tyranny.[44]

Itō sternly rejected the study of Chinese classics as "false" learning with no practical value that could provide no proper understanding of constitutional government. He states:

> Most of the old learning was false learning based on little fact. From now on, you should study practical sciences, and by all means read Chinese books, but only as a means of enriching your knowledge of literature. Almost nothing in Chinese literature by itself has any practical application.[45]

Itō was a statesman who kept his distance from nationalist ideologies and activism. Seeing that opponents of the new treaties with the Western countries routinely sprinkled their political speech-making with traditionalist themes from the Chinese classics, he urged changing such ways of thinking through scientific education, namely "practical science."

Extolling empiricism

The first feature of Itō's practical science was its apolitical orientation, and so it makes sense that the second was conformity to facts, as his statements indicate. His practical and fact-based view of learning has much in common with the empiricism and pragmatism of philosophers of the West. He was, in fact, interested in the British empiricist perspective, finding it congenial to what he himself believed, as the following "allegory" shows:

> Wanting to learn how the camel lives, a Frenchman went directly to a zoo, it is said. Camels are kept in zoos, but you cannot study their lives at the zoo because it is not their natural habitat. What did a German do? He confined himself to his room to study the life of camels through books. But the Englishman—he went to Egypt, where he visited the habitat of camels and observed firsthand how they actually lived. That is a superficial allegory, but it illustrates the need to take a thoroughly practical approach to the advancement of Japan.[46]

Here we can see how, just as he rejected the study of Chinese classics, regarding them as "false" learning, he rejects conceptual and speculative approaches—which he sees as symptomatic of the French and German approach—and extols the down-to-earth, practical empiricism of the British.

Personal experience

The third feature of practical science that Itō viewed as important was its utility. Knowledge of any value was something that could be applied in the real world. That is why empiricism is so important, he said, for only when it is based on facts can knowledge be applied to reality. This view of science leads to the view of learning as a tool:

> What is learning? It is no more than a tool for the young to use when they become adults to engage in the profession they choose. Learning is not an end in itself. You first acquire learning as a guide to getting on in the world. Only when you apply to reality what you have learned will you gain experience. With the accumulation of experience you can succeed in any profession you choose. I greatly hope you will achieve [all you deserve].[47]

Here, Itō asserts that learning is "no more than a tool" and a "guide to getting on in the world." He seems to reduce learning to utilitarianism—but let us examine what he was trying to convey by this remark. To do so, we need to recall his early days.

That Itō was able to become a man of distinction and achievement despite being born into a low-ranking farming family is beyond doubt the result of the education he received. Together with his intense desire to learn, his fortuitous encounters with Kuruhara Ryōzō and Yoshida Shōin, who became his mentors, and his travel to Britain to study even before it was legal made it possible for Itō to absorb a wide-ranging knowledge of the world. Those opportunities enabled him to start climbing the ladder of success toward the end of the Tokugawa shogunate. Having knowledge helped him overcome the class system and enabled him to grow beyond narrow-minded nationalist ideologies and anti-foreign sentiments.

Drawing from his own experience, Itō believed that individuals could become independent and self-reliant by acquiring knowledge through learning and by drawing on it to succeed no matter what one's class origins. That was the ideal course, but to realize it the individual must put his knowledge to actual use in society. Knowledge serves as a medium connecting individuals with society. Through knowledge, individuals can realize their full potential, act in society, and even work on society and reform it. In emphasizing "practical science," Itō appears to have sought to assert how people can fulfill their potential as members of society and establish their own identity as individuals through knowledge and its practical application.

Policy insights from the people

During much of 1899, Itō traveled all over Japan on a campaign to help his countrymen gain a better understanding of the Constitution. In his speeches, he called for popular government, that is, government by "civilized people."

The "civilized people" Itō wanted to cultivate were primarily apolitical business people, those engaging in daily economic activities instead of "indulging" in political activities. On the other hand, such business people were precisely the kind he sought to mobilize for political action. Asking rhetorically in a speech, "Is there anyone in any occupation who is not related to government?" Itō argued that business people need political involvement to perform the responsibilities of their work.

According to the logic of his thinking, everyone should devote themselves to their respective professions, but their participation in government is also necessary to improve the conditions for their work. If political factors arise that either obstruct their economic activities or, conversely, foster the development of their activities, they need to get involved in policy formation designed either to get rid of or promote those factors.

Itō believed that the practical application of specialized knowledge would yield abundant ideas and insights that could be used in formulating policies promoting the country's economic growth. He very likely aimed at constructing a national decision-making system enabling such policy insights to be reflected in the actual government/political process. The political forum for that purpose was the parliament, and Itō created the Seiyūkai party to bring to the parliament policy insights originating in the people's experience. The story of how the Seiyūkai was founded will shed further light on how he envisioned the way popular experience could inform the Diet.

Notes

1 *Itō-kō zenshū*, vol. 1 (*Bunshū*), pp. 182–3.
2 *Itō-kō zenshū*, vol. 1 (*Bunshū*), p. 183.
3 "Inoue Kaoru monjo," no. 303–1.
4 When Inoue convened a conference to revise the unequal treaties in Tokyo in May 1886, one of the items in the revised treaty draft called for foreign judges to be authorized to

participate in Japanese trials. In the wake of the general hue and cry over the humiliation of such a treaty condition, Inoue was forced to resign as foreign minister.
5 Letter from Itō to Matsukata Masayoshi, dated August 19, 1891, *Matsukata monjo*, vol. 6, p. 442.
6 *Itō monjo* (Hanawa), vol. 2, p. 145.
7 Letter from Itō Hirobumi to Itō Miyoji, dated October 11, 1891, in the collection of Kensei Kinenkan (Parliamentary Museum), reference number 11-3-5-s-10. Subsequent quotations in this section are from this letter.
8 A reference to the epochal shift in the locus of power from direct imperial rule based in Kyoto to military hegemony exercised by the Minamoto shoguns in Kamakura in the late twelfth century.
9 Among the first studies to see the Meiji Constitution in such a positive light after the end of World War II is Toriumi 1988. A more recent and excellent overview of the history of constitutional government under the Meiji Constitution is Naraoka 2006.
10 An abortive coup d'état launched by reactionary elements in the navy on May 15, 1932.
11 Remarkable progress has been made in research on this topic, the pioneer study being Banno 1971. Other important works include Takahashi 1995, Sasaki 1995, and Itō Yukio 1999.
12 *Yamagata-den*, vol. 3, p. 319.
13 A fresh look at the Ōkuma-Itagaki cabinet from the perspective of politician–bureaucrat relationships is presented in the second chapter of Shimizu 2007.
14 *Itō-den*, vol. 3, pp. 377 ff.
15 Japan's first general-interest magazine, *Taiyō* (The Sun) was published between January 1895 and February 1928 with a total of 531 issues. Its circulation in the early stage of publication was "nearly 100,000 copies" according to Hakubunkan.
16 *Ozaki Saburō nikki*, vol. 3, p. 201.
17 Temple dedicated to the Mōri family, former daimyo of the Chōshū domain.
18 Hijikata Hisamoto (1833–1918), former Tosa samurai and minister of the Imperial Household Department from 1885 to 1898, happened to be on the same train Itō and his retinue were taking to Utsunomiya in July; he was indignant to overhear Itō openly criticize Tanaka Mitsuaki (who had just succeeded Hijikata as Imperial Household minister) before the reporters. Sasaki 2003, p. 330.
19 Letter from Itō to Yamagata, dated June 29, *Yamagata monjo*, vol. 1, p. 126.
20 February 11, 1899 speech *Enzetsushū*, vol. 1, pp. 18–19.
21 Ibid., p. 13.
22 April 12, 1899 speech, *Enzetsushū*, vol. 1, pp. 169–70.
23 Ibid., vol. 2, p. 255, March 22, 1899 speech.
24 Ibid., pp. 181–2, March 19, 1899 speech.
25 Ibid., p. 255, May 22, 1899 speech.
26 Ibid., vol. 3, p. 47, May 31, 1899 speech.
27 Ibid., p. 123, June 10, 1899 speech.
28 *Tōkyō nichinichi*, November 15, 1899.
29 March 21, 1899 speech, *Enzetsushū*, vol. 2, p. 220.
30 Ibid., vol. 1, p. 151, April 10, 1899 speech.
31 Ibid., vol. 2, pp. 26–7, May 31, 1899 speech.
32 Ibid., vol. 3, pp. 11–12, May 31, 1899 speech.
33 Ibid., vol. 2, p. 264, May 30, 1899 speech.
34 On this point, Sasaki Takashi regards the purpose of the Itō campaign as making the people (*jinmin*) into a nation (*kokumin*) and shaping a nation-state (Sasaki 2002, pp. 17–18). However, Sasaki does not discuss the substance of "nation" and "state" in detail.
35 May 18, 1899 speech, *Enzetsushū*, vol. 2, pp. 159–60.
36 *Tōkyō nichinichi*, October 19, 1899.
37 May 30, 1899 speech, *Enzetsushū*, vol. 2, p. 265.

38 At the time of the tax increase in 1899, the income tax rate was raised and the tax exemption for corporations until then was also revised. The proportion of annual revenue coming from income taxes thereafter increased. This reform was intended to shift the emphasis in the taxation system from land tax to income tax. (Zeimu Daigakkō Kenkyūbu 1996, p. 46) As discussed in the next chapter, Itō's scheme to draw businessmen into the Seiyūkai can be seen as an attempt to create a link between raising their awareness as taxpayers and as citizens with responsibility to the state.
39 May 18, 1899 speech, *Enzetsushū*, vol. 2, pp. 160–1.
40 Ibid., vol. 3, p. 183, July 16, 1899 speech.
41 Ibid., vol. 2, p. 265, May 30, 1899 speech.
42 Ibid., vol. 3, p. 40, May 31, 1899 speech.
43 *Itō den*, vol. 2, p. 154.
44 April 12, 1899 speech, *Enzetsushū*, vol. 1, pp. 174–5.
45 Ibid., vol. 3, p. 40, May 31, 1899 speech.
46 Ibid., vol. 1, pp. 157–8, April 10, 1899 speech.
47 Ibid., vol. 3, pp. 38–9, May 31, 1899 speech.

4 Creating a society for knowledge

The Seiyūkai

From oligarch to party politician

The founding of the Seiyūkai (Rikken Seiyūkai—Friends of Constitutional Government) party in September 1900, with Itō Hirobumi as its first president, marks the birth of Japan's first political party capable of taking the reins of government. Although it was dissolved in 1940, right before the start of the Pacific War, it is the forerunner of today's conservative political camp. Today's Liberal Democratic (Jiyū Minshutō) party, which was formed from the merger of smaller conservative parties in 1955, became Japan's largest political party and has held a nearly continuous grip on power for the last six decades.

That Itō, once the proponent of "transcendental" government aloof from party politics, should be instrumental in setting up a political party himself is counted as one of the major turnabouts in the political history of the Meiji era. Scholars agree that the founding of the Seiyūkai was groundbreaking, but they have not accorded much attention to Itō's role in its emergence. He was a "transcendentalist," they say (citing remarks he made at the time of the establishment of the Constitution), who rejected any notion of a party-controlled cabinet. They conclude that Itō did not originally set out to form the Seiyūkai; it was, rather, the unavoidable consequence of other developments.

This image of Itō is shared by many historians, and scholars of this period generally attach little importance to his place in the establishment and management of the Seiyūkai. Political historian Mitani Taichirō believes the de facto leaders and those who exercised real power in the new party were the former Kenseitō leaders, especially Hoshi Tōru. Historian Masumi Junnosuke attributes the Seiyūkai emergence to Itō Miyoji's efforts to bring Itō Hirobumi and the Kenseitō together. Thus historians tend to see Hoshi and Itō Miyoji as the driving forces behind the emergence of the Seiyūkai. In the preface I cited philosopher of law Nagao Ryūichi's comment that, to regard Itō Hirobumi as the key figure in the establishment of the Meiji Constitution is "uninformed amateurism misled by Itō's dashing but superficial performance." Just as scholars see Inoue Kowashi as the real drafter of the Constitution, so Hoshi Tōru and Itō Miyoji are considered the prime architects of the Seiyūkai.

As these scholars see it, the Seiyūkai was, for Itō, not the legitimate offspring of his own firmly held political creed, but rather a "changeling" that would threaten to tear apart the political system he had been trying to build through the late 1880s and 1890s. Considering the internal trouble and subsequent collapse of the fourth Itō Hirobumi cabinet formed soon after the founding of Seiyūkai, as well as Itō's failure in its management in the early phase and his resignation as party president in 1903, many historians regard the founding of the Seiyūkai as the beginning of Itō's political downfall. A few studies have appeared that call attention to his leadership in launching the party, but their publication has been sporadic and the viewpoints and propositions they offered have not been taken up and expanded upon.[1]

A re-evaluation of Itō

In sharp contrast is a recent argument by Itō Yukio, that forming the Seiyūkai was part of Itō's plan to completely revamp the administrative system and bureaucracy, both of which had been reformed in the late 1880s, and bring them in line with the needs of the new post-industrial revolution era emerging around 1900.[2] Squarely facing the big, new developments taking place following enactment of the Constitution, including rising political awareness among the leading figures in local regions and the growing social influence of businessmen and industrialists, Itō Hirobumi appears to have seen in the Seiyūkai a means to expand participation in government by these groups and thereby to realize more fully the strengths and opportunities of constitutional government. In his mind, not only could the party be instrumental in bringing fundamental changes to the way constitutional government was exercised, it was also central to his endeavor to reform the country's administration as a whole, including the internal organization of the government. Professor Itō points out that Itō Hirobumi's first priority was to make Japan a stronger nation, and the reforms he wanted in internal affairs were all directed toward that goal. It was for that reason, he contends, that Itō tried so hard in Japan's foreign affairs to restrain what he considered a premature and unwise push for expansion into the Asian continent. He believed Japan should, rather, seek cooperation with the Western powers, beginning with entente with Russia.

Itō Yukio's work is pioneering in at least two respects: first, he was able to see in the founding of the Seiyūkai Itō Hirobumi's vision of the state and his strategies for both domestic and foreign policy; second, he gathered sufficient evidence to overturn the long-held image of Itō as an opportunistic, spur-of-the-moment politician and present him as a statesman with solid, far-sighted principles and convictions. Inspired by Professor Itō's new insights into Japan's political history, this chapter looks again at the formation of the Seiyūkai, but from a different perspective. Here we focus more specifically on Itō Hirobumi's thinking. We have seen how he traversed the country, going directly to the people in his campaign to raise political awareness about the Constitution and the duties of citizens in a modern state; what lay behind the campaign was the long-range program he had been working on since the drafting of the Constitution by which to make Japan an independent, constitutional state. In the 1880s, he had been involved in setting up its framework; he now turned to bringing it alive with the spirit of a people who supported constitutionalism. As he took up this next challenge, how did he envision the role of the Seiyūkai in constitutional government, and how did the party actually turn out?

Keeping a distance from party politics

Itō Hirobumi was not the only one giving speeches around the country in 1899. Itagaki Taisuke of the Kenseitō (Constitutional party) and Ōkuma Shigenobu of the Kensei Hontō (True Constitutional party)[3] as well as a number of others were also busily campaigning in various parts of Japan. All over the country prefectural assembly elections were scheduled for that September. These were the first elections to be held since the prefectural and county codes had been revised in March to effect a shift from indirect to direct election of prefectural assembly members. For the political parties, therefore, it was urgent to go directly to the people to gain their support. A report in a widely read mass-circulation magazine described intense campaigning, saying that it looked more like the clamor of national assembly elections than prefectural voting. "The national political parties," it said, "are now openly involved in prefectural assembly elections. Banking on the power of their respective headquarters, they are jockeying for advantage in this election so they can expand their party's influence."[4]

In October 1898, internal struggle between the liberal and progressive factions of the governing Kenseitō caused the Ōkuma-Itagaki cabinet to collapse, and that made the competition between the constitutional parties all the more frenetic. Politicians rushed from one region to another fighting furiously to secure more support for their parties. The *Jiji shinpō* newspaper carried a cartoon satirizing the wrangling politicians. It shows Itō, Itagaki, Ōkuma, and other well-known

Figure 4.1 Caricature of political figures on nationwide electoral campaign. From right: Itagaki, Itō, and Ōkuma. *Jiji shinpō*, May 24, 1899.

Source: Chūō Kōron Shinsha, p. 155.

figures in a tour group; Itō is armed with a big gold sake cup; Itagaki is sitting backwards on the rump of a horse, meaning that he follows along blindly; and Ōkuma is blowing on a conch shell, which tells us that he is bragging.

Ōkuma and Hoshi campaigns

The movements of two of the party bigwigs—Ōkuma of the Kensei Hontō and Hoshi of the Kenseitō—offer a glimpse of the intensity of the election campaigns in 1899.

First, Ōkuma. Around the same time as Itō launched his stumping tours, Ōkuma also set out on a speech-making campaign and his destination was the Tōhoku region. He arrived in Fukushima on April 16 and in Sendai on April 18, and at these two places he held gatherings where he was able to whip up great enthusiasm among his party supporters for the cause of tax reduction. His schedule was especially tight in Sendai, where he attended a total of five meetings and delivered four speeches in a single day.[5] One Ōkuma biography relates that the trip to Sendai was his first political tour since the "bombing incident." Ōkuma himself called it his "first battle" since the incident.[6] Ten years earlier, in 1889, an attempt had been made on his life by an ultranationalist opposing the revision of the treaties with the Western countries and he had lost his right leg in the explosion. The fact that he showed renewed courage for the "battle" reveals not only his own enthusiasm for the election fray but also the palpable tension among the political parties.

Ōkuma's visit to Sendai was indeed described in the press as a "political battle." Kenseitō rival Hoshi Tōru had arrived in Sendai on April 6, several days prior to Ōkuma's visit. For Ōkuma's Kensei Hontō, the Tōhoku region along with the Hokuriku region (the Sea of Japan side of Honshū), was the main base of electoral support, so Hoshi had obviously gone to Sendai to undermine the rival party's support base.[7] Ōkuma hastened to Sendai to fend off incursions on his political turf and to solidify his support base. A newspaper article announced in excited tones, "The political battle being waged in Tōhoku between the former Liberal and former Progressive parties, spurred on by their 'banners and drums,' is one of the most spectacular shows of recent times."[8] After that, in late May, Ōkuma traveled to the Kansai region and went through the routine again, speaking out against higher taxes in the grueling quest to win support for his party.

As for his rival, following the April stint in Tōhoku, Hoshi went to the Hokuriku region in late June. His objective was not just to vie for the support base there for the Kensei Hontō, but also to defend his own party against the challenge of the Kokumin Kyōkai (Nationalist Association), a nationalist group on its way to setting up a party that would try to erode the political base of the Kenseitō. Many in the association's leadership were connected in some way or other with the region, and the association had poured enormous energy into expanding its influence there.[9] In July, the Kenseitō held a gathering in Utsunomiya, Hoshi's own constituency. Itō Hirobumi was invited to attend. Ostensibly it was a group of local businessmen who asked him to come, and he delivered a speech for them,

Figure 4.2 Hoshi Tōru (1850–1901).
Source: Photograph courtesy of the National Diet Library of Japan.

but in actuality Hoshi had made arrangements to have both Itō and Itagaki at the meeting. Having two such prominent political figures come to Utsunomiya would, he anticipated, only widen his sphere of influence. It was a move that demonstrated Hoshi's "determination to go into battle with all the money and muscle he could muster," reported the *Yomiuri shinbun* (July 14, 1899).

A different kind of campaign

Inter-party rivalry had become so contentious by that time that money (*kinryoku*) and muscle (*wanryoku*) had become popular bywords. "Money" meant pork-barrel-style maneuvering for the benefit of one's own district, which made it a powerful tool for spreading party influence in a regional electorate. Hoshi is often mentioned as the first modern politician in Japan to resort to that tactic. After the Utsunomiya meeting, he went to Hokkaido, and toward the end of July he visited Tōhoku again. Rumor had it that Hoshi was going to Yamagata with a plan to extend the national Ōu railway line to Sakata as a gift to local businessmen.[10]

The high pitch of political competition also unleashed rampant incidents of "muscle," ranging from intimidation to murder. When Hoshi arrived in Aomori on July 29 after a stumping tour in Hokkaido, he was assaulted by a thug. (Two years later he would be assassinated.) Other party leaders also became targets of the increasingly frequent acts of violence. "Only recently Mr. Miura [Gorō] was injured by someone from the former Liberal party in the Hokuetsu [Niigata-Toyama] area," a newspaper reported, "and now Mr. Hoshi has been attacked by a former Progressive party member. Money and muscle have come to dominate the political world. Where have justice and equity gone?"[11] With partisan battles fought with money and violence, justice and fairness had vanished.[12]

Itō had to conduct his own speech-making tours in this boisterous political context. He was determined to steer clear of the fracas, as is evident from the places he chose to deliver his speeches. He avoided locales where he might get involved in inter-party squabbling, so he did not visit, for example, any part of the Tōhoku region, where the election race was especially brutal. He did go to the Hokuriku region where the parties were battling in earnest. The original plan had been to go in August, but his advisor Itō Miyoji urged him to postpone the visit; going to the front lines of the party battle in a place like Kanazawa shortly before the prefectural elections, he said, would put Itō Hirobumi right into the maelstrom. Hirobumi followed Miyoji's advice and went to Hokuriku in October, after the elections were over.[13]

In these and other respects, the Itō campaign differed from the campaigns of the other political parties, whose primary purpose was to come out on top in the elections. I myself conclude that, even though he campaigned across the nation like the other politicians, Itō Hirobumi's objectives were different, as he himself explained many times during his campaign. What those objectives were, can be seen by examining the main points of his speeches.

Constitutional government and party-led government

The term constitutional government ordinarily calls to mind a parliamentary democracy. Popular participation in government is guaranteed by the constitutional provision for a parliament. And, insofar as responsibility in the exercise of parliamentary government is shouldered by political parties, constitutional government is ultimately synonymous with party government. That perfectly sound logic is indeed how people's rights activists early on regarded constitutional government under the Meiji Constitution. Later many members of the oligarchy adopted the same view and became party politicians.[14] What about Itō Hirobumi, on the verge of becoming a party politician himself—did he think the same way?

The people's duties to the emperor

Interestingly enough, in this period (around 1899), Itō Hirobumi repeatedly showed the distance he felt between party government and himself. He said, for instance, "I don't hope for a party cabinet, but I am not one to obstruct it either."[15]

Behind that noncommittal wording was a firm resolve to change the way party politics was playing out in Japan. In other words, by preserving a distinction between constitutional government and party government, he thought that the former could operate to keep balance in the workings of the latter. To explain his thinking at that point, let us recall his fundamental view of government.

We know that Itō was talking about "civilized government" (*bunmei no seiji*), which in his view must be led by the people. That meant fostering in the people, through education, the capability to participate in governing. A civilized, educated people could do so under a system that guaranteed popular participation in government, and that system was constitutionalism. Chapter 2 discusses Itō's view at the time when the Constitution was enacted—that a populace empowered by improved education and "culture" must be the basis for the development of the state. Establishing the kind of constitutional state Itō envisioned depended on incorporating the energy and vitality of such an enlightened people not only into economic activities but also into the political processes of the state, thereby making "the people's public life" more vital and active. In speeches he made during the 1899 circuit, Itō publicly urged greater popular participation in government. In one, he described the idea of constitutional government in terms of rights:

> What is meant by constitutional government is, first, that it distinguishes the sphere above and the sphere below, that is, the sphere of what the monarch should do and that of what the people should do. It makes clear the rights for the monarch to exercise, and the rights for the people to enjoy. That should be the basis on which to run national government.[16]

Here Itō sees joint governance by the emperor and the people as the principle underlying a constitutional system. His focus, however, is on the people's participation and their responsibility. The parliamentary system and the right to vote were bestowed upon the people by the emperor in the Constitution. The Constitution "is granted by the Emperor to his subjects, and it will remain unchanged and unchangeable because the Emperor's words are final and cannot be nullified." Itō assured people, in other words, that they "will never be robbed of the rights granted by the Constitution."[17]

The Meiji Constitution has acquired the general image of a set of laws and principles conferred single-handedly on the people by the sovereign that curbed their rights and reserved extensive prerogatives for the emperor. What Itō particularly emphasized, however, was how the Constitution gave the people the right to and guarantee of opportunity to participate in government. Once those rights were granted, they could never be revoked, even by the sovereign. For Itō, that was where the Constitution's true value lay.

Stressing that theme, Itō assured his audiences that they had political rights that no one, not even the emperor, could violate, and he explained that for their part the people had the obligation to the emperor to make full use of their rights in the interest of making their country prosper. To be loyal to the emperor, he said, was "to enjoy your rights spelled out in the Constitution and fulfill your duties toward the country."[18] He also called on the people to stay politically alert, saying, "You cannot afford to be asleep [passive]. If you are asleep, you will be unable to fulfill your duty to the country."[19]

Purpose of constitutional government

Itō's constitutionalism was premised on the politicization of the people. That, in turn, was related to the main purpose of a constitutional system, which was to bring a politically awake people into an orderly system and with that realize an ideal form of government, that is, joint governance of the nation by the emperor and the people. The primary objective of constitutional government, he said, is to ensure that "the Emperor, who reigns over the country, and the people, who are the constituents of the country, will be in harmony and get along well together."[20]

Harmony between the emperor and the people was the objective as well as the spirit of constitutional government. For that purpose the emperor entrusted the exercise of his own sovereignty to representatives of the people. Their responsibility, therefore, was to "conduct government for the Japanese people in a benevolent way like gentle spring rain moistening the soil, always keeping in mind that the impartial emperor has charged them with the exercise of his sovereignty."[21] Ideally, then, the emperor, as an impartial and nonpartisan overseer, consigned to the people the exercise of his rights of sovereignty and the people, mindful of his will, would carry out their tasks fairly and without bias. The result would be a "harmonious unity" of people and emperor.

This was the kind of nation Itō expected to take shape under the imperial Constitution. He envisioned "harmonious unity" prevailing not just between emperor and people but also between, for example, the legislative branch and the executive branch. "The workings of the Constitution rely on harmony. Disharmony impedes the progress of the nation."[22] It was one of his favorite themes, and he seemed tireless in arguing the need for harmony between the cabinet and parliament also; indeed, among all the powers and forces at the state level. "The state must be the sole focus of politics today," Itō said;

> if you are charged with the affairs of the state, that must be your only concern, and so you must always distinguish matters of state from the affairs of a prefecture or county. I am eagerly awaiting the day when you will cease pouring such energy into niggling conflicts at the local and regional levels and combine your efforts to carry out state projects successfully.[23]

The first nationwide prefectural assembly elections to be held since the new law mandated a direct election system were scheduled for September 1899, in the midst of Itō's speaking tours. The election campaigns that year were heated, and acrimonious inter- and intra-party conflict kept getting worse. Itō did not see politics as inherently, inevitably conflict-ridden; he saw it, rather as a process of reconciliation and cooperation moving toward the creation of a state founded on unity among its people. For that reason, as he watched the melee during the campaigns, he was vehement in appealing for an end to political infighting and urging collaboration among parties to "promote state projects."

Need for a new kind of party

Believing in the possibility and need for collaboration, and knowing that rough-and-tumble politics was not only unnecessary but damaging, Itō was understandably very critical of the way political parties had been conducting their business. It follows that one of his slogans when he founded the Seiyūkai was change in the way the parties operated. As Itō saw it, Japan's party politics was degenerating into "revenge politics."[24] He compared it to the brutal wars between the warrior clans of the twelfth century or their successors in the fourteenth century, which were a far cry from modern, civilized politics. "We cannot let them reduce the parliament of the Empire of Japan to a stockade within which everyone is locked in battles of revenge."[25]

> Everyone has their own opinions about what the interests of the nation are, and political parties are no more than groups of people who share the same opinions. The way our political parties are carrying on now, in ceaseless combat, reminds us of the fighting between the Minamoto and Taira or Nitta and Ashikaga. They go too far; it is no way to behave under our civilized, constitutional government. Political parties should be given less weight. Party members take their own parties and other parties, also, too seriously. That political opinions vary is inevitable, given the huge number of people in our country, but if too much importance is attached to parties, as is happening today, we are going to end up with a savage situation like the Taira-Minamoto war. Truly, that would be extremely bad for the nation.[26]

The admonition that "political parties should be given less weight" has to do with Itō's ideas on the need to accommodate change. He knew that "with the parliament in place, separation into different parties is unavoidable."[27] But, on the other hand:

> Things are constantly in motion, so politicians have no choice but to look at situations in terms of specific merits and demerits. When they see things in those terms, they may have to say yes this year to something to which they said no last year.[28]

Itō wants politicians not to make judgments based on fixed, rigid principles, but to study the constantly changing domestic and overseas environments and judge and act according to the prevailing circumstances. Knowing that the nation's interests change from one moment to another, he says, you can see that it is sound policy to cooperate with yesterday's foes rather than try to strengthen your own group by creating a faction or forming a party. Speaking of the spirit of compromise under constitutional government, Itō comments:

> Why does constitutional government work so well in Britain but poorly in other countries? I asked and was told that the British have a strong spirit of compromise. Other peoples don't. People with little spirit of compromise may be unsuitable for constitutional government.[29]

For Itō the real value of constitutional government lay in its built-in means to reconcile and orchestrate the various factors that made up the state. And the wonderful quality of constitutional government lay in its guarantee to all of them of the means and authority to participate in the exercise of sovereignty. But at the same time each and every factor that made up constitutionalism was required to operate in the spirit of compromise. Political parties were no exception. They, above all, had to proceed through compromise. In theory constitutional government does not require political parties, but in reality there has never been an instance of constitutional government without them.

> Every country that has constitutional government also has political parties. That is not an argument, it is an ineluctable fact. Political parties might not be necessary in theory, but the facts and history show that every country with constitutional government also has political parties. We are bound to accept the reality that they are going to arise.[30]

If it is unavoidable that parties will form, thought Itō, they need to be a lot better than what Japan had produced so far—parties that he saw drowning in squabbling and vituperation. Here was a statesman who considered popular participation in government and awareness by the people of their responsibility toward government as the nucleus of constitutional government. He wanted somehow to move the parties onto a higher plane, to make them responsible and responsive, able to coordinate the interests of the people and functioning as trustworthy mediators between people and government. Itō says, "I believe if political parties take greater care to make accommodations with one another as much as possible, constitutional government will proceed apace."[31] He was determined to do something about it, and the way he chose was to found a political party himself.

Forming the Seiyūkai

In 1898, Itō was leading his third cabinet, formed in January that year. On June 10, following the rejection of a tax increase bill, Itō dissolved the lower house of the Diet. Then, apparently anticipating the creation of the Kenseitō out of the merger of the major opposition Liberal and Progressive parties soon after, he immediately announced at a cabinet meeting his intention to start a new party. Because of the timing of this announcement, his move is usually explained as a foil to the opposition party merger,[32] an opportunistic and spur-of-the-moment strategy against the Kenseitō.

Yet during his third cabinet, Itō had been working steadily to expand suffrage and revise the election law and tax system, policies that were aimed at transforming the political fabric of the nation by involving the people more substantially in government. Any appraisal of the intent behind his new party movement must take those endeavors into account.

In May 1898 the Itō cabinet had submitted to the Imperial Diet a bill for revision of the House of Representatives election law, which, if it had passed, would have greatly increased the number of voters by modifying voting qualifications.[33] The same bill also provided for the abolition of the property qualification for eligibility to stand for election. "If elections are to let voters choose those whom they judge to be trustworthy," he declared in one of his speeches, "high tax payment is not necessary as a qualification to run for office."[34]

If the revised law had passed, it would have brought the number of voters up from the current 440–50 thousand to two million, underlining the "necessity to expand urban representation in the Diet in line with the growth of commerce and industry."[35] Itō had two goals in mind. One was related to the surge of growth in industry in the years after the Sino-Japanese War of 1894–5. In line with his basic conviction that change in the structure of the economy must be accompanied by political change, and with industry booming, he wanted to change the composition of voters by shifting the main body of the electorate from landowners to urban industrialists and people in business and commerce.

The other goal was to get rid of the overzealous political talkers who so dominated the parties. Itō detested demagogues and rabble-rousing political bullies. In "On Education" (1879) he talked about the need to discourage such people and to promote "scientific" thinking among the people and the importance of policy formation based on logical, scientific thinking. This was a major theme of his political career. We will see in Chapter 7 how that theme underlay what he tried to do as resident-general in Korea, and he reiterated it in a June 16, 1899 speech, too, expressing his "wish to make those with an inclination for political debate stay closer to the facts."[36] He continued:

> Since the enactment of the Constitution a large number of people have appeared burning with zeal to talk politics. What is truly deplorable is that those avid debaters indulge only in empty political rhetoric and do not think about industry and practical things. I wish those political talk enthusiasts would pay more attention to the economic conditions of Japanese society and the actual state of the Japanese people's sanitation and education in Japan and check the progress that is being made by studying statistics, and so on. I want to see them conduct their discussions on the basis of facts as they possibly can.[37]

Viewing government and the private sector as inseparable, Itō tried to mobilize the knowledge accumulated by government officials and people with specialized expertise for government. He also sought to incorporate the practical and specialized knowledge of private-sector businessmen in politics and government. If the preponderance of leaders in the parties were such people, he thought, the demagogues would eventually be driven out of party politics.[38]

The bill of the revised election law was shelved and did not pass, yet Itō did not give up on his determination to get people in business and commerce actively involved in politics and to do something to reform the firebrand style of many party members. He continued to work toward those objectives, which, ultimately, led to his founding of the new party.

Fence-sitting businessmen

After the House of Representatives was dissolved on June 10, Itō immediately set out to rally the business community in support of his plan to form a political party. On June 14, he invited a group of businessmen to the Imperial Hotel for a meeting to secure sponsorship for the party. He met with the distinguished entrepreneur Shibusawa Eiichi to ask for his cooperation.[39] Shibusawa did not want to take a leading role, but, since he agreed with Itō's policies, he said he would "openly back the party, and also would not hesitate to tell other people," as well. Thus Shibusawa promised to give indirect support and then signed a written pledge at Itō's request.[40] True to his word, Shibusawa set up organizations within the Tokyo Chamber of Commerce that would back the policies Itō was pushing, including the League for Raising the Land Tax (December 1898) and the League for Revising the House of Representatives Election Law (January 1899). When the Seiyūkai was founded in September 1900, Shibusawa organized a businessmen's conference, which issued a final resolution that states, "All persons present hereby agree to give their full support to the Seiyūkai, which is the result of Marquis Itō's statecraft, and are resolved to form close ties with it."[41]

Figure 4.3 Shibusawa Eiichi (1840–1931).

Source: Photograph courtesy of the National Diet Library of Japan.

Itō's appeal to business and commerce did not turn out as planned, however. Only a small number of businessmen actually joined the party. The resolution, in fact, contained an additional statement acknowledging the risks involved and offering a way out:

> Given the abuses that have been perpetrated in association with the political parties, those persons working with banks and companies are not necessarily required to become members if they deem that their joining the party might be detrimental to the management of their business.[42]

Much to Itō's righteous indignation, Shibusawa himself did not join.

Interference by Iwasaki Yanosuke

It is undoubtedly true, as is often proposed, that one factor in the disappointing numbers when the party was launched was the tradition in Japan's business culture of non-involvement in politics. For the most part entrepreneurs disdained "dirtying their hands" by contact with politics, and this might have brought on

Figure 4.4 Iwasaki Yanosuke (1851–1908).

Source: Iwasaki-ke Denki Kankōkai, ed. *Iwasaki Yanosuke den*, vol. 2. Tōkyō Daigaku Shuppankai, 1971.

second thoughts about joining the Seiyūkai. Just as important, however, specific forces were also at work that impeded Itō's efforts to draw in people from the business and finance communities. Inoue Kaoru, Itō's ally, had been worried from the start about the likelihood that Iwasaki Yanosuke (1851–1908), governor of the Bank of Japan, would try to interfere.

On June 19, 1898, immediately after Itō announced his plan to form the party, Inoue said in a letter to Itō, "People in business circles are at the mercy of the inclinations of Iwasaki [Yanosuke]," and described what was going on:

> During his [Iwasaki's] career ... he has been intimately tied to Ōkuma [Shigenobu] through their friendship over the past several years, and moreover, those working hardest among [Ōkuma's] Progress party members come mainly from Fukuzawa [Yukichi]'s academy. In addition, the relationship between Fukuzawa and Iwasaki is such that Iwasaki has provided close to 100,000 yen in financial assistance to Fukuzawa over these few years ... [43]

Inoue thus feared that Iwasaki, who had close ties with Ōkuma and Fukuzawa and was a Progressive party sympathizer, would use various means to get in the way of Itō's efforts. Describing Iwasaki's influence in the financial world, Inoue wrote:

> It is only natural that bankers and company managers, though well aware of the need to correct the despicable practices we have seen so far in the other political parties, should be afraid that the combined forces of Iwasaki's financial power and the Bank of Japan will come up against them and sabotage their immediate financial and business dealings. It is impossible to expect them to stand together in support of Itō's new party.[44]

Some members of the business world were definitely sympathetic to the Seiyūkai, and it is not known exactly how Iwasaki might have disrupted their enterprises. (Iwasaki, by the way, resigned as governor of the Bank of Japan in October 1898.) Yet it was recognized in the above resolution that many were worried that joining the party might hamper them in the management of their enterprises.

Their worries were justified, as we can see from the case of Taki Hyōemon, a large taxpayer and member of the House of Peers. Taki sent Itō a letter on September 2, 1900 requesting membership in the Seiyūkai. He even wrote, "I am planning to ask a number of business leaders I know well in Tokyo, Osaka, Kyoto, and other places near and far to join too." Not long after he became a member, however, on July 6 the following year, he wrote to Itō that he was leaving the party: "Indeed, like others, there have been many occasions on which my party membership has created serious problems in my relations with banks and in my business and House of Peers activities. I can no longer endure these difficulties."[45]

The "problems" he suffered were probably maneuvers by pro-Ōkuma (i.e. Kensei Hontō) politicians and businessmen backed by Iwasaki. Itō, who wanted nothing to do with such scrapping among the parties, had sought to bring members of the financial and business communities—the very people who had long kept out of politics—into the heart of government and build a new kind of constitutional state premised on mutual accord and balanced interests. He ended up being engulfed by the political maelstrom. The October 1900 issue of the magazine *Taiyō* carried an article that reported:

> Even today, in a certain company many executives come from the former Kaishintō [Reform party], and former Jiyūtō [Liberal party] members complain that they are often handicapped. . . . Solid and serious businessmen are determined to carry on their enterprises independently, acting on their own convictions and without any thought of relying on politicians. They are wise enough not to join a political party and thereby make other parties their enemy.[46]

As the article shows, by this time the impact of Japan's growing political parties was also affecting the business world.

New party with the Kenseitō as the base

Having failed to recruit adequate support in commerce and industry himself, Itō felt he had no choice but to turn to Hoshi Tōru, the skilled and clever leader of the Kenseitō (Constitutional party, the former Liberal party). As noted earlier, Hoshi and Itō Miyoji are often cited by historians as the driving force behind the Seiyūkai, and no doubt they did play a key role in laying the preliminary groundwork. In July 1899, when Itō visited Utsunomiya at the invitation of local businessmen, it was Hoshi who acted as intermediary. Itagaki Taisuke too was invited at that time. The *Yomiuri shinbun* newspaper made fun of the gathering, saying it had looked like a meeting of former Liberal party members convened in Utsunomiya.[47]

Itō's speech-making in the Hokuriku region in October was also rumored to be connected with Hoshi's earlier tour of the region in June. The *Ishikawa-ken shi* [A History of Ishikawa Prefecture] recounts that Hoshi's visit to Hokuriku was "apparently meant to boost the momentum of the Kenseitō and invigorate the business world of the city of Kanazawa," and suspects that "a tacit agreement made at that time between Hoshi Tōru and the business community was a major factor behind Marquis Itō Hirobumi's later visit."[48]

On June 1, 1900, Matsuda Masahisa, Hayashi Yūzō, and Suematsu Kenchō from the Kenseitō Executive Council and Kataoka Kenkichi, speaker of the House of Representatives, asked Itō to become head of the Kenseitō. He waited more than a month and then, on July 8, turned them down. He appeared determined to keep away from the current parties and stick to his goal of creating a new one. He had a vision of the kind of party he wanted to form and he worked that summer on preparing a set of rules for it.[49]

On August 23 he invited Hoshi and other ranking members of the Kenseitō to meet with him at which he "notified them in private of the platform of the new party."[50] Apparently they were so impressed that, in response, the Kenseitō leaders offered their entire party to Itō, without any strings attached. On August 25, at the Kōyōkan, an exclusive restaurant in the Shiba district of central

Creating a society for knowledge: the Seiyūkai

Figure 4.5 Group celebrates the new Seiyūkai (1900). Itō (front row, tenth from right) with main party members.

Source: Chūō Kōron Shinsha, p. 175.

Tokyo, the Seiyūkai founding committee was formed. A formal announcement was made of the inauguration of the new party and party platform. Thus the Seiyūkai was born out of the merger of Itō's vision and the people and organization led by Hoshi. The fact was, however, that Itō's new party could never have gotten off the ground without the ready-made base that the Kenseitō provided. Itō tended to pursue his ideals with a tenacity that caused him to neglect the nuts-and-bolts aspects of running a political organization. As will be discussed in the next chapter, this fervid concern with ideals affected his management of the party soon after its founding. The confusion of those days reflects the secondary place he gave to the down-to-earth requirements of party organization.

Itō was in some respects too optimistic. A statesman-politician—Itō was both—should be held responsible for the results of his actions and words. Having lofty ideals does not necessarily guarantee high-quality performance. Keeping in mind the problematic side of Itō as a politician-manager, let us further investigate the ideals and concepts he injected into the Seiyūkai.

From "faction" to "society"

Itō made up his mind to form a party himself because of dissatisfaction with the existing parties. He began the process but failed to rally the desired participation from the business and finance world, so, in the end, there was no way to organize the Seiyūkai except within the framework of existing political factionalism.

I have so far referred to the Seiyūkai as a political party, but Itō himself resisted using the word party (*tō*) for his new organization. He chose to call it a society (*kai*), hence Seiyūkai. When Itō Hirobumi revealed its name to Itō Miyoji in a letter dated July 28, 1900, he wrote:

> I want to do away with the usual "party" (*tō*) designation. I'm set on calling it the Rikken Seiyūkai. . . . [This] is merely a means to get around using a term that is so abhorrent to bureaucrats and businessmen and make it easier for them to join us. As long as it causes no inconvenience in this superficial world, I want to avoid using the word. *Tō*, after all, originates in *hōtō* (Ch. *pengdang*), or cliques or factions organized by self-serving bureaucrats in ancient China. People hate using it. I beg you to understand.[51]

Thinking that *tō* had the bad connotations of self-serving *hōtō* and would not be an appealing choice, Itō here wanted to avoid it in the interest of getting maximum possible support from officialdom and business circles. Itō Miyoji replied, "I think you are worrying unnecessarily. It would be of no use, anyway, to allow into our party anyone so obdurate as to consider today's political parties similar to the *hōtō* of faraway China."[52] Ultimately, however, Itō Hirobumi prevailed and the name Seiyūkai was adopted.

It was not a matter of mere terminology. To Itō a "society" (*kai*) matched his idea of a type of political organization that was different in conception from the political parties that had arisen so far.

Draft rules

A week before the above letter, Itō had sent Itō Miyoji his draft of rules for the new party. The draft included the following six items:[53]

1 Selection and appointment of cabinet ministers are based on the Emperor's prerogative. We shall not oppose the cabinet solely because cabinet members from outside the party are appointed.
2 The cabinet is an advisory body to the Emperor and a body of responsible government. We shall not interfere in it from within the party solely because party members are selected as cabinet ministers.
3 We aim to reform administration by selecting suitable persons to the appropriate posts in each section of the government. We shall fairly designate people from outside the party as well. We shall not select people solely because they are party members.
4 We shall act for the public benefit and shall not become involved in local interests without reason.
5 If we wish to publicly comment on current issues as the opinion of party members, the party president shall decide whether or not to do so.
6 Regarding elections and activities in the Parliament, suitable persons shall be put in charge and shall receive guidance from the party president.

In contrast to the more businesslike and practical official party platform announced one month later, on August 25, the above list candidly expresses Itō's philosophy for a political organization. The philosophy boils down to three points: preserving a distinction between the party and the cabinet/government; distinguishing between the central government and local autonomy; and strong party leadership in the party under the president. A close reading of Itō's speeches, comments to the press, and other documents suggests what he was aiming for in these three areas.

Relation to the government

His view of the relation between the party and the government can be better understood by looking at a speech given during his 1899 speech-making campaign. Explaining that the members of the lower house of the Diet represent all the people of the nation and that "their *honzon* (literally, "main [Buddhist] image"; that is, their principal focus of attention) is the people." He says:

> The members of the House of Representatives must sincerely consider the opinions of the people—who are the *honzon* [i.e. to whom they are responsible]—and they must perceive the people's interests and work to faithfully perform what the people wish them to do in the national parliament.[54]

One of Itō's favorite passages from the work of the British thinker Edmund Burke is the admonition Burke made to local electorates, which Itō repeated in his own words: "Act not as your representative but as a representative of the whole nation." Moreover, in the speech introduced immediately above, Itō refers to Burke when he enjoins each member of the lower house to gather in parliament to act as a representative of the interests of the whole nation, not as a mouthpiece for individual interests.

The Japanese parliament, Itō observed, did not function that way at all. He deplored the real-life parliament, which had degenerated into an arena of vicious infighting among parties clawing for the upper hand. Although it should be a place for careful deliberation by the representatives, it had turned into a "fighting arena." "Parties must think deeply and well, and deliberate on what are the best ways to proceed to benefit the nation."[55] He pointed out that even before parliamentary deliberations on an issue began, "the parties are already deliberating the same issue separately in their own offices," and bemoaned what "looks as if there are two parliaments."[56]

Those are not the circumstances under which a party cabinet should be formed, he declared. "As long as the parties meet separately and each makes its own demands regarding the country's administration, a party-based cabinet is totally out of the question."[57] He couldn't bear the idea of the executive branch of government being exploited by a self-serving party that had secured exclusive privileges. In his view, a person who takes the helm of state may have used party politics to the maximum to beat his rivals and get to where he was, but once in power, he should have a fair and equitable outlook and run the government for the sake of the whole nation. "You may vie with other parties for political power," he said, "but once you have entered the realm of national government you should be neutral and fair." He goes on to say:

> In governing the people and administering the affairs of state, if the ruling party works only for its own interests, those in opposition will suffer. Such unfairness is not permissible in government. Whoever and whatever party may come to power must set their own interests aside, deal with things fairly, not discriminate against other parties, and focus only on public projects, the lives of the people, and the interests of the nation.[58]

In short, Itō did not necessarily believe that a political party could or should be the leading actor in seeking and ensuring the wellbeing of the nation. When appointing members of the cabinet, the executive branch charged with achieving objectives in the public interest, selection of candidates should not be at the discretion of the ruling party alone, even though the party is important in the process. Itō's concept of a political party seems to transform it into an important political group, which, with a base in the parliament, supplies competent personnel to the cabinet. In that concept, the party is an organization to train and maintain a pool of political experts.

Central government and local autonomy

On the distinction between central government and local autonomy, Itō held that the competition for party dominance should be confined to the realm of national government and that in outlying parts of the country, government should be based on the principle of cooperation. He says:

> Disputes over different political opinions should be carried on at the level of national government, but local-level projects and other local endeavors will proceed smoothly if the leading figures in villages get along well and work together in cooperation.[59]

According to Itō, political parties should operate at the central government level and disputes among them "should not be extended to villages."[60] In reality, the reverse was true. As a result of the prefectural code revision, there were fierce and incessant conflicts among parties engaged in local pork-barrel politics. "These days the evil effects of political parties have been sharply felt throughout Japan."[61] This is one reason why he says, "Debates between the parties should as a matter of course be argued for the purpose of national government."[62] And since government should concern itself with the wellbeing of the entire nation, a strict distinction between central government and local autonomy made sense:

> I think we have to call [local] autonomy "local administration" rather than "local government." Almost all matters related to the entire nation naturally

fall under the purview of government. Political parties often talk about so-called tactics and policies, and those should all be designed to work for the entire nation of Japan.[63]

Itō thus distinguishes between central and local, and between government and autonomy, and he regards political parties as being in charge of central government. That being so, he insists that the parties should not involve themselves too deeply in local affairs. He said, and this is a good example of the way he sought to relativize party politics, "Political party-style debates should not intrude too far into local matters. What local places need most for their well-being is amity among the people there."[64]

Absolute obedience to party president

The items Itō drafted for the party rules described strong powers of leadership vested in the head of the party. He held to this autocratic style of party leadership as an organizing principle during the early phase of the Seiyūkai. It is one of the points he kept bringing up in his campaign speeches, often referring to Benjamin Disraeli (1804–81), a nineteenth-century British statesman:

> Disraeli ... says that a British prime minister should be obedient to his own party and that the party members should be absolutely obedient to him, their party head. They are required to obey the command of the head, he says. When many convene in parliament there needs to be discipline and order. The members, he says, resemble a lawful and well-organized military unit. The necessity for a leader is obvious.[65]

One of Disraeli's achievements was to transform the Conservative party into a popular party with a strong support base in the masses. Itō knew this well, and it would not be strange if, out to reform Japan's parties and create a responsible party capable of governing Japan, he saw something of Disraeli in himself. As he indicates in the passage quoted above, the aspect of Disraeli's approach to governing that most resonated with Itō was the British statesman's insistence on establishing party discipline through absolute obedience to the party head.

On October 21, 1899, during his speech-making in the Hokuriku region, Itō was invited to speak at a gathering of the Kenseitō in the city of Takaoka. He cited Disraeli in that speech: "The head of a political party must faithfully follow the party's policy and at the same time, the party members must be absolutely obedient to the command of their head."[66]

In Itō's view party reform was needed before all else to establish the absolute authority of the party head. It was in a party with autocratic leadership that Itō found the potential for a party-based cabinet. He said, "If a cabinet is ever formed based on a political party, the head of that party must be capable of unifying the party well enough to enable it to fulfill the heavy responsibility of handling state affairs."[67]

He considered party unity as absolutely essential to achieving national prosperity. He talked of the House of Representatives as representing the entire nation, but the reality was that the representatives would find it extremely difficult to free themselves from special local interests and those of certain groups and classes. For Itō, that is where the party came in. It would function to screen the interests the Diet members represented and sift out those public interests that should be addressed by the political party.

To that end a party head needed to be powerful enough to determine the final opinion of the party as a whole and act on it. He would deliberate with the heads of other parties in parliament until they reached a compromise. In that way, agreement would be reached on national issues in the open forum of parliament. The party members would absolutely follow what their head had agreed to and decided on. These were probably the sorts of concerns Itō had when he advised party leaders that they needed to leave off their backstage (*kuromaku*) power-brokering and come forth and openly lead. He spoke at a meeting of people in favor of revising the election law:

> I wonder if Japanese political parties have any genuine leader. Everyone knows about the power their so-called heads have, but they have no seat in parliament. Thinking about it, I myself was once called a *kuromaku*, and observing how things are today I cannot help thinking that our party leaders are just that—they are *kuromaku*. ... The parties are going to have to stop that kind of thing under constitutional government, which is open and public government.[68]

Salon-like party

Itō prescribed strong party leadership, but at the same time he suggested that the Seiyūkai be a loosely knit, club-style organization. In his July 28 letter to Itō Miyoji cited earlier, he also noted his idea that "party headquarters, unlike the other parties, should be organized like a club with adjunct clubs set up in other regions." Itō Miyoji was opposed to the idea, however, saying, "Organizing clubs in place of headquarters and branch offices would be just impossible to do, and they would be bad for the party's unity and communication."[69] Instead, he suggested that the headquarters and branch offices should be the core organizations, and parallel to them, clubs could be set up as places for social purposes, which could open the party's doors wider to people. Hoshi Tōru agreed. "So please reconsider," Itō Miyoji requested as he tried to persuade his boss.

Itō Hirobumi's stipulation that loosely connected clubs be used in lieu of headquarters and branch offices seems inconsistent with his repeated insistence on strict party discipline. Why did he prefer an open, salon-like party milieu to a rigidly hierarchical one? Behind the seemingly strange combination of powerful party leadership and salon-type organization was Itō's idea of a political party as a "society" or "think-tank."

The party as think-tank

The founding of the Seiyūkai in 1900 has long been considered the outcome of Itō's conversion from "transcendentalist" statesman to party politician. But, as the foregoing discussion demonstrates, his true intention was to throw himself into the whirl of party politics in order to reform it from within.

Far beyond devotion to transcendentalism or party politics, it was an ideal of constitutional government that dominated Itō's thinking. Once the Constitution was enacted, he was unwavering in his efforts to develop a constitutional system intended to unify the people and bring peaceful accord to the country. He believed the relation between political parties and constitutional government should foster goodness and harmony:

> Partly to improve political parties, I want the people to learn to tell good government from bad. Only if the people can tell the difference can the evils of political parties be swept away and can the parties become agencies to perform their legislative functions and usher in unity between high and low. If the parties work otherwise and spread disunity between high and low, they will not be working as they should under the Constitution. The purpose of constitutional government is to bring harmony between ruler and ruled, hence unity between high and low.[70]

In a statement published in the inaugural issue of the party organ *Seiyū* before the Seiyūkai was founded on September 15, Itō explained the purposes for which he established it. Far from the excited sloganeering that might be expected for the kick-off moment in the battle to take control of the country, his statement was a sober call for prudence and self-restraint by party members. He stressed anew that the organization was not a machine to take the helm of state but a public body created to achieve "national harmony":

> Political parties are duty-bound to exert themselves to the utmost in the task of serving the state. In order to clean up the administration and thereby further the nation's prosperity, the ruling party must set qualifications and select as candidates for [cabinet and government] office people with adequate knowledge and experience who come from both inside and outside the party. The ruling party must never give posts to certain people because they are party members regardless of whether they are competent or not. In dealing with matters relating to local interests or the interests of organizations, members of the ruling party must apply the yardstick of public benefit. Party members must never be swayed by private considerations in favor of individuals and organizations from one's hometown, accept their requests, or give them party assistance. Together with my fellow members I wish to eradicate such vulgar and ignoble practices.[71]

The admonition not to give cabinet and government posts to people just because they are party members was a warning against the scramble for official posts that led to the collapse of the Ōkuma-Itagaki cabinet. Also, it followed a reminder that "the power to appoint and dismiss cabinet ministers is the constitutional prerogative of the Emperor," suggesting Itō's additional concern to forestall the arbitrary selection of candidates for cabinet posts by a party cabinet that would infringe on the emperor's right to appoint cabinet ministers.

On the other hand, the stipulation that appointees to official posts must "have knowledge and experience" and should come from both inside and outside the party underscores the importance Itō placed on the competence and skills of the people in government. He was determined to stamp out the routine practice of selecting people just because they were members of the majority party.[72]

Itō thought he could exert a restraining influence on the parties and clean up some of their more corrupt and abusive practices by transforming himself into a party politician. That was one of the reasons he was so assiduous about strict discipline within his party. Most of what has been described, however, makes the party movement look somewhat passive. But there was an active side to it as well.

A supplier of political experts

The active side of the party, embedded in its founding, was its role as an agency to supply political experts. Itō's declaration that cabinet ministers should be "people with adequate knowledge and experience who come from both inside and outside the party" expressed his conviction that political parties should play the role of discovering and training educated, knowledgeable, capable people and making them available for government service. In short, Itō saw the Seiyūkai as a gathering place of competent people. What kind of people were they? Itō took great pains, unsuccessful as they were, to get businessmen to join, but not because he was trying to create a political party of capitalists. It was their expertise and experience that he wanted to put in the service of government. Such people would be part of a body—the Seiyūkai—that could consider all the pros and cons, and advantages and disadvantages, in issues affecting the nation by gathering and deliberating on the knowledge and opinions of people from all segments of society. He expressed this idea in a speech delivered at a Seiyūkai meeting in 1901:

> In a constitutional system the people naturally have to be concerned about what is beneficial and what is harmful for their nation. Even so, the entire population cannot reflect on political matters all the time. Farmers need to tend their fields; industrialists need to think about supply and demand and about promoting industry, and they have to keep trying to expand their businesses; merchants have to keep checking quantities of agricultural and industrial products. All of them together should work with the aim of increasing their profits. Increasing profits for individuals means greater prosperity for the nation. At the same time, some of the population should go into matters of government as their occupation. It is essential, for example, for someone to plan how farm products should be distributed and investigate how to produce certain goods at home so we do not have to depend on other countries to supply them. Such people keep focused on commerce and industry,

but they are also able to weigh the strong and weak points in the government's current policies.

It is not good, needless to say, for the whole population to get caught up in political fever, and so we must have some individuals who represent the population and can judge matters on fair and even ground for the benefit of industry. Political debate should be left to officials, members of parliament, journalists, and the like. I'd like to see all in the general public performing their own duties while remaining alert and aware of political affairs. These, I believe, are policies to follow under constitutional government.[73]

Itō had made similar remarks during his 1899 speech-making tours. The main points were that the "civilized" people he wanted to nurture in Japan included businessmen and working people who were not involved in politics and whose productivity contributed to the nation's economic growth. People should give first priority to their occupations but they should not forget to be "alert and aware" of political affairs. At the same time, he did not want to see "the whole population . . . caught up in political fever"; the people should be able to leave political matters to "officials, members of parliament, journalists, and the like."

Ideal form of the Seiyūkai

For Itō, in a "civilized" nation people performed the duties of their work while staying away from political entanglements, and at the same time they maintained interest in political affairs and participated in certain ways in government. Their own individual interests were linked to the interests of the state, and, in that sense, all types of business were related to government. Some would decide to use their professional skills directly to help government, and such persons would be "representatives" of the people. This was the ideal he advocated.

Itō's ideal political party would have been an organization where such representatives of the people gathered, deliberated, and studied state policies together. He envisioned the Seiyūkai functioning in this manner. He wanted it to serve as a mediator, first to draw up specific policies in answer to the demands on the government that arose out of daily economic activities, and then to convey them to the nation's political leaders. He wanted the party to be a repository of know-how and expertise in policy-making to be used for the benefit of the state and the public. In the end, Itō's Seiyūkai was not just a political organization for policy realization but also something that resembled a modern think-tank.

It is very likely that Itō sought both near-autocratic power for the party president along with a somewhat club-style form of organization in order to make those two functions compatible. A loosely connected set-up of club-like headquarters and regional branches, all open to the public, would insure that knowledge, even from the farthest communities of people, would be accessible and freely distributed. To achieve the policy goals worked out within such an arrangement, the party members would act in concert in parliament under the strong leadership of the party president. The Seiyūkai, as Itō envisioned it, can thus be seen as the perfect apparatus for garnering and disseminating knowledge and giving it practical application.

Notes

1 Among such studies are works by George Akita, Oyama Hironari, and Motoyama Yukihiko. Raising objections to the commonly held image of Itō, they treat him as a bona fide party politician, not as a "transcendentalist" who changed his mind as the result of compromise and reconciliation with political party forces.
2 Itō Yukio 2000, p. 26.
3 The Kenseitō (Constitutional party), established from the merger of Ōkuma's Shinpotō (Progressive party) and Itagaki's Jiyūtō (Liberal party) in June 1898, split in October the same year into the new Kenseitō party (former Jiyūtō) and the Kensei Hontō (True Constitutional party—former Shinpotō).
4 *Kokumin no tomo* 1899.
5 "Count Ōkuma's Tour in Sendai," *Mainichi shinbun*, April 21, 1899.
6 *Ōkuma kō hachijūgo-nen shi*, vol. 2, p. 338.
7 Ariizumi 1983, p. 267.
8 "Political Battle in Tōhoku," *Mainichi shinbun*, April 14, 1899.
9 *Ishikawa-ken shi*, vol. 4, p. 482.
10 *Mainichi shinbun*, July 29, 1899.
11 Ibid., July 31, 1899.
12 On this point, see Miura Gorō's memoir, Miura 1988, pp. 294 ff.
13 *Itō monjo* (Hanawa), vol. 2, p. 393 and vol. 8, p. 317.
14 Among admirable recent studies that probe the establishment of party government under the Meiji Constitution are Iokibe 2003, Naraoka 2006, and Murai 2005.
15 May 17, 1899 speech, *Enzetsushū*, vol. 2, p. 127.
16 Ibid., vol. 3, p. 81, June 2, 1899 speech.
17 Ibid., vol. 2, p. 258, May 22, 1899 speech.
18 Ibid., vol. 3, p. 97, June 9, 1899 speech.
19 Ibid., vol. 2, pp. 258–9, May 22, 1899 speech.
20 Ibid., p. 66, May 15, 1899 speech.
21 Ibid., vol. 1, p. 185, April 12, 1899 speech.
22 Ibid., pp. 46–7, February 10, 1899 speech.
23 *Tōkyō nichinichi shinbun*, October 29, 1899.
24 May 15, 1899 speech, *Enzetsushū*, vol. 2, p. 77.
25 Ibid.
26 Ibid., pp. 78–9.
27 Ibid., p. 90, May 16, 1899 speech.
28 Ibid., p. 91.
29 Ibid., vol. 1, p. 47, December 10, 1898 speech.
30 Ibid., vol. 2, pp. 174–5, May 19, 1899 speech.
31 Ibid., vol. 1, p. 47, December 10, 1898 speech.
32 For details on the process of the Seiyūkai founding, see Itō Yukio 2000 and also the classic studies by Kobayashi 1990, Masumi 1965–80, vol. 2, and Yamamoto Shirō 1975.
33 In addition to existing voters, who directly paid an annual national tax of fifteen or more yen, the law would have enfranchised all who paid a land tax of five or more yen or income or business tax of three or more yen annually.
34 June 7, 1898 speech, *Enzetsu zenshū*, pp. 56–7.
35 Ibid., p. 53.
36 June 16, 1899 speech, *Enzetsushū*, vol. 3, p. 163.
37 Ibid., p. 162.

38 The idea of expelling the *sōshi*, or political bullies who abused the cause of social justice, from political parties was clearly expressed in his speech of August 25, 1900 to the Seiyūkai's founding committee. "We must get rid of *sōshi*-like activities. Allowing unpropertied, do-nothing scoundrels to join in counteracts our goal of influencing government to make the jobs and businesses of law-abiding people increasingly prosperous." (*Seiyū* 1900, vol. 1, p. 7) For a study of the close ties between Meiji-era political parties and *sōshi*, see Watanabe 2001.
39 *Itō den*, vol. 3, p. 373.
40 Shibusawa Eiichi memorandum, "Seiyūkai shoshiki no shitasōdan" [Preliminary Discussion on the Organization of the Seiyūkai], *Hiroku*, vol. 1, p. 7.
41 *Shibusawa denki shiryō* supplement, vol. 1, p. 154.
42 Ibid.
43 *Itō den*, vol. 3, p. 375.
44 Ibid.
45 *Itō monjo* (Hanawa), vol. 6, p. 132.
46 October 1, 1900 issue, Oyama 1967, pp. 83–4.
47 *Yomiuri shinbun*, July 14, 1899.
48 *Ishikawa-ken shi*, vol. 4, pp. 484–5.
49 Letter from Itō to Yamagata, dated July 1, 1900. *Yamagata monjo*, vol. 1, p. 129. In this letter Itō wrote, "Besides the enclosed paper I have formulated party rules, but they still need polishing and so I will show them to you one of these days" (p. 130).
50 *Hara nikki*, vol. 1, p. 297.
51 *Itō den*, vol. 3, pp. 446–7.
52 Ibid., p. 448.
53 "Itō monjo," Shorui-no-bu (Documents), p. 166.
54 May 15, 1899 speech, *Enzetsushū*, vol. 2, p. 68.
55 *Tōkyō nichinichi shinbun*, October 22, 1899.
56 Ibid., p. 124, May 17, 1899 speech.
57 Ibid., p. 127.
58 Ibid., pp. 129–30.
59 Ibid., p. 84, May 16, 1899 speech.
60 Ibid., p. 85.
61 Ibid., pp. 85–6.
62 *Tōkyō nichinichi shinbun*, December 3, 1899.
63 May 15, 1899 speech, *Enzetsushū*, vol. 2, p. 60.
64 Ibid., pp. 128–9, May 17, 1899 speech.
65 Ibid., vol. 1, p. 109, February 20, 1899 speech.
66 *Tōkyō nichinichi shinbun*, November 2, 1899.
67 May 17, 1899 speech, *Enzetsushū*, vol. 2, p. 127.
68 Ibid., vol. 1, pp. 114–15, February 20, 1899 speech.
69 Letter dated August 5, *Itō den*, vol. 3, p. 448.
70 June 16, 1899 speech, *Enzetsushū*, vol. 3, pp. 174–5.
71 *Seiyū*, vol. 1, pp. 1–2.
72 Itō is not trying here to justify the present "transcendental" oligarchic government. As an attempt to protect administrative authority against the emerging political forces, the Yamagata cabinet revised the Civil Service Appointment Ordinance and established the Ordinance Pertaining to the Status of Civil Officials (March 1899), making it no longer possible to appoint vice ministers, bureau chiefs, and prefectural governors without certain qualifications. Itō was opposed to that new system and insisted on its removal (Shimizu 2007, pp. 114 ff.). Itō regarded the political party as a place for pooling competent political personnel, but he did not think of political parties and officialdom as incompatible. Rather, he probably thought they should augment each other as suppliers of political experts.
73 *Seiyū*, vol. 11, p. 9.

5 Consolidating the national structure

The constitutional reforms of 1907

Seiyūkai setback

Itō created the Seiyūkai in the hope that it would take the lead in promoting the spirit of constitutional government, which to him meant the spirit of compromise and reconciliation. For Itō, constitutional government provided the means for, and therefore encouraged, the people's participation by giving them a stake in government and its policies; it would foster the political integrity of the state and build up national strength. He believed that compromise and concession must be the guiding principles for any political party that aimed at achieving such a government, not the rancorous strife that had characterized party politics until then.

An episode that illustrates the heart of Itō's thinking involves the meeting of Itō and Tokutomi Sohō (Iichirō), an influential journalist and the owner and chief editor of the monthly *Kokumin no tomo* magazine and the *Kokumin shinbun* newspaper. This occurred in early 1898, when the third Itō cabinet was formed. Tokutomi recorded the exchange that opened this first-time meeting between them:

> The moment Itō saw me he said, "Mr. Tokutomi, you are pro-imperial (*kinnō*), are you not?" So I replied, "I am sure there is no one among the Japanese people who is not pro-imperial." At this he said, "That is good to hear. You, too, are a member of my party, then," and after that we talked about all sorts of things.[1]

At that time, Itō was already formulating plans to found a new party grounded in his political creed, which was to overcome confrontation and achieve national reconciliation and harmony under the pro-imperial banner in the name of the Japanese people. His comment to Tokutomi is further affirmation of his belief that the motif of a political party must be unity and conciliation, not rivalry and contention.

Yamagata's interference strategy

When Itō set up the Seiyūkai, he urged its members to take that creed seriously from the outset. As the new party set sail he called for restraint in partisanship and the tempering of political struggle. But almost as soon as it was launched, the party became mired in confusion.

It all began when Prime Minister Yamagata Aritomo suddenly offered to transfer ruling power to the Seiyūkai. Not long after Itō announced his plans to form the party and laid out its platform on August 25, 1900, Yamagata informed Itō that he planned to step down as prime minister, now that the North China Incident (Boxer Rebellion) had been settled. He then tried to persuade Itō to form a new cabinet. His real motive was to erode the base of the Seiyūkai; his carefully calculated scheme was aimed at destroying the party by manipulating it into a position of national power before its foundations and management were firmly established. Yamagata was betting that the new party would flounder.

Itō turned down the offer for the time being. He knew what Yamagata was up to, but, more important, as we saw in the previous chapter, installing a party-based cabinet was not his primary objective. According to *Itō Hirobumi den* [A Biography of Itō Hirobumi], when Yamagata proposed that the Seiyūkai take power, Itō responded:

> The real purpose of organizing a political party is, as you, Your Excellency, have acknowledged, to rally those who truly wish to act on their devotion to the country, partly to rid the established parties of their evil practices and partly to assist the government. Only when a party is not in power can it achieve that goal and let constitutional government display its beauty.[2]

No mere platitude, that statement reflected Itō's deepest convictions.

Itō was an idealist, and it showed in his vision for the new party. He refused to believe that acrimonious power struggles were inherent in the nature of party politics. But almost by definition a political party has to scramble for political power. His right-hand man Itō Miyoji declared that his boss's "ideas look good on paper but have no practical substance."[3] Itō Hirobumi struggled to get his ideas across to Yamagata, Hoshi, Itō Miyoji, Hara Takashi, and others, assiduously guiding them with his drafts of the Seiyūkai platform and rules—the documents that laid out the aims behind the founding of the party. The "political friends" (*seiyū* as in Seiyūkai) who responded to his call to join rallied around him and urged him to take the helm of government, but even while lying in the same bed, they were dreaming different dreams, concerned more with themselves than with Itō's ideals.

On September 26, the Yamagata cabinet resigned en masse. On September 29, the emperor summoned Itō and ordered him to form a cabinet. Itō firmly demurred, claiming that "there is no need for the Yamagata cabinet to resign; also the Seiyūkai is not yet completely organized, and with the current state of foreign affairs in flux, a reshuffle of responsible officials at this time" would not be advisable.[4] Hara, who had by then taken over from Itō Miyoji the nuts and bolts leadership involved in setting up the new party, consulted Inoue Kaoru, and together they tried to persuade Itō Hirobumi to comply with the imperial order.[5]

Cabinet appointment troubles

On October 7, Itō was once again called to the imperial palace and once more ordered to form a cabinet. Unable to keep refusing, he decided to become prime minister. It would be his fourth term.[6] Then he had to decide whom to appoint as ministers of state. Having no aspirations for a full-fledged party cabinet, Itō regarded a political party as just one of several important sources from which to draw ministerial candidates. It was the prime minister's duty, he believed, to look widely for competent persons inside and outside his political party as long as the choice satisfied the iron law of appointments: "the right man in the right place."

Trying to follow that rule frustrated Itō from the start. Originally he had planned to bring in Inoue Kaoru from outside the Seiyūkai as finance minister, but Watanabe Kunitake (1846–1919), who took inordinate pride in his own efforts to help Itō get the party going, objected. Watanabe had expected that, naturally, he would take the post of finance minister. With that expectation apparently squashed, a thoroughly irritated Watanabe went to work writing critical articles about Itō and the Seiyūkai, that were carried in several newspapers on two consecutive days: October 9 and 10.

Fearing that a key member might walk out right after the party was established and expose him for mismanagement, Itō talked with Watanabe and tried to explain his thinking instead of sanctioning him for his precipitous action. Watanabe sheathed his sword, so to speak, and apologized to Itō. (As it turned out, Watanabe would be appointed finance minister when the new cabinet started.) This was not an auspicious beginning, and the scramble to repair the damage revealed that Itō's philosophy of personnel selection had by no means been embraced by all his colleagues, even some very close to him.

As if on cue, another misstep followed on the heels of the first. Through Prince Saionji Kinmochi (1849–1940), Itō conveyed to Hara Takashi that he would not be appointed to the cabinet, upon which an indignant Hara complained: Had not Itō brought him into the Seiyūkai precisely because, as Itō had said, he needed Hara in the new cabinet and wanted him to join the party first? This was "totally unexpected," cold treatment, wrote Hara, criticizing Itō in his diary:

> All in all, Itō is so weak-kneed that he let four executive council members of the former Jiyūtō (Liberal party) join the cabinet. He also decided to make Katō Takaaki foreign minister at the request of Matsukata [Masayoshi] and make Watanabe Kunitake finance minister, bowing to threats from the latter. Because of those ad hoc decisions, he has ended up breaking his promise to me.[7]

Hara vented his wrath at Itō for trying to be everybody's friend and ending up unable to exert strong leadership. Itō himself was in anguish over exactly the same issues. On October 13, he wrote to Inoue:

> Such is the state of affairs inside the Seiyūkai. It is just terrible. What I grieve most about is that none of these people look at things from the point

Figure 5.1 Hara Takashi (1856–1921).

Source: Photograph courtesy of the National Diet Library of Japan.

of view of the security and benefit of the state. They want higher posts for themselves, proffering whatever reason they like, like honor or disgrace. They dredge up one groundless pretext after another. I see no one contemplating plans and measures for national government out of serious concern for the future of the state. Instead all they do is seek out each other's help in their greedy pursuit of fame and profits. Working with such people, how can I loyally serve [the emperor] and carry out my vital responsibilities when the nation is having such a hard time? I can do nothing but beg for heaven's compassion. How very deplorable it all is![8]

Itō might have supposed that his philosophy of personnel selection was known and accepted by everyone, but, to his surprise, when he began the process of appointments, it proved inordinately difficult to control the party members' desire for cabinet posts. In the above letter he confided his depressing plight to Inoue and asked him again to please take the post of finance minister. His entreaty was in vain. The following morning, Inoue's reply arrived, declining the offer:

I am afraid you may think me a bad friend if I leave you, the old marquis, to bear the burden of responsibility by yourself at this time of national difficulty.

As you organize a cabinet, if I was short-sighted enough to let an awkward situation occur again—like the one that put me into conflict with [Itō] Miyoji two years ago[9]— that would not only be painful for you but it would mean hardship for the nation at a time when it is in jeopardy. I have carefully considered your offer and decided I will not be able to accept such an important post. I beg your understanding in accepting my firm decision to decline.[10]

Now, observing the unruly state of the Seiyūkai, Inoue thought that if he accepted the post he might end up in the same embarrassing position that Itō Miyoji had been in two years earlier, and, if so, he feared it would ruin his relationship with Itō Hirobumi; hence his refusal to accept the offer. In the end, it was Watanabe who became finance minister.

Short-lived cabinet

The fourth Itō cabinet was finalized on October 19. All but three cabinet ministers—Foreign Minister Katō Takaaki, Army Minister Katsura Tarō, and Navy Minister Yamamoto Gonnohyōe (Gonbei)—were Seiyūkai members, meaning that it was virtually a single party cabinet. However, as we may infer, the cabinet was far from standing firmly behind Prime Minister Itō. The most contentious issue was the appointment of Watanabe as finance minister, which the party's executive council had unanimously opposed. As expressed by Hara in his diary, that appointment added to the dark cloud gathering over Itō's leadership.[11]

The new Itō cabinet started off during the fifteenth session of the Diet, which opened on December 25. The primary issue pending was a tax increase to finance overseas troop deployment to confront the Boxer Rebellion (June 1900 to September 1901) in China. The bill easily passed in the House of Representatives, where the Seiyūkai held the majority, but was rejected by the House of Peers. Yamagata Aritomo watched with sympathy for the House of Peers, saying, "Things have turned out like this, I suppose, because the government has treated the House of Peers so very coldly in everything."[12] The predominantly Seiyūkai cabinet came into being with a base in the House of Representatives and the principle of popular government. But under the Meiji Constitution, the House of Representatives was only one of the multiple organs of the state; only one of several functional divisions. More experience was needed in the practice of popular government if the House of Representatives was to gain greater political unity. At that point, however, all Itō could do was to turn to the "head of the empire" who held the rights of sovereignty spelled out in the Meiji Constitution. On March 12, an imperial edict was issued requiring the House of Peers to pass the tax increase bill. Thus the government bill was finally enacted, by the order of the emperor.

Itō's tax bill issue was resolved, but the Seiyūkai remained in turmoil. Right after the House of Peers vetoed the tax increase bill, Tsuzuki Keiroku, a member of the party's executive council, voiced his opposition to the bill, sparking a move to expel him from the party.[13] The bill was passed, but the troubles over Watanabe's appointment as finance minister remained. At a cabinet meeting on

April 15, when Watanabe requested the termination of government projects funded through public debt, he was opposed by five ministers from the Seiyūkai—Suematsu Kenchō, Kaneko Kentarō, Matsuda Masahisa, Hayashi Yūzō, and Hara Takashi. A bitter confrontation ensued. Facing implacable disunity within the cabinet, Itō resigned on May 2, ending the fourth Itō cabinet.

Itō's Seiyūkai cabinet thus came to an end without producing any noteworthy results. On May 20, soon after his resignation, Itō had a private talk with Yamagata, to whom he reiterated his deeply-held political philosophy:

> We have been elevating the status of the people since the Restoration, and so now it has become necessary to listen to their opinions. If their opinions are heard, it is inevitable that political parties will be formed. If indeed that is the case, we cannot ignore them.[14]

The fourth Itō cabinet had failed, and the reason was the extreme difficulty of bringing harmony to the widely disparate voices of the people. At that time, Itō was unable to reconcile even the opinions of his close associates.

Disappointment over the Anglo-Japanese Alliance

Itō failed to forge unity in the Seiyūkai even after he stepped down as prime minister. A new cabinet was formed by Katsura Tarō (1848–1913), the first non *genrō* politician to become prime minister. (Katsura himself would become a *genrō* in 1912.) Katsura's cabinet was not aligned with any party and was composed mainly of Yamagata-faction members. People disparaged it as the "little-Yamagata cabinet."

The Seiyūkai leaders naturally intended to launch an attack on this re-emerging "transcendental" cabinet, which distanced itself from any political party, once the disorder within the party was settled. Itō prevented them from doing that. In September he departed for the United States to be present at a ceremony at Yale University, where he was to be awarded an honorary doctorate. But the real purpose of his trip was to visit Russia on his return in order to negotiate a Russo-Japanese entente, discouraging an Anglo-Japanese alliance that Japan's government had been pushing. Itō had no intention of interfering with Katsura's foreign policy; in fact, he communicated regularly with the Tokyo government, informing them of his activities and negotiations with Russian officials. But Katsura pre-empted him by concluding the Anglo-Japanese Alliance in December 1901, while Itō was still in the middle of negotiations with Russian foreign minister Vladimir Lambsdorff (1845–1907).

Itō must have been greatly disappointed, but he made it a rule to follow government policy once it had been decided. Just then in Japan, a confrontation between the Katsura cabinet and the Seiyūkai was heating up over what to do with the reparations China was to pay Japan from the Boxer Rebellion. On November 29, Itō, then in Russia, sent a telegram to Inoue Kaoru with a message to the members of the Seiyūkai. It read, "The kind of international competition we're seeing today requires a strong and lasting government, and unless it is because of something

Figure 5.2 Katsura Tarō (1848–1913).
Source: Photograph courtesy of the National Diet Library of Japan.

vital to the nation, no one who opposes the cabinet should be given any sympathy." When Inoue showed Hara this message, Hara reacted strongly:

> If all we need is to make the present cabinet strong and lasting, what on earth was the point in our joining this party, which we did to improve the cabinet and contribute to the state? If what his Excellency [Itō] is saying is right, we have no choice but to throw off all other considerations and blindly follow the government.[15]

Itō's warning against opposition to the cabinet seemed to Hara an absurd idea coming from an obstinate man who knew nothing about politics.

Discontent with Itō's leadership among party politicians like Hara reached a peak at the Seiyūkai convention of May 21 and 23, 1903. Until then the Seiyūkai had kept the government in a corner by opposing its proposals for navy expansion and land tax increase. And now, contrary to the party line, Itō was moving in the background seeking out the possibility of a compromise with Prime Minister Katsura. At the convention, when Itō let it be known what he was up to, this was the last straw for many of the party members. Their vexation with the party management exploded. Ozaki Yukio, for one, openly criticized Itō's arbitrary decision to seek compromise and, fed up, left the party.

On June 13, Itō had a private talk with Hara. Asked to explain his position vis-à-vis the government, Itō replied, "All I'm doing is regarding good as good and bad as bad. It's not wise to be committed to oppose from the outset." He told Hara "not to be too hasty to take power." Irritated by Itō's lukewarm position, Hara retorted:

> A man like your Excellency who has already achieved great feats may desire nothing more, but that's not the case with me. Your Excellency is also getting on in years, and so, unless you find a successor quickly, [the party] will be torn apart.[17]

Hara's remark was just one more indication that party members no longer trusted Itō's leadership. One after another, they started leaving the party.

Privy Council president

Itō decided to resign as head of the Seiyūkai and took the post of president of the Privy Council on July 13. This was the result of maneuvers by Yamagata and Katsura to separate Itō from the party and sideline him with duties in other matters. With his party management at an impasse, Itō "returned to attendance on the emperor, his only safe refuge, following the path of retreat prepared by Yamagata and Katsura."[17]

Clearly Itō's experiences as the first president of the Seiyūkai and his short fourth term as prime minister were bitter ones. Holding close his ideals about the constitutional state and popular government, Itō indeed suffered a setback in the nuts-and-bolts maneuvering of actual politics. Students of the period have tended to emphasize this setback and view this series of events as the beginning of Itō's political downfall. Such a view focuses too narrowly on the day-to-day political realities, obscuring the deeper significance of his ideas and actions. What motivated Itō at that time was a long-term and more fundamental vision of the state, and a fair historical judgment of Itō must take that vision into account.

Several recent studies look positively at Itō's leadership in the Seiyūkai and his fourth cabinet. Historian Itō Yukio, for instance, argues that Itō Hirobumi at that time hoped to bring about internal government reforms and sought to streamline and coordinate the administrative and financial aspects of the state. He cites Itō Hirobumi's attempt to restore the prime minister's authority to appoint key government posts by modifying Yamagata's revised Civil Service Appointment Ordinance and the Ordinance Pertaining to the Status of Civil Officials that the latter had adopted. Pursuing a similar line of research, historian Shimizu Yuichirō highlights, for example, Itō Hirobumi's idea of placing Seiyūkai members in the chief secretary posts of the ministries as a way of creating a more integrated governing structure, centered around a political party.

These and other recent works understand the Seiyūkai as central to Itō Hirobumi's broader vision of the state. The party was a means through which Itō attempted to revamp the governing structure. He also sought other avenues for reform. In around 1900, he set out to make far-reaching institutional reforms aimed at overhauling the Meiji Constitution system he had initially created, thus enabling the emergence of the structure he envisioned for the Meiji state. It seems evident that the Seiyūkai was part of his large-scale plan for reform. In 1907 the whole picture of Itō's reforms emerged—what I refer to in this book as the constitutional reforms (reforms of laws under the Constitution) of 1907.

The Imperial Household Research Committee and constitutional reform

Before Itō became first Seiyūkai president, in September 1900, he had presided over the Imperial Household Research Committee, which had been installed in August 1899 in the imperial court. As the committee's first chief, he served until the following year.

Revamping the imperial household system

The committee was founded as a research and deliberative organ, with a view to restructuring the imperial household system. Regarding this project, Itō had high ambitions. In February of the previous year (1898) he presented to the emperor a ten-point proposal concerning the imperial household system. He pointed out weaknesses in the current system and recommended changes, including handling of ceremonial occasions within the imperial family, demotion from noble to subject status, reform of the imperial household economy, and guidance for the crown prince.[18] Later, he privately submitted to the emperor another proposal to set up a research committee focused on seeking ways to perfect the imperial household system. This was given official approval and led to the installation, on August 24, 1899, of the Imperial Household Research Committee in the imperial court.

On September 11, Itō summoned the committee's vice-president, Hijikata Hisamoto, and general-affairs officials (including Hosokawa Junjirō, Takasaki Masakaze, Itō Miyoji, Ume Kenjirō, Hozumi Yatsuka, Hanabusa Naojirō, Tada Kōmon, Sannomiya Yoshitane, Hirohashi Masamitsu, and others) and spoke to them about the purpose of the committee. In legal terms, he said, the imperial household was separate from the government, but "in reality the separation remains unclear as ever."[19] He proposed clarifying the legal status of the imperial household and its members. He then reported the twelve items the emperor had ordered to be studied and determined. They were: (1) procedures for weddings, funerals, and mourning of the imperial family and other court ceremonies; (2) treatment of imperial family members; (3) rewards for imperial family members and meritorious subjects; (4) bestowal and promotion of peerage titles; (5) regulations concerning petitions; (6) an imperial family act (*kōzokurei*); (7) religion of imperial family members; (8) imperial property and taxes; (9) civil suits relating to imperial property; (10) the Peerage Act; (11) the court rank system; and (12) special inquiries made concerning the imperial household system.[20]

136 *Consolidating the national structure*

The fact that the items overlap with those of the ten-point proposal Itō had presented to the emperor the previous year is another indication of his initiative in creating the committee. Several years earlier, in March 1884, and prior to the enactment of the Meiji Constitution, he had set up a research committee in the court to study, in its entirety, the system underlying the structure of the nation. In February 1889, when the Meiji Constitution as well as the Imperial Household Law (Kōshitsu Tenpan) and other constitution-related laws[21] were promulgated, they concerned (in the main) government affairs. General rules for the imperial household were decided, but laws governing imperial household affairs to be established parallel with the laws relating to national government were left for the future, following the policy of addressing "Imperial Household affairs with great care in a gradual fashion."[22] That is to say, the structure of the Meiji state was characterized by a dual legal order revolving around the Meiji Constitution and the Imperial Household Law; it had by then a body, so to speak, but its head and limbs were still incomplete.

For Itō, who saw himself and was seen by others as the central figure in the enactment of the Meiji Constitution, it was crucial to make the imperial household system into a solid institution to support the tasks left undone when the Constitution was established and fine-tune the dual system of Meiji Constitution-Imperial Household Law. So once again, ten years after the enactment of the Constitution, Itō installed a research committee in the court and began to work out how to remodel the imperial household system.

Itō resigned as Imperial Household Research Committee president when he founded the Seiyūkai party in September 1900. He should not, he believed, stay in a position in the court when he was the head of a political party. Hijikata Hisamoto, vice-president, succeeded him as committee president, but the committee's activities essentially came to a halt. It did not regain its vigor until July 1903, when Itō stepped down as head of the Seiyūkai and was reappointed as committee president with Itō Miyoji as its vice-president. After that, the committee made steady progress. Meanwhile, the Russo-Japanese War started and ended (1904–5). In 1907 results of the committee's work began to be made public, piece by piece. In February that year, the Kōbunshiki Order, which had stipulated forms of laws, orders, and state seals, was abolished and replaced by the amended version, the Kōshikirei Order (formally, Order concerning Forms of the Imperial Rescripts, Statutes, and Other State Documents). The new edict was accompanied by the promulgation of an expanded Imperial Household Law, and the legal form of imperial household ordinances (*kōshitsurei*) concerning imperial household affairs was established.

The Imperial Household Research Committee was dissolved on February 11, with the promulgation of the enlarged Imperial Household Law. After that, a large quantity of basic legislation on the imperial house was issued as *kōshitsurei*.[23] In other words, 1907 marked the emergence of the dual constitutional order consisting of the system of laws for state affairs, whose supreme law was the Meiji Constitution, and the imperial household affairs law system, whose supreme law was the Imperial Household Law.[24]

The year the framework of the dual Meiji legal system was established, 1907, marked an important juncture in Japan's legal history. Constitutional scholar Ōishi Makoto describes this juncture as "constitutional reform," saying that even if the Constitution itself had not been changed, "the constitutional order can be changed by revising or abolishing constitution-related laws that are ordinary legislative laws."[25] During the Meiji era, the Imperial Household Research Committee's work was indeed an ambitious attempt at constitutional reform.

Completing the system of national laws

The committee's activities have been studied from the viewpoint of the history of the Constitution, and of the legal system, and also from the standpoint of political history, especially concerning the emperor system and military affairs. First, a study by Kawata Keiichi, done from the perspective of constitutional and legal history, makes an important contribution by pointing out that the imperial household system underwent steady reform beginning with the promulgation of the expanded Imperial Household Law.[26] The Kōshikirei Order established the conditions for issuing imperial edicts and rescripts, procedures for revision of the Meiji Constitution and the Imperial Household Law, and for the promulgation and enactment of laws and regulations, including imperial house ordinances. A unified system of national laws was thus established, argues the author, bringing revolutionary change to the way the state was structured. Previous to the changes, the internal affairs of the imperial household had been treated as separate from the government. Until then, the Imperial Household Law had never been made public. This separation of government and imperial household was now over and the imperial household was repositioned as an organ of the state. The completion of the dual legal system of 1907 thus carried the understanding that the imperial court, long concealed behind its bamboo screen, was now legally established as a system of government on a par with the central government.

Following upon research focusing on the improvement and completion of the system of national laws, more attention has turned to the actual working of the laws. In particular, in the field of political history, scholars have been looking closely at the institutional independence of the military.

The Kōshikirei Order, drawn up by the Imperial Household Research Committee, required that all laws and imperial edicts be countersigned by the prime minister, thereby strengthening the latter's powers. Apprehensive about this order, Yamagata Arimoto and others schemed and eventually established Military Ordinance (Gunrei) No. 1 titled "On Military Ordinances" (Gunrei ni Kansuru Ken; 1907), which codified the practice of *iaku jōsō*, whereby the military would submit reports on military affairs directly to the emperor. This, historians assert, laid the institutional foundation for Shōwa-era militarism, by allowing for the independence of the military.[27] Taking that point into consideration, we may say that the constitutional reforms of 1907 produced not only the dual Meiji Constitution-Imperial Household Law system but also a three-pronged system, the third prong being the military.

138 *Consolidating the national structure*

The Imperial Household Research Committee was therefore not engaged solely in revising the imperial household system, despite its name. The work of the committee was also directed at the reform of the cabinet system and the systematic integration of the national laws, that is, a revamping of Meiji constitutionalism itself. In the process, the committee's activities offended Yamagata and others, with the result, completely unintended by Itō, that the military was able to achieve an independent status. Did the 1907 constitutional reform represent the completion of the Meiji Constitution system, or was it the prelude to its collapse? Before making any judgment, let us take a closer look at the activity of the Imperial Household Research Committee and clarify what Itō sought to achieve through constitutional reform.

Constitutional reforms of 1907 (1): integrating the emperor into the state

Itō was reappointed as president of the committee on July 13, 1903, upon which the committee resumed its activity. On August 17, the vice president Itō Miyoji sent Itō Hirobumi a document titled "Guidelines for the Start of Research" (Chōsa Chakushu no Hōshin).[28]

The document dealt with diverse matters, but its essence boils down to the following:

> The argument that because the imperial household affairs are the Emperor's private affairs, the Imperial Household Law is a family code stipulated by the imperial household itself, does not agree with the history of our empire of Japan. . . . It is necessary therefore to clarify that the imperial household is a distinctive element of the state and establish that it has its own unchangeable standards.

The document defined the imperial household as an organ of the state and stated that the goal of the dual legal system: the Imperial Household Law "is a fundamental law of the state with the same force as the constitution of the empire."

Ariga Nagao

Itō Miyoji needed someone to start the work of implementing the document. He recommended to the committee, and then delegated to the task, Ariga (also Aruga) Nagao (1860–1921), who was appointed as a general-affairs official (*goyōgakari*). In a letter to Itō Hirobumi upon his appointment as vice-president, Itō Miyoji wrote, "Ariga Nagao, whom you have been helping since last year, has no particular job in the Japanese mainland, I hear, and so, why not hire him for the Research Committee?" He added, "Use him as a right-hand man and he is sure to be of great service."[29] He evidently placed extraordinary trust in Ariga.

Itō Hirobumi apparently complied. Within a week, Itō Miyoji wrote a letter of thanks, saying, "I appreciate your consideration in helping to secure his

Consolidating the national structure 139

Figure 5.3 Ariga Nagao (1860–1921).
Source: Chūō Kōron Shinsha, p. 215.

appointment, and Ariga himself is deeply grateful."[30] That was how Ariga came to work under Itō Hirobumi, but the connection between the two went back much farther, to Itō's study in Vienna under Lorenz von Stein in 1882.[31] Ariga was one of the many Japanese to follow Itō seeking to study under Stein, but he stood out among the others as perhaps the "best" of Stein's Japanese students, and he was instrumental in introducing his teacher's ideas to Japan. The *Sutain-shi kōgi* [Stein's Lectures] (1889), edited by Kaieda Nobuyoshi, the most widely circulated volume of Stein's scholarship in the Meiji era, is based on Ariga's translation of the professor's lectures. Like Stein, who was a prolific writer in law, politics, and economics, Ariga produced a variety of books, including *Shakaigaku* [Sociology] (1883–4), *Kokkagaku* [The Theory of the State] (1889), *Gyoseigaku* [Public Administration] (1890), *Nihon kodaihō shakugi* [Commentary on Ancient Japanese Law] (1893), *Nis-Shin sen'eki kokusaihō ron* [A Study of International Law and the First Sino-Japanese War] (1896), and *Nichi-Ro rikusen kokusaihō ron* [A Study of International Law and Russo-Japanese Land Battles] (1911). Ariga's approach was a remarkable embodiment of Stein's style of research.

After Ariga died, the *Gaikō jihō* [Diplomatic News] journal he had founded carried many memorials. One of them was written by Takada Sanae, a friend from their college days who would later become president of Waseda University. In his eulogy Takada recalled how Ariga, after graduating from the university, "belonged to Prince Itō's circle ... He was in the Privy Council for a long time, and if I remember correctly he was once a secretary to Prince Itō."[32] His place as an associate of Itō was firmly established by his appointment as a general-affairs official in the Imperial Household Research Committee. A close advisor to both Itō Hirobumi and Itō Miyoji in the committee, Ariga initiated numerous productive activities that fulfilled their expectations. We can get a glimpse of his activities in a letter from Itō Miyoji to Itō Hirobumi concerning the "Guidelines for the Start of Research":

> Some people have already started research in line with our guidelines, and as soon as they come up with something I will show it to you. I also instructed Ariga Nagao to conduct research on a variety of things and since he had prepared a fairly large number of papers, I sent him back to Tokyo recently.[33]

It is quite possible that Ariga was involved in preparing the new guidelines. An interim report on the research submitted in October 1904 was written by Ariga under the title "Kōshitsu-ben," a proposal concerning the implementation of the Imperial Household Law.[34] In other words, Ariga was the de facto architect of the modern imperial household system.

Ariga had been a member of the Kōten Kōkyūjo (Institute for Research on Imperial Classics), where he was engaged in the study of the history of the imperial household system. In 1900, before he was appointed to the Imperial Household Research Committee, he delivered a lecture on "Relationships between the Government and the Imperial Household,"[35] one of a series on the major issues currently facing Japan. He divided the issues into three categories: relationships between the government and the military; relationships between the government and the imperial household; and relationships between Japan and Taiwan.[36] In his lecture on relationships between the government and the imperial court, Ariga touched on the Imperial Household Research Committee founded the previous year, emphasizing that the matters before the committee were not "a few household affairs . . . but fundamental issues that can affect the organization of the entire state."[37] We can read into this the high hopes he had for the committee. When he was appointed the following year he must have felt that he had arrived— he was finally working where he was meant to be.

Based on his experience with the committee, Ariga wrote some valuable historical material that offers a systematic explanation of constitutionalism in Japan. It takes the form of a series of lectures he gave to a constitutional research group from China from February 1908 to July 1909, which had been arranged through the good offices of Itō Hirobumi.[38] Transcripts of the lectures, titled "Kensei kōgi" [Lectures on Constitutionalism], are included in the "Itō Miyoji Kankei Monjo" [Itō Miyoji Papers] in the collection of the Japanese National Diet Library's Kensei Shiryōshitsu (Modern Japanese Political History Documents Room). The documents provide details about the constitutional reform he himself had been involved in the previous year as well as its significance and its limits. Drawing on these documents, we can get an idea of what sort of nation was envisaged as a result of the 1907 reform.

The emperor as an organ of the state

The main task of the Imperial Household Research Committee was to reconsider the separation of the government and the imperial court when the Meiji Constitution was drawn up and to position the imperial household as an important organ of the state. That purpose was not firmly established when the committee was created, however. In fact, Itō's original goal was quite the opposite. In his address to the core committee members when he became president, he said that under the law, the imperial household should be clearly separate from the government, but that "in reality the line dividing them remains as vague as ever." Thus, when the committee was set up, Itō intended to work on completing the separation between the government and the imperial court, in accordance with the principle behind a series of mid-Meiji-era reforms, and to place the Meiji Constitution at the apex of the structure of the nation.

Things changed completely, however, after the committee resumed its activity in July 1903. The "Guidelines for the Start of Research," submitted the following month, repositioned the imperial household as an element of the government and the Imperial Household Law as a fundamental law of the state. President Itō's initial instruction to the committee members was reversed.

The committee's aim, however, in discarding the idea of separating the government and imperial court, and instead placing the imperial household within the framework of the government, was not to strengthen the emperor's role in government or institute direct imperial rule. On the contrary, it intended to further institutionalize the imperial throne and the imperial household and incorporate them into the government. The idea was, in other words, not that the people should selflessly serve the emperor but that the emperor should serve the government.

In his 1900 lecture on the relationship between the government and the imperial court, Ariga stated, "The Emperor reigns over the country not in order to govern the private property of the imperial household but to fulfill his public service duties according to the will of the imperial family's ancestral deity [Amaterasu Ōmikami]."[39] Unlike the case in many European monarchies, in Japan the state never once became the property of the emperor. The emperor's public obligation that he had to fulfill by the order of the sun goddess Amaterasu Ōmikami was to govern the land. He (or she) reigned but did not own the state.[40]

Material in the "Kensei kōgi" reinforces the view that the Imperial Household Research Committee's real aim in incorporating the imperial court into the government did not contradict Itō Hirobumi's constitutional policy. One good example is Ariga's comparison of the government to a corporation (March 29, 1908). With constitutional government in place, Ariga said, it was now necessary to distinguish between the government and the imperial court, and he likened the situation to the growth of a corporation. When a business is founded by a private individual it belongs, at first, to the founder and is directly managed by him. He is, in a sense, managing two households—his company and his own family. He is in direct control of both, as the head of each.

As the business grows, however, the company gradually moves out from under the owner's autocratic management. In this way, "the head, while continuing to deal directly with the affairs of his family, moves into indirect management of the commercial business." In other words, the household head maintains direct charge over his family affairs, but the company president only indirectly controls the company as its scale of management expands and it gains sure footing commercially. Indeed, although the company is his company, its affairs are no longer managed within the sphere of his independent decision-making but are dealt with by agencies determined by the company's bylaws.

In this way, for the manager, his household and company become two different kinds of organizations. At the same time, he has two roles—he is a household head and he is also a company president. He is both a private person and a public person. According to Ariga, the constitutional system made just that distinction; it clarified the private–public aspects of the emperor. One aspect was head of the imperial household, and that should be separate from the emperor's aspect as head of state.

This may appear to contradict the Imperial Household Research Committee's guiding idea of the imperial household "as an element of the government." But the contradiction is resolved if we understand that the committee was seeking not to mobilize the imperial household as the ruler of the state but to enable the government to institutionalize it, namely, to make the imperial household a part of the national system. The committee-driven series of reforms to the imperial household was aimed at incorporating it into the state as a state institution. This attempt to separate the imperial household from the government was, therefore, confined solely to the level of institutions. So Ariga's argument is persuasive: the underlying objectives of the committee were to prevent the imperial prerogative from dominating politics and to more fully institutionalize the imperial household. That was exactly what Itō Hirobumi had had in mind in his work on the Meiji Constitution.

Separation of government and court

We have established that the Imperial Household Research Committee's constitutional reform was aimed not so much at clarifying the separation of the imperial court from the government as at making the court a part of the government by integrating it further into the state system as a national institution. The issue of how to distinguish court and government was to be addressed later. We should at this point examine the emperor as the head of the state.

Ariga saw the emperor in state politics as unambiguously bound by law. In 1901, he had stated in *Kokuhōgaku* [A Study of National Law], that "The head of state must not engage in conduct that is contrary to the Constitution."[41] In his April 28, 1908 lecture to a Chinese constitutional research group, he showed that he continued to maintain that position: "To begin with, the Emperor's prerogatives must comply with the Constitution, . . . and therefore, an order of the monarch that is not in accordance with the provisions of the Constitution is not a legally valid imperial order."[42]

The difference in opinions over the character of the emperor in the Meiji Constitution between the monarchist orthodox school and the constitutional school is well known. Proponents of the former attached importance to the phrase in Article 4 stating that "The Emperor is the head of the Empire, combining in Himself the rights of sovereignty," while the latter focused on the ensuing phrase in the same article, "and exercises them according to the provisions of the present Constitution."[43] Ariga, a staunch constitutionalist, was a member of the latter persuasion. Hozumi Yatsuka (1860–1912), a leading advocate of the orthodox school, made his position clear after the Constitution was enacted in an essay titled "Teikoku kenpō no hōri" [Principles of the Constitution of the Empire],[44] whereupon Ariga countered with "Hozumi Yatsuka-kun Teikoku kenpō no hōri o ayamaru" [Hozumi Yatsuka Is Mistaken about the Principles of the Constitution of the Empire],[45] insisting that the emperor was an organ of the state.

Even though Ariga was on the side of the constitutional school, in those days he disapproved of the progressive development of parliamentarianism.[46] He believed that under constitutionalism the cabinet should govern the country; constitutional government meant responsible government by the cabinet. Regarding the relationship between government and emperor, it was this matter of responsibility that served as the "standard by which to separate the government from the imperial court" (March 15, 1908). Matters that entailed responsibility were not to be handled by the imperial court but by the government as state affairs. Relegated to indirect governing, the emperor would be kept away from political responsibility, thus assuring the reliable and smooth government of the country. Ariga added, "Constitutional government is a convenient form of government; if the monarch is an enlightened ruler, good results will immediately follow. And if the monarch is very young, or weakly, or mentally unstable, such circumstances need not come to light" (November 29, 1908).

In this way, Ariga sought not only to position the imperial household as a state organ, but to fully integrate it into the institutional system, thus distancing it from the exercise of any real political power. By so doing, he expected to formalize the nature of rule by the emperor and the imperial household and thereby keep them away from political responsibility. In Ariga's view, it was individual ministers of state and the cabinet as a whole who bore ultimate responsibility for government.

Constitutional reforms of 1907 (2): responsible government and control over the military

Ariga stressed (as recorded in a lecture to the Chinese group) his belief that any system is moved by human intellect, and that the most important factor in designing a national system is how to bring intelligent discernment into full play. He said:

> A constitution is only a rough framework of what should be done; it is the task of intellect to work with it so as to achieve the objectives of the state. This is mental work that only humans can perform. Crucial to establishing a system of government is to enable people to perform that task adequately. That is the aim of a government system.
>
> (November 13, 1908)

Under a constitutional system, as with any other, the greatest concern is how to run the state effectively. Ordinarily the first principle of constitutionalism is to firmly establish limits on state power, but Ariga believed in a more aggressive approach. Arguing that the national system codified by the Constitution was no more than a rough framework, he asked how it could be managed and put to effective use. In other words, he saw institutional dynamism as essential to a successful constitutional state.

Ariga's theory of constitutionalism can be summed up as an institutional principle of state action—a system meant not so much to restrain the state as to make the state work. The role of the cabinet was to manage the actions taken by the state. "A 'negative' [Ariga used this English word] cabinet cannot possibly facilitate the development of the state. The state needs a 'positive' cabinet" (December 13, 1908). By "positive" cabinet he meant a cabinet that would supervise government. Ariga distinguished between administration and government, saying that the former "carries out major state-level projects according to law or imperial ordinance," whereas the latter "formulates certain policies beyond law and imperial ordinance" (April 7, 1908). Hence the duty of the cabinet was not simply to execute the law and imperial ordinances but to establish guidelines for state management, including the execution of laws and imperial ordinances, that is, to establish the direction of national government (April 7, 1908). In support of responsible government, therefore, Ariga highlighted not only the duty of ministers of state to advise the emperor but also the duty of the cabinet headed by the prime minister to supervise national government and take all responsibility for it.

The Kōshikirei Order and revival of the strong premier

Ariga defined constitutional government as cabinet-led responsible government.[47] So another "hidden" task of the Imperial Household Research Committee was to bring responsible government into being.

By that time the Meiji Constitution had been in place for almost twenty years, and circumstances at home and abroad had changed greatly. Japan's constitutional system was at a crossroads. Political parties had gained power and parliamentary government had steadily taken root, but there was a growing problem that threatened to tear the government apart: the rise of the military. The divisive momentum had arisen in a very short period, as a result of rapid expansion of the army and navy driven by war with China and with Russia, and Japan's acquisition of control in Taiwan and Korea. As a means to counter that rise, the underlying intent behind the Imperial Household Research Committee's response to these developments was to concentrate governing power in the cabinet and thereby prevent Japan's arduously crafted national system from breaking apart.

An important part of the committee's mission was to incorporate the imperial household institution into the national system. For that purpose it formulated the Kōshikirei Order and, accordingly, revised the Cabinet Organization Order (Naikaku Kansei). The Kōshikirei Order was an important set of Constitution-related regulations that laid down the modes of promulgating all sorts of public documents issued by the government, and it integrated national laws into a unified system. The Kōshikirei Order stipulated that each time the Imperial Household Law was revised, the revision had to be promulgated (Article 4). The *kōshitsurei*, or ordinances concerning imperial household affairs, including regulations stemming from the Imperial Household Law, gained recognition as a legitimate form of law (Article 5). Hence a dual system of laws, the one dealing with government affairs and the other with imperial household affairs, was established. It is also notable that Article 3 of the Kōshikirei Order stipulated the promulgation procedures if the Meiji Constitution was amended.

According to Kawata Keiichi, the Kōshikirei Order was also drafted by Ariga.[48] This is not implausible; the concepts in the order rest on the ideas that mark Ariga's thinking about the cabinet. As historians have pointed out for some time, the Kōshikirei Order was designed to return the office of prime minister to the level of strength laid out many years before in the Cabinet-Ordinance (Naikaku Shokken) of 1885. The Cabinet-Ordinance, created when the cabinet system was put in place, stated in Article 1, "The Prime Minister as the chief of cabinet ministers reports important state affairs to the Emperor and, after listening to his wishes, indicates the direction of government policy and supervises competent government agencies." Article 4 stated, "Laws and regulations established by the legislative and executive powers shall be countersigned by the Prime Minister." The Official Powers of the Cabinet was abolished in 1889, however, replaced by the Cabinet Organization Order (1889–1947). Article 4 of the latter contains this significant passage:

Cabinet Organization Order

Article 4
Imperial ordinances relating to law and administration in general shall be countersigned by the Prime Minister and competent ministers. Those imperial ordinances that relate to the affairs of a specific ministry shall be countersigned by the minister of that specific ministry.

This article reduced the prime minister's status and authority considerably, making him merely the head among ministers of the same rank in the cabinet. Thus weakened, the prime minister's power was revived by provisions of the Kōshikirei Order, the pertinent parts of Articles 6 and 7 of which are excerpted here:

Kōshikirei Order

Article 6
1. An imperial edict shall accompany promulgation of a law.
2. The imperial edict in the preceding paragraph shall include a statement to the effect that the parliament has approved. After the Emperor signs, the edict shall be stamped with the imperial seal and then the Prime Minister shall write the date and countersign alone or with other ministers of state or a competent minister.

Article 7
1. An imperial edict shall accompany the promulgation of an imperial ordinance.
2. The imperial edict in the preceding paragraph shall be signed by the Emperor and then stamped with the imperial seal. The Prime Minister shall then write the date and countersign alone or with other ministers of state or a competent minister.

These provisions restored the requirement that all laws and regulations adopted by the legislative and executive branches be countersigned by the prime minister. At the same time, the Cabinet Organization Order was revised, removing Article 4 of the order (cited above) and spelling out the prime minister's authority to enact cabinet ordinances and lead and supervise the Superintendent General of the Metropolitan Police and prefectural governors. In this way, the Cabinet Organization Order was changed so significantly that it put the prime minister once again in a strong position of power over national government. That was exactly what the Imperial Household Research Committee had been seeking. Where Ariga showed his real worth was in working out the theoretical underpinnings for their purposes and designing ways to put them into practice.

Challenge to the right of *iaku jōsō*

The underlying motive behind the Kōshikirei Order was to revise the Cabinet Organization Order and to bring the prime minister back to a position of power and strong leadership in a cabinet-led responsible government. This was the unspoken but most fundamental mission of the Imperial Household Research Committee's constitutional reform.

The committee had a specific adversary in mind when it established the Kōshikirei Order, and that was the military. The order requiring that all laws and regulations have the prime minister's countersignature was designed specifically to counter the military's practices of submitting military affairs proposals directly to the emperor, free from all Diet and cabinet constraints (*iaku jōsō*).

The committee's concern was clearly indicated in the document titled "Gunrei gunsei no kubetsu o akiraka ni suru koto" [Clarifying the Difference between Military Ordinances and Military Administrative Regulations] (156)—referred to as the "Difference" document hereafter—included in "Itō Miyoji Kankei Monjo" [Itō Miyoji Papers] in the National Diet Library's collection. (This document is reprinted in *Suiusō nikki* [Suiusō Diary][49].) Written on the ruled paper printed with the name of the Imperial Household Research Committee, the "Difference" document stated that military ordinances (*gunrei*), which should be restricted to matters pertaining to the emperor's "supreme command of the Army and Navy" as stipulated in Article 11 of the Meiji Constitution, had been expanded so much that even matters relating to the "organization and peace standing of the Army and Navy," in Article 12, had fallen almost completely under the emperor's supreme command. It called for clarification of the difference between military ordinances (supreme command-related affairs) and military administrative regulations (military administrative affairs: *gunsei*). The document is not dated but the wording in the text indicates that it was compiled around February 1901. Most likely, Itō Miyoji did the research and prepared the document at Itō Hirobumi's order in the early days of the Imperial Household Research Committee. This suggests that from the outset of its activities the committee prioritized the task of controlling the military, in addition to improving the imperial household system. Let us examine the specific content of the "Difference" document.

Why was it necessary to distinguish between *gunrei* and *gunsei*? This was because military ordinances originated from the military authorities' proposals submitted directly to the emperor and were issued without any cabinet involvement. Further, it was not required that they be made public. The military's right of *iaku jōsō*, in the narrow sense, stemmed from the need to assure that at times when battles were being fought, an "agency with the authority to issue military ordinances" (*iaku*), such as the Army General Staff Office, would directly "submit to the Emperor, the Commander in Chief" (*jōsō*) a report and request instructions on the progress of the battle and command of troops. But the military, which abhorred interference in its affairs by civil officials and the Diet, expanded the interpretation of *iaku jōsō* to include matters of military organization and organizational management in peacetime. The grounds on which the military based its interpretation was Article 7 of the Cabinet Organization Order:

Cabinet Organization Order

Article 7
Matters submitted [to the Emperor] concerning military secrets and supreme command-related affairs shall be reported by the Army Minister and Navy Minister to the Prime Minister except those that the Emperor wishes to be placed under the discretion of the Cabinet.

Hence, matters relating to "military secrets and supreme command-related affairs" only had to be reported by the army and navy ministers to the prime minister ex post facto, as a rule, without being sent to the cabinet. The question was, what were "military secrets and supreme command-related affairs"? In this regard, the "Difference" document stated:

The provision of Article 7 of the Cabinet Organization Order allows the army and navy authorities to make their own interpretations. For this reason, as long as the Army Minister and Navy Minister categorize certain military administrative affairs as military secrets and supreme command-related matters, regardless of the validity of their view, they take a position independent of the Cabinet. Yet, perversely, he who is placed in the position of having to listen to their opinions is the Prime Minister, the person in charge of integrated national government.

148 Consolidating the national structure

In other words, it was left up to the military authorities to decide what were "military secrets and supreme command-related affairs." Even ordinary military administrative affairs were arbitrarily submitted directly to the emperor and made into military ordinances. As a result, the document suggested, the military made itself independent of the cabinet, hindering the management of an integrated national government under the prime minister.

According to the document, the earliest example of such hindrance was the Order Concerning the Quota of Army Personnel (Rikugun Tei'in Rei) enacted in November 1890. Because of this order, army-related government agencies, and even schools under their jurisdiction, were classified as "confidential military and supreme command-related affairs." Matters such as these, large and small, were increasingly submitted by the army minister to the emperor for approval without cabinet deliberation. From then onward, a vast number of regulations concerning army-related government organizations and their various schools were established by those procedures.

An alarming case involved an incident in April 1896 over an Imperial Ordinance Concerning Wages for Employees who Fill Vacancies of Army Noncommissioned Officers and Ministry-appointed Civilian Officers. Then Army Minister Ōyama Iwao (1842–1916) had independently submitted a wage proposal to the emperor for approval and later, matter-of-factly, sent it to the cabinet for deliberation and approval. But it was an item that required a change in the budget and, moreover, the wage demanded by the army exceeded the employees' monthly wage determined previously by the cabinet. Then Prime Minister Itō Hirobumi was infuriated and refused the army minister's request for cabinet deliberation. A notification was sent under the prime minister's name to caution the army and navy against abuse of their *iaku jōsō* right of direct appeal to the emperor.

To rectify this hitch in the way national institutions were meant to work, the "Difference" document called for a strict distinction between purely supreme command-related affairs and military administrative affairs, while recognizing that some matters straddled the two categories. Concerning administrative affairs, the document disallowed the military's right of direct appeal to the emperor and recommended that the prime minister submit all appeals to the emperor. The "Difference" document also stated:

> Article 7 of the Cabinet Organization Order refers to some military secrets apart from supreme command-related affairs, but in anything that relates to military administrative affairs, nothing must be kept secret from the ministers of state. Therefore, the scope of the military's right of direct appeal to the Emperor has to be restricted to supreme command-related affairs and the term "military secrets" must be deleted.

Thus, the document proposed revision of the Cabinet Organization Order by removing "military secrets."

As we have seen, the plan to derail the trend toward separating military administration from the cabinet was incorporated into the activity of the Imperial

Household Research Committee from the very beginning. Indeed, it was part of the driving force behind the 1907 establishment of the Kōshikirei Order and the revision of the Cabinet Organization Order.

Itō's resolute stance

When the Kōshikirei Order was announced, the government showed little interest in it. The cabinet adopted the draft, but Home Minister Hara Takashi wrote bluntly in his diary, "I saw no big difference from the old one [Kōbunshiki Order]."[50] Even other cabinet members did not see into the basic intent of the Kōshikirei Order. The order was a powerful medicine, and to be effective, it had to be treated very carefully and kept as inconspicuous as possible.

The medicine soon began to take effect. As the intent of the Kōshikirei Order became apparent, there was a strong reaction from some quarters—the military, most notably the army. Earlier, in March 1907, Navy Minister Saitō Makoto submitted to the emperor a draft of an authorization to deploy defense units at Jinhae Bay and Yongfung Bay in Korea, and then, in accordance with the newly enacted Kōshikirei Order, Saitō meant to have it countersigned by the prime minister and the navy minister and issue it as an imperial ordinance. Dubious of these procedures, which were so different from before, the emperor— on March 23—telegraphed an inquiry to Itō Hirobumi, then in Korea as resident-general, and three days later he sent a messenger to Korea to consult with Itō.[51]

Itō made three points in his reply. First, establishment of defense units was a matter of national administration and should be officially declared by an imperial ordinance. This was because the setting up of those units meant creating a new regulation, which would constitute a matter of the national budget. In addition the defense units would have to issue a great many orders and prohibitions to both Koreans and Japanese residing where the units were stationed. The ordinance therefore would have almost the same effect as a law. Matters to be submitted by the military directly to the emperor, on the other hand, should "pertain exclusively to the realm of military ordinances; by their nature they neither increase nor decrease the budget, nor do they affect the people's rights and duties," Itō asserted.

Second, the Cabinet Organization Order required imperial ordinances to be countersigned by the prime minister. Deployment of defense units was no exception, and the countersignature of the navy minister as the competent minister also had to be added under the new system.

Third, in some previous cases only the countersignature of the competent minister had been enough, but due in part to the revision of the Cabinet Organization Order and in part to the Kōshikirei Order, it was "even clearer" now that the prime minister's countersignature was needed. Therefore, "Continuing to follow the previous practices and failing to adhere to [the Kōshikirei Order] would reduce the Kōshikirei Order to an impractical and useless regulation." Itō's reply to the emperor concluded by saying "I regret to say, it is not right to promulgate an imperial ordinance on organizing defense units with the countersignature of the navy minister alone, ignoring the Kōshikirei Order."[52]

Itō Hirobumi's determination to clarify the *iaku jōsō* was very firm. Prior to his reply to the emperor, he had told Itō Miyoji to draft that reply, but the draft did not satisfy him. A letter from Miyoji to Hirobumi, dated April 10, reveals that he admonished Miyoji for circuitous phrasing and urged him to straightforwardly discuss "a clear distinction between the *iaku jōsō* and imperial ordinances."[53] Replying, Miyoji made this excuse, "Lest the wording might be inappropriate or disrespectful in response to the imperial inquiry, I tried to use indirect, roundabout words and terms, ending up with that obscure language."

In the same letter, Miyoji wrote that the emperor had asked him about the possibility that a certain matter would be first submitted by the military to the emperor and then issued as an imperial ordinance. "Is it all right, the Emperor asked, that at first he approves a proposal submitted to him with the signature of a competent minister alone and then has the prime minister countersign as a formality before issuance?" In response to the imperial query, Itō Miyoji replied, "With all due respect, allow me to say that Your Majesty seems not to understand well the difference between military ordinances [relating to the supreme command] and administrative regulations [relating to political, administrative affairs]." All that were to be proclaimed, whether they were military-related or not,

> must be deliberated on in the Cabinet first and then the Prime Minister will submit them to Your Majesty. When they are proclaimed, countersigning is necessary in order to clarify who is responsible. Countersigning as a formality only at the time of issuance, therefore, would be impossible under constitutional government.

This reply undoubtedly echoed Itō Hirobumi's thinking.

Yamagata rallies

The abortive attempt to get an ordinance for defense-unit deployment in Korea finally prompted the army to see the underlying intent of the Kōshikirei Order. On May 13, Yamagata Aritomo wrote to Army Minister Terauchi Masatake (1852–1919), "That kind of change will throw the high command chain into confusion and destroy the very basis of military administration."[54] He launched a movement against the Kōshikirei Order. Eventually a military ordinance was drafted as a law that would guarantee the military's right of direct appeal to the emperor.[55]

A rough draft was apparently prepared by early August. On August 10, Yamagata wrote to Terauchi complaining that nothing had yet appeared in the press concerning the military ordinance and demanded to know what had happened.[56] (Yamagata at that time was away from Tokyo, living in Ōiso, the resort town south of Tokyo.) By now impatient about the delays in promulgating many supreme command-related ordinances, Yamagata pressed the army minister for prompt action. Nine days later, on August 19, a request jointly signed by the army

Figure 5.4 Itō (left) with Yamagata Aritomo.
Source: Chūō Kōron Shinsha, p. 235.

and navy ministers was submitted to the emperor for his approval of Military Ordinance No. 1 titled "On Military Ordinances." The reason given was:

> Orders concerning supreme command-related matters from now on will be issued as a special form, namely, as Military Ordinances and will be countersigned by the competent minister alone. Thereby, they will be made distinct from regulations on administrative matters and the exercise of the prerogative of supreme command will be made clearer.[57]

Two weeks later, on September 2, Yamagata met with Itō Hirobumi, who had come back from Korea for a short time, and he pressed Itō to accept the establishment of the military ordinance as a law to demarcate the boundaries between supreme command-related and administrative matters.[58] Itō was forced to agree.

Military Ordinance No. 1, "On Military Ordinances," was sanctioned and enacted on September 11. It consisted of four articles:

> Article 1 Those laws relating to the Supreme Command of the Army and Navy that are sanctioned by the Emperor shall be Military Ordinances.

> Article 2 Those Military Ordinances that require public announcement shall be accompanied by an Imperial Edict. The Edict shall be signed by the Emperor and stamped with the Imperial seal. Then, the competent Army and Navy Ministers shall write down the date and countersign.

Article 3 Military Ordinances shall be publicly announced through official gazettes.

Article 4 Military Ordinances shall immediately come into force except those whose date of implementation is specifically set.

With this No. 1 Ordinance, those supreme command-related matters that were submitted directly to and sanctioned by the emperor were now issued under the term *gunrei*, or military ordinance. Of military ordinances, those that were to be publicly announced required the countersignature of the army and navy ministers alone. The enactment of the Kōshikirei Order ended up creating much commotion, which, finally, was "settled by firmly establishing the legal status of the military."[59]

Itō Hirobumi's idea of the nation

The present chapter examined in some depth the several systems that the Imperial Household Research Committee established in 1907, arguing that the constitutional reforms of 1907 were aimed not so much at perfecting the dual system of national law revolving around the Meiji Constitution and the Imperial Household Law, as at bringing together the central government and imperial court into one national system and centralizing its operation under the cabinet.

Primary objective of constitutionalism

The main factors behind the reforms were new internal and external developments affecting the national system since the enactment of the Meiji Constitution, including a firmer foundation of parliamentary government, growing influence of political parties, increasing independence of military administration, and the military's imperialistic pursuit of expansion to the continent. In the face of these developments, the Itō-led Imperial Household Research Committee sought to prevent the national system from dissolving and to reintegrate it.

The real architect on the committee behind the new institutional framework was Ariga Nagao. Having absorbed Itō's ideas on overhauling the institutional configuration of the Meiji Constitution, Ariga devoted himself to research and drafting bills of various sorts, a point I would like to acknowledge here.

Let me first note that Ariga and Itō shared views on institutions and constitutionalism. For Ariga, institutions should not be a straitjacket but something for people to use, a means that supported their endeavors; something that would prompt people to act in order to achieve worthy results. Likewise, the bedrock principle of constitutionalism should be to facilitate national activity, not constrain it.

Those ideas echoed what Itō had been saying for a long time. The reader will recall his remark cited in Chapter 1 to an audience in Taiwan, "Only when the state has institutions does it function." For Itō, like Ariga, institutions, or systems, were something that gave vigor and life to a state and kept it moving. The best and most effective institution that would bring vigor to national life and strengthen the state was constitutionalism. In 1907, the year the present chapter has focused on, Itō presented the following opinion concerning the constitutional state:

> The issues to resolve and objectives to achieve by establishing the Constitution in our country lie not merely in reconciling and harmonizing the interests of all classes at home, but also in infusing fresh energy into, and creating new forces in, the public life of the people under constitutional government. As in many constitutional monarchies, [the purpose of constitutionalism] is to provide fresh vigor and drive in fulfilling the responsibility of the state itself in addition to harmonizing the interests of the people of the many classes in the country.[60]

If we combine that citation with what we have discussed so far in this book, we can confirm that from early on, Itō believed that the vigor of the people was the key to the autonomy of the state. Institutions were something that, above all else, connect the state and the people and thereby trigger a chain reaction of vigor among them. What Itō saw as the essence of institutions was their capacity to mediate between the state and the people in various forms, most typically in forms that encourage the people's social and economic activities, raise their civic awareness, and promote their participation in government—and the circulatory effects of all three. The primary objective of constitutionalism was to guarantee and promote popular participation in government. Ever since the Meiji Constitution came into being, Itō had worked to reach that objective, and part of that effort was the founding of the Seiyūkai.

Itō's two faces

The other organization Itō founded to perfect the constitutional system was the Imperial Household Research Committee. In the committee, at Itō's request, Ariga designed the plan to integrate the emperor and imperial rights into an institutional framework and establish a cabinet-led government. Itō took pains to reiterate the importance of the latter when the committee was set up. He referred to the same theme over and over again during his 1899 nationwide speaking campaigns. During one of those speeches, for example he described his concerns at that time as focused on two things: "What is most urgent to me now is, one, to establish a government that will continue to exist for a long time, and two, to strengthen and improve political parties."[61]

In Itō's mind the establishment of a strong government was linked closely to the development of more responsible, effective political parties, as we have seen. The previous chapter described Itō's plan in founding the Seiyūkai to create an improved form of political party that would train and maintain a pool of experts on government. A political party should be an organization able to supply competent personnel to the cabinet. This relationship must not be reversed—the party should serve the cabinet but not vice-versa. He rejected the logic by which the majority party in parliament inevitably forms a cabinet by itself. He abjured

154 Consolidating the national structure

the thought of the cabinet as a battleground, something to be seized by the winner in a struggle for power. To Itō, the cabinet was an office of wisdom where policies were discussed evenly, fairly, with the nation always foremost in mind:

> As men of old have said, legislative affairs should be discussed as thoroughly as possible among representatives of the people; when it comes to administrative work, because the government is not an office of public discussion, it can only rely on the talent and ability and wisdom and knowledge of inside people. [Once a decision is made] it should be carried out systematically under strong leadership, and that is the secret of good administration.[62]

The cabinet was the brain of the state that supervised all administrative affairs. It could well be called an office of wisdom and knowledge. That was what Ariga described as a "positive cabinet."

Around 1900, Itō assumed the "two faces" of Imperial Household Research Committee president and Seiyūkai party president. He sought to perfect the national system by making reforms aimed at cabinet-led government and at parliament-led constitutionalism, two conceptually distinct functions of the state. The reform effort by the Imperial Household Research Committee, although its activity was temporarily interrupted, produced significant results in 1907. It is generally held that the committee created the legal system for imperial household affairs in addition to the existing government affairs law and thereby established the dual legal order centering on the Imperial Household Law and the Meiji Constitution. On the other hand, what president Itō envisioned for the form of the state was a powerful cabinet-led government. For that purpose he put Itō Miyoji and Ariga to work in establishing the Kōshikirei Order and revising the Cabinet Organization Order.

Did Itō really give way to the military?

This scheme invited sharp reaction from the army, with the result that Military Ordinance No. 1 was enacted to institutionalize the military's *iaku jōso* practices, hence the birth of another major law. The 1907 constitutional reforms by the Imperial Household Research Committee unexpectedly produced—at least on the surface—a threefold legal system: the laws of government, imperial household, and military affairs.

That result must have been source of bitter disappointment to Itō. The constitutional reform he had been pushing forward was frustrated at the very last stage because he gave way and accepted the military ordinance. He failed to put the finishing touches on the national system he had envisioned. Ariga, in his lecture given to the Chinese constitutional research group on May 9, 1909, stated that: "Of the things that are being done now in Japan there is one I consider very wrong," and that was, he said, that the military treated even matters of military administration as supreme command affairs and made them military ordinances. "That is where you have to be careful when you study the current Japanese system," he warned the Chinese. To put military administration strictly under cabinet control had been a vitally important objective for the committee, which it finally failed to achieve. Ariga's remark undoubtedly echoed Itō's thinking.

But was the establishment of the military ordinance in any way a one-sided concession by Itō? Is it true that Itō, who was so resolute toward the emperor on this matter, let himself be forced into conceding without any resistance? We cannot fully understand this issue unless we consider Japan's activities abroad as well as the domestic political situation. Itō was the resident-general of Korea at that time and the military ordinance problem in fact originated in Korea. Itō's constitutional reform could not possibly be fully explained without factoring in Japan's rule of Korea. In the following chapters we will examine Itō's vision of the state in the context of the political situations in East Asia as well as in Japan.

Notes

1 Tokutomi 1990, p. 19.
2 *Itō den*, vol. 3, pp. 463–4.
3 *Itō nikki*, vol. 1, p. 531.
4 *Hara nikki*, vol. 1, pp. 299–300.
5 Ibid., p. 300.
6 Ibid., p. 300.
7 Ibid., p. 301.
8 *Itō den*, vol. 3, p. 472; *Seigai den*, vol. 4, p. 777.
9 The awkward situation Inoue recalled had taken place two years earlier, during the third Itō cabinet. At that time, a rumor had been circulating that Itagaki Taisuke would join the cabinet in return for the Jiyūtō alliance with Itō. Sandwiched between Inoue, then finance minister, who opposed that arrangement, and then agriculture and commerce minister Itō Miyoji, who supported it, Itō Hirobumi had, after a lot of painful thinking, ruled out Itagaki as a cabinet member. Itō Miyoji had then resigned from his post.
10 *Itō den*, vol. 3, p. 475.
11 *Hara nikki*, vol. 1, p. 301.
12 Letter from Yamagata to Matsukata Masayoshi dated March 1, 1901, *Matsukata monjo*, vol. 9, p. 176.
13 *Seigai den*, vol. 4, p. 765.
14 *Hara nikki*, vol. 1, p. 337.
15 Ibid., p. 370.
16 Ibid., vol. 2, pp. 67–8.
17 Mitani 1995, p. 45.
18 *Itō den*, vol. 3, pp. 335 ff.
19 Ibid., pp. 420–1.
20 Ibid., pp. 425–6.
21 House of Representatives Election Law, Parliamentary Law, Public Accounts Law, and House of Peers Act.
22 *Meiji tennō-ki*, vol. 6, p. 185.
23 They include the Imperial Household Conference Ordinance (1907), Accession to the Throne Ordinance, Regent Ordinance, Investiture of the Crown Prince Ordinance (these three in 1909), Imperial Family Members' Positions (*shin'i*) Ordinance, Imperial Family Members Ordinance, Imperial Household Property Ordinance (these three in 1910), and the Imperial Household Accounting Ordinance (1912).
24 Ōishi 2005, p. 291.

25 Ibid., p. ii. What Ōishi actually has in mind here is a series of reforms in the system of government starting with the administrative reform under the Hashimoto Ryūtarō administration (1996–8).
26 Kawata 2001, Chapter 5.
27 Regarding the history of research in this field and achievements to date, see Itō 2000, pp. 227 ff.
28 *Itō Miyoji*, vol. 2, pp. 10 ff.
29 Letter by Itō Miyoji dated July 18, 1903, *Itō monjo* (Hanawa), vol. 2, p. 434.
30 Ibid., p. 434, letter by Itō Miyoji dated July 23, 1903.
31 See Chapter 2 above, pp. 49–51; for details see Takii 1999.
32 Takada 1927, p. 102.
33 Letter dated August 17, 1903, *Itō Miyoji*, vol. 2, pp. 9–10.
34 Kawata 2001, p. 198.
35 No. 167 of the *Kokka Gakkai zasshi*, journal of the Kokka Gakkai (The Association of Political Social Sciences), an organization founded in the faculty of law of the Imperial University in 1887. Itō Hirobumi played an important role in its establishment.
36 His lecture on relationships between the government and the military was published as a supplement to nos. 157–61 (1900–1) of the *Kokka Gakkai zasshi*. The lecture on relationships between Japan and Taiwan was carried in no. 172 (1901) of the same journal, entitled "Legislative Illusions on Taiwan," accompanied by a discussion on the Takano Incident, in which Takano Takenori, chief of the Taiwan high court of justice, was arbitrarily dismissed by the Japanese government in 1897.
37 Ariga 1901, p. 2.
38 Itō Miyoji 1910, p. 3.
39 *Kokka Gakkai zasshi* 167, pp. 22–3.
40 This argument was also reflected in Ariga's remarks about the emperor's relations with government officials. "Government officials have never been the Emperor's private retainers"; they were public servants; see *Kokka Gakkai zasshi* 167, p. 12. See also "Kensei kōgi," Ariga's collection of lectures to a Chinese research group visiting Japan in 1909, "The Emperor and what is called the Emperor's government are distinct" (March 14, 1909). The following citations, giving only dates, are also from "Kensei kōgi."
41 Ariga 1901–1902, vol. 1, p. 225.
42 "Kensei kōgi."
43 Ōishi 2005, pp. 277 ff.
44 Hozumi 1889.
45 Ariga 1889.
46 November 21, 1908 lecture, included in "Kensei kōgi" mentioned above.
47 Earlier in *Daijin sekinin ron* [A Study of the Responsibility of Ministers of State], published in 1890, Ariga had proposed that the ministers of state with the job of advising the emperor govern the country, thus preventing the emperor from bearing any responsibility. Ariga 1890, pp. 287 ff.
48 Kawata 2001, p. 201.
49 Kobayashi Tatsuo 1966. Itō Miyoji called his residence Suiusō, or "rain-falling-on-green-leaves cottage."
50 November 13, 1906 entry, *Hara nikki*, vol. 2, p. 207.
51 *Meiji tennō-ki*, vol. 11, p. 798.
52 Ibid., p. 798 and *Hiroku*, vol. 1, pp. 441–2.
53 Kobayashi Tatsuo 1966, pp. 823–4.
54 "Terauchi monjo," no. 360–1.
55 Regarding how the *gunrei* (military ordinance) was established, see Yui 2009, pp. 52 ff. and Itō Takao 2000, pp. 227 ff. For an empirical analysis of the legal-historical significance of military ordinances, see Gotō 1996, pp. 63 ff.
56 "Terauchi monjo," no. 360–1.

57 "Gunmukyoku gunrei keishiki seitei no ken" [On the Establishment of the Form of Military Ordinances by the Bureau of Military Affairs], in "Mitsudai nikki 1907."
58 Letter from Yamagata to Terauchi, dated September 2, 1907, "Terauchi monjo," no. 360–2.
59 Itō Takao 2000, p. 230.
60 Itō Hirobumi 1907, p. 127.
61 *Enzetsushū*, vol. 2, p. 100.
62 Ibid., vol. 3, p. 160.

6   Itō and China

Two months in Korea and China

The Seiyūkai was the product of Itō Hirobumi's ideas and goals, some of which took shape as a result of a trip he made to China in 1898. This chapter will revisit his pre-Seiyūkai years to explore how his time in China affected his thinking about establishing a political party. Chapter 3 followed Itō as he campaigned around Japan in 1899, just ten years after the promulgation of the Meiji Constitution. In his effort to carry out an overhaul of the constitutional system, he made a series of speech-making tours to take his ideas about constitutional government directly to people around the country. His founding of the Seiyūkai the following year was, in a way, the conclusion of that campaign. But another tour that fed into the Seiyūkai project was his trip to China.

On August 19, 1898 Itō left Japan on a two-month visit to Korea and China. In China, he was warmly welcomed by Kang Youwei (1853–1927) and other leaders of the movement for constitutional monarchy who were working toward remodeling China following the example of Meiji Japan. While in China, Itō accidentally found himself on the fringes of a coup d'état engineered by Empress Dowager Cixi (1835–1908) and her associates to oust Kang and his reformer group. Itō had the rare experience of being on the spot while an epochal event in China's modern history, now known as the Hundred Days' Reform, was unfolding.

What impact did that experience have on him? How did it affect his political vision and his view of foreign affairs? This chapter looks at what I believe to be the considerable imprint of the visit to the continent on his scheme for creating a new kind of party.

Itō went to China immediately after his third cabinet was dissolved. Power shifted to the new Kenseitō (Constitutional party) cabinet headed by Ōkuma Shigenobu (leader of the old Constitutional Reform party) as prime minister and with Itagaki Taisuke (head of the old Jiyūtō or Liberal party) as home minister—the Ōkuma-Itagaki cabinet. Itō must have been upset and bitter that Yamagata's strategy had been so effective in thwarting his attempt to form a political party. Two months later, he left Nagasaki in a ship bound for Korea and China.

Itō had gone abroad a number of times, and each time he gained new knowledge, sharper political insights, and a broader vision of nation building and overcame some crisis in his career in public service. As had been the case with his very first trip outside Japan (to Britain in 1863), as well as when he joined the Iwakura Mission in 1871, and again when he toured Europe to study constitutional government in 1982, the 1898 visit to China opened his eyes to realities that provided a huge learning experience.

Itō first landed in Korea at Incheon on August 22 and on August 25, he arrived in Seoul, where he had an audience with Gojong, the first emperor of the Korean empire (1897–1900). A new regime had just taken over from the centuries of Joseon dynasty (1392–1897) rule in October the previous year. He described the occasion in a letter to his wife Umeko: "The extent of the hospitality shown me by Korea's emperor and government was greater than anyone else has ever received."[1] Determined to become an independent state, Korea had chosen to make a clear break and cease its subservience to China's emperor. Now it, too, called itself "empire." The monarch of this old and now new country may have seen Itō as an ideal source of advice on how to run the fledgling modern government. Who better? Itō was the architect of Meiji Japan, a freshly minted independent empire that had swiftly managed to make a place for itself in the international community led by the Western powers. Little did Emperor Gojong dream that the man in front of him would return as resident-general after Japan had made his country a protectorate several years later.

Itō stayed in Korea until September 8; his hosts continued to entertain him lavishly. In the above-mentioned letter to Umeko, he wrote, "We have banquets

Figure 6.1 Emperor Gojong (1852–1919).

Source: Chūō Kōron Shinsha, p. 291.

daily. Almost every day and night, I'm invited to one party or another. My sweat runs down copiously, but fortunately I am never tired or weakened from all this bustling about each day." He seemed very satisfied with the extravagant hospitality. As he reported in a different letter, his stay in Korea "felt like a dream."[2]

An audience with Emperor Guangxu

Itō received dream-like hospitality in China, as well. Arriving at Tianjin on September 11, he wrote to Umeko, "The hearty welcome I have been given by people in China high and low is beyond description." The reception accorded him, surprising even to Itō himself, was not simply a demonstration of the courtesy and generosity toward guests inherent in Korean and Chinese cultures. The leaders in both countries, struggling to launch new kinds of government, eagerly welcomed his visit with hopes that he would support and guide them. One passage in the letter to Umeko describes the tenor of his first days in China:

> Day and night I'm entertained with food and drink and am very busy meeting many Chinese coming to ask me to do my utmost for China. One after another they come, just endless. From what I've heard so far, their emperor seems to be a smart and bright monarch. He's only 27 years old. When I go to Beijing, they say, the emperor will want to ask me about all kinds of things.[3]

In China, as in Korea, Itō was treated as a master instructor in modernization. As his letter suggests, he was perhaps not averse to receiving the ceaseless stream of requests to help China. Once in Beijing, the Chinese emperor, Guangxu (1871–1908), would be waiting to ask him for advice on all manner of things. It was with such expectations that he arrived in Beijing on September 14.

This was right at the time when Kang Youwei's reform movement was at its strongest in Beijing, the capital of Qing-dynasty China. The emperor had embraced the movement's precepts as official policy and the mood for sweeping reforms to bring constitutionalism to China had reached a high pitch. The timing was perfect. When Itō arrived, he was idolized as a hero. He was the man who had given Japan constitutional government, bringing it out of its long slumber as a country of lowly "eastern barbarians," and transforming it into a "civilized" country now more powerful than China. According to the *Guowenbao* newspaper published by Yan Fu (1853–1921), one of China's most influential enlightenment thinkers at that time, there was a plan underway in Beijing to ask Itō to stay on in China as an advisor.[4]

The day after he arrived at the capital, Itō met with Yikuang (Prince Qing 1838–1917, his name "Qing" is not the same as the dynasty name), a great-grandson of Emperor Qianlong (r. 1735–96) who was to be the first and last prime minister of the imperial cabinet under the Qing dynasty. Five days later, on September 20, Itō had an audience with Emperor Guangxu. "They tell me that the treatment accorded me at the audience was more meticulous and courteous than anyone had seen before," Itō wrote to Umeko. "Later I was invited to a banquet given by Prince Qing of the

First Rank [Yikuang], an imperial family member equivalent to a premier. This also was an event that was unprecedented, I hear."[5] Indeed, the Guangxu emperor had Itō seated beside him, an extraordinary honor.[6]

Empress dowager's 1898 coup

But the emperor's aunt, Empress Dowager Cixi, still exercised great power and one day after Itō's audience with the emperor, there was a coup. Sensing impending crisis and determined to stop the radical reforms, Empress Dowager Cixi and her conservative supporters put her nephew, the emperor, under house arrest. Kang Youwei and Liang Qichao (1873–1929) fled, ultimately finding refuge in Japan. Kang's younger brother Kang Guangren (1867–98), together with Tan Sitong (1865–98), and others, was executed. Zhang Yinhuan (1837–1900), right-hand man of the Guangxu emperor and mediator between Itō and the emperor, was exiled to a remote area in western China.

A letter to Umeko, on September 26, describes the excitement of the coup, as Itō vividly related what had happened:

> . . . all of a sudden, on the 21st, the situation radically changed. The empress dowager is now at the helm of government. Why this happened is because the emperor was so intent upon reform that he tried to do everything following the model of Japan, even making people change their clothing and so forth to Western style. When she found out what they were trying to do, the empress dowager was infuriated, I hear. One theory holds that there was a plot to depose her. It's very hard to tell what to believe in China.[7]

Witnessing the overnight collapse of the reform movement, when only a short time before its leaders had extolled him so vigorously, Itō was utterly serious when he said "It's very hard to tell what to believe in China." In the same letter to Umeko he wrote that he had asked Li Hongzhang (1823–1901) to spare Zhang Yinhuan's life. The circumstances of that request demonstrate the kind of international status and reputation Itō had achieved.

On September 25, a banquet was held for Itō at the residence of Hayashi Gonsuke (1860–1939), Japanese provisional chargé d'affaires to China. Among the guests invited was Li Hongzhang. In the middle of the party a messenger arrived from the British minister to China, conveying to Itō the rumor that Zhang Yinhuan would be executed the next day. The messenger relayed the word of the British minister that "he wishes Prince Itō to exert every effort to prevent the execution." Apparently, it was in response to this that Itō asked Li to spare Zhang's life.[8] In the above letter to Umeko, Itō said there appeared to be some tension between Li and Zhang but that "I know both men; it's very sad for me to hear that one of them is to be executed. So, last night I asked Li Hongzhang to do anything in his power to save Zhang Yinhuan." Clearly the British minister had known Itō Hirobumi to be a person who could be instrumental in rescuing Zhang.

Despite Itō's unexpected presence while upheaval was going on in Beijing, he kept largely to his original itinerary. He left Beijing for Tianjin on September 29, stayed there for a few days until October 2, and then left for Shanghai, arriving on October 5. There he was given the same enthusiastic welcome. Writing to Umeko after reaching Shanghai, he said,

> Wherever I go in China all kinds of people come to see me; not just government officials but everyone, including scholars and merchants, expressing their warm welcome. They really put themselves out to bring forth the best food and drink so they can hear what I have to say.[9]

On October 13, he left for the Wuhan region, going upstream on the Yangtze river to meet the scholar-official Zhang Zhidong (1837–1909), viceroy of Huguang province, in the commercial city of Hankou. Hearing about Itō's visit to Shanghai, Zhang Zhidong had sent a messenger to invite him to a meeting and Itō had accepted. Their meeting in Hankou, along with the 1898 coup, were to have a significant effect on Itō, as we will see later in this chapter.

Itō left Hankou on October 17 for Nanjing. Arriving on October 19, he met with Liu Kunyi (1830–1902), viceroy of Liangjiang (governor-general of the two Yangtze provinces and surrounding areas, Nanjing included). Liu was as powerful a regional political leader as Zhang Zhidong. Itō returned to Shanghai on October 22. From there, according to the original plan, he was scheduled to go on to South China. But in Shanghai, an order from the emperor of Japan for him to return home immediately awaited him. The Ōkuma-Itagaki cabinet had collapsed, and it was a cabinet that had been formed on Itō's recommendation to the emperor. Itō hurriedly prepared to leave China, and arrived at Nagasaki on November 7.

Back in Japan, Itō learned that the emperor had commanded Yamagata Aritomo to form a cabinet. The movement for party cabinets that Itō had led was thoroughly discredited and a "transcendental" cabinet made up of Chōshū-Satsuma oligarchs was put in place. "This adverse turn of events," says historian Masuda Tomoko, "was a sign that Itō's star had fallen, when so recently he had prided himself on having the deep trust of the emperor and being preeminent among the *genrō* (elders)."[10] So, as Masuda asserts, Itō felt that he had little choice but to go the way of a party politician and stand up to the Yamagata bureaucratic faction.

From our discussion so far, it is evident that Itō's decision to create the Seiyūkai should not be seen as the product of an opportunistic transformation driven by political calculations or lust for power. On the contrary, as was clear in his speeches championing the Constitution the following year, his political party was founded on the ideals of constitutional and civilized government. Those ideals had been firmly rooted in his outlook since before the establishment of the Meiji Constitution. For Itō, party-based government was not a matter of wrangling for political power but of political ideals—a vision of government. In my view, his experience in China in 1898 lent depth to his ideals and a strategic dimension to his vision of government.

Lessons of the 1898 coup in China

What did Itō Hirobumi learn from his travels in China in 1898? He realized that in thinking about China, he needed to separate its economy from its government. The political situation there was going to grow even more chaotic, he could see, but in economic terms the country had tremendous potential, and so it was of the utmost importance that Japan strengthen its economic ties with China. Let us consider more closely how Itō regarded the Chinese government and economy.

Itō's position vis-à-vis the reformists

The coup undoubtedly sparked in Itō a certain distrust of the Chinese government. Yet even before that, Itō had felt that something was wrong in the way reforms were being pursued in China. Indeed, a fierce power struggle was raging below the surface between Kang Youwei, Liang Qichao, and other reformers on one side and the conservative faction behind the Empress Dowager Cixi on the other. For the reformers, the situation was degenerating. They had dismissed Li Hongzhang as minister of the Zongli Yamen, the office in charge of foreign affairs, on September 7, and, in response, the Empress Dowager had ordered military forces to ready themselves for armed suppression of the reformers. The reformers had sought the help of Yuan Shikai (1859–1916), commander of the Xin-jun, or New Army, in backing the reformist emperor, with a plan to place the empress dowager under house arrest.

So Itō arrived when Beijing was at a hair-trigger moment. Kikuchi Hideaki observes that the reformers, caught in a difficult position, had in fact pinned great hopes on his arrival.[11] Itō recognized the weak situation the reformers were in and perceived that the leading figures in the Zongli Yamen foreign office were not necessarily supporters of the reforms. He kept his distance from the reformers. More than anything else, their dismissal of Li Hongzhang, who had been Itō's negotiation partner of many years and a man Itō respected as an experienced, moderate statesman, made him wary of the reform movement.

By September 18, the empress dowager's coup had become an imminent possibility. Kang Youwei called on Itō at the Japanese legation and pleaded with him to persuade the empress dowager to support the reforms. Itō replied in vague terms, leaving Kang greatly disillusioned, and declaring, "the Marquis [Itō] despises our country."[12] When, after the coup, Zhang Zhidong appealed to the Japanese government to help Kang flee to Japan, Zhang is reported to have told the Japanese side, "On the day of Marquis Itō's arrival in Beijing Itō disappointed Kang, and Kang secretly told the emperor not to see Itō or to trust Japan."[13] We cannot take this account entirely at face value, but Kang must have been clutching at straws and desperate to meet Itō to try to get his help in a tense situation. Perceiving that he had been given the cold shoulder, and having had such high hopes of Itō's help, he must have felt intense resentment.

Now let us look at Itō's thinking at the time of the coup as revealed in the "Itō monjo," a collection of Itō documents that contains records of his meetings with

Yikuang and Emperor Guangxu, titled "Itō Hirobumi Shinkoku kankei shiryō" [Materials on Itō Hirobumi's Relations with China] (375).[14] The records are written on ruled paper printed with the identification "State of Japan, Legation in China." Itō is recorded as saying:

> When it comes to national interest, you should be most prudent and careful. Never act rashly. Place experienced experts in command to formulate reform policies, and place young, spirited officials below to help them. Let them do their jobs and success will be yours. Should you ignore this point and try to bring about drastic reforms quickly, your efforts will only create confusion and disturbance.

Itō's caution against precipitous reform and his counsel to get "experienced experts" and "young, spirited officials" to work together probably disappointed the reformers. But had they known him better, they would have recognized in his advice the gradualism that had marked his political philosophy from the outset. He had given similar advice in Japan over the years, and now he was offering it to China as well.

Advice to Yikuang, Prince Qing

Even more important among the remarks recorded in the documents related to Itō in China is what Itō told Yikuang concerning the training of personnel. Recalling the time when, as Japan's prime minister, he had been asked by Yikuang (via the Japanese minister to China) for advice on military reforms, Itō told him:

> I replied at that time that the keystone of the military system is the quality of its officers, and that good officers should be trained in military academies. The top priority, therefore, is to build a military academy directly under the emperor of your country, I said. The same applies to all areas of reform, not just the military system. The important thing is to weigh the degree of urgency among items, correctly prioritize them, and implement them one by one. Make this approach your policy and you will succeed no matter how difficult the issue at hand may be.

In the last part of the above statement, true to form, he counsels gradualism, saying that the secret of success is not haste but to proceed step by step. Moreover, his advice in the first part of the statement reflects another dimension of his political creed: humans are the essence of institutions. In other words, the success or failure of a system depends on the intellect and learning of those who operate it. Regarding a military system, too, Itō said to Yikuang, "Once a military academy is set up and officers' education has improved, there is no need to worry about crude methods of training the ranks." That is to say, to firmly establish a system Itō considered it vital to train those who would support it, no matter how roundabout that approach might appear.[15]

His approach to systems, seeing them in terms of education, was based on his people-centered perspective—the idea that it is people who make systems function. The message he wanted to get across to Yikuang was the importance of nation-building on a foundation of people. In answer to the prince's questions "What is the path to a wealthy nation? Is it the custom duties at ports?" Itō declared, "No, no. How can the basis of national enrichment possibly lie in customs duties? The source of a nation's wealth is in the development of industry by the people."[16]

This, as he candidly explained to Yikuang, was the heart of nation-building. It was the vigor and vitality of the people, not makeshift reforms in institutions, that ensured that the nation would stand. Thinking thus, Itō advised the prince to reform the school system and reinvigorate the spirit of the people. Time and again in 1899, when Itō was touring Japan on his campaign to promote the Constitution, he would come back to this theme—that the nation was sustained by the physical and mental vitality of its people.

Concern about mixing religion with the state

By this time, China's leaders recognized the necessity for schools to teach practical science based on Western learning as the foundation of industry. Many such schools had been established. Building them was a pillar of Kang's reform movement. But there was a great disparity between the Chinese reformers and Itō as to what kind of schools to build and how.

Unlike "Western-affairs" (*yangwu*) movement leaders, Kang Youwei advocated improving elementary and middle schools and building new ones with the goal of expanding education among the people.[17] Itō Hirobumi was already critical of that policy before he reached China. On board the ship that took him from Korea to Tianjin, he is reported to have commented, "I have a feeling that China's reform still has a very long way to go," and, he argued:

> If I were to plan for China's future, I would leave elementary and middle schools aside for the time being and set up specialized colleges to train the experts China so badly needs . . . and use them for projects that would benefit the country.

According to Itō, there was "education for personal growth" and "education for national growth," and China urgently needed the latter. Top priority had to be given to specialized education to "produce the personnel China's government needs so badly and assign them to essential national projects."[18] Clearly, he was thinking about how to change the thinking of young people currently receiving higher education, and how to turn them into a national elite who could lead in modernizing the country. Education for the masses could be improved, step-by-step, only after that.

Itō and Kang Youwei had very different philosophical starting points. Itō's view of education—and government—reform was fundamentally different from

Kang's. Kang's reform movement is usually seen as a philosophical reaction to the Western-affairs faction's *Zhongti-xiyong* ("Chinese essence, Western technology") theory of limited modernization. That theory viewed China's traditional culture as the "body" or "substance" of the state, and allowed some westernization/modernization only as far as it was utilitarian or functional. A closer examination, however, reveals that Kang Youwei also advocated ideas similar to the *Zhongti-xiyong* idea. According to the scholar of Chinese philosophy, Murata Yūjirō, Kang Youwei's discourse is characterized by reference to Chinese culture as the "essence." That is, Kang extracted Confucianism from classical Chinese writings and sought to make it the state orthodoxy, within the framework of which to achieve national reform.[19]

To Itō, this mingling of religion and education, and, by extension, of religion and government, ought to be avoided at all costs. During his constitutional stumping tours in Japan the following year, Itō declared in speeches, regarding the employment of government officials, "What religion they embrace does not matter today. They are perfectly free to [privately] perform canonical religious functions of any religion. It makes no difference whether it is Buddhism, Shintoism, or Christianity."[20] Itō insisted that educated people should be able to take government positions according to their abilities, regardless of religion. Education and government must be carried out as secular pursuits and be always neutral toward religion.

It is safe to suppose that the reason Itō always kept his distance from the reformation movement in China was that he was dubious about its orientation toward religion, namely Confucianism. After he returned to Japan, in an imperial audience to report on his travels in Korea and China, he advised the emperor, "From now on, the Imperial Household should be impartial to all religions and all religious sects and never take any discriminatory measures against them."[21] His firsthand view of the reformation movement in China must have alerted Itō to the danger of a state strongly influenced by religious ideas.

Meeting with Zhang Zhidong

Despite his proximity to the violent overturning of the government in Beijing, Itō went on traveling in China according to plan. Kang Youwei's plea for help notwithstanding, he did not feel sympathy for the reform movement and was skeptical of its future. In Itō's eyes, a coup seemed inevitable.

Rescuing reformer intellectuals

On the other hand, Itō did what he could to rescue people endangered in the wake of the coup, one of them being the Chinese emperor's right-hand man Zhang Yinhuan, whose life he tried to save. Still in China, on October 10, Itō sent a message to the Japanese government via the Japanese consulate-general in Shanghai asking that it request the Chinese government to protect the life of Huang Zunxian (1848–1905), a Chinese diplomat stationed in Japan who had just been dismissed.[22]

Huang was an enlightened and liberal diplomat as well as an accomplished poet. Drawing on his experience and knowledge acquired during his tenure in Japan, Huang published a book titled *Riben guozhi* [Treatises on Japan], in 1895. In the preface he included scathing criticism of his fellow Chinese who "laughed at Japan for having brought in and utilized Western culture and science out of a need for defense against external threats." The book marked "a significant turning point in the history of Chinese understanding of the world."[23] Itō may have harbored serious doubts about China's reformation movement, but he was deeply anxious about the purge of individual reformist intellectuals after the movement failed.

Consider the case of Liang Qichao, who was as powerful a leader of the movement as Kang Youwei. With Itō's assistance, Liang found refuge in Japan. He had been meeting with Tan Sitong when they heard about the coup, and, at Tan's urging, Liang fled to the Japanese legation. Helped by Itō, he boarded a Japanese warship and escaped to Japan.[24] There he sought to absorb modern Western political and economic ideas mainly through Japanese translations of European and American texts. Later on he was influential in helping China to accept and adopt certain ideas and procedures from the West, and, in so doing, he helped to lay the foundations for the introduction of constitutionalism to his country.[25]

Itō apparently sensed strong potential in Liang. Hayashi Gonsuke, then Japanese acting minister in China, recalled in his memoirs how Itō had said to him, "Liang is an exceptional young man, an admirable lad," and giving Hayashi his instructions, he added, "Help Liang, will you? Help him flee to Japan. Once he is in Japan, I will take care of him. Young Liang is a soul too good for China."[26] Itō's feeling toward Liang seemed much more sympathetic than toward Kang Youwei. At that time, even as he mouthed the ideas of his mentor, Kang, Liang was growing suspicious of the religious tendencies coming into their movement and Kang's inclination to put Confucianism at the base of government and education. It made him understand more clearly the urgent need to master the sciences of the West.[27] No doubt Itō was aware of the change; he could see in Liang a resistance to religion and a move toward to modern, practical, and useful knowledge from the West.

As it turned out, as Hayashi said in his memoir, "Everyone expected Itō to provide protection for Liang, but it was Ōkuma who ended up taking the role of protector. Itō didn't care much about such things."[28] Indeed, after Liang and Kang fled to Japan, Itō avoided contact with them and it was Inukai Tsuyoshi who, via Ōkuma, harbored them instead. Itō and the Japanese government were caught between the political activities of Liang and Kang, both openly critical of the Chinese government, on the one hand, and China's demands that Liang and Kang be turned over to its government, on the other. The Japanese side was perplexed as to what to do. They finally reached an agreement with Inukai, protector of Kang and Liang, that Kang would be given 7,000 yen and deported to the United States and that Liang would stay in Japan with a monthly payment of 250 yen. Itō conveyed this agreement to Yamagata and urged him to "make those payments so we can wash our hands of them."[29]

Itō wanted to settle the problem on the basis of internationally acceptable rules. He must have wanted Liang to pursue Western studies while in exile in Japan; otherwise Liang would have had to leave the country. Ultimately, seeing intellectual promise in Liang, Itō gave his assent for the latter to stay in Japan. When a Chinese envoy came in October 1899 demanding that Kang be handed over, Itō blustered that the envoy "was extremely rash." With regard to the Kang Youwei issue, Itō explained, he had repeatedly made the argument to Li Hongzhang and others in Beijing immediately after the coup that "if Kang flees to Japan as a political exile, under international law our government will never be able to arrest and extradite him."[30] So, whatever his real motives, Itō stuck to his insistence that issues must be solved by civilized proceedings and the rule of law.

Zhang Zhidong

Despite having to hurry back home to Japan in early December 1898, after hearing of the collapse of the Ōkuma-Itagaki cabinet, Itō benefited by his travels to many parts of China. One highlight was his visit to Zhang Zhidong, a political figure on a level with that of Li Hongzhang. As the viceroy of Huguang province, Zhang supervised the development of the region with masterly skill, and he was also a renowned advocate of the *yangwu* modernization movement, the campaign for reform that had preceded Kang's movement. In March 1898, about six months before Itō arrived in China, Zhang had published a book titled *Quanxue pian* [Exhortation to Learning] that had become quite famous even before Itō's visit. The treatise "advocates moderate reform, and criticizes Kang Youwei's reform for its radicalism."[31] More important, as a work that expounds on the idea of "Chinese essence/Western technology," it was instrumental in prodding China's officialdom to finally recognize the "effectiveness" of Western science and technology and the need for China to master them. For that reason the book played a crucial ideological role in justifying efforts to modernize in late Qing China, including sending students abroad for training, abolishing the imperial examination system for government officials, and introducing constitutionalism.[32]

On October 13, having been invited to meet with Zhang, Itō left Shanghai for Hankou. Acting Consul-General Odagiri Masunosuke (1868–1934) in Shanghai must have been behind the invitation.[33] For quite some time Odagiri had been closely watching the steady economic growth taking place in Huguang province under Zhang's jurisdiction, especially the local steel industry centered on Hanyang Steel Mill, Asia's first modern steel works. He was eager to get Itō and Zhang together.

There are indications that, even before his trip to China, Itō also had shown interest in the economic conditions of the area administered by Zhang. *Hisho ruisan*, a classified collection of the private documents of Itō Hirobumi, contains a report on industry in Hanyang and Wuchang titled "Report on Projects of the Viceroy of Huguang."[34] Further, *Segai Inoue-kō den* [Biography of Inoue Kaoru] indicates that, as of 1897, Inoue Kaoru had decided to look into Chinese mines as a possible source of fuel for the Yahata Steel Works and had sent Nishizawa

Figure 6.2 Zhang Zhidong (1837–1909).
Source: Chūō Kōron Shinsha, p. 261.

Kimio to China to visit the mines. When Nishizawa came back, he is said to have reported not only to Inoue but also to Itō Hirobumi about the results of his inspection,[35] and after Itō returned from China, negotiations for a business tie-up between the Daye mine in China and the Yahata Steel Works made rapid progress. The Itō-Zhang meeting must have led to the start of the negotiations, as will be discussed later.

Itō already had some knowledge of Zhang Zhidong's thinking prior to their meeting. Journalist and businessman Kishida Ginkō (1833–1905) was a passionate and active advocate of friendship between Japan and China. As soon as he heard about Itō's trip to China, he had written to Itō about Zhang's new book *Quanxue pian*. His letter explained that the book consisted of two parts (the "Inner Chapters" and the "Outer Chapters"), one "discussing Confucian-style conservatism" and the other "introducing a wide range of topics relating to the West including reformation, introduction of Western science, studying abroad, newspaper reading, agriculture/industry/commerce, military science, mining, railways, and so forth, the model for which is mainly Japan."[36] Itō must have received Kishida's letter while he was in Tianjin, and would thus have learned something about Zhang's thinking before he headed for Hankou.

Intellectual resonance

Zhang met Itō for the first time on October 14. A grand banquet was held on October 16, and Itō left the following day. What did they talk about during their brief encounter? Acting Consul-General Odagiri later reported that after Itō had gone back to Japan, Zhang seemed to reproach himself, saying that, when Marquis Itō had visited, there had been things he had wanted to talk about with him but could not because of the recent coup in Beijing. He had apparently regretted letting the once-in-a-lifetime opportunity slip away just entertaining him in the customary way.[37]

Zhang no doubt did miss a valuable opportunity. Although his thinking differed from that of Kang Youwei and Kang's group of reformers, Zhang was also reform-minded and might have been considered in the same camp. He probably had to be careful about what he said just then, with the coup having taken place just days before. He might have felt compelled to censor himself when speaking to Itō.

Odagiri's account would seem to imply that the meeting between Zhang and Itō ended with little more than formalities and without any substantial discussion. But more may have been achieved. Before Itō hurried back to Japan he wrote to Zhang.[38] In his letter he said that, having read *Quanxue pian*, a copy of which Zhang had given him when they met, he admired his wealth of knowledge and was impressed with his acuity. Itō also said that the time had already passed when radical reforms of the type Kang advocated might have been effective for China, that drastic, precipitous reforms must be avoided not only for the good of China but for the future of East Asia, and that he realized that many people in China and elsewhere believed that Zhang, more than anyone else, could take the lead in building a stronger China. That Itō went out of his way to write such a letter as he prepared for his quick return to Japan suggests that the two men, when they met, had found themselves to be kindred spirits. Zhang's comment, recorded by Odagiri and mentioned above, was in all likelihood more an expression of disappointment that there had not been enough time to talk than regret that the meeting was fruitless.

It seems that a friendship developed between them at that time. Above all, the two resonated in regard to the idea that modernization should be achieved by gradual rather than radical reform. It was possibly through their discussion on education in particular that they discovered the extensive common ground between them.

Spirit of flexibility

During his stay in China, Itō spoke many times about the importance of education. To Yikuang he counseled the promotion and expansion of technical education. After saying goodbye to Zhang and going on to Nanjing, Itō met with another powerful regional leader, Liu Kunyi, viceroy of Liangjiang, to whom he stressed the need to establish technical schools. Heeding this advice, Liu sent a group to Japan the following year to "observe the status of education on agriculture and technology." Consul Odagiri, who had mediated between Liu and Itō, sent a letter to Itō, saying, "I have a request from the viceroy [Liu], entreating Your Excellency to kindly instruct [the group] when they arrive in Tokyo."[39] Itō was unable to comply, however, because he was away from Tokyo on his speech-making tour.

Itō no doubt discussed education with Zhang Zhidong. I touched upon Zhang's thoughts on education earlier in reference to *Quanxue pian*. In that treatise Zhang wrote, "Self-strength derives from power, power comes from wisdom, and wisdom comes from learning."[40] He called for the "wide establishment of schools across the country,"[41] and argued for a middle-of-the-road approach to educating people without too much emphasis either on "Chinese essence" or "Western technology." The book is generally viewed as an attempt to revive Confucianism by introducing a limited degree of Western technology and justifying acceptance of Western civilization on a superficial level. If that was the case, one wonders how Zhang could have found common ground with Itō, who regarded Confucianism as a holdover from the past.

Kawajiri Fumihiko, author of a rigorous study of the context in which *Quanxue pian* was produced, proposes that we reconsider Zhang's thought: "[Zhang Zhidong's] idea of 'Chinese essence, Western technology,' directed mainly at reformers in the province of Hunan, can be seen as an argument in support of the active introduction of Western sciences and institutions."[42] Indeed, in the "Shexue 3" section in the Outer Chapters of *Quanxue pian*, Western sciences are classified into two categories: *zheng* (essentially political economics) and *yi* (including mathematics, optics, and medicine). From what age and for how long these subjects must be taught so that students can master both categories are considered with great care.[43] Given that content, it is hard to believe, therefore, that Zhang's real intention was merely to graft "Western technology" onto "Chinese essence."

Evidence that Itō and Zhang had a common appreciation for the benefits of, and need for, Western science, and therefore communicated with each other very well, can be found in Zhang's criticism of Kang Youwei. Zhang wrote *Quanxue pian* as a counter-argument to Kang's *Kongzi gaizhi kao* [A Study of the Reforms of Confucius], published in the year that Zhang's book came out. At the beginning of *Quanxue pian*, Zhang wrote, "Three types of theories are advanced to save China from revolution. One calls for protecting the country, another for protecting Confucianism, and the third for protecting the Chinese race (*baozhong*). These three are inseparably connected. In fact they constitute a single approach. Protection of the ethnic group must come after protection of Confucianism, and protection of Confucianism must come after protection of the country." Protection of the country, of Confucianism, and of the "race"—that was also Kang's original theme. How did Zhang use it to criticize Kang? The answer is revealed in the priorities Zhang clearly asserts in his book. According to Murata Yūjirō:

> What worried [Zhang] most was the upsurge of the Kang group's movement to "respect Confucius, protect his teachings" and their call for "protecting the race," and "sociability" *(hequn)*. In Zhang's view, those undertakings swerved away from the more important "protection of the country."[44]

Thus Itō and Zhang found themselves of the same mind in opposing a radical reform movement that embraced religion (Confucianism), advocating instead moderate reform, which gave priority to protection of the country.

That Itō and Zhang were of very like minds is suggested by another anecdote. The dialogue between the two men was held in English. Zhang's interpreter was his secretary in charge of foreign languages, Gu Hongming (1857–1928). As a young man, Gu had spent more than ten years studying in several European countries. He was an accomplished intellectual, well versed in both Eastern and Western cultures, and the author of an English work titled *The Spirit of the Chinese People* (1915—translated into Japanese as *Shinajin no seishin* in 1940). According to his recollections, when he served as interpreter for the Itō-Zhang meetings, Gu presented Itō with a copy of his English translation of *The Analects of Confucius*. Itō accepted it, but asked, somewhat cynically, what significance the teachings of Confucius, written thousands of years before, had for the twentieth century. Gu replied that three times three equals nine, was as true thousands of years ago as it is in the twentieth century. Zhang Zhidong broke in and reproached him:

> Don't you know about the revolution in mathematics in the twentieth century? Today, when you get a loan from a foreign country, the value of the loan is not 3 times 3 equals 9 but 3 times 3 equals only 7, and when it comes time to repay, it becomes 3 times 3 equals 11.[45]

Itō might have said exactly the same thing. He and Zhang probably shared many ideas, and they both had a spirit of flexible adaptability with which to keep up with developments in the world.

Request from the Yahata Steel Works

One of Itō's purposes in visiting Zhang was to discuss a specific business arrangement. It had to do with obtaining iron ore for Japan's state-run Yahata Steel Works. Preparations to open the steel works were in full swing at that time. (It started up operations in February 1901.) One high-priority goal of the Meiji state was to establish a Japanese steel industry. Tremendous efforts were going into preparing for and building the Yahata Steel Works—a state project and Japan's first modern steel plant. One factor still not resolved was how to secure a continuing supply of good quality iron ore in large quantities. At first the Akatani iron mine in Niigata prefecture was considered a possible source, but the mine had yet to be developed, and so a more reliable source of iron ore had to be found. The best candidate was considered to be the Daye iron mine located in the province of Hubei under Zhang Zhidong's jurisdiction. It was there that Asia's first modern steel works, Hanyang Steel Mill, had been constructed under the leadership of Zhang himself.

There is a voluminous work called *Seitetsusho tai Kan'yahyō konsu kankei teiyō* [The Steel Works Compendium Related to the Hanyeping Coal and Steel Company], compiled by the Tokyo branch office of the Ministry of Agriculture and Commerce (Yahata) Steel Works in 1917. According to this record, when Wada Tsunashirō (1856–1920), director of the steel works, heard about Itō's plan to visit China in 1898, he asked Itō for help in purchasing iron ore from China. So it was that Itō brought up the request when he met with Zhang. The compendium describes the series of events as follows:

> At his meeting with Viceroy Zhang in Wuchang in Hubei province, the prince [Itō; he was marquis when he visited China] proposed a business tie-up between Japan and China. As the start, Itō explained, China would purchase coking coal from Japan and in exchange would sell Daye iron ore to Japan, and the viceroy agreed. Later, in 1899, to push negotiations forward, Director Wada himself went to China. Before he left [Japan], in case Viceroy Zhang might not agree, the director had Prince Itō write a letter to Zhang asking the viceroy to negotiate and saying that he was sending Steel Works director Wada to China to conclude a Japan-China business tie-up and to sign a contract for the purchase of Daye iron ore. Carrying this letter, Director Wada went to China.[46]

According to this source, at the October 1898 meeting Itō and Zhang made a private agreement on the sale-and-purchase exchange of Chinese iron ore and Japanese coal; to conclude the contract, Director Wada went to China carrying a letter written by Itō to Zhang. I have not confirmed the whereabouts of that letter yet, but what was discussed at the meeting can be confirmed in a Chinese document. According to the "ninth month" entry for "the 24th year of the Guangxu era" (1898) in the *Zhang Wenxiang gong nianpu* [Chronology of Lord Zhang Wenxiang (Zhidong)],[47] at the Zhang-Itō meeting they talked about an exchange of Japanese coking coal and Chinese iron ore. The entry records that Itō proposed shipping "Japanese coal to E [abbreviated form of Hubei province] and when the ship returns it will carry back Daye iron ore that is 'sold in exchange' (*daixiao*)," and Zhang Zhidong replied that he would have the proposal discussed immediately.[48]

Daye iron ore was to become an indispensable resource for Japan's steel industry. It was so important, in fact, that it was included in the notorious Twenty-one Demands on China (1915). It all started with this initial agreement between Itō and Zhang.

The Itō-Zhang meeting marked a remarkable encounter between two great statesmen, and also provides a glimpse of the significance of such encounters in determining the subsequent Japan–China relationship. The relationship between the Yahata Steel Works and the Daye iron mine is usually regarded as the beginning of Japan's economic aggression in China and, therefore, as representing an aspect of Japanese imperialism.

Was Itō at that time looking at China with the gaze of a plunderer? We can provide some answers to this by studying the remarks he made after he returned home, and extrapolating from them something of his views on China.

Views on China and plans for Japan

The following year, as he traveled throughout Japan campaigning for constitutionalism, Itō's speeches contained remarks about his experiences in China. They reveal that he had much sympathy for China's reformers—he proved as much by his efforts to rescue Liang Qichao and other talented young Chinese from the purge following the coup—but he was skeptical of the wisdom of rushing into reforms that merely addressed the needs of the moment; effective reform required a measured, step-by-step process that would encourage compromise with the existing order and environment and gradually adapt them to new situations. Comments in these speeches indicate his regret not so much about the failure of Kang's reform movement as about the political situation in China, where both reformers and conservatives too often tended to go to extremes:

> The manners and customs, the old practices, and the kind of science they are pursuing are not compatible with reforms that bring in new elements arising in this constantly evolving world . . . [and] they are in no state to be able to accept my advice and act on it. . . . I returned home with a sense of great regret.[49]

Another comment, although made in reference to Koreans, undoubtedly reflected his experience in China:

> Using education to guide them, we must find ways to imprint in their minds how important it is to keep progressing while maintaining peace at the same time. Specifically, they must not be allowed to become too antagonistic toward their royal house or to the government. On the contrary, they should be encouraged to work side by side with the royal family. That is the only way they will achieve truly solid reforms. As in China, in Korea, too, if they rush headlong into progress through revolution, they will end up causing all kinds of obstructions and inviting censure from the world powers. These points they need to keep in mind, and they must be inculcated with the idea that unless they are adequately trained, they will not achieve any of their objectives.[50]

Disappointment with poor governance

An overly ambitious, precipitous rush into reform was the reason Kang's Hundred Days movement failed. Political reform and achievement of Chinese independence from the Western powers would have contributed greatly to the security of East Asia, but "that is almost impossible now, for the situation has become so hopeless," wrote Itō. What was happening to China? It was being divided up among the European nations. Sooner or later Japan, too, Itō warned, "might end up confronting the European powers across a narrow strip of water."[51] Deeply disappointed with the governance of China, Itō was pessimistic about its political outlook.

Hopes for China's economy

Itō was extremely impressed, on the other hand, with the potential for economic growth in China:

> While the [Chinese] government is in great turmoil, as I have described, its people are diligent and probably more profitably engaged in business than

almost any other people in the world. The possibility of wealth for the Chinese is vast; simply making changes in financial policies and other improvements would enable the Chinese empire to keep on growing without much difficulty.[52]

Itō was thus very optimistic about China's economic potential. He was certain that if that potential could be developed, the country had the promise of becoming a prosperous nation one day. Itō's high expectations were backed by the awareness that a powerful economic sphere was emerging through the combination of the Chinese labor force and a massive inflow of Western capital. Even if the Chinese could not do it themselves, "more and more Europeans are coming in to promote industry and build railways, and those projects are going to be very large-scale."[53]

Apart from the politics and government of the Chinese nation, Itō was all in favor of actively pursuing the Chinese market. During his campaign tour in northern Kyushu, bilateral economic relations with China were a hot topic. If industrial projects in China grew bigger, he said in a speech, "Not only coal mining but all kinds of businesses will thrive here [in northern Kyushu], and more factories will have to be built as well. They all will serve to make this region more prosperous."[54] Demand from China was certain to grow rapidly and for economic reasons Japan could not afford to pass up the opportunity:

> No matter what the situation for the Chinese government, or the state of Chinese sovereignty, one thing certain is that demand from the Chinese people is going to keep growing day by day, and Japan is in the best possible place to meet that demand.[55]

We must not, he said, be so foolhardy as to let the European countries make economic inroads into China ahead of Japan.[56] "Japan is the most conveniently situated close to [China], and the development of our industrial export trade is vital to the very survival of our country."[57]

Without a doubt, Itō was thinking of a plan to link the northern Kyushu region industrial base centered on the Yahata Steel Works with the Hubei economic zone in China, which was controlled by Zhang Zhidong. From his experience in China, Itō had formulated a strategy for Japan to steer clear of China's government and politics while actively engaging with its economy.

Imperialist or evangelist?

Can we describe Itō's views on dealing with China as imperialistic? At least, judging from the following statement, we can say that his proposals for economic expansion in China were not rooted in an ambition to gain overseas territory. In his view:

> Today issues between countries have nothing to do with territory. Even if a territorial issue does arise it amounts to no more than a way to make your

own trade and industry more profitable. No matter how much you expand your territory, it's pointless unless it brings profit.[58]

Itō was restrained about continental expansion; it was much more important to focus on economic gain. Yet, one might ask, would he not have supported colonizing territories overseas if they promised to be economically profitable? Concerning Japan itself, he had argued against closing the country to foreign capital. As quoted in Chapter 3, he said:

> Without wealth the culture of the people cannot advance. For patriotism to grow, it should serve the creation of wealth. People say we have to protect the land, but what is the use of protecting it if it remains just barren soil?[59]

More important to him was economic wellbeing. To close the doors to foreign capital would not benefit Japan—or any country—in the long run, he insisted. Let us consider again another remark he made (also quoted in Chapter 3) in connection with this subject:

> European countries and the United States not only have abundant capital but they are rich in knowledge and experience. Some of their people may come to Japan and start enterprises together with Japanese, and others by themselves, and if they start businesses by themselves our people should observe how they do it so that we will be able to compete with them. I believe the competition will advance Japan's commerce and industry and that [Japanese] will benefit greatly from observing the experiences of [Westerners].[60]

As Itō saw it, there was no problem letting powerful Western capital flow in as long as the Japanese also absorbed the knowledge, know-how, and experience that Westerners brought with them. These would, eventually, lead to Japan's industrial growth. More than territory, he gave priority to economic and social advancement driven by the inflow of new knowledge. Behind that way of thinking was Itō's confidence in Japan's well-established government and the constitutional system he himself had built. Governance in China was unstable and unpredictable. Thoughtless expansion into that country, he warned, carried the risk of involvement in political turmoil and heavy damage to Japan's interests.

Nonetheless, some of his speeches made at that time contain remarks that encouraged Japanese cultural expansion into other parts of East Asia. In an address delivered at the Japan Overseas Education Society (Dai Nippon Kaigai Kyōiku Kai) on February 14, 1899, he argued that it was a moral obligation for "our country, a pioneer [of modernization] in Asia to bring 'civilized' (modern) science to China and Korea."[61] In the same speech he advised caution:

> Projects that Japanese are involved in have often been accompanied by disorder in Korea. Lack of discretion on the part of Koreans might be partly responsible, but that is precisely the kind of thing in which they must be guided.[62]

Later, Itō would take charge of government in Korea as its resident-general, regarding himself as an "evangelist of civilization." As we can see in the above speech, these ideas were already growing in his mind in 1899.

Building a nation of commerce

What significance did Itō's experience in China have for his vision of the Seiyūkai party? On this point, to summarize the discussion so far, creating the party was a step toward realizing popular government, something Itō had been trying to achieve since the enactment of the Meiji Constitution. He wanted a system where political demands—demands that arose out of the daily business activities of educated people with skills in practical science—would be heard. The basic idea behind the founding of the Seiyūkai was to create an apparatus to elicit the opinions and demands of the people and transform them into policy.

True to his political gradualism, Itō did not intend the whole nation to participate in government in one leap. What he had in mind, as of 1900, was to rally urban merchants and industrialists first. His vigorous attempt to enlist the influential business leader Shibusawa Eiichi in the nascent Seiyūkai was indicative of the importance Itō placed on this group of people. Itō saw the Japan of the future as a nation founded on industry and commerce. That required businessmen, mobilized throughout Japan from large cities and regional areas, to participate in policy-making. The Seiyūkai was to be the tool of a policy to make his vision for the nation into reality.

Itō's strategy for making Japan a nation of industry, commerce, and international trade, the administration of which he would entrust to the Seiyūkai, can also be seen in his choice of places to visit during his 1899 speaking tour. He went mainly to locations in western Japan and the Hokuriku region of northwestern Honshu. In western Japan, his focus was mainly northern Kyushu, where he anticipated the establishment of a Japan–China trade relationship centering on the Yahata Steel Works and the Daye iron mine. He also aimed to open up new markets in China.

The same intentions applied to his tour in the Hokuriku region. There he visited *habutae* (plain weave) silk-textile factories in Fukui and Kanazawa and inspected ports, strongly suggesting his strategic judgment that the region could become a frontline base for economic expansion into the continent through the export of *habutae* silk. There, too, he voiced his belief that Japan could and should be developed into a nation of commerce. "In the world today the focus of effort in any country is mainly development of trade with other countries . . . the goal of government policy, of foreign policy, is growth of commerce and industry," he said. About the *habutae* silk industry, he commented:[63]

> In recent years, I hear that the production of *habutae* silk has advanced dramatically, and if the product of this fast-growing industry is exported to foreign countries it will certainly benefit people in agriculture. To give an example, I believe that if commerce and industry thrive, that will greatly benefit the agricultural sector of silkworm-raising.

Itō believed that promoting industry and encouraging international trade would bring profit to domestic industry as a whole, agriculture included, thereby making the nation wealthier. The key to the nation's prosperity was to invigorate the activities of people in commerce and industry and let their interests be more directly reflected in government policy. One of his causes was revision of the election law in order to foster channels between business people and government, as well as to build a political party that would give them a forum and include them in the purview of government. In a speech given in the Hokuriku region, Itō expressed this idea as follows:

> Partisan people may see revision of the election law as just a matter of people's rights. In my opinion, however, commerce and industry should not stay at their current level but be encouraged to grow more and more. Thinking of the rise or fall of our nation, I submitted [the proposal for election law revision] in the hope that many representatives from commerce and industry will be sent to the parliament.[64]

The nation he aspired to build through the Seiyūkai was a nation founded on commerce. The tours in China and across Japan were strategic, all part of his strategy for furthering his vision of a nation of commerce through what he considered correct party politics.

Hands off political change in China

In the wake of the Boxer Rebellion, the ensuing invasion of Western armies, and the Russo-Japanese War, a new reform movement surged forth in China out of fear that the country would fall prey to the imperialists. Constitutionalism was one of the central pillars of the late-Qing New Policy (*Qing mo xinzheng*) launched in 1901 as a sweeping modernization movement orchestrated from above.

Constitutional research groups from China

In late 1905, the Qing government dispatched two constitutional research groups overseas, one to Europe and the United States, led by Duan Fang, and the other to Japan, led by Zai Ze. The Zai group stayed in Japan in January and February 1906. Itō continued to enjoy fame as a statesman who had adopted and established the first constitutional system in East Asia, and because of his reputation, the Chinese side sought his counsel when the first research group came to Japan in 1906. They met with him and also attended lectures by Tokyo Imperial University professor Hozumi Yatsuka and other scholars of constitutional law. In December 1907 another group, which was initiated by Yuan Shikai's request to the Chinese emperor, arrived in Japan and conducted constitutional research for over a year.[65] As mentioned earlier, it was Ariga Nagao, who had supported Itō Hirobumi's efforts in constitutional reform through the Imperial Household Research Committee, who contributed greatly to the Chinese group's research at that time. From February 1908 to July 1909, Ariga gave a total of sixty lectures to the group leaders, first Da Shou and then Li Jiaju (who became group leader after Da left Japan in May 1908). The lectures are recorded in "Kensei kōgi" [Lectures on Constitutionalism].

It was at Itō's direction that Ariga lectured to the Chinese research group. When the second group came they asked not only Prime Minister Katsura Tarō, but Itō as well for help. And through Itō's good offices, Ariga served as the lecturer for the second Chinese group.[66]

Itō's doubts about China

At the time when Ariga was giving lectures to Da Shou, Itō Hirobumi was resident-general in Korea, busy with the reform of its government. Did Itō have any plans to try to bring political stability to the East Asian region through guidance in constitutionalism, thus spreading the fruits of the Meiji constitutional system to China and Korea? Just before departing Japan for Harbin—in other words just before he was assassinated—according to Itō Miyoji, Itō Hirobumi was proactive regarding a constitution for China, telling Miyoji, "Next year I will to go to Beijing and will try to help them create a constitutional system for their country."[67]

Contrary to Itō Miyoji's account, however, Itō Hirobumi himself appeared determined to steer clear of involvement in any moves by China to embrace constitutional government. When, in January 1906, he met with Zai Ze, leader of the first research group, he started by supporting the idea of China becoming a constitutional state after the model of Japan, but toward the end of the meeting he made remarks indicating second thoughts. That is, when Zai asked specifically what steps China should take, and in what order, to establish its constitution, Itō began by saying, "That question is too big for me to answer" and then he went on. China's land was vast, he said, with many different peoples, cultures, and languages. Its transportation system was poor, making it difficult for its own people to interact. Being so different from the homogeneous land of Japan, China would have a hard time putting legal institutions in place uniformly throughout the country.[68] In short, Itō voiced doubts that a constitutional system could function well in a country that lacked the homogeneity required for a strong nation-state.

He was worried, moreover, that trying to graft a constitutional system onto a society burdened with the conditions that prevailed in China might invite chaos and disorder instead of good government, and such a scenario could be detrimental to the interests of Japan. By August 1909, Itō bluntly declared in one of his speeches, "I have had doubts from the very beginning about the chances of success for a constitutional system in China":

> In a country like Japan, which has well-developed transportation networks, there is no difficulty convening a parliamentary session every year. We are surrounded on all sides by the sea, for one thing, and water transport is easy and convenient, and our railways make it even easier to get around. In a country like China, however, even though its territory is vast, the railway

network is inferior, maritime transport serves only a part of the country, and people have to use river transport to get into the mountainous interior. How in the world could Chinese leaders summon parliamentary members to assemble within a short period of time?[69]

In addition to the harsh logistics of travel in China, Itō cited the rigidity of the Chinese habit of respecting old institutions. He described Japan's step-by-step progress in constitutional government, which began with local assemblies, to dispassionately observe how difficult it would be for China to shift to a constitutional system. If China were to adopt constitutional government now, he believed, it would end up creating political chaos instead of supporting progress and the damage done could easily reverberate in neighboring countries. In his words:

> How an attempt at constitutional government in China would affect peace in Asia is a most grave concern. Its territory being so immense and its old customs and practices so embedded and resistant to change, its regional governments frail and its transportation systems underdeveloped—is there any chance at all that a set of laws that are at odds with the old customs could be instituted and implemented in any way? If those laws [the constitution] failed to be enforced, what would happen in the enormous country of China lying just across the sea from Japan? I cringe to even to think of it.[70]

Itō was saying, in effect, that constitutional government is better suited to a medium- or small-size country, with a homogeneous population, than to a large-size, multi-ethnic country or empire. To attempt a system that provided for popular participation in government in such a multicultural society would become a source of internal disturbances. In Itō's view, the success, or not, of a constitutional government depended on how it was managed; good management would bring prosperity and inadequate management could cause a country to break apart. He seemed to see constitutionalism as a double-edged sword. Oriented toward the good of the people, Itō's basic concern was how to prevent Japan from being affected by political instability in China, and he concluded that if China tried to install a modern constitution, the results would adversely affect Japan.

Itō remained reluctant to get involved in Chinese political reforms. He believed that the country's institutions were too deeply rooted in the long-held customs of the people to be changed with ease. It would simply take too long and the effects would be too damaging.

Yet, at the very time that the late-Qing political reforms were underway, Itō was on the front lines in the process of institutional reform in Korea, with its society no less traditional than that of China. As its resident-general, Itō had been engaged in the project of modernizing Korea since 1906. Was he saying "yes" to Korean reforms and "not interested" in the case of China? Were Itō's seemingly contradictory ideas and actions the product of a double standard that kept him from imperialistic aggression in one country while facilitating colonization in another? To answer those questions, in the next chapter we will examine the logic behind the way Itō set out to govern Korea.

Notes

1 Letter from Itō to his wife Umeko, dated September 3, 1898, Suematsu 1997, p. 347. It may be noted that the main record of this trip consists of his letters to Umeko.
2 Letter from Itō to his wife Umeko, dated September 13, 1898, *Itō den*, vol. 3, p. 396.
3 Ibid., pp. 396–7.
4 Ding and Zhan 2004, vol. 1, p. 258.
5 Letter from Itō to Umeko, dated September 26, 1898, *Itō den*, vol. 3, p. 399.
6 Wang 1987, p. 103.
7 Letter from Itō to Umeko, dated September 26, 1898, *Itō den*, vol. 3, p. 399.
8 *Gaikō*, vol. 31 (1), p. 697.
9 Suematsu 1997, p. 352.
10 Masuda 1996, vol. 1, pp. 238–9.
11 Kikuchi 2005, p. 107. On Itō and the 1898 coup, see also Peng 1976, Chapter 5.
12 Kikuchi 2005, p. 107.
13 Zhang Zhidong, "Kang Youwei zhi shishi" [Facts about Kang Youwei], *Gaikō*, vol. 31 (1), p. 738.
14 The amanuensis of the record is Mori Taijirō (pen name Kainan), the secretary who always accompanied Itō on his travels. Itō greatly enjoyed writing *kanshi*, or classical Chinese-style verse, and Mori was an eminent *kanshi* poet. Mori was charged among other things with touching up Itō's poems.
15 Itō was convinced of this from very early in his career. During his 1882–3 tour in Europe to study constitutions, for example, he expressed this idea: "To reshape the mindset of the people, there is no way but to start with reform of school [and university] education," as cited earlier, in Chapter 2; Letter to Inoue Kaoru dated October 22, 1882, *Itō den*, vol. 2, pp. 320–1.
16 At that time Itō expanded on this point as follows:

> The main duty [of the government] is to adopt methods that will help people develop sources of moneymaking on their own initiative. It should be known that when the people are wealthy, the country is enriched. Customs duties are no more than a means of transferring part of private assets to the coffers of the state. It is a serious mistake to regard customs duties as the source of a nation's wealth.

17 Itō Akio 1977, pp. 26–7.
18 "Itō-kō no Shinkoku kyōiku dan" [Marquis Itō's Account of Chinese Education], *Kokumin shinbun*, September 29, 1898; Peng 1976, p. 292.
19 Murata 1992, p. 32.
20 *Enzetsushū*, vol. 1, pp. 181–2.
21 *Meiji tennō-ki*, vol. 9, p. 560.
22 *Gaikō*, vol. 31 (part 1), p. 679.
23 Hirano 2007, p. 286.
24 Ding and Zhan 2004, vol. 1, pp. 265 ff.
25 Hazama 1999.
26 Hayashi 2002, pp. 92–3.
27 Takeuchi Hiroyuki, "Ryō Keichō no Kō Yūi e no nyūmon jūgaku o megutte" [Liang Qichao's Study under Kang Youwei], in Hazama 1999, p. 27. With regard to ideological differences between Kang and Liang, see Murata 1992.
28 Hayashi 2002, p. 95.
29 Letter from Itō to Yamagata, dated February 12, 1899, *Yamagata monjo*, vol. 1, p. 125.
30 "Itō monjo," no. 378.
31 Onogawa 1969, p. 146.
32 Tao 2007, p. 80.
33 For a substantial study of Odagiri, see Yu 1998.
34 Hiratsuka 1969.
35 *Segai den*, vol. 5, p. 297.

36 Letter from Kishida Ginkō to Itō, dated August 22, 1898, *Itō monjo* (Hanawa), vol. 4, p. 317.
37 *Gaikō*, vol. 31 (part 1), p. 726.
38 *Itō den*, vol. 3, pp. 401–2.
39 Letter from Odagiri to Itō, dated March 23, 1899, *Itō monjo* (Hanawa), vol. 3, p. 197.
40 *Quanxue pian*, Outer Chapters, "Yizhi diyi 1," Kawajiri 1994, p. 7. I drew on this essay by Kawajiri for Zhang's thought and his place in those times.
41 *Quanxue pian*, Outer Chapters, "Shexue 3," Nishi 1997, vol. 2, p. 112.
42 Kawajiri 1994, pp. 7–8.
43 Nishi 1997, vol. 2, pp. 115 ff.
44 Murata 1992, pp. 33–4.
45 Gu 1995, p. 19.
46 Ministry of Agriculture and Commerce 1917, p. 9 and Saigusa and Iida 1957, p. 257.
47 Hu 1967.
48 Yu 1998, p. 202. In 1900 when Japan again proposed a further acquisition of concessions of the Daye iron mine, Zhang Zhidong, wanting to save face for Itō, agreed although with the condition that the maximum amount of iron ore supplied to Japan be limited to 50,000 tons. Wu 2009, vol. 2, p. 619.
49 *Enzetsushū*, vol. 2, p. 171.
50 Ibid., vol. 1, p. 206.
51 ibid., vol. 2, pp. 171–2.
52 Ibid., vol. 1, pp. 200–1.
53 Ibid., vol. 2, p. 36.
54 Ibid., p. 36, May 13, 1899 speech at reception held by Bakan businessmen's group.
55 Ibid., pp. 205–6, May 20, 1899 speech in Fukuoka.
56 Ibid., p. 211.
57 *Tōkyō nichinichi shinbun*, November 10, 1899.
58 *Enzetsushū*, vol. 2, p. 214.
59 *Tōkyō nichinichi shinbun*, November 15, 1899; see Chapter 3, p. 90.
60 *Enzetsushū* 1899, vol. 2, pp. 181–2.
61 Ibid., vol. 1, pp. 204–5.
62 Ibid., p. 206.
63 Speech given at Shōshūkan hall in the city of Fukui, as reported in *Tōkyō nichinichi shinbun*, October 19, 1899.
64 *Tōkyō nichinichi shinbun*, October 19, 1899.
65 Xiong 1998 and Soda 2009.
66 Itō Miyoji 1910.
67 Ibid.
68 Xiong 1998, p. 137.
69 *Hiroku*, vol. 2, p. 250.
70 Ibid., pp. 251–2.

7 Fostering governance in two countries

Itō's dual role and the resident-generalship

In Chapter 5 we discussed Itō's 1907 constitutional reforms in Japan. From 1903, as reappointed president of the Imperial Household Research Committee, he had set out to establish a modern imperial household system, but he was also working on reforms to achieve a national system of responsible government centered on the cabinet. Itō's main objective was to strengthen the cabinet and it is likely that he used the committee as a cover for that purpose.

Meanwhile, in March 1906, Itō had been appointed the first resident-general in Korea and since then had been hard at work on policy for its governance as a protectorate. In July 1907, Japan's Korea policy underwent a major change following the "Hague Secret Emissary Affair." Korean emperor Gojong, in order to draw the world's attention to Japan's action in making Korea a protectorate and to protest at the illegality of this maneuver, had secretly sent three representatives to the Second Peace Conference in The Hague, which was being held between June 15 and October 18. Gojong's plan was thwarted when the envoys were refused access to the conference, and in the face of the outraged response of the Japanese government, and Itō as well, Gojong was forced to abdicate. In the wake of these events, the Third Japan–Korea Treaty was signed in late July, giving the Japanese resident-general wide authority in Korean domestic administration, including the power to approve legislation and administrative sanctions and appoint and dismiss government officials. The Korean military was disbanded the following month and Japan essentially annexed Korea that year.[1]

Thus 1907 was a pivotal year in the establishment of Japanese rule in Korea and was undoubtedly a busy time for Resident-General Itō. In addition to governing Korea, as president of the Imperial Household Research Committee he was simultaneously leading the effort to make government reforms in Japan.

This chapter focuses on Itō's administration of Korea, the final stage of his career as a statesman. A career that had been brilliant to that point ended with a phase that is remembered as disgraceful. When he had first visited Korea, it had been as a high-profile figure acclaimed for the prodigious feat of transforming Japan into a constitutional state. As it turned out, instead of continuing his achievements in that noble intention, he is judged to have paved the way for

Japan's annexation of Korea and thereby orchestrated the prelude to Japan's expansion into the continent. For that role (on October 26, 1909) he was assassinated in Harbin, Manchuria by An Jun-geun (1879–1910), a member of the Korean independence movement. It may have been the terrorist act of an independence activist, but ever since, Itō has been a symbol of Japan's colonization of Korea.

Itō's governance in Korea as resident-general has long been regarded as a part of the process of colonizing Korea—a passive interpretation that sees little in what he did besides laying the groundwork for annexation of that country. Some scholars have attempted to dig deeper, to question that assumption, and to understand more about his administration there,[2] but the conventional view that he spearheaded the Korean annexation is still deep-seated.

Based on an examination of primary historical sources that shed light on the inner layers of Itō's thinking and strategy for the administration of Korea, the conclusions of the present study diverge from the commonly held views. Of specific interest here is how the idea of governing Korea was incorporated into his grand vision of the Japanese state—the idea upon which he pursued his activities for constitutional reform in his role as the president of Japan's Imperial Household Research Committee—and how that idea fit into the overall framework of his thinking. Even while he was resident-general of Korea, Itō was also president of the committee, so he was therefore involved in core administration-building in both Korea and Japan. One individual was spearheading government reform at the same time in two different countries. The questions I would like to examine here are: Were the two reform projects linked to each other? If so, how?

Before addressing these questions, we may well also ask, why did Committee President Itō become resident-general of Korea in the first place? Was it because, as many have argued, he was driven by the ambition to become the first head of a new agency.[3] Or did he have a clear plan that led to the colonization of Korea? Or, alternatively, was there some other reason? Let us start by looking at how Itō became the resident-general of Korea.

1904 proposal and the First Japan–Korea Treaty

In March 1904, soon after the outbreak of the Russo-Japanese War, Itō visited Korea. The official reason for his visit was to inquire after the Korean emperor's wellbeing, but the real purpose was to persuade him to go along with Japan's policy toward Korea and to cooperate with Japan. He presented the Japanese viewpoint, which was that a primary cause of the war was Japan's determination to protect Korea from Russia, and that Japan therefore expected Korea to work with Japan. To that end he met with Emperor Gojong on March 18 and March 20. Their previous meeting had been five years earlier in August 1898, when they met during Itō's Korea–China tour. At that time, Itō had received a hearty welcome, but this time their meetings were filled with tension. Itō presented a ten-point proposal to Gojong. The six major points of that proposal recommended that Korea should: (1) move toward reforming government and society based on the model of Europe and the United States to achieve self-reliance and thereby contribute to securing peace in East Asia; (2) not expel foreign nations and religions or adopt a stance opposed to Western civilization; (3) take measures to either adjust or abolish old manners, customs, and practices that would hinder the survival of the country; (4) these points having been the principles that Japan has followed over the last thirty-or-so years, China and Korea should follow suit, taking a path that leads to a stronger Korea moving in harmony with Western civilization; (5) drive the presence of Russia, which aims to invade our countries on the pretense of being a "Western" culture, from the region; (6) in view of the recent development of transportation facilities and the more active international communication that it is enabling, Korea too should develop the civilized modes of interaction through the "exchange of tangible and intangible things and expansion of production of goods necessary for people's lives, gradually increasing wealth and thereby achieving greater independence . . . and ensuring the survival of the country through competition," and should never let barbaric elements use violence and obstruct those efforts.[4]

Itō may have had the underlying motive of justifying the war with Russia that had just broken out, but still, these items sound today like a paean to "civilization." Five years earlier he had been welcomed in Korea as the standard-bearer of a new civilization; in 1904 he returned as an out-and-out evangelist for civilization.

Thus began the fateful relationship between Itō Hirobumi and Korea, Itō having positioned himself as the advocate of civilization. Leaving Emperor Gojong to meditate upon this discourse on civilization, Itō returned to Japan on April 1. After that, the Japanese government moved forward steadily with steps that would lead to Korea becoming a protectorate. A "General Plan for Korea" (Tai-Kan Shisetsu Kōryō), passed by the Japanese cabinet on May 31 (1904), stated that Japan would be vested with the "real power of protection over Korea in political and military affairs." It also provided for Japanese supervision not only of Korea's diplomatic affairs, but also its finances, railways, means of communication, and Japanese control over land development. From the outset, Japanese policy vis-à-vis Korea was intended to include control over the country's administration. This will be made abundantly clear later as we discuss Itō's governance as resident-general.

The First Japan–Korea Treaty of August 1904 stipulated the appointment of a Japanese financial advisor and a diplomatic advisor selected from among third power nationals recommended by the Japanese government. According to that provision, Megata Tanetarō, director-general of the Tax Bureau of the Japanese Ministry of Finance, and Durham Stevens (1851–1908), an American hired by the Japanese Ministry of Foreign Affairs, were appointed as financial and diplomatic advisors respectively. By that time, people in Japanese political circles seem to have assumed that Korea would be made a protectorate. Hara Takashi, for example, wrote in his diary that when he visited Navy Minister Yamamoto Gonnohyōe at the naval ministry, they "discussed our Korea policy in passing. There was absolutely no other way than to make [Korea] a protectorate." At that time Hara heard from Yamamoto and Saionji Kinmochi about Itō's scheduled trip to Korea, and wrote in his diary, "If [Itō] is resolved to determine the destiny of Korea, that is a very good thing; otherwise he's going to end up a failure like Count Inoue [Kaoru] did some years ago."

Inoue Kaoru, Itō's long-time ally, had been posted in Korea for about a half year, starting in October 1894, during which he had been working on guiding reforms in Korean government administration (the second round of the Gabo Reform of 1894–6). No sooner had he gone back to Japan in June 1895, however, than Emperor Gojong issued an edict nullifying the reforms and reversing everything Inoue had done. Hara's diary suggests that he and other informed political leaders had been speculating that Itō was going to Korea to finish something of great importance, something Inoue had tried to do but failed, and that Itō would take charge of governing the protectorate.[5]

Second Japan–Korea Treaty

On April 8, 1905 the cabinet formally determined that Japan had the right to establish a protectorate over Korea.[6] After Russia recognized that right at the Portsmouth Peace Conference, Japan set about making full-fledged plans to turn Korea into a protectorate. Then Itō visited Korea again. This time, too, the ostensible reason was to inquire after the Korean emperor's wellbeing, but his real task was to sign the Second Japan–Korea Treaty (called the Eulsa Protectorate Treaty in Korea) that would give Japan the right to declare Korea a protectorate of Japan. On November 15, he met with Emperor Gojong and pressed him to entrust Japan with the handling of Korean diplomatic affairs. Gojong protested that such an action would reduce Korea to a status similar to Hungary vis-à-vis Austria.[7] Itō responded that Hungary had no emperor, that Gojong would remain Korea's emperor, and that Korea would "undergo no change in its national polity."[8]

Gojong tried to protest further, "I cannot decide this matter myself right now. I need to consult government officials and also to ascertain the will of the people." Itō dismissed that response:

> Yours is not a constitutional government. Your country is an absolute monarchy where the emperor decides everything, is it not? But you talk about the will of the people, et cetera, and I surmise that you are thinking of instigating your people to oppose Japan's proposal.[9]

In 1897, the Empire of Korea had replaced the Joseon dynasty (1392–1897), and in his retort to Gojong, Itō was exploiting a new Korean law legitimizing despotic rule by the emperor (Article 2). He also knew that the emperor was suspected of secretly giving instructions and funds to the Korean anti-Japanese movement operating in the wings outside government circles.

Gojong's reply was vague and evasive. He tried to get around the negotiations. On November 17, Itō visited the imperial court three times, but Gojong refused to see him on the grounds of ill health. Instead the emperor ordered his cabinet ministers to "negotiate and reach a compromise." Seizing the opportunity to exploit the imperial order to "reach a compromise," Itō forced the Korean ministers to agree to the protectorate treaty.[10] The last resistance Gojong managed to make was to insert a sentence preceding the text of the treaty: "We agree to the provisions below until the objective of enriching and strengthening Korea begins to bear fruit." Itō accepted that wording and took up a brush to write it in himself.[11]

The Second Japan–Korea Treaty stipulated that the resident-general would be stationed in Seoul as the representative of the Japanese government "to manage solely foreign policy matters" (Article 3). This provision stated the official position, but the Japanese government had different intentions—its leaders were resolved to gain control over Korea's domestic administration. According to the Hara diary entry cited above, Itō appears to have been eager to take up the post of resident-general and to govern Korea. On November 19, right after the treaty was signed, Itō received a request from Prime Minister Katsura Tarō to draft the Residency-General Organization Ordinance:

> Now that the Korean protectorate treaty has been concluded, an Imperial ordinance concerning the Residency-General and the Residency needs to be issued as soon as possible. Please send me Your Excellency's opinion by telegram as promised.[12]

Itō set about drafting the organization ordinance. Describing the process of drafting, he wrote:

> Since I reported on the 8th of this month [December] after returning [from Korea], I met with cabinet ministers and *genrō* elders and then decided on *the major direction for our policy toward Korea*. I began drafting the organization ordinance, instructions, and other items for the Residency-General and got them all ready within two or three days. After consultations with the Privy Council, the Imperial proclamation was finished and the core members of the Residency-General appointed. So now we have accomplished the first step.[13] (emphasis added)

The ordinance on the organization of the residency-general and the residency was issued on December 21. With that, Itō's "major direction for our policy toward Korea" was transmitted into action.

Control over the Japanese garrison in Korea

Despite the direct involvement of such a prominent political figure as Itō, the particulars of the residency-general caused considerable controversy in some quarters of the Japanese leadership. The target of attack was Article 4 of the ordinance:

> Organization Ordinance on the Residency-General and the Residency
>
> Article 4 The Resident-General may order the Commander of the [Japanese] garrison in Korea to use force when he considers it necessary to maintain peace and order in Korea.

This gave the resident-general the authority to give orders to the commander of the Japanese garrison stationed in Korea. In itself, that was perhaps a sensible measure, given the rapidly rising anti-Japanese sentiment in Korea following the protectorate treaty. The problem was that resident-generalship was going to be filled by Itō, who was a civilian.

Field Marshall Yamagata Aritomo had been kept informed of developments in Korea by Hasegawa Yoshimichi (1850–1924), commander of the garrison in Korea. On November 27 (Itō was still in Korea), about three weeks before the residency-general organization ordinance had been issued, Yamagata spoke his mind to Army Minister Terauchi Masatake, "To appoint a military officer as resident-general would be the most suitable thing to do at this time."[14] The army contingent had long assumed that the resident-general of Korea would be an army man, and Itō had pushed that choice aside and taken the post himself.[15]

As soon as Itō had been appointed resident-general on December 21, Hasegawa wrote to Terauchi in Tokyo, saying:

> Article 4 states that the Resident-General can *order* the Commander to send out troops. Is the Commander then directly subordinate to the Resident-General? Even the commanders of divisions are under the direct authority of the Emperor. So are the commanders of armies, of course. Does the Resident-General have the authority to control the Commander [of the Japanese troops in Korea], who also comes immediately under the Emperor? I believe no one except the Emperor does.[16]

The critical issue was whether it was in any way possible for the military, which was directly subordinate to the emperor, to be bound to obey the orders of the resident-general. In another era—in the 1930s and early 1940s—even the suggestion of such a thing would have been tossed aside as an infringement on the power of the supreme command. The fact that Itō was able to override such voices of protest from the army in late 1905 was because of directives that came from the emperor.

On January 14, 1906, the Meiji emperor summoned Army Minister Terauchi Masatake and Chief of the Army General Staff Ōyama Iwao and told them he was giving Resident-General Itō the authority to employ the garrison in Korea. You must see to it, he said to them, that the garrison is used in accordance with the national defense strategy. The imperial order proved very effective. Garrison Commander Hasegawa was left with no choice but to accept control by the resident-general. In a letter to Terauchi, he said, "Inasmuch as the order has been given by His Majesty the Emperor, how can I disagree?"[17] When Itō arrived in Seoul on March 2, he took up the single post that, under the Meiji Constitution, gave a civil official the authority of command over the army, and he had created that post himself.

Itō's reasons

Reviewing all the events that led up to Itō's assumption of the post of resident-general, we can see two possible reasons why he, first, created the post, and then stepped into it himself. One was his concern for the "civilization" or modernization of Korea, and the other was the matter of control over the Japanese army.

Since his Korea–China tour of 1898, Itō had apparently been increasingly aware of Japan as a pioneer in modernization in East Asia. His involvement in China's affairs had been limited. He was convinced of the importance of the Chinese market, but, certain that China's political chaos was not going to subside for some time, he deliberately avoided getting involved.

Not long after he returned to Japan, however, he began actively talking about Japan's moral obligation to take the lead in the modernization of East Asia. Chapter 6 briefly mentions the speech he made on February 14, 1899 at the invitation of the Japan Overseas Education Society (Dai Nippon Kaigai Kyōiku Kai), an organization that set up and ran the Keijō Gakudō (Seoul Academy) and other schools to further Japanese language education in Korea. In that address he said:

> When we speak of education overseas, we must consider the need not only to educate Koreans but Chinese as well. To introduce modern science from our country is not only fairly easy for them, it will also be effective quite quickly. Further, from our point of view, if our country, a pioneer in modernization in East Asia, provides guidance to China, which has vast lands and a large population but whose modern sciences are still immature, it would benefit us as well. Our help in such things will, in the long run, bring greater wellbeing to both sides. Also, we should be aware that our country is morally obligated to do so.[18]

The audience was made up of people involved in the promotion of education in Korea, and they may have been somewhat bewildered to hear Itō urging them to extend their activities to China. That part of his speech was probably prompted by his thoughts of the knowledge-hungry intellectuals he had come into contact with in China in 1898, such as Liang Qichao and Zhang Zhidong. Essentially, however, at that moment Itō was giving voice to his sense of mission to spread "civilization" in East Asia. We have also seen how a few years later, in March 1904, right after the outbreak of the Russo-Japanese War, Itō tried to inspire Emperor Gojong with the allure of "civilization." Two years after that, Itō landed on the Korean peninsula as resident-general, all set to put his words into action to bring "civilization" to the Koreans.

The other reason that Itō worked on setting up the residency-generalship, and then took it on himself, had to do with his determination to gain control over the army. A noteworthy recent interpretation of how command of the garrison was given to the resident-general explains it in the context of conflicting plans for the future. In that view,[19] it was a consequence of a confrontation between Itō and the army and between Itō and new-generation bureaucrats, such as Katsura Tarō, Komura Jutarō, and Gotō Shinpei, over Japan's policy toward the continent and the plan for Korean annexation. The resident-general's right to control the army is seen as a means, not an end. Can we not say, however, that gaining and using that right was, for Itō, itself an end, not a means? That is the perspective taken in this book, the aim of which is to reconstruct Itō's thinking during his career.

What is crucial to consider in that context is the matter of constitutional reform in Japan. At that time, Itō was concurrently president of the Imperial Household Research Committee in Japan. Not long after he became resident-general he formulated the Kōshikirei Order, which was intended to give the cabinet control over military administrative affairs, among other constitutional reforms. His effort to restrain the army invited a backlash, and the upshot was the establishment of the military ordinance law. Around the same time, Itō was seeking to put the Japanese troops in Korea under his control. It seems to me that these reforms relating to the government–army relationship in Japan and Korea can be understood as different dimensions of the same intention. Below, we will re-examine Itō's approach to governing Korea, from these perspectives—civilization and control over the army.

The showdown with Confucian tradition

Itō hoped to make Japan a nation of civilized people and he considered nation-building in collaboration with the people to be the central task of civilized government. What about Korea? What was the philosophy with which he set about governing the protectorate of Korea?

Philosophy of government in Korea

One day in October 1906, Nitobe Inazō (1862–1933), educator, agricultural economist, and author of *Bushido: The Soul of Japan* (1900), went to see Itō at the request of Kiuchi Jūshirō (1866–1925), the person in charge of agriculture, commerce, and industry at the residency-general. Nitobe hoped to persuade Itō to promote Japanese emigration to Korea. The first thing Itō said was, "There seems to be a lot of enthusiasm for bringing people from Japan into Korea, but I am opposed to the idea." Nitobe protested, "But what possibility is there of Koreans developing this country by themselves?" To this Itō is said to have replied:

> Koreans are a great people, you know. In the history of their country there was a period when it was far more advanced than Japan. There is no reason that people with such a history cannot run their country themselves. They are in no way less competent than we are. They are not to blame for the circumstances they are in today. It's their government's fault. If only their country is governed well, then the people will not lack, qualitatively or quantitatively.[20]

What Nitobe recorded was Itō's vision of the potential of the Korean people for self-government, and his hope to develop that potential as far as possible so they could achieve this. To that end, Itō placed top priority on political reform in Korea, believing that reform would work by itself to advance the civilization of its people. Let us examine the content of Itō's "civilization" policy.

Itō's statements and specific instructions at the start of his tenure as resident-general may be accessed through the Council for Korean Administration Reform, the forum where Itō convened and presided over Korean cabinet ministers' meetings. The record of the proceedings of the "cabinet meetings" held there is included in volume six of *Nik-Kan gaikō shiryō shūsei* [Collected Materials Related to Japanese–Korean Relations], edited by Kim Chong-myong.[21] I have attempted to reconstruct Itō's philosophy on the governing of Korea, drawing mainly on his remarks recorded in the council.

Although officially, Japan's control of Korea was confined to diplomatic powers and foreign relations, the General Plan for Korea adopted by the cabinet in May 1904 makes it clear that the Japanese government had decided long before to place a wide range of its administrative and economic affairs, including finance, infrastructure, and industry under its direct control. In taking up his assignment in Korea, Itō justified the usurpation of Korea's powers as a nation by regarding himself as a "missionary of civilization." His was the task, he held, of guiding Koreans to modernize, to become a "civilized" people. During the first days after he became resident-general he declared, "I have assumed this post because I want to bring Korea into the ranks of the civilized countries of the world."[22]

Democracy, rule of law, gradualism

In explaining to Koreans specifically what he meant by "civilized country," Itō focused on three elements: democracy, rule of law, and gradualism. To him, democracy meant popular government, a notion he kept coming back to during his constitutional campaign tours in Japan. He brought up the same idea again and again in Korea, too. When, in a private audience with Emperor Gojong on March 25, 1906, only a few days after Itō took office, the emperor asked, "What do you think Korea should do to develop its power and prosper?" Itō replied, "The only thing you can do is rely on the resources of your people."[23] Later, he spoke to the Korean cabinet ministers about people-oriented governance, saying, "The government's primary objective must be to favor the people. The government has no choice but to stop obsessing over ways to favor the bureaucracy."[24] In one sense, Itō saw no difference between governance in Japan and governance in Korea, for, in both, the people had to pursue civilization, to modernize, in order for the nation to advance and to increase production and promote industry. That aspect of Itō's philosophy was similar to the idea of democracy embedded in the Confucian idea of benevolent rule, or the way of the king (*wangdao*).[25]

In the same audience with Emperor Gojong, Itō referred to the second element, the rule of law. If the economic power of the people is to grow, he said:

> It is essential above all to ensure the safety of their lives and property. . . . If people's lives and property are constantly in danger of loss or damage due to greedy and corrupt government officials they will never be able to concentrate on their work and increase their wealth.[26]

This was a call for restraints on the arbitrary abuse of state power. His message was clear: without the rule of law, a country cannot hope to achieve a people-oriented government and cannot expect to grow stronger as a nation.

Itō firmly believed that the rule of law was the norm in the civilized world, and he did not accept policies that deviated from this.[27] Under such government, Koreans could shed the old ways of sycophantism to bureaucrats and officials, its people would grow into self-reliance, and Korea would achieve autonomy and independence. These ideas filled Itō's mind and his statements, at least during the early phase of his time as resident-general.

His approach to realizing them, of course, was gradualism. At the first meeting of the Council for Korean Administration Reform, talking about reforms in the Korean education system, he said, "It's no good to start out with a plan for drastic reform, because it will only fail." Instead he counseled the group to "devise plans for small reforms at the beginning that can then be gradually expanded."[28]

Gradualism was the very fiber of Itō's being as a statesman. It marked his political style: having a broad, firm vision of the big reforms needed, he would carry them out slowly, in steps, careful always to watch and calculate current trends.[29] That was the way he had pressed forward in introducing constitutionalism in Japan, and he went about governing Korea in the same way. He respected Korea's existing order and values wherever possible, even as he sought gradually to make Korea a modern nation. However, while his gradualist approach was effective in establishing a parliamentary system in Japan, it created confusion in Korea. That is one of the aspects of his rule in Korea that we will now consider in looking at Itō's policy for education there.

Enthusiasm for educational reform

From the outset, Resident-General Itō demonstrated his enthusiasm for educational reform. "Improving education costs money and takes time, but if we don't start we can't expect any results. We need to start the education project as soon as we can."[30] The extent to which the role and importance of education occupied Itō's mind in governing Korea offers yet another glimpse into his mindset at that time.

At the first session of the Council for Korea Administration Reform, Itō stressed the importance of education to his administration of Korea. Two major effects of education, he said, would be to facilitate military conscription and create taxpayers. "To implement military conscription . . . requires more widespread education and the cultivation of knowledge."[31] Further, "children who are educated will have a natural understanding of why people must pay taxes."[32] The idea behind these pronouncements on improved education was the creation of a loyal people who would fulfill their obligations to the state.

One could say that Itō tried to use education to create a governable people. But, as we will recall from his February 1889 speech to the Japanese peerage, he was well aware that creating a better-educated population could be a double-edged sword for the ruler. The ideal population to govern was not only willing to pay taxes to the state but also had a strong public spirit and kept a watchful eye on how their taxes were used. His vision for Korea was very much in that mold.

At the council meeting in December 1908, Itō said: "As I see it, people in all the provinces of Korea are abandoning the old custom of kowtowing to government officials ... That is a sign that confidence in what we call people's rights is beginning to take hold."³³ This remark cannot be interpreted as just bluffing. He thought that as they grew better educated, people would naturally become increasingly aware of their rights and start denouncing corrupt government officials. And as a result, he continued, "Officials who behave badly will become steadily fewer."³⁴ He warned, nonetheless, that with the rise of a more enlightened people, the way they are ruled must become more rational, too. This was his line of thinking in governing Japan, and it was no different in the case of Korea.

As for content, Itō saw education as a means to create the human resources needed to promote industry and create social and economic benefits. At the council's December 1908 session he described something from his own experience:

> I started studying the Chinese classics as a little boy and learned about the golden age of the Zhou dynasty [eleventh–third century BCE]. And when I visited the West for the first time and witnessed the formidable development of Western culture and institutions, I saw the genuine Way of Zhou being practiced there. I thought that was the way a state should be.³⁵

Itō carried that impression with him when he went back to Japan from Europe. To the council members this was an exhortation to free Korea from traditional East Asian learning, based on the Chinese classics, and shape a new social structure based on Western learning.

Western science was practical science that brought tangible benefits to society; this, Itō said, just as he had argued in Japan, must be the model for education in Korea, too. Education must be useful, socially applicable, and equip people to succeed in business and industry. Only through education could people rise out of their threadbare existence.

Combatting the influence of Confucianism

Itō's views on education allowed no tolerance for Korean traditional knowledge revolving around Confucianism. He criticized it as socially harmful and irredeemably anachronistic.

In July 1906, Itō denounced Emperor Gojong on several counts: in a letter the emperor had called him "Marquis" Itō instead of "Resident-General"; a document had been discovered that contained the phrase "island barbarian enemies Itō and Hasegawa" uttered by Gojong; and the Korean imperial court had made contact with and provided funds to rioters. He compelled Gojong to agree to the formation of an investigation committee charged with reforming the Korean court, and he ordered restrictions that would regulate and oversee the comings and goings of people in the imperial court.³⁶

This was one of the ways by which he sought to keep Confucian scholars away from the court, reform the governing structure of Korea, and change the attitude of the ruling class. Itō regarded the Confucian teachings embraced by the Korean elite as nefarious, empty theory that was bringing ruin to the country. Koreans were being left behind in the world, reduced to a condition of misery, almost entirely "because of their [excessive] respect for those ancient teachings." Abolish them, he said:

> Today, people with their eyes open follow the way of civilization so that they can increase the wealth of the country and the wellbeing of the people; to abandon such harmful and useless ancient customs would be an act of loyalty that would benefit Korea, would it not?[37]

From the Korean perspective, however, this was deeply disturbing. It had long been the duty of a "man of virtue" to invite Confucian scholars and listen to their words.[38] "Receiving scholars warmly is an old custom in our country."[39] Each country has its system of knowledge and intellectuals to consult in order to justify and rationalize the way it is governed. In that sense we can talk about "knowledge as a constitutional factor."[40] In Korea, for many centuries, that knowledge had been Confucianism.

Itō sharply dismissed any such protests from the Korean side. His retort:

> No matter that scholars may go and dwell deep in the mountains and valleys, no matter how long they may meditate before the trees, how can they possibly get any idea of what is going on in the world and become clear-sighted enough to understand how to manage a modern state. . . . Instead of inviting a Confucian scholar who has been secluded on some faraway mountain to discuss national administration, you would do better to search for, find, and discuss it with the ashes of Confucius.[41]

In his private life Itō was a literary type who had a deep attachment to the Chinese classics. But he believed it intolerable for the official organization of government to be swept along by such a premodern system of thought. To Itō, a viable state in the modern world had to be founded on Western knowledge of science. Confucian teaching came out of the Zhou dynasty, an archaic political and social system that arose back in the mists of Chinese time. To cling to that ancient discourse as if it were infallible and to try in today's world to form judgments based on it was the height of anachronism. Confucian scholars, Itō remarked, "are simply unable to deal actively with the changes of the times."[42]

It was not just Confucian scholars that Itō wanted to banish. One of the incidents that prompted him to regulate who came and went at the court concerned an unsuccessful attempt by Gojong to invite Iino Kichisaburō (1867–1944), the leader of a new Japanese religion, to the court. Iino, a self-styled oracle, had made many predictions about the progress of the Russo-Japanese War and had won the admiration of Japanese military leaders, including Kodama Gentarō, chief of the general staff of Japan's Manchuria Army during the war, and Tōgō Heihachirō, commander-in-chief of the Japanese Combined Fleet. Later, for a certain period of time, Iino used his "divine power" to gain a measure of influence in Japanese political circles, acquiring a reputation as a kind of Japanese

Rasputin. Emperor Gojong heard unfounded chatter about how Iino's influence was strong enough that Itō, Yamagata, and other *genrō* elders would prostrate themselves before him. Thinking this might be a way to control Itō, Gojong had sent a secret messenger to invite Iino to the court.[43]

Itō said of Iino, "He may not be a fortuneteller, but neither his scientific knowledge nor his personality has any value at all." So it must have irritated Itō that Gojong thought Iino was the "most far-sighted intellectual who ever lived." Perhaps more infuriating was the rumor that Iino looked down on "Yamagata, Itō, and other elder statesmen as they knelt and obeyed his instructions."[44] In addition to Confucian scholars, others like "unruly women diviners" frequented the court, making it extremely difficult to push the emperor toward modern, enlightened thinking. With its mélange of odd characters, the Korean court seemed to Itō like an "abode of evil."[45] The ban on free entry into the court was a symbol of Itō's determination to cleanse the court and every other public space not just of Confucianism but every old custom and replace them with scientific knowledge based on the model of the West. It was a metaphor for Itō's endeavor to install what he considered to be the ideal way of governing Korea and his strategy of bringing the Korean court up to date, making it a beacon of enlightened people going forward in a new civilization.

Limited funds

"Civilization" meant the spiritual and intellectual modernization of the Korean people as much as it did material and economic modernization. Educational reform and new kinds of knowledge were therefore among Itō's top priorities.

Some say that Itō's education policy, although it received great public acclaim, was not actually given that much importance. Even if that appears to be the case, it was not because Itō was just making empty pronouncements. Rather, it reflects how delicate an issue educational reform in Korea was. Itō understood that changing the heart and soul of education involved adjustments in the mental and emotional make-up of people, which can never happen overnight. It had to be an extended step-by-step process that would take a long time. Itō's preferred approach, and his only choice, was gradualism, and that remained a consistent element in his policy throughout his tenure in Korea:

> I do not put much hope in the Koreans of today, but as we build schools and educate Koreans of future generations, we will see a vast difference in every respect between those who received education and those who did not. A steady, slow spread of education over many years will eventually make all Koreans into a civilized people.[46]

This was part of a speech he made to the Korean cabinet ministers in June 1908. By that time the anti-Japanese movement had grown so active that his protectorate policy was stymied. But he did not abandon his vision of making the Koreans "a civilized people" some time in the future through the "steady, step-by-step spread of education."

Regardless of policy, the realization of educational reform in Korea did not proceed as Itō had envisioned. The factors that shaped his gradualist policy and eventually frustrated it were financial, human, and social.

At the first session of the Council for Korea Administration Reform, Itō made it clear that his approach to education reform would be gradualist, and he also identified the problems he foresaw. "What we need most is funds, followed by teachers and textbooks,"[47] Itō said. Funds for the reform of education and the necessary human and material resources to launch it were short. Another issue concerned the social conditions that would affect the new type of education.

Regarding funds, Itō expressly ruled out the option of getting education-related revenues from Korean society to finance the reform. He was able to come up with an interest-free loan from Japan. The council's first session agreed to receive ten million yen from the Japanese government to use for the "promotion of industry." Since the fund included an amount to be used for educational improvement, Japan ended up financing the educational reform in Korea.

Of the ten-million-yen fund, only 500,000 yen was allotted for the improvement of education, however. "Education improvement" was given no place in the aforementioned General Plan for Korea, which had been formulated by the Japanese government in May 1904 as a guideline for governing Korea. We can presume, therefore, that the council hesitated to take out of the Japanese loan a larger amount and put it into education when no such allocation had been stipulated in the General Plan. However it came about, the educational reform had to begin with very limited financing.

Double standard vis-à-vis local traditions

As for teachers and textbooks, I will focus on the former. Itō remarked, "Right now there are not many teachers. No matter how many schools we may build, if we don't have qualified teachers, it will be like painting a dragon with its eyes missing."[48] Indeed, the shortage of teachers was a big factor limiting how far Itō could implement his education policy. Beyond the numerical shortage of teachers, of greater concern to Itō was their quality and attitude. He instructed Japanese teachers in Korea to respect the national characteristics of Koreans. Speaking to Japanese who had just arrived to teach there, Itō urged them to learn the language and not to denigrate the Korean religion or traditions:

> Religions, whether Buddhism, Confucianism, or Christianity, are the same in that they inspire people, and so there is no reason to regard this religion as good and that religion as bad. In our country the freedom of religion is guaranteed by the Constitution, but in Korea there are no regulations concerning religion. You must be careful in this regard and refrain from reckless criticism of religious people for what they say and do.[49]

On every possible occasion, Itō the statesman talked about popular sentiments and old practices in Korea. His basic approach to Korean popular culture and customs appears to have been non-interference, if not protection. He was prudent, for example, when speaking about regulations against traditional medicine and about the issue of cutting off the traditional male topknot (*sangtu*). Concerning the former, he said, "Should you ban the practice of Chinese-medicine doctors, there would be no doctors in Korea. . . . Gradual steps are preferable in regulating the practice of medicine. Radical measures will do no good at all."[50] Regarding cutting off the *sangtu*, he considered it better to let the custom die out naturally as people voluntarily stopped wearing the topknot rather than to prohibit it by law.[51]

In the area of general education, therefore, he gave ample leeway to Korean traditions and popular customs, and this formed a sharp contrast with the strict regulations he placed on the Korean imperial court. One can say that Itō divided Korean society into the popular realm of traditional life and the rational realm of government organization and exercised a double standard by taking a gradualist approach toward the former and trying to rid the latter of its mystical and religious dimensions as quickly as possible. He supported freedom of religion and was generous in his attitude toward people's faith. Perhaps we should say that his underlying motive was to separate religion from government and remove the former from the public realm and confine it to the private realm.

Therefore, if he encouraged respect for Korean traditions and old practices, that did not mean he wanted to maintain them in the cultural foundations of government in Korea. On the contrary, they should and would disappear eventually with the progress of modernization. What Itō wanted from children's education in Korea was the onset of gradual change that was allowed to steadily make its way into the mindset of the people and turn them toward a modern future.

Nationalist movement and private schools

When it came to the practical implementation of reform, Itō's gradualism was often forced off course. One of the major sources of disruption was anti-Japanese activity, specifically nationalist movements and resistance by the so-called righteous armies (*ŭibyŏng*).[52] In the area of education, Korean intellectuals were, quite apart from the measures Itō was mapping out, enormously enthusiastic about better education and they were developing vigorous projects to set up schools—so much so that their ideas and plans ended up conflicting and competing with Itō's.[53]

The serious disagreements between the objectives and views of the Korean nationalist education movement and those of Itō are a case in point. The nationalist movement was dedicated to fostering patriotic nationalism. In addition to promoting literacy for practical social purposes, the movement's private schools put strong emphasis on raising political awareness among the population and, thereby, nurturing nationalism.

Resident-General Itō's ideas on education, by contrast, as enunciated in his 1879 proposal "Kyōiku-gi" (On Education), emphasized the importance of science over so-called political discussion: "Too many people versed in political debate would hinder the wellbeing of the people," he had said in the proposal, and the idea remained a constant in Itō's thought. So he had little sympathy for overheated popular passions like nationalism.

> The pressing task now is first to protect Korean people so they do not suffer from want of food and clothing, and then to provide them with education to develop and improve their skills. Clamoring in vain for independence and nationalism while living in idleness will accomplish nothing for the country.[54]

That view, expressed in a speech in Korea in 1908, also indicates his belief in Korea's need for better science education to improve the material conditions of people's lives and his conviction that the schools were not a place for political discussion—"clamoring in vain for independence and nationalism." He was reiterating in Korea what he had asserted about private school education in Japan, and seeing in Korea some of the same issues he had seen earlier in Japan.

During the 1880s in Japan the movement for popular rights had risen to an unprecedented peak. By supplying it with activists, private law schools like Keiō and Waseda (then Tōkyō Senmon Gakkō), became bases of the movement. It was to counter that movement that Itō founded the Imperial University (1886), now the University of Tokyo, which offered training in what was called study of the state, centered on national administration, and he introduced new institutions and theories by which to recruit graduates of the university for government posts. Itō's maneuvering to remove the teaching of politics from private schools in Japan met with considerable success, as we saw in Chapter 2. He must have intended to do the same in Korea, but he was not successful. To understand why, it is necessary to review what happened during the course of education reform in Korea during Itō's time as resident-general.

At the first session of the Council for Korea Administration Reform in March 1906, Itō laid out his plan, to take effect in small steps over the years ahead, for improving and broadening education, but only three months later he revised the plan. At the sixth session, on June 23, when he had just come back from a two-month stay in Japan, he replaced Shidehara Taira (1870–1953), councilor of educational administration assigned to education reform in Korea, with Mitsuchi Chūzō (1871–1948). The reason Itō gave was that Shidehara "may be suitable as an instructor but he is not a competent writer." Itō complained that a textbook project Shidehara was working on was going far too slowly. But there was something more urgent going on than the speed of Shidehara's work, and it was putting pressure on Itō. He was impatient to move forward: "We need to get started on the expansion of education as quickly as we can. If we don't provide for the education of children, there is nothing we can do to plan for the development of Korea."[55]

Itō's sudden shift in education policy, from the unhurried pace laid out three months earlier to an urgent call for quick action on reform, was most likely caused by the serious political instability in Korea. During the two months that he was away from Korea, riots had broken out in various parts of the country. When he got back he was startled to see how far the situation had deteriorated. It looked so bad that he sat down to write a will, in case he should be killed.[56] He must have decided that, given the situation, he had to revise the initial plan.

For some time there were no signs that the disorder was calming down. Even two years later, in June 1908, Itō was still worried. He told a gathering of Korea's provincial governors that yes, the private schools were being built in rapidly increasing numbers, but they did not contribute to the material improvement of people's lives. They encouraged only unproductive, empty theorizing. What Korea needs—what we must do—he said, is to "provide the people with education that will enable them to engage in practical business activities."[57]

Itō finally turned to legal measures to clamp down. In August 1908, the Private School Act, Private School Supplementary Provisions, Academic Societies Act, and School Textbook Approval Regulations were established under the leadership of the Residency General. These laws and regulations had to be followed in order to start a private school and to supply textbooks. Under these strict controls, many of the private schools were shut down.[58]

But Korean nationalism only grew stronger and disruptive anti-Japanese activities showed no sign of abating. Itō seems to have found himself at an impasse. Toward the end of that year, recognizing that with each action his office took it lost more popular support, he acknowledged that, "We cannot carry out reform in Korea without doing something to change the attitudes of the people. Radical measures are not the answer." So once again, he saw that it was necessary to change tack in education reform.[59]

He does not seem to have planned in which direction he would change course. He apparently chose to wait and see how things would develop, without taking any active measures for the time being. There were voices calling for the establishment of business schools, for example, but Itō responded that they needed first to look at supply and demand for the graduates; they could set up business schools, but what would their graduates do? He doubted that Korean society was yet able to use them. Regarding a proposal to send Korean students to Japan, he said that more important than education per se was, at that point in time, the creation of a national ethos that would support the development of industry.[60] There is some truth to that remark, but one finds it somewhat incongruous in light of his firm views on the critical role of education. He could not but revert to the initial long-term plan for primary education and guidance of the people toward gradual acceptance of business education. Or perhaps one could simply say that Itō was at a standstill.

Handling of Korean intellectuals

Although his approach wavered, Itō's determination to install a system of general education in Korea remained on course. His approach, however, was not consistent with what he had done in Japan or advised in China. In Japan, his first project had been the reform of higher education and the training of an elite to lead government. His focus was on intellectuals. In China, too, he thought priority should be given to specialized higher education so as to produce people needed by the government who could be assigned to important state projects. With these points in mind, let us look at how Itō dealt with Korean intellectuals.

His remarks at the thirty-ninth session of the Council for Korean Administration Reform, held on April 29, 1908 provide insights on this matter. "Don't forget that all things in human society rest on 'people' (*hito*)," said Itō. When he said "people" he meant "people of ability." Itō argued that, as long as they had administrative skills, a wide range of people should be appointed to government jobs regardless of their ideologies or intellectual preferences. As he saw it, the existing selection and recruitment process for local government officials in Korea was overly influenced by personal connections, by who one's friends were. On that point the anti-Japanese movement had good reason to rail, he felt, against favoritism and unfair employment practices. To renovate Korea's officialdom and win greater public support, Itō took the position that the government had to "open its doors wide to people of ability."

Who were these "people of ability"? According to Itō, they were "people with some knowledge of Western science and the ability to handle clerical matters." As for Confucian scholars, Itō wanted them to stay far away from government. "Confucianists may not be bad, but they don't do clerical work. Popularity does no good . . . Promising young men should be chosen" rather than old Confucian scholars who "have a glib tongue but can't make their hands and legs work." Initially, Itō was even willing to offer government jobs to able people from among the anti-Japanese activists, thinking that might help reform a system dominated by Confucian scholars.[61]

Itō had always been good at bringing into the government political foes and opposition party members, people the government thought were dangerous, and had successfully marshaled their skills for use within the government. This was part of his political style—thinking of ways to work with opponents instead of crushing them. Saionji Kinmochi, Mori Arinori, Mutsu Munemitsu, Itagaki Taisuke, Ōkuma Shigenobu, and other very capable men whom the government had considered dangerous were all recruited or restored to government posts through the good offices of Itō Hirobumi.

He tried to keep to that style in Korea, too. He appointed Yi Yong-sik, known as the "boss of the Confucianists," to the post of education minister.[62] Hoping to incorporate Koreans with modern ideas and knowledge into the protectorate government, Itō tried to find common ground with anti-Japanese intellectuals in the nationalist education movement.

Failure to win over the Confucianists

Itō's attempt to win Korean intellectuals to his side was frustrated. The wall of nationalism between them was too high to surmount. Even in Japan, Itō had never attached much importance to nationalism. He had kept his distance from anti-foreign Japanese nationalism and championed an open-door policy for the promotion of industry. The nationalist education movement in Korea, however, was suffused with ideas of anti-Japanese resistance and calls for national independence. Itō and Korean intellectuals had different worldviews, and that difference stood in the way of any mutual understanding.

The nationalist education movement did share some of Itō's modernization goals, but he failed to win its support. As a last resort he tried to conciliate the Confucian scholars, the traditional ruling elite. Itō had no particular liking for classical Chinese studies, but he did have a sound knowledge of its literature, and that enabled him to interact with Confucian scholars through the activity of writing classical Chinese-style poems. While he scorned the "empty arguments" of the Confucian way of governing the state, he sought to get along with Confucian scholars—the "brains that rule the public mind of today's Koreans"—and use them for his cause.[63]

On January 12, 1909, Itō made a speech to an audience of some 400 people, including county magistrates, *yangban* officials, and Confucian scholars, all gathered at the official residence of the resident-general's secretary in Daegu. The speech included a "love call" to Confucianists. Itō said:

> What Japan wants for Korea today is a complete change in the old way of doing things. It wants Korea's people to be guided in the direction of learning and industry so that they will enjoy the benefits of civilization, and [Japan] will join forces with them.

Japan, China, and Korea were all "countries that maintain the support of the people through the ethical teachings of Confucius and Mencius," he said. Korea has never been inferior to China or Japan, materially or spiritually. He tried his best to urge the Confucianists to think in new ways and accept modernization as a good thing for Korea. In the middle of the speech, someone from the audience stood up and came forward loudly remonstrating against Itō until they were finally subdued. Red with anger, Itō concluded:

> I have asked you in all sincerity to follow the imperial orders issued from the Korean Emperor. All people throughout Korea have no choice but to try to change the old course. If some among you want to resist Japan individually, come out and try!

Ultimately, then, Itō's attempted dialogue with Korean intellectuals ended with intimidation.[64]

Governing Korea and military reforms in Japan: extension of constitutional reform

Even while he was struggling to cope with the situation in Korea, Itō remained president of the Imperial Household Research Committee in Japan. Considering whether and how this aspect of Itō's work was reflected in his administration of Korea, we must ask whether it was related to his efforts at constitutional reforms in Japan. As noted earlier, it is likely that he regarded Korea as a place to put into practice his plans for managing Japan's military.

Military ordinance: a concession?

A significant issue with regard to control of the military emerged over deployment of the Japanese naval garrison units at Jinhae Bay and Yongfung Bay in Korea. The deployment issue sparked controversy because it exposed the real intent of the Kōshikirei Order (February 1907) and led eventually to the Military Ordinance (Gunrei) Law (September 1907), discussed in Chapter 5. Following the issuing of the Kōshikirei Order, Itō sought to establish a system in Korea to place military administrative affairs under the control of the Korean cabinet, as was the case in Japan. Itō probably wanted to reproduce in Korea the government–military relations model that the 1907 system had aimed to achieve in Japan. If so, Itō's administration of Korea may have been partly intended to set a precedent for government reform in Japan. With that point in mind, let us re-examine the establishment of the military ordinance and its application.

Going back to the question that was raised toward the end of Chapter 5: Was the establishment of the military ordinance really just a concession for Itō? Could it have represented also a step forward for him? I suspect that Itō and Yamagata reached some sort of tacit agreement concerning the ordinance at the top-level meeting held between them on September 2, 1907. This possibility is suggested by a passage in the September 11, 1907 entry of the Hara Takashi diary. (Hara was then home minister in the first Saionji cabinet.) That was the day when Military Ordinance No. 1 ("On the Military Ordinances") was approved by the emperor. The passage reads:

> This morning I attended the regular cabinet meeting where the Prime Minister reported on the provisions of the Military Ordinance. This matter concerned the codification of the practice of *iaku jōsō* [whereby the military submitted reports and proposals on military affairs directly to the emperor], which had sparked controversy before. Field Marshall Yamagata had given to the Emperor a proposal to expand the army far more than previously, and so an Imperial order had been issued that substantial discussions be held with Itō and Yamagata and the results be reported to the Emperor. Saionji [Kinmochi] conferred with Itō and Yamagata. Itō put forth a fair argument that [Yamagata's proposal] ran counter to the Constitution. The Prime Minister [Saionji] agreed and reported accordingly to the Emperor. An Imperial sanction made in accordance with the report had the effect of reducing the existing power [of *iaku jōsō*] . . .[65]

The passage indicates no disgruntlement on Hara's part at the establishment of the ordinance; in fact, he seems even to have welcomed the restrictions it placed on the power of the military leaders. How much Hara knew about the behind-the-scenes progress on that matter is not known, but his positive reception of the military ordinance, coming as it did from a member of the cabinet, is noteworthy. The Hara diary suggests that some of those in key government posts regarded the military ordinance as a sign of some success in incorporating military affairs into the constitutional system.

Figure 7.1 Saionji Kinmochi (1849–1940).
Source: Photograph courtesy of the National Diet Library of Japan.

The military ordinance and the Itō-Yamagata summit

Now let us consider again, based on the context described above, the way the military ordinance came into being. At the end of March 1907, Navy Minister Saitō Makoto had delivered to the emperor a proposal for an ordinance that would allow the deployment of naval garrison units at Jinhae Bay and Yongfung Bay in Korea. The procedures Saitō had followed were different from previously, and so the emperor sent an inquiry by telegraph, and later a messenger, to Itō Hirobumi, who was then in Korea as resident-general, asking for an explanation. In response, Itō emphasized the necessity of a strict application of the newly-enacted Kōshikirei Order, as we saw in Chapter 5.

Stressing the authority of the Kōshikirei Order, Itō noted that the ordinance in question had to be countersigned by the prime minister as well as the navy minister. Yamagata, the leader of the army faction, was vehemently opposed, saying that would disturb the authority of the supreme command system. As a countermeasure, the army prepared a draft for a military ordinance providing for exceptions to the application of the Kōshikirei Order and submitted it to the emperor on August 19, 1907. Upon receiving it, the emperor ordered Prime Minister Saionji to consult Itō and Yamagata. On the August 22, the emperor sent Grand Chamberlain Tokudaiji Sanetsune to Army Minister Terauchi Masatake to inquire about the military ordinance draft. The question that concerned the emperor was "whether all the proposals of the kind that came under *iaku jōsō* heretofore would be issued as military ordinances (*gunrei*) or whether some of them would be excepted and have to be submitted to the cabinet for approval."[66] In other words, would the applicable range of *iaku jōsō* be maintained or would it be reduced?

The following day, August 23, Terauchi went to the palace to answer the inquiry.[67] What was discussed is not known. Did the army propose then that the existing practice of *iaku jōsō* be codified as it was? An agreement of some kind concerning the matter was very likely reached at the September 2 Itō-Yamagata meeting. Itō is thought to have made a concession, as noted earlier, but was it a one-sided concession? Was a give-and-take deal not struck between the two top leaders, one military, the other civilian? Consider what Yamagata wrote about the meeting in a letter to Terauchi:

> This morning, Shunpo [Itō's alias] visited me at the villa. After we talked about the situation in Korea and foreign and domestic affairs, I opened the subject of the military ordinance. Demarcation between high-command related affairs and military administrative affairs is very complex, and so the Army authorities came up with a clear demarcation and reported it to the Emperor. [Itō] said it was fine to determine a clear distinction and then asked about the matter of

Figure 7.2 Terauchi Masatake (1852–1919).

Source: Photograph courtesy of the National Diet Library of Japan.

countersignature [by the prime minister]. In any case, I explained, an order [to the army] without the signature of the army minister would slow down, and even hamper, the operation and activities of army units and troops.[68]

From the above letter we should note the following points. First, Itō and Yamagata did not differ markedly about determining a distinction between high-command related affairs and military administrative affairs. Second, Itō's greater concern lay in the matter of countersignature, that is, he persisted with the idea that military administrative affairs would require countersignature by the prime minister. Third, Yamagata's response, "In any case," sounds evasive. Pressed by Itō to agree on the need for the prime minister's countersignature, Yamagata complained, saying that army unity and morale would suffer if the army minister's countersignature was not required—complaint yes, but not a straightforward refusal. While their discussion on the countersignature was left somewhat up in the air, he continued, "An overall agreement was reached. As for details you [Terauchi] should explain. I told him [Itō] not to be too unrelenting or press you too hard."

Yamagata's concessions

From what Yamagata wrote in the letter it is hard to imagine him having one-sidedly pressed Itō for a concession. One suspects that under pressure from Itō, Yamagata, too, was forced to make some concession, as suggested by his evasiveness on the matter of countersignature.

It is not known what Terauchi told the emperor the following day in answer to the imperial inquiry of August 22, 1907, but we can assume that Yamagata gave up any expectation that all items, which until that point had been submitted directly to the emperor, would become military ordinances and instead compromised, allowing that some of them would be distinguished from the others and submitted to the cabinet. That was probably how Terauchi answered the emperor. Of course Yamagata wanted to narrow as much as possible the range of items that would be distinguished from high-command related items, and so, when pressed by Itō to widen the range, he tried to get around it, deflecting a direct answer with vague words. Itō, for his part, did allow the Military Ordinance Law to be enacted, but he most likely succeeded in drawing a concession from Yamagata regarding its application. Very likely to his satisfaction, Itō appears to have reduced the range of opportunity to exploit *iaku jōsō* and thereby secured a foothold for the cabinet to get involved in the administrative aspects of military affairs.

A retrospective account of an army officer during the early Shōwa era supports that interpretation. Hayashi Yasakichi (1876–1948), a major who worked in the military affairs department of the army ministry at that time (1907), recalling the issuance of the Kōshikirei Order, wrote:

> Well, if that kind of thing were to happen today it would surely end up as a bloody pistol affair. We were much more moderate in those days (laughter) and did our best to fix the situation any way we could.

He thus told about the background of the adoption of the Military Ordinance Law. When the ordinance law was enacted, Hayashi reported to Yamagata, only to be admonished. He recalled:

> I was sure Field Marshal [Yamagata] would give us a pat on the back. He didn't. On the contrary, he stormed, "You might think you now have a convenient law, but don't try to abuse it. If you do I won't let you off!" . . . With this thunder from Yamagata-san, we consulted the Cabinet Legislation Bureau and examined all the imperial ordinances issued till then. We decided such and such were military ordinances because they were mostly related to the high command and such and such were imperial ordinances [based on the Kōshikirei Order] because they were mostly related to administrative affairs. We thus divided them neatly between [Military Ordinance-based] military ordinances (*gunrei*) and [Kōshikirei Order-based] imperial ordinances (*chokurei*).[69]

From this account we know that Yamagata himself warned his men against the excessive issuing of military ordinances and that, following Yamagata's "thunder" they consulted the Cabinet Legislation Bureau and separated military from administrative ordinances. Indeed, after the Military Ordinance Law was enacted, many of the imperial ordinances that had been issued with the advice of the army minister alone began to be revised based on the Kōshikirei Order, that is, jointly signed by the army minister and the prime minister. (Such revised ordinances included those concerning army wages, military police, army uniforms, army officers' ranking, replenishment of army personnel, etc.) Military ordinances themselves decreased in number. Hayashi's account agrees with these facts.

Looked at in this way, the Military Ordinance Law can be seen as having been effective in reducing the range of high-command related items and as resulting from the army's desperate attempt to protect its rights, rather than something that frustrated Itō's 1907 efforts at constitutional reforms or established the legal basis for expansion of the imperial prerogative of supreme command.

That Itō let the Military Ordinance Law be enacted was a concession, it is true, but he also became very confident that, by further enhancing the effects of the constitutional reforms, he would be able to restrain the *iaku jōsō* system even more and place military administration gradually under more constitutional constraints. The place where he had intended to put such ideas into practice was Korea. So we can see that a major factor behind Itō's becoming the first resident-general in Korea was the 1907 constitutional reforms in Japan.

Legal restraints on military activities

When Itō assumed office as resident-general, he himself had prepared the draft of the ordinance on the organization of the residency-generalship and the residency, and the ordinance stipulated that the resident-general had the power to command the Japanese garrison force in Korea. That Itō was audacious enough to make himself—a civilian—the first resident-general prompted an angry response from the army.

From the start, therefore, the relationship between Itō's administration of Korea and the army was strained. That provided the backdrop for the controversy over the deployment of new garrison units on the peninsula. Moreover, Itō made so many moves to restrain army attempts to expand that one suspects that he chose Korea as the frontline for that purpose. Thinking along those lines, let me describe some of the policy measures he instituted.

First of all, Itō sought to limit the activities of the Japanese army garrison in Korea by law. In July 1906, at a session with Korean cabinet ministers, there arose an argument over the expropriation of land in Korea by the Japanese army. At that time Itō criticized the way the army had until then expropriated land for military use and proposed that a Korean county representative and a Japanese official together arrange to provide compensation directly to landowners for land thus expropriated.[70] He made it a policy that sufficient compensation should be paid to landowners. He made this proposal in response to the Japanese navy's request to expropriate some plots of land near Jinhae Bay. The Japanese navy's attempt to build a garrison unit at the bay was the first challenge to the aspirations Itō had in mind when he took up the post of resident-general.

The following month, in August, the martial law restrictions that had been imposed by the Japanese army to maintain public order and safety in Korea were relaxed. The number of punishable acts was reduced and capital punishment was eliminated.[71] Itō wanted to remove the strong military tinge in the administration of Korea and shift it more toward civilian rule. This was not entirely to appease Koreans who wanted a different sort of government; more immediately it was connected to the series of constitutional reforms he had been striving toward back in Japan in order to inhibit the autonomy of the military and bring it under the rule of law.

Having power of command over the Korea garrison army, Itō exercised it in various ways. According to Itō Yukio, he was involved even in personnel appointments in the navy. In June 1907, Navy Minister Saitō Makoto sounded out Itō about whether it would be all right to appoint Major General Miyaoka Naoki to command the Jinhae Bay garrison unit. "It's perfectly appropriate," replied Itō.[72]

Itō kept a watchful eye on the organizational matters of the garrison army and also on the details of commands and instructions within the army. Around the same time, when Itō came across a passage he did not agree with in an instruction manual the Korea garrison army commander Hasegawa had issued to his men, Itō told Hasegawa to delete the passage. Hasegawa withdrew the instruction, revised it, and then reissued it. In a letter to Terauchi, Hasegawa complained, "The Resident-General's attitude toward the Army these days is irritating."[73] In light of the government–military relationship heretofore, what Itō was doing was hard for the garrison army commander to understand.

Checking army expansion

Itō also exercised his authority over the garrison army to prevent reckless activities by its troops. A good example concerns a branch office of the residency-general that was set up in Gando (Jiandao in Chinese), an area sharing the border with

China, in August 1907. The official reason for setting up the branch was to protect Koreans living in the area. The ulterior motive is said to have been to build a base for dealing with Russia's anticipated southern advance.[74] A close look at Itō's instructions issued to the branch office, however, suggests that his own purpose was to prevent excessive actions by the Japanese army.

On October 25, 1907, Lieutenant Colonel Saitō Suejirō, head of the Gando office, proposed to Itō that they place Korean residents in Gando under Korean jurisdiction. "If we do that," Itō responded, "it might be taken to mean that we have tacitly recognized Gando as part of Chinese territory," and as long as the Korean–Chinese border issue remained unsettled "we must be careful not to give them [Chinese] any ideas that would work against our interests."[75]

Earlier, Itō had instructed Saitō, "Behind the Gando issue lies the bigger matter of determining the border, and therefore, you must take the greatest care to ensure that nothing you do gets in the way of settling this bigger matter." Saitō needed to be careful never to let the Chinese "mistake any Japanese action for an invasion and occupation." For that purpose, "when you hear a complaint from Koreans you should immediately send a written notice about it to the Chinese officials and make it their responsibility." Itō sought to prevent any problem in the small area of Gando from "spreading to the entire Manchurian region and escalating into a serious situation."[76] Itō saw the Gando branch office as the threshold of Korea, beyond which the Japanese army must not go.

Finally, on the matter of Itō's ideas vis-à-vis the military, let us consider Itō's reflections at the time of specific military actions. After the Third Japan–Korea Treaty was signed and the Korean army dissolved, resistance by the anti-Japanese militia intensified. Itō called on his home government to send more troops to quell the riots. On the other hand, he called for prudence in military action.

On June 12, 1909, Itō summoned the army officers and made a speech.[77] Introducing himself as the resident-general representing Japan in Korea, under the direct orders of the emperor, he emphasized his duty to protect Korea. The instructions he was issuing, he said, were part of that duty. First of all, he warned them to "never cross the national border in normal times unless otherwise expressly stipulated by the Treaty." Second, he instructed them "to take the utmost care not to inflict any injury on local residents, since the rioting is not in the least a civil war but merely local disturbances." The third warning he gave them was to refrain from going too far in putting down the riots by the "righteous army" activists. As he saw it, among those who took part in the resistance led by the militia, "most joined it under duress, and local people may have some anti-Japanese sentiments but do not openly engage in armed resistance against Japan." He stressed the necessity of distinguishing real rioters from bystander civilians. Itō thus warned the Japanese garrison army against excessive actions and urged them to be disciplined in their relations with Koreans.

The breakdown of Korean rule

Itō Hirobumi was like Janus; he faced two directions at once—toward Korea as a missionary of modernization and toward Japan as a reformer under the Constitution.

Leader facing two ways

The pivot of Itō's political ambitions was guiding Japan toward emergence as a civilized state through people-centered government. The same can be said of his policies for Korea. He tried to guide the Korean people toward becoming a civilized nation exactly the way he did in Japan. His means to that end were democracy, constitutionalism, and gradualism. There is some indication that, following the Third Japan–Korea Treaty, the thrust of Itō's governing policy in Korea shifted from cultural policies to the encouragement of self-government.[78]

On the other hand, within the deeper layers of Itō's approach to governing was his consistent "civilization policy"—namely, his belief that by enabling the people to avail themselves of knowledge and education and by ensuring rational, modern government, the nation would naturally grow in power and prosperity. He governed Japan on the basis of that philosophy, and it was the same philosophy that underlay his administration of Korea. That was what lay behind his urging—in a speech given not long before the end of his years as resident-general (in early 1909) during the southern-Korea tour when he accompanied Emperor Sunjong to a large audience that included Confucian scholars—that Korea put "the old way of doing things" aside and pursue learning and industry so as to "enjoy the benefits of civilization."[79]

One major focus of reform to be achieved by introducing modern, civilized practices was the imperial court of Korea. During the period of the establishment of the Meiji Constitution Itō had tried to depoliticize the imperial court in Japan, and as of 1907 he was in the middle of making it an organ of the state. By so doing, he wanted to change the Japanese imperial system so that the emperor would be a constitutional monarch, like European monarchs. He took the same approach to the Korean emperor and imperial court and initiated the modernization of their institutions and lifestyles, presumably hoping that the Korean public would follow suit.

Earlier, in November 1905, Itō had browbeaten Emperor Gojong and the Korean cabinet ministers into signing the Second Japan–Korea Treaty, but later, after fulfilling his aims, as he was leaving Korea for a temporary return to Japan, Itō was told by Emperor Gojong:

> Your hair is grey now, probably as a result of your long devoted service to your country. I earnestly hope that you will entrust Japanese government affairs to younger politicians and that your still grey hair will be spent to assist me. By the time your hair has turned as white as snow, I am sure that you will have made great contributions to our country, with enormous effects. The reason I press for your assistance, old though you have become, is that I have greater trust in you even than in my government ministers.[80]

The Korean emperor's attitude toward Itō had undergone a complete change. He now entreated Itō to assist him until his "hair has turned as white as snow." Innately good-hearted, Itō must have been deeply moved.

Komatsu Midori, a close associate of Itō's, wrote that when Itō was asked, "Of all people today, whom do you respect the most?" he had immediately replied

"The Emperor of Japan and the Emperor of Korea" and cited what Gojong had said to him.[81] In Japan, Emperor Meiji had transformed himself into a constitutional monarch at Itō's prodding and, understanding Itō's government policy well, had played a key role in Itō's grand design.[82] Initially Itō must have felt that Gojong, in the same way, would change and work together with him in modernizing Korea.

Such expectations were to be dashed. Ultimately, Gojong resisted Itō's policy at every point, and even maintained contact with, and provided assistance to the anti-Japanese movement. Itō imposed the court ban to facilitate its modernization, but it did not accomplish the intended purpose because he paid too little attention to the weight of Korean court culture.[83] That failure symbolized Itō's greatest mistake in governing Korea—his failure to find local partners who would support his reforms.

Resident-General Itō had another face, that of reformer of institutions in Japan under the Constitution. For that side of Itō, it seems plausible that Korea might have been the place to put into practice the kinds of constitutional reforms he had led in Japan in 1907. Certainly Itō kept on transmitting specific examples from Korea of how military administrative reforms should be carried out in Japan, the most eloquent of such examples being his handling of the issue of deployment of Japanese naval garrison units at Jinhae Bay and Yongfung Bay in Korea. Civilian though he was, Itō was given the power to command the garrison army in accordance with the Residency-General Organization Ordinance, and he supervised the activities and military administration of the Japanese army stationed in Korea. We can surmise that, by demonstrating in Korea what the government–military relationship should be like, Itō wanted to set a precedent for Japan.

In this way, Itō's governing of Korea was shaped by the fact that he faced two directions at once, toward Korea and toward Japan. That way of facing two directions simultaneously emerged out of his idea for changing Japan's national system, the reform he had been grappling with before he became resident-general. For Itō, governing Korea had much to do with domestic reform in Japan.

Circumspect on annexation

The last matter I would like to consider in this book is Itō's view of the annexation of Korea. It has often been pointed out that from the beginning of his tenure as resident-general, Itō supported the immediate annexation of Korea. The basis for this view is a telegram Itō sent to Japanese foreign minister Hayashi Tadasu on April 13, 1907 saying, "If the Korea situation continues on in the way it is going now, *annexation* [written in katakana] will grow more difficult each year" (...*toshi o heru ni shitagōte "anekizēshon" wa masumasu konnan naru ni itaru beshi*). This line has been interpreted to indicate that Itō advocated immediate annexation as the only way to solve the problems in Korea.[84]

Read in its full context, however, that interpretation may be a bit hasty. Itō's focus was rather on Japan's concession to Russia over Japanese special interests in Manchuria and Inner Mongolia. What he really wanted to say was that if Japan were to goad Russia by persisting in expanding its sphere of influence, Japan's protectorate policy toward Korea might be adversely affected. It is possible that he used the word "annexation" as a rhetorical flourish meant to persuade the foreign ministry to make concessions on the Manchuria and Mongolia issue.

Indeed, in foreign affairs Itō's concern in those days was not so much with the problem of Korea as it was with finding a satisfactory solution to the Manchuria issue. He was seriously worried that a local Gando problem might spread to all of Manchuria. He therefore instructed the military officer stationed in the Gando area to compromise with China over the issue of sovereignty, even if it meant that they had to sacrifice some of Japan's responsibility as protector of the local Korean residents.

Itō's concern was not limited to the Gando problem. He was firmly opposed to any move to bring Manchuria under Japan's sphere of influence. At a conference on the Manchurian issue held on his initiative at the prime minister's official residence in Tokyo in May 1906, Itō criticized the Manchuria regional office of the army for attempting to put Manchuria under Japan's control. He persuaded the government to decide that the Kwantung government-general's office in Manchuria would be reorganized as a peacetime organization and that military offices would be abolished, one by one. At that point Itō's argument against Japan's management of Manchuria prevailed, overcoming Chief of General Staff Kodama Gentarō's aggressive position on the matter.[85]

Other than the rhetorical "annexation" flourish in the 1907 cable, Itō does not seem to have expressed any hint of support for annexation. In public, he persisted in counseling caution: "There is no need to annex Korea. Annexation would be extremely difficult and burdensome."[86]

Changing his mind

On March 30, 1909, however, Foreign Minister Komura Jutarō (1855–1911) passed to Prime Minister Katsura Tarō a pair of proposals—a "great policy toward Korea" and an "outline of facilities in Korea"—urging that the cabinet adopt a resolution to annex Korea. Katsura had no objection but the question was: What would Itō say? Both Katsura and Komura knew very well that Itō was opposed to annexation.

The two decided to talk with Itō in person and persuade him to accept annexation. On April 10, armed with steely determination to get his approval, they visited Itō, who was back in Tokyo. Much to their surprise, Itō readily agreed.[87] The greatest obstacle having been removed, the cabinet adopted a resolution, on July 6, to annex Korea.

Why did Itō approve annexation at that time? To understand why he did, it is necessary to consider another diplomatic issue that was solved along with the annexation. According to Yi Sŏng-hwan, the policy of Korean annexation "was pursued simultaneously and almost in parallel with Japan's Gando policy."[88] China had instructed the Japanese government (March 23) that it would claim ownership of Gando at the International Court of Arbitration in The Hague. So there was the likelihood that the territorial dispute over Gando might develop into an international issue. Aware that the international community might be roused to interfere in Japan's overseas expansion, Yamagata Aritomo proposed to the Japanese government that Gando be abandoned and that Korea be secured instead.

In this way, Japan compromised with the Chinese government, which had insisted on settling the Manchuria issue, including Gando, all at once; Japan decided to secure Korea, separating it from the Manchuria issue.[89] It thus chose to annex Korea in exchange for ceasing its pursuit of interests in Manchuria, even if only for the time being.

That was the background of Itō's approval of the Korean annexation. His fundamental concern had been how to prevent his country's military expansion into Manchuria. As the resident-general of Korea he imposed on himself the task of keeping the Japanese army within Korea. Because this task was fulfilled when

Figure 7.3 Itō Hirobumi with Korean Crown Prince Yi Un, 1908.

Source: Chūō Kōron Shinsha, p. 341.

the Japanese government gave up the idea of managing Manchuria, he gave the nod for Korean annexation.

Post-annexation plan

After agreeing to the annexation in May, Itō turned in his resignation as resident-general to Prime Minister Katsura. What plans did he have for the government of post-annexation Korea? Or was he eager to make Korea a thing of the past that was no longer his concern?

There is a copy of a memo among the papers of Suematsu Kenchō (1855–1920), a multi-talented statesman and Itō's son-in-law (husband of his second daughter). The full text of the memo dictated by Itō reads as follows:

> Ten representatives shall be elected from each of the eight provinces of Korea to form the lower house of parliament
>
> Fifty elders shall be elected by vote from among *yangban* military and civilian officials to form the upper house of parliament
>
> The government ministers of Korea shall be made up of Koreans and be a responsible cabinet.
>
> The government shall be subordinate to the viceroy.
>
> Because it is a total merger [of Japan and Korea] an entente will not be needed; a declaration will do.
>
> How shall we treat the Korean Imperial Household?
>
> How shall we deal with other countries?[90]

This memo outlines the annexation process and post-annexation structure of government. As Itō Yukio's investigation suggests, the memo might have been written sometime after Itō Hirobumi approved the annexation in April 1909.[91] The first half of the memo indicates that the main structure of government, as Itō conceived it, would consist of a two-house parliamentary system (including an assembly of representatives of the people) and a cabinet made up of Koreans supervised by the viceroy, who would replace the resident-general. Most notable is the fact that Itō Hirobumi envisioned a parliament and a responsible cabinet of Koreans even after annexation. He embraced the idea that, even after Korea was no longer a state, it would have an independent colonial parliament and its autonomy would be fully guaranteed.

Allowing a parliament meant allowing popular participation in the political decision-making process, which might lead to self-rule by the people of colonial Korea. In Korea, as well as in Japan, Itō Hirobumi supported a civilized form of government, made up of competent persons whose practice of government would always be watched by the people. It seems to me, therefore, that the idea emerging from the memo reflects Itō's dream that when the Korean people became capable of self-rule through education, and parliamentary government took firm root, Korea would regain its independence and a genuine alliance would form between Japan and Korea.

Was Itō Hirobumi prepared to continue his work and bring that dream into reality? Or did he wish to be liberated from the nightmare of involvement with Korea? The answer was buried deep in history when he was shot and killed in Harbin in northern China on October 26, 1909.

Notes

1. Moriyama 1987.
2. See Moriyama 1987 and Itō and Lee 2009. However, neither of these works (including my own essay published in the latter, "Chi no kyōdō toshite no Kankoku tōchi," pp. 193–217) paid any attention to Itō's simultaneous engagement in constitutional reforms in Japan at that time.
3. Journalist Tokutomi Sohō called him "hatsumono-gui," or a glutton for the "first harvests of the season."
4. *Itō den*, vol. 3, pp. 639 ff.
5. July 28, 1904 entry, *Hara nikki*, vol. 2, p. 106.
6. Gaimushō 1965, vol. 1, "Bunsho no bu" [Documents], pp. 233–4.
7. At that time Austria and Hungary were united under the Austrian monarch. They maintained separate parliaments and governed their regions autonomously, but three ministers acted to oversee their joint financial, military, and foreign policy operations.
8. *Itō den*, vol. 3, p. 687.
9. Ibid., p. 689.
10. Kimura 2007, p. 361.
11. *Shūsei*, vol. 1, p. 48.
12. Ibid., p. 52.
13. Letter from Itō to Hayashi Gonsuke, dated December 29, Tōa Dōbunkai 1973, vol. 2, p. 92.
14. "Terauchi monjo," no. 360–42.
15. Yamamoto Shirō 1976.
16. "Terauchi monjo," no. 38–14, emphasis (using italics here) by Hasegawa.
17. "Terauchi monjo," no. 38–16, letter dated January 26, 1906.
18. *Enzetsushū*, vol. 1, pp. 204–5.
19. See Ogawara 2010, pp. 95–126 and the works mentioned there.
20. *Nitobe zenshū*, vol. 5, pp. 550–1.
21. *Shūsei*, vol. 6.
22. Ibid., part 1, p. 247, seventh session of the Council for Korea Administration Reform, held on July 3, 1906.
23. Ibid., pp. 163–4.
24. Ibid., p. 450, fourteenth session of the Council for Korea Administration Reform, held on April 9, 1907.
25. Initially, Gojong himself had ruled in a Confucian "king's way," upholding the principle that "It is the people who should be the center of the country" (Kimura 2007, pp. 87 ff.). Gojong's people-centered idea and that of Itō were fundamentally different, however, in that the former was traditionalism featuring a return to the ancient way whereas the latter was modernism based on the promotion of industry.
26. *Shūsei*, vol. 6, part 1, p. 164.
27. Ibid., p. 390, twelfth session of the Council for Korea Administration Reform, held on November 16, 1906.
28. Ibid., p. 138, first session of the Council for Korea Administration Reform, held on March 13, 1906.
29. Accounts testifying to this characteristic of Itō's approach are too numerous to mention. They include those by Shinagawa Yajirō and others, which have already been

introduced in this book. Such accounts about Itō's resident-general days may also be found in Komatsu 2005, p. 49.
30 First session of the Council for Korea Administration Reform, held on March 13, 1906, *Shūsei*, vol. 6, part 1, p. 133.
31 Ibid., p. 132.
32 Ibid., p. 133.
33 Itō viewed Korean popular resistance to government officials as a consequence of the development of people's rights in Korea.
34 Sixty-third session of the Council for Korea Administration Reform, held on December 8, 1908, *Shūsei*, vol. 6, part 3, p. 1,123.
35 Ibid., p. 1,143, sixty-fifth session of the Council for Korea Administration Reform, held on December 25.
36 Ibid., vol. 6, part 1, pp. 232 ff., private audience, July 2, 1906.
37 Ibid., pp. 232 ff., seventh session of the Council for Korea Administration Reform, held on July 3, 1906.
38 Gojong protested: "In our country since ancient times we have had the custom of inviting and listening to scholars selected from the 'forest' [world] of the Confucian literati." (*Shūsei*, vol. 6, part 1, p. 237) The idea of "one lord and the whole people equal under his rule," derived from the people-centered theory of Confucianism, was basic to the philosophy of governing for the Korean ruler. For that reason, the imperial court in Korea was open to the outside so that the sovereign could hear the voice of the people. See Hara 2003.
39 Remark by the finance minister Min Yeong-gi at the seventh session of the Council for Korea Administration Reform, held on July 3, 1906, *Shūsei*, vol. 6, part 1, p. 247.
40 I discussed this point in detail in Takii 1999.
41 Private audience, July 27, 1906, *Shūsei*, vol. 6, part 1, p. 313.
42 Ibid., p. 314.
43 Letter from Itō to Yamagata Aritomo, dated April 1, 1906, *Yamagata monjo*, vol. 1, p. 141.
44 Seventh session of the Council for Korea Administration Reform, held on July 3, 1906, *Shūsei*, vol. 6, part 1, p. 246.
45 *Itō den*, vol. 3, p. 726. For details on the Korean court and divination, see Shin 2008, p. 209.
46 Transcription of speech delivered on June 5, 1908, *Shūsei*, vol. 6, part 2, p. 886.
47 Ibid., part 1, p. 133.
48 Ibid., pp. 133–4.
49 "Advice to Japanese Teachers in General Education," April 14, 1907, *Itō-kō zenshū*, vol. 2, "Academic Speeches," p. 246.
50 Third session of the Council for Korea Administration Reform, held on April 9, 1906, *Shūsei*, vol. 6, part 1, p. 181.
51 Ibid., part 2, p. 899, forty-first session of the Council for Korea Administration Reform, held on June 9.
52 For nationalist movements, see Yi Sŏng-hwan, "Itō Hirobumi no Kankoku tōchi to Kankoku nashonarizumu" [Itō Hirobumi's Administration of Korea and Management of Korean Nationalism], in Tsukiashi 2009. On the resistance movement of the righteous armies, see Shin 2008 and Ogawara 2010. The latter studies might be read with caution, however, as they seem to excessively idealize the premodern people's consciousness of order under the guise of the righteous armies.
53 On education reform movements by contemporary Koreans, see the Yi study mentioned in the preceding footnote, as well as Yoon 1982, Kim 1996, and Satō 2000.
54 Transcription of speech delivered on June 17, 1908, *Shūsei*, vol. 6, part 2, pp. 926–7.
55 Sixth session of the Council for Korea Administration Reform, held June 25, 1906, *Shūsei*, vol. 6, part 1, p. 221.
56 *Itō den*, vol. 3, pp. 717–18.
57 Transcription of speech, *Shūsei*, vol. 6, part 2, pp. 926–7.
58 Satō 2000, p. 233.

59 Sixty-fifth session of the Council for Korea Administration Reform, held December 25, 1908, *Shūsei*, vol. 6, part 3, p. 1,142.
60 Ibid., pp. 1,138 ff., sixty-fifth session of the Council for Korea Administration Reform, held December 25, 1908.
61 Ibid., part 2, pp. 836–9, see thirty-ninth session of the Council for Korea Administration Reform, held on April 29, 1908.
62 Komatsu 2005, pp. 165 ff.
63 Sixty-fifth session of the Council for Korea Administration Reform, held on December 25, 1908, *Shūsei*, vol. 6, part 3, p. 1,141; Che 2009.
64 "The Purpose of Japan is to Help Strengthen Korea," January 12, 1909, *Itō-kō zenshū*, vol. 2, "Political Speeches," pp. 488–90.
65 *Hara nikki*, vol. 2, p. 257.
66 *Meiji tennō-ki*, vol. 11, p. 787.
67 Ibid.
68 Letter from Yamagata to Terauchi dated September 2, 1907, "Terauchi monjo," no. 360–2.
69 Hayashi Yasakichi, "Heiken seiken no bunkai un'yō ni tsuite" [Analysis and Operation of Military Authority and Government], in "Makino monjo," no. 126.
70 Eighth session of the Council for Korea Administration Reform, held on July 12, 1906, *Shūsei*, vol. 6, part 1, p. 271.
71 Matsuda 2011, p. 14.
72 Itō Yukio 2009, p. 503.
73 Letter from Hasagawa to Terauchi, dated July 2, 1907, "Terauchi monjo," no. 38–24.
74 Moriyama 1987, pp. 229 ff.
75 *Gaikō*, vol. 40 (2), p. 138.
76 Ibid., pp. 120–1.
77 "Kuratomi monjo," no. 30–1.
78 Moriyama 1987.
79 "The Purpose of Japan is to Help Strengthen Korea," January 12, 1909, *Itō-kō zenshū*, vol. 2, "Political Speeches," pp. 488–9.
80 *Shūsei*, vol. 6, part 1, pp. 74–5.
81 Komatsu 1934, p. 30.
82 Itō Yukio 2009.
83 In this way Itō tried to reform the Korean imperial system in the same way he had transformed the Japanese emperor into a constitutional monarch. The parallels between the reforms in the national systems of Japan and Korea could be seen in the cabinet reforms also. In June 1907, a Korean cabinet organization ordinance took effect. It was designed to reduce the power of the emperor and expand the power of the prime minister, head of the cabinet. The new ordinance gave authority to the prime minister to submit confidential matters to the emperor and put administrative agencies under his control, to issue cabinet ordinances and appoint and dismiss junior officials, and to punish cabinet agencies or revoke their orders. The ordinance also required the army and navy ministers to report to the prime minister first when they submitted reports to the emperor on military secrets or ordinances. That reform of the Korean cabinet system was made in line with the Japanese cabinet system reform carried out earlier.
84 *Gaikō*, vol. 40 (1), p. 124.
85 Kobayashi Michihiko 1996, p. 163.
86 Speech delivered at the Japanese Club in Seoul on July 29, 1907, *Itō-kō zenshū*, vol. 2, "Political Speech," p. 459.
87 *Itō den*, vol. 3, p. 838.
88 Yi 1991, p. 90.
89 Ibid., p. 91.
90 Horiguchi 2003, vol. 2, p. 387.
91 Itō Yukio 2009, pp. 551 ff.

Afterword

The 100th anniversary of Itō Hirobumi's death was in 2009. That year also marked 120 years since the promulgation of the Constitution of the Empire of Japan (Meiji Constitution), which was accomplished largely through Itō's efforts. Yet, in 2009, virtually nothing was done to commemorate either the death of the architect of the Meiji Constitution or the promulgation of this first modern constitution in East Asia. Symposiums honoring Itō and the birth of the Meiji Constitution were held in Yamaguchi prefecture, in the cities of Hikari (Itō's birthplace) and Hagi (capital of the Chōshū domain). But except for those events and the publication of an excellent work on Itō by historian Itō Yukio, no national event, within the academic community or outside it, was organized to reassess the historical significance of Itō or the Meiji Constitution.

Considering the generally held images of Itō Hirobumi and the Meiji Constitution, the reason for that disregard is not hard to understand. For one thing, all too often the Meiji Constitution is seen as a diabolical charter endorsing the official prerogatives vested in the emperor that paved the way for Japan's militarist era of the 1930s and 1940s. And so, as the creator of that charter, Itō is irrevocably associated with militarism. The negative aspects of that image are further accentuated by his role as the first resident-general of Korea and the opening of the path to Japan's annexation of the peninsula. He has thus been identified as the figure who most pointedly symbolizes Japan's four decades of rule in Korea, which lasted until 1945.

The Itō Hirobumi I have depicted in this book is intended to be distinct from such regretful images. I have written about how he championed a "new civilization" for Japan, his achievements as a "statesman of institutions," and his contributions to "popular government," but overarching all these was Itō's commitment as a statesman-advocate of knowledge (*chi no seijika*).

Itō had an extraordinary appetite for learning. In his early twenties, when the country was still under the rule of the Tokugawa shoguns (1603–1867) and the laws prohibiting citizens from traveling overseas were still in effect, he journeyed to Britain to acquire knowledge of the "new civilization" beginning to impinge on Japanese shores. He returned home a year later, equipped with a new and wider perspective on Japan and the world. The knowledge he had acquired enabled him to rise above his status and reach the top of his profession, despite the confines of the rigid class system. This experience convinced Itō that the basis of nation-building had to be an educated people free to choose occupations and able to improve and use their skills, regardless of the social class they were born into. His endeavors following the Restoration of 1868 were aimed at creating a cluster of core institutions to achieve that purpose. By the end of his life he had been responsible for putting in place the Meiji Constitution, the Imperial University (now the University of Tokyo), the Imperial Diet, the Seiyūkai political party, a responsible cabinet, the Imperial Household Research Committee, and the residency-general of Korea.

These institutions were conceived as leading ultimately to a functioning popular government. From the outset of the Meiji era, he urged the introduction of a parliamentary system that would guarantee the participation of the people in government. He was modern Japan's leading champion of democracy. In Chapter 1, I noted Tsuda Umeko's recollection of how intensely interested Itō was in Alexis de Tocqueville's *Democracy in America*. De Tocqueville's classic does not uncritically glorify democracy. The author was born an aristocrat, shortly after the French Revolution, and while he believed democracy to be inevitable in the course of history, he tended to be pessimistic about its effect on the human

Figure 8.1 Fukuzawa Yukichi (1835–1901).

Source: Photograph courtesy of the National Diet Library of Japan.

spirit. By contrast, Itō was born into a poor farming family and when he was young, they became, by adoption, legal members of a low-ranking samurai family. These circumstances might well have influenced Itō's positive attitude toward the development of democracy and egalitarian society, which, in turn, became the ideals guiding his efforts to rebuild Japan's political system.

My portrayal of Itō may seem to draw similarities with people's rights (*jiyū minken*) movement ideologues or enlightenment thinkers like Fukuzawa Yukichi, but he clearly differed from them. First, he was a gradualist in terms of change in the social order and in his worldview. A responsible statesman, Itō would not have encouraged the immediate installation of a parliament or legislation enfranchising a broad segment of new voters within a short period of time. If a system or institution was transplanted to Japan from abroad, he did everything possible to make certain that some Japanese immunity function did not kick in to reject it. Perceiving democracy as an irrevocable trend in the constantly shifting flow of history and keenly aware of the political conditions in and outside Japan, as well as the still nascent economic strength and political maturity of the Japanese people at the time, Itō sought to move slowly toward a parliamentary system.

Second, the kind of knowledge he wanted the Japanese to acquire was practical. Itō had zero tolerance for speculative, ideological learning. Rather, he believed in the power of empirical, usefully applicable knowledge to create efficiency and expedience, and to bring economic prosperity. He rejected as unproductive the arguments of the people's rights movement activists and dogmatic Confucian and Kokugaku (National Learning) scholars. In that respect Itō and Fukuzawa were similar, but they differed in how practical knowledge should be put to use. Fukuzawa believed in the strict separation of the government and private sectors and advocated freedom of economic activity by the private sector without government involvement. Itō was interested in forming connections between the two sectors through the mediation of knowledge, thereby forming a public sphere. He conceived of the Seiyūkai as a kind of think-tank that would hear and consider practical needs and demands—which he described as "knowledge"— of various kinds arising from the private-sector business sphere, develop them into public policy items, and channel them to parliament. It was with much the same idea in mind that he founded the Imperial University and within it the Kokka Gakkai, a forum where scholars as well as politicians, bureaucrats, businessmen, and others involved in some way in governing the country could gather and exchange information and insights. For Itō, knowledge was something to be circulated among all people, and the state should function as a kind of forum to facilitate that circulation, a forum that relativized the lines between the government and private sectors.

Itō's limitations as a politician can be seen in his tendency to focus so intensely on new and practical knowledge that he failed to appreciate important developments right around him. His apparent inability to understand and appreciate nationalism is a case in point. He censured nationalist movements in Japan, considering them to be reckless and exclusivist, and even in Korea as resident-general he never truly grasped the motivation or nature of Korean anti-Japanese nationalism. Because of that lack of understanding, he ultimately failed in the governing of

Korea. Itō seems to have thought that sentiments like nationalism, which he saw as irrational, would naturally subside as a society modernized. As far as he was concerned, his governance in Japan and Korea was consistent; in both countries he crusaded for modernization and established government institutions to facilitate the development of a modern society. For Koreans, however, Itō was an outsider. It was unbearable that an outsider should try to force his version of civilization upon them. Yet Itō seems never to have understood that sentiment, because he persisted in believing that there was no essential difference in the ways that Japanese and Koreans should best be governed. To him, the Koreans were as much potential partners in his endeavors as were the Japanese.

But if Itō had a blind spot in failing to grasp the Korean mindset, it was reciprocated by both the Japanese and the Koreans. Neither appeared to have fully understood Itō's thinking, particularly his vision of engaging the people in the business of the nation through institutions set up to receive, discuss, revise, or act on their needs, ideas, and preferences. How many Japanese of his time were in tune with his goals? How many really understood his passionate campaign to build popular government based on the Meiji Constitution, to do away with partisan politics in government through the agency of the Seiyūkai, and to implement institutional reforms in his capacity as president of the Imperial Household Research Committee and resident-general of Korea? They were not many. In that sense, while he was a well-known and popular politician in Japan, he was a proudly independent, and isolated, statesman in his time. He was also a great thinker, but the thought of Itō Hirobumi as statesman, politician, and pioneering student of Western institutions has long been neglected. It may be that a thorough and objective reconsideration of his thought and his conceptions of state and society had to await more recent times, when, finally, there has emerged more robust public discussion on change in government leadership and in government structures, opening minds to a new appreciation of the way he saw his country and the future of its people.

Itō Hirobumi has been, for me, a towering peak—a mountain I have been trying to scale since I embarked as a young man on my doctoral studies. This book is the English translation of a work published in 2010 as a *shinsho* paperback. *Shinsho* editions are publications for general readers on topics of interest written by academic specialists. Mine, however, is a bit different. It is the product of fifteen years of research and writing, a long and arduous process of studying primary sources and documents while trying to answer my own questions. In the end, rather than trying to convey in layman's language what I already knew, I produced an academic work based on very considerable research that presents what is mostly unknown even in the academic community.

In researching and writing this book, I received assistance and advice from so many people that I cannot mention all the individual names here. They include those involved in the study sessions, associations, and Itō commemorative symposia where I had opportunities to talk about topics that are part of this book, as well as those who helped me with my documentary research, and the friends and colleagues who assisted me in finding and interpreting Chinese documents.

I must, however, mention three names. One is Itō Yukio, professor at Kyoto University. Professor Itō's first seminar at Kyoto University, which dealt with Itō

Hirobumi, was a major factor in my decision to shift my specialization from German legal history to the study of this major political leader. I had written my master's thesis on Lorenz von Stein, but because of my encounter with Professor Itō I turned my research focus to the study of the thought of the towering Meiji statesman Itō, a figure in whom I had been interested for some time, especially in connection with his studies under von Stein. Professor Itō's *Itō Hirobumi: Kindai Nihon o tsukutta otoko* [Itō Hirobumi, the Man Who Created Modern Japan],[1] published in 2009, the 100th anniversary of Itō Hirobumi's death, is now *the* authoritative biography. It recreates Itō Hirobumi not only as a statesman but also as a private person, involved in family and other relationships. It is unrivaled among works on Itō Hirobumi published so far. The publication of this book by my mentor, naturally, put pressure on those like me planning to publish a book on the same subject, but it was valuable because it helped me to define and crystallize the image of Itō that had been developing in my mind—the image of Itō Hirobumi the thinker—that had been long overlooked. I realized that, rather than as a statesman, I wanted to present him as a political thinker of modern Japan whose powerful insight and grandeur of vision was comparable even to that of Fukuzawa Yukichi. It is up to the reader to decide whether I have been successful.

Another person to whom I would like to express special thanks is Kobayashi Michihiko, professor at the University of Kitakyushu. Professor Kobayashi, together with Professor Itō Yukio, advised and encouraged me at study meetings. Professor Kobayashi came with me to investigate documents held by the Yahata Steel Works of Nippon Steel and elsewhere and gave me a number of valuable leads. For instance, when I had probed the history of Sino–Japanese relations, an area with which I am not very familiar, and was at a loss as to where to explore further, he suggested that Itō's relations with Zhang Zidong were probably important to examine. This advice offered me a breakthrough and enabled me to write Chapter 6. The epilogue of one of Professor Kobayashi's major works, *Nihon no tairiku seisaku* [Japan's Continental Policy],[2] includes this passage: "A good scholarly study consists of connected steps in a carefully reasoned argument backed up by empirical evidence; the steps of the argument are so closely interrelated that the entire structure will never break apart." I hope this book, too, has such a firmly coherent structure.

Finally I would like to express my appreciation to Shirato Naoto of the Chūō Kōron Shinsha publishing company's "Chūkō shinsho" editorial department. He met me in the spring of 2005 to request that I write this book, hoping that I would produce a biography of Itō Hirobumi to be published to coincide with the 100th anniversary of his death. I accepted, but I could not finish it in time for the anniversary year. I completed it the following year.

Takii Kazuhiro
March 2010

Notes

1 Itō Yukio 2009.
2 Kobayashi Michihiko 1996.

References

Unpublished Documents

"Inoue Kaoru monjo"
   "Inoue Kaoru kankei monjo" 井上馨関係文書 [Inoue Kaoru Papers]. In the collection of Japanese National Diet Library's Kensei Shiryōshitsu (Modern Japanese Political History Documents Room).

"Itō Hirobumi shuki gaiyū nikki"
   "Itō Hirobumi shuki gaiyū nikki" 伊藤博文手記 外遊日記 [Itō Hirobumi's Notes and Overseas Travel Diary]. In "Itō Hirobumi monjo (sono 2)" 伊藤博文文書 (その二) [Itō Hirobumi Papers (2)]. In the collection of Japanese National Diet Library's Kensei Shiryōshitsu (Modern Japanese Political History Documents Room).

"Itō Miyoji monjo"
   "Itō Miyoji kankei monjo" 伊東巳代治関係文書 [Itō Miyoji Papers]. In the collection of Japanese National Diet Library's Kensei Shiryōshitsu (Modern Japanese Political History Documents Room).

"Itō monjo"
   "Itō Hirobumi monjo" 伊藤博文文書 [Itō Hirobumi Papers]. In the collection of Japanese National Diet Library's Kensei Shiryōshitsu (Modern Japanese Political History Documents Room).

"Kensei kōgi"
   Ariga Nagao 有賀長雄. "Kensei kōgi" 憲政講義. In "Itō Miyoji kankei monjo" [Itō Miyoji Papers] in the collection of the Japanese National Diet Library's Kensei Shiryōshitsu (Modern Japanese Political History Documents Room).

"Kuratomi monjo"
   "Kuratomi Yūzaburō kankei monjo" 倉富勇三郎関係文書 [Kuratomi Yūzaburō Papers]. In the collection of Japanese National Diet Library's Kensei Shiryōshitsu (Modern Japanese Political History Documents Room).

"Makino monjo"
   "Makino Nobuaki kankei monjo" 牧野伸顕関係文書 [Makino Nobuaki Papers]. In the collection of Japanese National Diet Library's Kensei Shiryōshitsu (Modern Japanese Political History Documents Room).

"Mitsudai nikki 1907"
   "Mitsudai nikki Meiji yonjūnen" 密大日記明治四十年 [The Army's Secret Diary, 1907]. In the collection of the National Institute for Defense Studies, Ministry of Defense. Japan Center for Asian Historical Records, National Archives of Japan, C 03022854500.

"Sanjō-ke monjo"
   "Sanjō-ke monjo" 三条家文書 [Sanjō Family Documents]. In the collection of Japanese National Diet Library's Kensei Shiryōshitsu (Modern Japanese Political History Documents Room).
"Terauchi monjo"
   "Terauchi Masatake kankei monjo" 寺内正毅関係文書 [Terauchi Masatake Papers]. In the collection of Japanese National Diet Library's Kensei Shiryōshitsu (Modern Japanese Political History Documents Room).

Published References

In Japanese

Aoki 1970
   Aoki Shūzō 青木周蔵. *Aoki Shūzō jiden* 青木周蔵自伝 [Autobiography of Aoki Shūzō]. Heibonsha, 1970.
Ariga 1889
   Ariga Nagao 有賀長雄. "Hozumi Yatsuka-kun Teikoku kenpō no hōri o ayamaru" [Hozumi Yatsuka Is Mistaken about the Principles of the Constitution of the Empire]. *Kenpō zasshi* 6–8 (1889).
Ariga 1890
   Ariga Nagao. *Daijin sekinin ron* 大臣責任論 [A Study of the Responsibility of Ministers of State]. Meihōdō, 1890.
Ariga 1901
   Ariga Nagao. "Kokka to kyūchū no kankei" [The Relationship between the State and the Imperial Court]. *Kokka Gakkai zasshi* 167 (1901).
Ariga 1901–1902
   Ariga Nagao. *Kokuhōgaku* 国法学 [Science of National Law], 3 vols. Tōkyō Senmon Gakkō Shuppanbu, 1901–1902.
Ariizumi 1983
   Ariizumi Sadao 有泉貞夫. *Hoshi Tōru* 星亨 [Hoshi Tōru]. Asahi Shinbunsha, 1983.
Banno 1971
   Banno Junji 坂野潤治. *Meiji kenpō taisei no kakuritsu: Fukokukyōhei to minryoku kyūyō* 明治憲法体制の確立: 富国強兵と民力休養 [Establishment of the Meiji Constitutional System: Enrich the Country, Strengthen the Army, and Alleviate the Burden on the People]. Tōkyō Daigaku Shuppankai, 1971.
Che 2009
   Che Je-mok 崔在穆. "Itō Hirobumi no Kankoku Jukyō kan" 伊藤博文の韓国儒教観 [Itō Hirobumi's View of Korean Confucianism]. In Itō and Lee 2009.
Ding and Zhan 2004
   Ding Wenjiang 丁文江 and Zhan Fengtian 趙豊田, eds. (ed. and trans. by Shimada Kenji 島田虔次). *Ryō Keichō nenpu chōhen* (annotated Japanese translation of Liang Qichao nianpu changbian 梁啓超年譜長編 [Chronological Biography of Liang Qichao]), 5 vols. Iwanami Shoten, 2004.
Enzetsu zenshū
   Hakubunkan Henshūkyoku 博文館編輯局 (Hakubunkan Editorial Office), ed. *Itō-kō enzetsu zenshū* 伊藤公演説全集 [A Corpus of Prince Itō Hirobumi's Speeches]. Hakubunkan, 1910.

Enzetsushū
    Itō Hirobumi 伊藤博文. 伊藤侯演説集 *Itō-kō enzetsushū* [Collected Speeches by Marquis Itō Hirobumi], 3 vols. Tōkyō Nichinichi Shinbun, 1899.

Gaikō
    Gaimushō 外務省 (Japanese Ministry of Foreign Affairs), ed. *Nihon gaikō monjo* 日本外交文書 [Documents on Japanese Foreign Policy], 73 vols. Nihon Kokusai Rengō Kyōkai (U.N. Association of Japan), 1947–1963.

Gaimushō 1965
    Gaimushō (Japanese Ministry of Foreign Affairs), ed. *Nihon gaikō nenpyō narabini shuyō monjo* 日本外交年表並主要文書 [Chronology and Important Select Documents in Japanese Diplomacy], 2 vols. Hara Shobō, 1965–1966.

Gotō 1996
    Gotō Shinpachirō 後藤新八郎. *Hōsei-shi gunji-shi kenkyū gyōseki shū* 法制史・軍事史研究業績集 [A Collection of Studies on the History of Legal System and the History of Military Affairs]. Private edition, 1996.

Hara nikki
    Hara Keiichirō 原圭一郎, ed. *Hara Kei nikki* 原敬日記 [The Diary of Hara Kei (Takashi)], 6 vols. Fukumura Shuppan, 1965–1967.

Hara 2003
    Hara Takeshi 原武史. *Jikiso to ōken* 直訴と王権 [Direct Petitions and Royal Authority]. Hara Shobō, 2003.

Hayashi 2002
    Hayashi Gonsuke 林権助. *Waga nanajūnen o kataru* わが七十年を語る [An Account of My Seventy Years]. Yumani Shobō, 2002.

Hazama 1999
    Hazama Naoki 狭間直樹, ed. *Kyōdō kenkyū Ryō Keichō: Seiyō kindai shisō juyō to Meiji Nihon* 共同研究 梁啓超：西洋近代思想受容と明治日本 [Collaborative Research on Lian Qichao: Meiji Japan and Acceptance of Modern Western Thought]. Misuzu Shobō, 1999.

Hirano 2007
    Hirano Satoshi 平野聡. *Dai Shin teikoku to Chūka no konmei* 大清帝国と中華の混迷 [The Great Empire of Qing and the "Central Flower" in Chaos]. Kōdansha, 2007.

Hiratsuka 1969
    Hiratsuka Atsushi 平塚篤. *Hisho ruisan: Gaikō hen (ge)* 秘書類纂 外交編（下）[Classified Collection of Itō Hirobumi's Private Papers: Foreign Policy (Part 3)]. Hara Shobō, 1969.

Hiroku
    Hiratsuka Atsushi, ed. *Itō Hirobumi hiroku* 伊藤博文秘録 [Confidential Papers of Itō Hirobumi], 2 vols. Hara Shobō, 1982.

Hogohiroi
    Sasaki Takayuki 佐佐木高行. *Hogohiroi: Sasaki Takayuki nikki* 保古飛呂比：佐佐木高行日記 ["Hogohiroi," the Diary of Sasaki Takayuki], 12 vols. Tōkyō Daigaku Shuppankai, 1970–1979.

Horiguchi 2003
    Horiguchi Osamu 堀口修 (Nishikawa Makoto 西川誠, ed.). *Suematsu shishaku-ke shozō monjo* 末松子爵家所蔵文書 [Documents in the Collection of the Viscount Suematsu Family], 2 vols. Yumani Shobō, 2003.

Hozumi 1899
    Hozumi Yatsuka 穂積八束. "Teikoku kenpō no hōri" 帝国憲法の法理 [Principles of the Constitution of the Empire]. *Kokka Gakkai zasshi* 3: 25–32 (1899).

Inoue Kaoru Monjo Kōdokukai 2008
   Inoue Kaoru Monjo Kōdokukai 井上馨文書購読会 [Society for Reading the "Inoue Kaoru Monjo"]. "'Inoue Kaoru kankei monjo' shoshū Itō Hirobumi shokan honkoku, Zoku" "井上馨関係文書" 所収 伊藤博文書簡翻刻 (続) [Reproduction of Itō Hirobumi's Letters (Part 2), in "Inoue Kaoru kankei monjo" (Inoue Kaoru Papers)]. *Sankō shoshi kenkyū* 参考書誌研究 68 (2008).

Inoue Kowashi den
   Inoue Kowashi Denki Henshū Iinkai 井上毅伝記編集委員会 [Editorial Committee of *Inoue Kowashi den*], ed. *Inoue Kowashi den: Shiryō-hen* 井上毅伝: 資料編 [Biography of Inoue Kowashi: Documents]. Kokugakuin Daigaku Toshokan, 1966–.

Iokibe 2003
   Iokibe Kaoru 五百旗頭薫. *Ōkuma Shigenobu to seitō seiji: Fukusū seitōsei no kigen Meiji 14-nen–Taishō 3-nen* 大隈重信と政党政治: 複数政党制の起源 明治十四年-大正三年 [Ōkuma Shigenobu and Party Government: The Origin of Multi-Party System from 1879 to 1914]. Tōkyō Daigaku Shuppankai, 2003.

Ishikawa-ken shi
   Ishikawa-ken 石川県 [Ishikawa Prefecture]. *Ishikawa-ken shi* 石川県史 [A History of Ishikawa Prefecture], 5 vols. Ishikawa-ken Toshokan Kyōkai, 1974.

Itō Akio 1977
   Itō Akio 伊東昭雄. "Henpō ishin undō to sono shisō" 変法維新運動とその思想 [The Reformation Movement and Its Thoughts]. In Nishi 1977.

Itō and Lee 2009
   Itō Yukio 伊藤之雄 and Lee Sung-Hwan 李盛煥, eds. *Itō Hirobumi to Kankoku tōchi* 伊藤博文と韓国統治 [Itō Hirobumi and His Governing of Korea]. Minerva Shobō, 2009.

Itō den
   Shunpo-kō Tsuishōkai 春畝公追頌会 [Society for Honoring the Achievements of Prince Shunpo (Itō's alias)], ed. *Itō Hirobumi den* 伊藤博文伝 [A Biography of Itō Hirobumi], 3 vols. Hara Shobō, 1970.

Itō Hirobumi 1907
   Itō Hirobumi 伊藤博文. "Teikoku kenpō seitei no yurai" 帝国憲法制定の由来 [History of the Establishment of the Constitution of the Empire of Japan], in Ōkuma Shigenobu 大隈重信 comp., *Kaikoku gojūnen-shi* 開国五十年史 [A History of Fifty Years after the Opening of the Country], vol. 1. Kaikoku Gojūnen-shi Hakkōjo, 1907.

Itō Miyoji
   Shinteikai 晨亭会. *Hakushaku Itō Miyoji* 伯爵伊東巳代治 [Count Itō Miyoji], 2 vols. Shinteikai, 1938.

Itō Miyoji 1910
   Itō Miyoji 伊東巳代治. "Shinkoku kenpō to waga kuni" 清国憲法と我国 [The Qing Chinese Constitution and Our Country]. *Kokumin shinbun* 國民新聞, October 5, 1910.

Itō monjo (Hanawa)
   Itō Hirobumi Kankei Monjo Kenkyūkai 伊藤博文関係文書研究会 [Society for the Study of Itō Hirobumi Papers], ed. *Itō Hirobumi kankei monjo* 伊藤博文関係文書 [Itō Hirobumi Papers], 9 vols. Hanawa Shobō, 1973–1981.

Itō nikki
   Itō Miyoji. *Itō Miyoji nikki kiroku: Mikan Suiusō nikki* 伊東巳代治日記・記録: 未刊翠雨荘日記 [The Diary and Records of Itō Miyoji: Unpublished Suiusō Diary], 7 vols. Yumani Shobō, 1999.

Itō Shin'ichi 1979
> Itō Shin'ichi 伊藤真一. "Chichi Hirobumi o kataru" 父・博文を語る [Talking about My Father Hirobumi], in Muramatsu Takeshi 村松剛. *Nihon bunka o kangaeru: Muramatsu Takeshi taidanshū* 日本文化を考える: 村松剛対談集 [Thoughts about Japanese Culture (Muramatsu Takeshi Collection of Dialogues)]. Nihon Kyōbunsha, 1979.

Itō Takao 2000
> Itō Takao 伊藤孝夫. *Taishō demokurashi-ki no hō to shakai* 大正デモクラシー期の法と社会 [Law and Society in the Period of Taishō Democracy]. Kyōto Daigaku Gakujutsu Shuppankai, 2000.

Itō Yukio 1999
> Itō Yukio 伊藤之雄. *Rikken kokka no kakuritsu to Itō Hirobumi* 立憲国家の確立と伊藤博文 [Itō Hirobumi and the Establishment of Constitutional State]. Yoshikawa Kōbunkan, 1999.

Itō Yukio 2000
> Itō Yukio. *Rikken kokka to Nichi-Ro sensō* 立憲国家と日露戦争 [A Constitutional State and the Russo-Japanese War]. Bokutakusha, 2000.

Itō Yukio 2009
> Itō Yukio. *Itō Hirobumi: Kindai Nihon o tsukutta otoko* 伊藤博文: 近代日本を創った男 [Itō Hirobumi, the Man Who Created Modern Japan]. Kōdansha, 2009.

Itō-kō zenshū
> Komatsu Midori 小松緑, ed. *Itō-kō zenshū* 伊藤公全集 [Collected Works and Materials of Prince Itō Hirobumi], 3 vols. Itō-kō Zenshū Kankōkai, 1927.

Iwakura monjo
> Nihon Shiseki Kyōkai 日本史籍協会, ed. *Iwakura Tomomi kankei monjo* 岩倉具視関係文書 [Iwakura Tomomi Papers], 8 vols. Tōkyō Daigaku Shuppankai, 1968–1969.

Jikki
> Tada Kōmon 多田好門. *Iwakura-kō jikki* 岩倉公実記 [Authentic Chronicle of Prince Iwakura], 3 vols. Hara Shobō, 1968.

Kaneko 2001
> Kaneko Kentarō 金子堅太郎 (collation editing by Ōbuchi Kazunori 大淵和憲). *Ō-Bei giin seido torishirabe junkaiki* 欧米議院制度取調巡回記 [Account of the Inspection Tour of Parliamentary Systems in Europe and the United States]. Shinzansha Shuppan, 2001.

Kawajiri 1994
> Kawajiri Fumihiko 川尻文彦. "'Chūtai seiyō' ron to 'gakusen': Shin-matsu 'Chūtai seiyō' ron no ichisokumen to Chō Shidō *Kangakuhen*" "中体西用"論と"学戦": 清末"中体西用" 論の一側面と張之洞 "勧学篇" [The "Chinese Essence, Western Technology" Theory and Ideological Divisions: An Aspect of the Late-Qing Theory of "Chinese Essence, Western Technology" and Zhang Zhidong's *Quanxue Pian*]. *Chūgoku kenkyū geppō* 中国研究月報 48:8 (1994).

Kawata 2001
> Kawata Keiichi 川田敬一. *Kindai Nihon no kokka keisei to kōshitsu zaisan* 近代日本の国家形成と皇室財産 [Modern Japan's State Formation and Imperial Household's Assets]. Hara Shobō, 2001.

Kazoku Dōhō Kai enzetsushū
> *Kazoku Dōhō Kai enzetsushū* (1889–9) 華族同方会演説集. 6 vols, publisher unknown.

Kido monjo
    Kido Takayoshi Kankei Monjo Kenkyūkai 木戸孝允関係文書研究会 [Society for the Study of Kido Takayoshi Papers], ed. *Kido Takayoshi kankei monjo* 木戸孝允関係文書 [Kido Takayoshi Papers], 4 vols. Tōkyō Daigaku Shuppankai, 2005.

Kido nikki
    Kido Takayoshi 木戸孝允. *Kido Takayoshi nikki* 木戸孝允日記 [The Diary of Kido Takayoshi], 3 vols. Tōkyō Daigaku Shuppankai, 1967.

Kikuchi 2005
    Kikuchi Hideaki 菊池秀明. *Rasuto enperā to kindai Chūgoku* ラストエンペラーと近代中国 [The Last Emperor and Modern China]. Kōdansha, 2005.

Kim 1996
    Kim Tae-hoon 金泰勲. *Kindai Nik-Kan kyōiku kankeishi kenkyū josetsu* 近代日韓教育関係史研究序説 [An Introductory Study on the History of Modern Japan–Korea Educational Relations]. Yūzankaku Shuppan, 1996.

Kimura 2007
    Kimura Kan 木村幹. *Kōsō, Minpi* 高宗・閔妃 [Kojong and Queen Min]. Minerva Shobō, 2007.

Kobayashi 1996
    Kobayashi Michihiko 小林道彦. *Nihon no tairiku seisaku 1895–1914: Katsura Tarō to Gotō Shinpei* 日本の大陸政策 1895–1914: 桂太郎と後藤新平 [Japan's Continent Policy 1895–1914: Katsura Tarō and Gotō Shinpei]. Nansōsha, 1996.

Kobayashi 1966
    Kobayashi Tatsuo 小林龍夫, ed. *Suiusō nikki* 翠雨荘日記 [Itō Miyoji's Diary]. Hara Shobō, 1966.

Kobayashi 1990
    Kobayashi Yūgo 小林雄吾 (Yamamoto Shirō 山本四郎, ed.). In vol. 1 of *Rikken Seiyūkai shi* 立憲政友会史 [A History of Rikken Seiyūkai]. Nihon Tosho Sentā, 1990.

Kokumin no tomo 1899
    Kokumin no tomo 国民之友 5:22 (1899), pp. 63–64.

Komatsu 1934
    Komatsu Midori 小松緑. *Shunpo-kō to Gansetsu-kō* 春畝公と含雪公 [Prince Shunpo (Itō Hirobumi) and Prince Gansetsu (Yamagata Aritomo)]. Gakuji Shoin, 1934.

Komatsu 2005
    Komatsu Midori. *Chōsen heigō no rimen* 朝鮮併合之裏面 [Behind the Korean Annexation]. Repr. Ryūkei Shosha, 2005.

Masuda 1996
    Masuda Tomoko 増田知子. "Rikken Seiyūkai e no michi" 立憲政友会への道 [The Path to the Seiyūkai, the Friends of Constitutional Government], in Inoue Mitsusada 井上光貞 et al., eds. *Meiji Kenpō taisei no tenkai* 明治憲法体制の展開 [The Development of the Meiji Constitution System], 2 vols. Yamakawa Shuppansha, 1996.

Masumi 1965–1980
    Masumi Jun'nosuke 升味準之輔. *Nihon seitōshi ron* 日本政党史論 [A Study of Japanese Political Parties], 7 vols. Tōkyō Daigaku Shuppankai, 1965–1980.

Matsuda 2009
    Matsuda Toshihiko 松田利彦. *Nihon no Chōsen shokuminchi shihai to keisatsu 1905–1945* 日本の朝鮮植民地支配と警察 1905–1945 [Japan's Colonial Rule of Korea and the Police 1905–1945]. Azekura Shobō, 2009.

Matsukata monjo
　　Matsukata Mineo 松方峰雄 et al., eds. *Matsukata Masayoshi kankei monjo* 松方正義関係文書 [Matsukata Masayoshi Papers], 20 vols. Daitō Bunka Daigaku Tōyō Kenkyūjo, 1979–2001.

Meiji tennō-ki
　　Kunaichō 宮内庁 (Imperial Household Agency), ed. *Meiji tennō-ki* 明治天皇紀 [Chronicle of Emperor Meiji], 13 vols. Yoshikawa Kōbunkan, 1968–1977.

Ministry of Agriculture and Commerce 1917
　　Nōshōmushō (Yawata) Seitetsusho Tōkyō Shutchōjo 農商務省 (八幡) 製鉄所東京出張所 (Ministry of Agriculture and Commerce [Yawata] Steel Works, Tokyo Branch Office). *Seitetsusho tai Kan'yahyō konsu kankei teiyō* 製鉄所対漢冶萍公司関係提要 [The Steel Works' Compendium Related to the Hanyeping Coal and Steel Company]. 1917.

Mitani 1995
　　Mitani Taichirō 三谷太一郎. *Nihon seitō seiji no keisei: Hara Takashi no seiji shidō no tenkai (zōhoban)* 日本政党政治の形成: 原敬の政治指導の展開 (増補版) [Formation of Japanese Party Government: Development of Hara Takashi's Political Leadership (Enlarged Edition)]. Tōkyō Daigaku Shuppankai, 1995.

Miura 1988
　　Miura Gorō 三浦梧楼. *Kanju shōgun kaikoroku* 観樹将軍回顧録 [Memoirs of Miura Gorō]. Chūō Kōron Sha, 1988.

Moriyama 1987
　　Moriyama Shigenori 森山茂徳. *Kindai Nik-Kan kankeishi kenkyū* 近代日韓関係史研究 [A Study of the History of Japan–Korea Relations]. Tōkyō Daigaku Shuppankai, 1987.

Murai 2005
　　Murai Ryōta 村井良太. *Seitō naikakusei no seiritsu* 政党内閣制の成立 [Establishment of the Party Cabinet System]. Yūhikaku, 2005.

Murata 1992
　　Murata Yūjirō 村田雄二郎. "Kō Yūi to 'Tōgaku': *Nihon shomokushi* o megutte" 康有為と"東学": "日本書目志"をめぐって [Kang Youwei and Eastern Learning: Focus on the *Riben Shumuzhi* (Bibliography of Japanese Books)], in *Gaikokugo-ka kenkyū kiyō* 外国語科研究紀要 [Research Bulletin of the Department of Foreign Languages, University of Tokyo College of Arts and Sciences] 40:5 (1992).

Nagao 2000
　　Nagao Ryūichi 長尾龍一. *Rekishi jūbako sumi tsutsuki* 歴史重箱隅つつき [A Peep into Historical Details]. Shinzansha Shuppan, 2000.

Naraoka 2006
　　Naraoka Sōchi 奈良岡聰智. *Katō Takaaki to seitō seiji: Nidaiseitō-sei e no michi* 加藤高明と政党政治: 二大政党制への道 [Katō Takaaki and Party Politics: Path to a Two-Party System]. Yamakawa Shuppansha, 2006.

Naraoka 2009
　　Naraoka Sōchi. "Igirisu kara mita Itō Hirobumi tōkan to Kankoku tōchi" イギリスから見た伊藤博文統監と韓国統治 [Resident-General Itō Hirobumi and His Governance of Korea as Seen by Britain]. In Itō and Lee 2009.

Nishi 1977
　　Nishi Junzō 西順蔵, ed. *Genten Chūgoku kindai shisōshi* 原典中国近代思想史 [Original Sources of Chinese History of Modern Thought], 6 vols. Iwanami Shoten, 1976–1977.

Nitobe zenshū
   Nitobe Inazō 新渡戸稲造. *Nitobe Inazō zenshū* 新渡戸稲造全集 [The Complete Works of Nitobe Inazō], 25 vols. Kyōbunkan, 1969–2001.

Ogawara 2010
   Ogawara Hiroyuki 小川原宏幸. *Itō Hirobumi no Kankoku heigō kōsō to Chōsen shakai: Ōkenron no sōkoku* 伊藤博文の韓国併合構想と朝鮮社会: 王権論の相克 [Itō Hirobumi's Korean Annexation Plan and Korean Society: Conflicting Views on the Royal Powers]. Iwanami Shoten, 2010.

Ōishi 2005
   Ōishi Makoto 大石眞. *Nihon kenpō-shi (Dai-ni-han)* 日本憲法史 (第二版) [A History of the Japanese Constitution (Second Edition)]. Yūhikaku, 2005.

Ōishi 2008
   Ōishi Makoto. *Kenpō chitsujo e no tenbō* 憲法秩序への展望 [Prospects of Constitutional Order]. Yūhikaku, 2008.

Ōishi et al. 1998
   Ōishi Makoto, Takami Katsutoshi 高見勝利, and Nagao Ryūichi 長尾龍一, eds. *Kenpō-shi no omoshirosa* 憲法史の面白さ [The Fascination of Constitutional History]. Shinzansha Shuppan, 1998.

Ōkubo monjo
   Nihon Shiseki Kyōkai 日本史籍協会, ed. *Ōkubo Toshimichi monjo* 大久保利通文書 [Ōkubo Toshimichi Papers], 10 vols. Tōkyō Daigaku Shuppankai, 1967–1969.

Ōkubo nikki
   Ōkubo Toshimichi 大久保利通. *Ōkubo Toshimichi nikki* 大久保利通日記 [The Diary of Ōkubo Toshimichi], 2 vols. Tōkyō Daigaku Shuppankai, 1969.

Ōkuma monjo
   Waseda Daigaku Daigakushi Shiryō Sentā 早稲田大学大学史資料センター (Waseda University Archives), ed. *Ōkuma Shigenobu kankei monjo* 大隈重信関係文書 [Ōkuma Shigenobu Papers], 8 vols. Misuzu Shobō, 2004–.

Ōkuma-kō hachijūgo-nen shi
   Ōkuma-kō Hachijūgo-nen-shi Kai 大隈侯八十五年史会 (Society for the History of Marquis Ōkuma's Eighty-Five Years), ed. *Ōkuma-kō hachijūgo-nen shi* 大隈侯八十五年史 [History of Marquis Ōkuma's Eighty-Five Years], 3 vols. Hara Shobō, 1970.

Onogawa 1969
   Onogawa Hidemi 小野川秀美. *Shin-matsu seiji shisō kenkyū* 清末政治思想研究 [A Study of Late-Qing Political Thought]. Misuzu Shobō, 1969.

Oyama 1967
   Oyama Hironari 小山博也. *Meiji seitō soshiki ron* 明治政党組織論 [A Study of Meiji-era Political Party Organization]. Tōyō Keizai Shinpōsha, 1967.

Ozaki Saburō nikki
   Ozaki Saburō 尾崎三良. *Ozaki Saburō nikki* 尾崎三良日記 [The Diary of Ozaki Saburō], 3 vols. Chūō Kōron Sha, 1991–1992.

Ozaki 1962
   Ozaki Yukio 尾崎行雄. *Gakudō jiden: Nihon kenseishi o kataru* 咢堂自伝: 日本憲政史を語る [The Autobiography of Gakudō (Ozaki's alias): Talking about a History of Japanese Constitutional Government]. In vol. 11 of *Ozaki Gakudō zenshū* 尾崎咢堂全集. Ozaki Gakudō Zenshū Kankōkai, 1962.

Peng 1976
   Peng Zezhou 彭澤周. *Chūgoku no kindaika to Meiji ishin* 中国の近代化と明治維新 [Chinese Modernization and the Meiji Restoration]. Dōhōsha Shuppanbu, 1976.

Saigusa and Iida 1957
> Saigusa Hiroto 三枝博音 and Iida Ken'ichi 飯田賢一, eds. *Nihon kindai seitetsu gijutsu hattatsushi: Yawata Seitetsusho no kakuritsu katei* 日本近代製鉄技術発達史: 八幡製鉄所の確立過程 [A History of Development of Japan's Modern Steel Technology: The Process of the Establishment of the Yawata Steel Works]. Tōyō Keizai Shinpōsha, 1957.

Saitō 1967
> Saitō Ryūsuke 斎藤隆介. *Shokuninshū mukashi banashi* 職人衆昔ばなし [An Account of Old Days of Craftspeople]. Bungei Shunjū, 1967.

Sakamoto 1991
> Sakamoto Kazuto 坂本一登. *Itō Hirobumi to Meiji kokka keisei* 伊藤博文と明治国家形成 [Itō Hirobumi and the Establishment of the Meiji State]. Yoshikawa Kōbunkan, 1991.

Sasaki 1995
> Sasaki Takashi 佐々木隆. *Hanbatsu seifu to rikken seiji* 藩閥政府と立憲政治 [The Oligarchic Government and Constitutionalism]. Yoshikawa Kōbunkan, 1995.

Sasaki 2002
> Sasaki Takashi. *Meijijin no rikiryō* 明治人の力量 [The Caliber of Meiji People]. Kōdansha, 2002.

Sasaki 2003
> Sasaki Takayuki 佐佐木高行. *Sasaki Takayuki nikki: Kazashi no sakura* 佐佐木高行日記かざしの桜 [The Diary of Sasaki Takayuki: *Kazashi no sakura*]. Hokusensha, 2003.

Satō 2000
> Satō Yumi 佐藤由美. *Shokuminchi kyōiku seisaku no kenkyū* 植民地教育政策の研究 [A Study of Colonial Education Policy]. Ryūkei Shosha, 2000.

Seigai den
> Inoue Kaoru-kō Denki Hensankai 井上馨侯伝記編纂会 [Marquis Inoue Kaoru Biographical Compilation Society], ed. *Seigai Inoue-kō den* 世外井上公伝 [Biography of Inoue Kaoru], 5 vols. Hara Shobō, 1968.

Seiyū 1900
> *Seiyū* 西友. Rikken Seiyūkai Kaihōkyoku, 1900.

Shiba 2002
> Shiba Ryōtarō 司馬遼太郎. *Tobu ga gotoku* 翔ぶが如く [Like Flying (a novel about Saigō Takamori and Ōkubo Toshimichi)], 10 vols. Bungei Shunjū, 2002.

Shiba and Banno 1995
> Shiba Ryōtarō and Banno Junji 坂野潤治. "Nihon to iu kokka" 日本という国家 [The State Known as Japan]. *Sekai* 世界, June 1995.

Shibusawa denki shiryō
> Shibusawa Seien Kinen Zaidan Ryūmonsha 渋沢青淵記念財団竜門社 (Ryūmonsha, Shibusawa Eiichi Memorial Foundation), ed. *Shibusawa Eiichi denki shiryō* 渋沢栄一伝記資料 [Shibusawa Eiichi Biographical Materials]. Shibusawa Eiichi Denki Shiryō Kankōkai, 1955–1960.

Shimizu 2007
> Shimizu Yuichirō 清水唯一朗. *Seitō to kanryō no kindai: Nihon ni okeru rikken tōchi kōzō no sōkoku* 政党と官僚の近代: 日本における立憲統治構造の相克 [Political Parties and Bureaucrats of Modern Times: Strife over Constitutional Governance in Japan]. Fujiwara Shoten, 2007.

Shin 2008
> Shin Chang-u 慎蒼宇. *Shokuminchi Chōsen no keisatsu to minshū sekai 1894–1919: "Kindai" to "dentō"o meguru seiji bunka* 植民地朝鮮の警察と民衆世界 1894–1919:

"近代"と"伝統"をめぐる政治文化 [The Police and the Masses in Colonial Korea 1894–1919: Political Culture over "Modernity" and "Tradition"]. Yūshisha, 2008.

Shūsei
　Kim Chong-myong 金正明. *Nik-Kan gaikō shiryō shūsei* 日韓外交資料集成 [A Collection of Materials Related to Japanese-Korean Relations], 10 vols. Gan'nandō Shoten, 1962–1967.

Siemes 1970
　Siemes, Johannes J. ジーメス, trans. Honma Hideyo 本間英世. *Nihon kokka no kindaika to Roesurā* 日本国家の近代化とロエスラー [Modernization of the Japanese State and Roeslers]. Miraisha, 1970.

Soda 2009
　Soda Saburō 曽田三郎. *Rikken kokka Chūgoku e no shidō: Meiji kensei to kindai Chūgoku* 立憲国家中国への始動: 明治憲政と近代中国 [China's Start as a Constitutional State: Meiji Constitutionalism and China]. Kyoto: Shibunkaku Shuppan, 2009.

Stein 1991
　Stein, Lorenz von ローレンツ・シュタイン. *Shakai no gainen to undō hōsoku* 社会の概念と運動法則 [The Concept of Society and the Law of Movement]. Minerva Shobō, 1991. Translation by Morita Tsutomu 森田勉 of the "introduction" in the *Geschichte der sozialen Bewegung in Frankreich von 1789 bis auf unsere Tage* (History of the French Social Movements from 1789 to the Present [1850]), 3 vols. Leipzig, 1850.

Suematsu 1997
　Suematsu Kenchō 末松謙澄. *Kōshi Itō-kō* 孝子伊藤公 [Prince Itō, Dutiful Son]. Matsuno Shoten, 1997.

Sufu 1977
　Sufu Kōhei 周布公平, ed. *Sufu Masanosuke den* 周布政之助伝 [A Biography of Sufu Masanosuke], 2 vols. Tōkyō Daigaku Shuppankai, 1977.

Suzuki 1999
　Suzuki Hiroyuki 鈴木博之. *Nihon no "Geniusu Roki"* 日本の"地霊 (ゲニウス・ロキ)" [Japan's "Genius Loci"]. Kōdansha, 1999.

Takada 1927
　Takada Sanae 高田早苗. "Ko Ariga Hakushi omoide no ki" 故有賀博士思出の記 [My Recollections of the Late Ariga Nagao]. *Gaikō jihō* 外交時報 543 (1927).

Takahashi 1992
　Takahashi Hidenao 高橋秀直. "Haihan seifu ron" 廃藩政府論 [A Study of "Anti-Han-Clique" Government]. *Nihonshi kenkyū* 日本史研究 356 (1992).

Takahashi 1993
　Takahashi Hidenao. "Seikanron seihen no seiji katei" 征韓論政変の政治過程 [The Process of the Political Crisis of 1873]. *Shirin* 史林 76:5 (1993).

Takahashi 1995
　Takahashi Hidenao. *Nis-Shin sensō e no michi* 日清戦争への道 [The Path to the First Sino-Japanese War]. Tōkyō Sōgensha, 1995.

Takahashi 1976
　Takahashi Korekiyo 高橋是清. *Takahashi Korekiyo jiden* 高橋是清自伝 [The Autobiography of Takahashi Korekiyo], 2 vols. Chūō Kōron Sha, 1976.

Takii 1998a
　Takii Kazuhiro 瀧井一博. "Cheko ni nokoru Itō Hirobumi no tegami: Buruno ni 'Kurumekki monjo' o tazunete (1)" チェコに残る伊藤博文の手紙ブルノに"クルメッキ文書"を訪ねて (1) [Itō Hirobumi's Letters Remaining in Czech Republic: Visiting

the "Johann Ritter von Chlumecky Papers" in Brno (1)]. *Shosai no mado* 書斎の窓 475. Yūhikaku, 1998.

Takii 1998b
Takii Kazuhiro. "Cheko ni nokoru Itō Hirobumi no tegami: Buruno ni 'Kurumekki monjo' o tazunete (2)" チェコに残る伊藤博文の手紙 ブルノに"クルメッキ文書"を訪ねて (2) [Itō Hirobumi's Letters Remaining in Czech Republic: Visiting the "Johann Ritter von Chlumecky Papers" in Brno (2)]. *Shosai no mado* 476. Yūhikaku, 1998.

Takii 1998c
Takii Kazuhiro. "'Gunaisuto monjo' saihō" 「グナイスト文書」再訪 [Revisiting the "Rudolf von Gneist Papers"]. *Shosai no mado* 480. Yūhikaku, 1998.

Takii 1999
Takii Kazuhiro. *Doitsu kokkagaku to Meiji kokusei: Shutain kokkagaku no kiseki* ドイツ国家学と明治国制: シュタイン国家学の軌跡 [Staatswissenschaften (Science of the State) and the Meiji State System: The Locus of Stein's Staatswissenschaften]. Minerva Shobō, 1999.

Takii 2003
Takii Kazuhiro. *Bunmeishi no naka no Meiji kenpō* 文明史のなかの明治憲法. [The Meiji Constitution in the History of Civilization]. Kōdansha, 2003.

Takii 2009
Takii Kazuhiro. "Chi no kyōdō to shite no Kankoku tōchi" 知の嚮導としての韓国統治 [Rule of Korea Guided by Knowledge]. In Itō and Lee 2009.

Takii 2010
Takii Kazuhiro. *Itō Hirobumi: Chi no seijika* 伊藤博文: 知の政治家 [Itō Hirobumi–Japan's First Prime Minister and Father of the Meiji Constitution]. Chūō Kōron Shinsha, 2010.

Tao 2007
Tao Demin 陶徳民. *Meiji no kangakusha to Chūgoku: Yasutsugu, Tenshū, Konan no gaikō ronsaku* 明治の漢学者と中国: 安繹・天囚・湖南の外交論策 [Meiji-era Sinologists and China: Foreign Policy Critiques by Shigeno Yasutsugu, Nishimura Tenshū, and Naitō Konan]. Suita: Kansai Daigaku Shuppanbu, 2007.

Tōa Dōbunkai 1973
Tōa Dōbunkai 東亜同文会 (East Asia Common Culture Society). *Zoku tai Shi kaikoroku* 続対支回顧録 [Memoirs about China, Sequel], 2 vols. Hara Shobō, 1973.

Tokutomi 1990
Tokutomi Iichirō (Sohō) 徳富猪一郎(蘇峰). *So-ō yume monogatari* [So-ō's Tales of Dreams] 蘇翁夢物語. Chūō Kōron Sha, 1990.

Toriumi 1988
Toriumi Yasushi 鳥海靖. *Nihon kindaishi kōgi: Meiji rikkensei no keisei to sono rinen* 日本近代史講義: 明治立憲制の形成とその理念 [Lectures on the Modern History of Japan: The Constitutional System of Meiji and Its Formation and Ideals]. Tōkyō Daigaku Shuppankai, 1988.

Toriumi 2005
Toriumi Yasushi. "Itō Hirobumi no rikken seiji chōsa: Shinshiryō o tegakari ni" 伊藤博文の立憲政治調査: 新史料を手がかりに [A Study of Itō Hirobumi's Research on Constitutional Government: Using New Materials as a Clue]. In Toriumi Yasushi et al., eds. *Nihon rikken seiji no keisei to henshitsu* 日本立憲政治の形成と変質 [The Formation and Transformation of Constitutional Government in Japan]. Yoshikawa Kōbunkan, 2005.

Tsuchiya 1962
    Tsuchiya Tadao 土屋忠雄. *Meiji zenki kyōiku seisakushi no kenkyū* 明治前期教育政策史の研究 [A Study of the History of Early-Meiji Educational Policy]. Kōdansha, 1962.

Tsuda 1970
    Tsuda Shigemaro 津田茂麿. *Meiji seijō to shin Takayuki* 明治聖上と臣高行 [Emperor Meiji and His Loyalist [Sasaki] Takayuki]. Hara Shobō, 1970.

Tsukiashi 2009
    Tsukiashi Tatsuhiko 月脚達彦. *Chōsen kaika shisō to nashonarizumu: Kindai Chōsen no keisei* 朝鮮開化思想とナショナリズム: 近代朝鮮の形成 [Korean Enlightenment Thought and Nationalism: Formation of Modern Korea]. Tōkyō Daigaku Shuppankai, 2009.

Waseda Daigaku hyakunen-shi
    Waseda Daigaku Daigaku-shi Henshūjo 早稲田大学大学史編集所 (Editorial Office of the History of Waseda University), ed. *Waseda Daigaku hyakunen-shi* 早稲田大学百年史 [Centennial History of Waseda University], 5 vols. Waseda Daigaku Shuppan, 1978–1997.

Watanabe 2001
    Watanabe Yukio 渡辺行男. *Shueichō no mita teikoku gikai* 守衛長の見た帝国議会 [The Imperial Diet as the Chief Guard Saw It]. Bungei Shunjū, 2001.

Xiong 1998
    Xiong Dayun 熊達雲. *Kindai Chūgoku kanmin no Nihon shisatsu* 近代中国官民の日本視察 [Japanese Observation by Modern Chinese Officials and People]. Seibundō, 1998.

Yamagata den
    Tokutomi Sohō 徳富蘇峰, ed. *Kōshaku Yamagata Aritomo den* 侯爵山県有朋伝 [Biography of Prince Yamagata Aritomo], 3 vols. Hara Shobō, 1969.

Yamagata monjo
    Shōyū Kurabu Yamagata Aritomo Kankei Monjo Hensan Iinkai 尚友倶楽部山県有朋関係文書編纂委員会 [Shōyū Club Editorial Committee of the Yamagata Aritomo Papers], ed. *Yamagata Aritomo kankei monjo*. 山県有朋関係文書 [Yamagata Aritomo Papers], 3 vols. Yamakawa Shuppansha, 2005–2008.

Yamamoto 1975
    Yamamoto Shirō 山本四郎. *Shoki Seiyūkai no kenkyū: Itō sōsai jidai* 初期政友会の研究: 伊藤総裁時代 [A Study of the Seiyūkai in Its Early Stage: Under Itō [Hirobumi's] Presidency]. Seibunsha, 1994.

Yamamoto 1976
    Yamamoto Shirō. "Kankoku Tōkanfu setchi to tōsuiken mondai" 韓国統監府設置と統帥権問題 [Establishment of the Office of the Resident-General in Korea and the Issue of the Imperial Prerogative of Supreme Command]. *Nihon rekishi* 日本歴史 336 (1976).

Yamamoto 1994
    Yamamoto Yūzō 山本有造. *Ryō kara en e: Bakumatsu Meiji zenki kahei mondai kenkyū* 両から円へ: 幕末・明治前期貨幣問題研究 [From *Ryō* to *Yen*: A Study of the Monetary Issue in the Bakumatsu-Early Meiji Era]. Minerva Shobō, 1994.

Yamamuro 1984
    Yamamuro Shin'ichi 山室信一. *Hōsei kanryō no jidai: Kokka no sekkei to chi no rekitei* 法制官僚の時代: 国家の設計と知の歴程 [The Time of the Legislative Bureaucracy: State-Planning and the Process of the Intelligence]. Bokutakusha, 1984.

Yamazaki 2006
 Yamazaki Minako 山崎渾子. *Iwakura Shisetsudan ni okeru shūkyō mondai* 岩倉使節団における宗教問題 [The Issue of Religion in the Iwakura Mission]. Kyoto: Shibunkaku Shuppan, 2006.

Yi 1991
 Yi Sŏng-hwan 李盛煥. *Kindai higashi-Ajia no seiji rikigaku: Kantō o meguru Nit-Chū-Chō kankei no shiteki tenkai* 近代東アジアの政治力学: 間島をめぐる日中朝関係の史的展開 [Political Dynamics in Modern East Asia: Historical Development of Japan-China-Korea Relations over Gando (Ch. Jiandao) Island]. Kinseisha, 1991.

Yoon 1982
 Yoon Keun-cha. 尹健次. *Chōsen kindai kyōiku no shisō to undō* 朝鮮近代教育の思想と運動 [Korean Modern Education Thought and Movement]. Tōkyō Daigaku Shuppankai, 1982.

Yoshida Shōin zenshū
 Yamaguchi-ken Kyōiku Iinkai 山口県教育委員会 (Board of Education, Yamaguchi Prefecture), ed. *Yoshida Shōin zenshū* 吉田松陰全集 [A Complete Collection of Yoshida Shōin's Writings], 11 vols. Iwanami Shoten, 1986.

Yu 1998
 Yu Naiming 于乃明. "Odagiri Masunosuke kenkyū: Meiji-Taishō-ki Chū-Nichi kankeishi no ichisokumen" 小田切万寿之助研究: 明治大正期中日関係史の一側面 [A Study of Odagiri Masunosuke: An Aspect of Sino-Japanese Relations in the Meiji and Taishō Eras], doctoral dissertation (1998), University of Tsukuba.

Yui 2009
 Yui Masaomi 由井正臣. *Gunbu to minshū tōgō: Nis-Shin Sensō kara Manshū Jihen-ki made* 軍部と民衆統合: 日清戦争から満州事変期まで [The Military and Popular Mobilization: The Period from the First Sino-Japanese War to the Manchurian Incident]. Iwanami Shoten, 2009.

Zeimu Daigakkō Kenkyūbu 1996
 Zeimu Daigakkō Kenkyūbu 税務大学校研究部 (National Tax College Research Department), ed. *Zeimusho no sōsetsu to zeimu gyōsei no hyakunen* 税務署の創設と税務行政の 100年 [The Establishment of Tax Office and the Centennial of Tax Administration]. Ōkura Zaimu Kyōkai, 1996.

In English

Akita 1967
 Akita, George. *Foundations of Constitutional Government in Modern Japan 1868–1900*. Harvard University Press, 1967.

Banno 1995
 Junji Banno, trans. J. A. A. Stockwin. *The Establishment of the Japanese Constitutional System* (The Nissan Institute/Routledge Japanese Studies Series). Routledge, 1995.

Beasley 1995
 Beasley, William G. *Japan Encounters the Barbarian*. Yale University Press, 1995.

Breen 1996
 John Breen. "The Imperial Oath of April 1868—Ritual, Politics, and Power in the Restoration." *Monumenta Nipponica* 51:4 (1996), pp. 407–29.

Matsuda 2011
 Matsuda Toshihiko. *Governance and Policing of Colonial Korea: 1904–1919* (Nichibunken Monograph Series no. 12). Kyoto: International Research Center for Japanese Studies, 2011.

Takii 2005
  Takii Kazuhiro. "The Constitution of Japan and Ito Hirobumi's Design." *Gaiko Forum* (English edition) 5:3 (Fall 2005).
Takii 2007
  Kazuhiro Takii, trans. David Noble. *The Meiji Constitution: The Japanese Experience of the West and the Shaping of the Modern State* (LTCB International Library Selection, no. 21). I-House Press, 2007.

In Chinese

Gu 1995
  Gu Hongming. *Zhang Wenxiang mufu jiwen* [Record of Zhang Wenxiang (Zhidong)'s Private Administration]. Shanxi Guji Chubanshe, 1995.
Hu 1967
  Hu Junzhuan. *Zhang Wenxiang gong nianpu* [Chronology of Lord Zhang Wenxiang (Zhidong)]. Wenhai Chubanshe, 1967.
Wang 1987
  Wang Xiaoqiu. *Jindai Zhong-Ri qishilu* [Revelations of Modern China and Japan]. Beijing Chubanshe, 1987.
Wu 2009
  Wu Jianjie. *Zhang Zhidong nianpu changbian* [Chronological Biography of Zhang Zhidong], 2 vols. Shanghai Jiatong Daxue Chubanshe, 2009.

Chronology

(Lunar calendar until January 1, 1873, when Japan adopted Gregorian calendar)

1841 (Tenpō 12)
Born in Chōshū domain (9th month).

1857 (Ansei 4)
Through good offices of Kuruhara Ryōzō, enters Shōka Sonjuku school in the village of Matsumoto (now city of Hagi, Yamaguchi prefecture) to study under Yoshida Shōin (9th month).

1859 (Ansei 6)
Yoshida Shōin executed (27th day, 10th month) in Edo (now Tokyo). Together with Chōshū comrades, Itō buries mentor's body at Ekōin temple at the Kozukahara execution site.

1862 (Bunkyū 2)
With Takasugi Shinsaku and others, involved in the burning of the British legation in Edo (12th day, 12th month); with Yamao Yōzō, involved in the assassination of Japanese classics scholar Hanawa Jirō.

1863 (Bunkyū 3)
1st month: Marriage to Irie Sumiko decided; 3rd month: Promoted to regular samurai status (*shibun*); 5th month: With Inoue Monta (Kaoru), Nomura Yakichi, Endō Kinsuke, and Yamao Yōzō, secretly departs for Britain despite law prohibiting citizens from traveling abroad; 23rd day, 9th month: Reaches London.

1864 (Genji 1)
3rd month: Leaves London with Inoue and reaches Japan (10th day, 6th month); 7th month: Chōshū retainers battle bakufu (shogunate) troops near imperial palace gates in Kyoto and the bakufu receives imperial order to send punitive expedition against Chōshū; 8th month: Combined squadron of four Western powers bombard Chōshū at Shimonoseki Straits.

Chronology 237

1866 (Keiō 2)
1st month: Satsuma-Chōshū alliance formed; 3rd month: Divorces wife Sumiko; 4th month: Marries Umeko, daughter of Kida Kyūbei of Jōnokoshi, Shimonoseki; 22nd day, 4th month: Granted permission to study in Britain with Takasugi but gives up the plan due to strained relations between Chōshū and the bakufu; 5th day, 6th month: The bakufu orders second punitive expedition against Chōshū; 8th month: Itō goes to Shanghai with English trader Thomas Glover to purchase steamship for Chōshū.

1867 (Keiō 3)
9th day, 1st month: Crown Prince Mutsuhito ascends throne (Emperor Meiji); 14th day, 10th month: The shogun returns political power to the emperor; 9th day, 12th month: Restoration of imperial rule proclaimed.

1868 (Keiō 4 / Meiji 1)
3rd day, 1st month: Outbreak of Boshin Civil War with the battle of Toba-Fushimi, Kyoto (ends in Hakodate, Hokkaido on 18th day, 5th month the following year); 1st day, 1st month: Itō assigned post of junior councilor (*san'yo*) with responsibility for foreign affairs in the Meiji government; 14th day, 3rd month: Charter Oath issued by the emperor; 27th day, 5th month: Appointed governor of Hyōgo prefecture; 27th day, 8th month: Emperor Meiji's enthronement ceremony held; 8th day, 9th month: Era name changed to Meiji; 11th month: Itō, hearing Himeji domain lord Sakai Tadakuni's offer for return of the land and people of his domain to the emperor (*hanseki hōkan*), submits proposal for nationwide *hanseki hōkan*.

1869 (Meiji 2)
1st month: Itō submits "Kokuze kōmoku" ("Principles of National Policy," also known as "Hyōgo ron," or Hyōgo Proposal); 6th month: The land and people of the feudal lords returned to the emperor; 7th month: New government organization order issued; assumes office as deputy vice minister of foreign affairs.

1870 (Meiji 3)
11th month: Goes to the United States with Yoshikawa Akimasa, Fukuchi Gen'ichirō, Yoshida Jirō, Kinashi Heinoshin, and others to study fiscal and monetary systems (returns to Japan 9th day, 5th month, 1871).

1871 (Meiji 4)
5th month: Based on Itō's proposal, called the New Currency Regulation, modern Japan's first monetary law is established; 14th day, 7th month: Imperial edict for the abolition of domains (*han*) and the establishment of prefectures (*ken*) issued; 12th day, 11th month: Leaves Yokohama as a deputy ambassador of the Iwakura Mission; 14th day, 12th month: Delivers speech at welcome ceremony in San Francisco ("rising sun" speech).

1872 (Meiji 5)
12th day, 2nd month: Leaves Washington for Japan with Ōkubo Toshimichi to obtain Letters of Credence necessary to negotiate with American officials to revise unequal treaty; 17th day, 6th month: Arrives in Washington with Ōkubo with the Letters of Credence; the same day: The mission decides not to enter into treaty negotiations with America; 7th month: Mission arrives in London; 3rd day, 12th month: Japan adopts Gregorian calendar, making that day January 1, 1873 (era name Meiji continues to be used).

1873
March 9: Arrives in Berlin; March 11: Meets with the German Kaiser (Wilhelm I) and Chancellor Otto von Bismarck; May 11: Arrives in Rome and writes to Kido and Ōkubo, both of whom returned home earlier, telling them of the wonders of Italian culture; September 13: Returns to Japan with Iwakura and other mission members; October 24: Saigō Takamori resigns as councilor (*sangi*); October 25: Itō assumes office as councilor and minister of public works; November 19: Assigned to investigate constitutions and laws.

1874
January: "Tosa Memorial" (Minsen Giin Setsuritsu Kenpakusho) calling for establishment of a national assembly submitted to the government (Left Chamber) by Itagaki, Soejima, and others.

1875
January (to early February): Osaka Conference (meeting of Itagaki, Kido, and Ōkubo arranged by Itō and Inoue Kaoru) held; April: Imperial decree issued stating that constitutional government will be established step by step; June 20: First session of the Assembly of Prefectural Governors held at Asakusa Honganji temple; July 5: Chamber of Elders (Genrōin) opened.

1877
February: Outbreak of Satsuma Rebellion, which ends when leader Saigō Takamori commits suicide on September 24.

1879
Submits proposal "On Education" (Kyōiku-gi) in September, and, on September 29, Education Order (Kyōikurei) issued.

1881
January: Meeting with Inoue Kaoru and Ōkuma Shigenobu in Atami; March: Councilor Ōkuma Shigenobu tries to secretly deliver to the emperor an opinion paper calling for a British-style parliamentary cabinet system through Minister of the Left Prince Arisugawa Taruhito; June: Inoue Kowashi submits to Iwakura Tomomi an opinion paper proposing a Prussian-style constitution granted by the emperor; July 30: The emperor permits sale of Hokkaido Colonization Office

assets; October 12: The "Political Crisis of 1881" (issues over the sale of Hokkaido Colonization Office assets and Ōkuma's opinion paper lead to dismissal of Ōkuma as councilor); three days later, Ōkuma hands in his resignation and leaves the government; October 11: Order to sell the Hokkaido Colonization Office assets cancelled; October 12: Imperial edict issued promising the establishment of a national assembly in 1890.

1882
March 14: Departs for Europe to study European constitutions.

1883
August 3: Returns to Japan; August 6: Visits the imperial palace to report to the emperor on the results of the constitutional study tour.

1884
March: Assigned as head of the Bureau for Investigation of Constitutional Systems, newly set up in the imperial court, and also as minister of the imperial household; July: The Peerage Decree issued; Itō granted the title of Count (*hakushaku*).

1885
February: Sent to China to settle issues arising from the Gapsin Coup, a failed three-day coup in Korea; April 18: Treaty of Tianjin signed between Itō and Li Hongzhang; December: Cabinet system established—abolishing the Grand Council of State (Dajōkan) and the Bureau for Investigation of Constitutional Systems—and the Cabinet Legislation Bureau set up.

1886
February: Order Concerning Forms of the Laws, Orders, and State Seals (Kōbunshiki) issued and the ministry organization system established; March: Imperial University (in Tokyo) founded; June: Itō issues an official notice to the imperial princes, cabinet ministers, the *chokunin* officials (appointed by the emperor), and peers that their wives should wear Western dress on formal occasions.

1887
March: Founds the Kokka Gakkai research association within the Imperial University; May: Gustave Boissonade, French scholar of law hired by the Japanese government, expresses opposition to precipitous revision of the unequal treaties with Western powers; July 26: Tani Tateki (Kanjō) criticizes the Itō government for its treaty revision draft and resigns as minister of agriculture and commerce; September 17: Foreign Minister Inoue Kaoru informs the Western countries of indefinite postponement of treaty revision conference and resigns (Prime Minister Itō holds the post of foreign minister concurrently until Ōkuma takes over in February of the following year).

1888
April 28: Privy Council opens and Itō, who has resigned as prime minister, becomes its first president.

1889
February 11: Meiji Constitution promulgated; February 26: Itō delivers speech on the constitution at the Kazoku Dōhō Kai (*Kazoku Dōhō Kai enzetsushū* [Kazoku Dōhō Kai Collection of Speeches], no. 5); February 27: Gives speech to the imperial princes and the peers; June: Publishes *Kenpō gikai* [Commentaries on the Constitution]; December 24: Cabinet Organization Order issued.

1890
November 25: First session of the Imperial Diet held.

1891
May 11: Ōtsu Incident (attempt to assassinate Russian Crown Prince Nicholai II, then visiting Japan); September 21: Itō gives lecture on constitutionalism in Yamaguchi prefecture.

1892
January: Tries to form a political party based on the existing government party (Taiseikai), without success due to the emperor's opposition; August: Second Itō cabinet formed.

1894
August: First Sino-Japanese War breaks out.

1895
April: Treaty of Shimonoseki signed with China, followed by diplomatic intervention by Germany, France, and Russia over the terms of the treaty, forcing Japan to accept the intervention the following month; Itō granted the title of Marquis (*kōshaku*).

1896
August 31: Resigns as prime minister.

1898
January: Third Itō cabinet formed; June 10: House of Representatives dissolved, Itō expressing his intention to found a political party at cabinet meeting; June 14: Itō invites businessmen to Imperial Hotel and sets up founders' council in preparation for new party; June 22: Shinpotō (Progressive party) and Jiyūtō (Liberal party) are merged to form Kenseitō (Constitutional party), a major opposition party; June 24: At a meeting of elders Itō proposes creation of a party to counter the Constitutional party but Yamagata and others oppose; same day: Itō has an audience with the emperor, submitting his resignation as prime minister, offering

to return his order of merit and peerage to the emperor, and recommending that Itagaki and Ōkuma form a new cabinet; June 30: Ōkuma-Itagaki cabinet formed; August 19: Itō leaves Nagasaki for tour of Korea and China; August 25: Arrives in Seoul and meets with Korean Emperor Gojong; September 14: Arrives in Beijing; September 15: Meets with Prince Qing (Yikuang) and Kang Youwei among others; September 20: Meets with the Chinese emperor Guangxu; September 21: Coup led by Empress Dowager Cixi; purge of Kang Youwei and other reformers; Itō arranges for Liang Qichao to board a Japanese warship to flee to Japan; September 29: Itō leaves Beijing for Tianjin; October 2: Leaves Tianjin for Shanghai (arriving there on October 5); October 13: Departs for Hankou to meet with Zhang Zhidong; October 19: Departs for Nanjing to meet with Liu Kunyi; October 31: Ōkuma submits his resignation as prime minister; November: Hearing the resignation of the entire Ōkuma cabinet, Itō cancels further tour in China and hurries back to Japan (arriving at Nagasaki on November 7); November 8: Yamagata cabinet formed.

1899
March: Prefecture and county system instituted; revision of Civil Servants Employment Order; order on the status of civil servants and order concerning the disciplinary punishment of civil servants established; April: Itō begins nationwide campaign tour to spread the idea of constitutionalism; April 9: Departs for Nagano (arrives April 13); May 8: Leaves on tour of Kansai and Kyushu regions; July 17: Revised treaties with foreign powers enforced; foreign residents no longer confined to closed settlements; August 24: The Imperial Household Research Committee set up in the court with Itō as president; September 21: General elections for prefectural assemblies start across the country; October 5: Chinese delegation led by Li Shengduo comes to Japan demanding that Kang Youwei be handed over; October 14: Itō departs on speaking tour of Hokuriku region.

1900
February: Election law revised but Itō's attempt at major expansion of the electorate prevented by Yamagata bureaucracy faction; July 28: Reveals to Itō Miyoji the name of the new party, Rikken Seiyūkai (Friends of Constitutional Government, Seiyūkai for short); August 25: Seiyūkai founding committee formed at the Kōyūkan restaurant in Shiba, Tokyo; September 15: Inaugural ceremony of the Seiyūkai held (the previous day Itō resigned as president of the Imperial Household Research Committee, succeeded as president by Hijikata Hisamoto); October 19: Fourth Itō cabinet formed, and except for the army, navy, and foreign ministers all other ministerial posts taken by Seiyūkai members.

1901
May 2: Itō submits resignation as prime minister because of disunity in the cabinet; June: First Katsura cabinet formed; July 11: Itō leaves Ōiso for speaking tour in Kansai; opening ceremonies of Seiyūkai chapters in Hyōgo, Okayama, and Yamaguchi on July 13, 15, and 18 respectively; July 20: Visits Wakamatsu steel

mill; July 22: Returns to villa in Ōiso; September 18: Departs for the United States, official purpose is to receive honorary doctoral degree at Yale University; December 2: Starts negotiating with Russian foreign minister Count Vladimir N. Lambsdorff for a Russo-Japanese entente; December 7: Amended draft of Anglo-Japanese Alliance approved at the elders' meeting.

1902
January: Anglo-Japanese Alliance signed in London.

1903
May: Compromise budget plan adopted at general meeting of Seiyūkai members (those dissatisfied with the decision quit the party one after the other); July 13: Itō becomes president of the Privy Council (and accordingly resigns as president of the Seiyūkai); three days later reappointed as president of the Imperial Household Research Committee and as advisor to the Imperial Family Economic Conference (Itō Miyoji becomes vice-president of the Committee); August: Okuda Yoshito and Ariga Nagao appointed as Committee's general affairs officials (*goyōgakari*) on the recommendation of Itō Miyoji.

1904
February 10: Japan declares war on Russia (Russo-Japanese War); March 7: Itō appointed as ambassador on special mission to inquire after the wellbeing of the Korean imperial family; March 20: Audience with the Korean emperor; May 31: Japanese government adopts a General Plan for Korea (Tai-Kan Shisetsu Kōryō); August: First Japan–Korea Treaty signed.

1905
April: Cabinet meeting decides on establishment of the right to protect Korea; September 5: The Portsmouth Peace Treaty signed; November: Itō goes to Korea to "inquire after the wellbeing of the Korean imperial family" (arrives at Pusan on November 8), the real task being to force the Korean emperor to sign a Japan–Korea treaty (to deprive Korea of its diplomatic sovereignty); November 17: Forces the Korean ministers to sign the Second Japan–Korea Treaty; December: Establishes the organization ordinance on the residency-general and the residency; December 21: Appointed as first resident-general of Korea.

1906
January: First Saionji cabinet formed, and China's constitutional research group led by Zai Ze comes to Japan (stays in Japan for one month, during which they study the Japanese constitutional system through lectures given by Kaneko Kentarō and Hozumi Yatsuka); March 2: Itō arrives in Seoul as resident-general of Korea; April 21: Leaves Seoul for a temporary return home; May 22: Elders' meeting on Manchuria issue held at the prime minister's official residence in Tokyo; June: Itō submits to the emperor proposals on regulations concerning investiture of the crown prince, school education for young

imperial family members, imperial household mourning and funeral ceremonies, state funerals, court ranks, hereditary assets of members of the peerage, enforcement of the peerage decree, enforcement of the peerage hereditary assets law, and enforcement of the imperial genealogy decree; June 23: Returns to Korea (during his absence, many riots occurred in various parts of Korea); July 1: Sends will to son-in-law Suematsu Kenchō and adopted son Yūkichi; July 2: Presses the Korean emperor to observe the Japan–Korea treaty and embarks on modernization of the Korean imperial court; July 7: Imposes a ban to regulate visiting of the imperial court by Koreans or non-Koreans; July 8: Establishes education-related laws concerning schools of various types; October 26: Issues regulations on real estate certification, legalizing the ownership of land by Japanese and other non-Koreans; November 9: Korean prime minister, Park Je-sun, requests the Japanese government to protect Koreans living in Gando; November 21: Itō leaves Seoul and, after visiting Jinhae Bay, returns to Japan temporarily and submits to the emperor drafts of the Kōshikirei Order and regulations concerning the investiture of the crown prince and school education for young imperial members.

1907
February 1: Kōshikirei Order issued, revising the Cabinet Organization Order (Article 4 was eliminated according to Article 1, paragraph 2 of the Kōshikirei Order); February 11: Supplement to the Imperial Household Law issued (national legal system established under the Meiji Constitution, Imperial Household Law, and Imperial House Ordinance as the highest laws, and general laws and imperial edicts subordinate to them); March 11: Departs for Korea; the Japanese navy formulates the garrison unit regulations (to be issued as military ordinance [*gunrei*]), while the Kōshikirei Order requires the prime minister's countersignature; Yamagata, in his May 13 letter to army minister Terauchi Masatake, expresses strong opposition to joint signature by the prime minister; June 14: Korean Cabinet Organization Order announced, modeled after the revised Cabinet Organization Order and Kōshikirei Order issued earlier in Japan; July: Hague Secret Emissary Affair; July 19: Korean Emperor Kojong steps down from the throne; July 24: Third Japan–Korea Treaty signed (Itō requested the Japanese government to dispatch military troops to maintain order in Korea); July 27: Peace Preservation Law established in Korea restricting freedom of speech, assembly, and association; August 1: Korean military dissolved; August 10: Itō leaves Seoul for Japan; August 19: Submits to Meiji Emperor the draft "On Military Ordinance"; the regency-general of Korea opens branch office in Gando; September 11: "On Military Ordinance" (Military Ordinance No. 1) approved by the emperor; September 21: Granted the title of Prince (*kōshaku*) together with Yamagata Aritomo and Ōyama Iwao; October 3: Returns to Seoul; the Japanese Crown Prince Yoshihito (later Emperor Taishō) visits Korea, attended by Katsura Tarō (then president of Oriental Society); December 14: Itō returns to Japan with Korean Crown Prince Yi Un.

1908

February: Ariga Nagao gives lectures on constitutionalism to China's constitutional research group leader Da Shou and later Li Jiaju (total of sixty lectures up to July 1909); April: Itō returns to Korea (arriving in Seoul on April 16); Newspaper Law (Korea) enacted, imposing stricter restrictions on freedom of speech; August 26: Private School Act, private school supplementary provisions, Academic Societies Act, and school textbook approval regulations enacted; November 14 and 15: Chinese Emperor Guangxu and Empress Dowager Cixi pass away (Itō fears the decreased prestige of the Beijing government may undermine the morale of local government officials and people); December 21: Korea garrison army commander Hasegawa Yoshimichi dismissed.

1909

January 7: Leaves Seoul, accompanying Emperor Sunjong on imperial tour of southern Korea; January 27: Accompanies Emperor Sunjong on imperial tour of northern Korea; February 10: Leaves for Japan; April 10: Prime Minister Katsura Tarō and Foreign Minister Komura Jutarō visit Itō to persuade him to accept Japan's annexation of Korea and Itō approves; May 21: Itō presents resignation as resident-general of Korea to Prime Minister Katsura; June 14: Resigns as resident-general of Korea, succeeded by Sone Arasuke; July 1: Leaves Ōiso for Seoul; July 6: Japanese cabinet adopts resolution to annex Korea; July 15: Leaves Korea for Japan from Incheon; July 22: Korean judicial power is transferred to Japan; August: Itō tours Tōhoku and Hokkaido accompanying the Korean crown prince; September 4: Gando treaty signed, formally recognizing Gando as part of Chinese territory; October 26: Assassinated by An Chung-gun in Harbin.

Index

"aikokushin" *see* patriotism
America's National Bank Act 21
Anglo-Japanese Alliance 132, 242
An Jun-geun 184
Ansei Purge 8
anti: -foreignism (*jōi*) 18; -government campaign 46, 54; -Japanese 186, 188, 195, 197, 199–200, 208, 210, 219; -Western ideology 11
Aoki Shūzō 28, 30–1, 34
Ariga Nagao 138–46, 152–6, 178–9, 242, 244
Assembly of Prefectural Governors 41–3, 71, 238
auditors 42–3
autocratic leadership 120

Bismarck, Otto von 15, 32, 35, 49–50, 238
Boxer Rebellion 128, 131–2, 178
British: legation 8, 15, 236; -style parliamentary cabinet system 3, 43–4, 238; -style party government 46
bunmei no seiji see civilized government
Burke, Edmund 65, 74, 118

cabinet: -led responsible government 144, 146; system 3, 44, 52, 66, 84, 138, 145, 216, 238–9
The Cabinet-Ordinance (Naikaku Shokken) 145
Cabinet Organization Order 144–9, 154, 240, 243
Central Chamber 22, 38
central government 118–20, 137, 152
Chamber of Elders *see* Genrōin
Chinese: classics 96–7, 193–4; labor force 175; market 175, 189
chokurei see imperial ordinances

Chōshū 8, 10–11, 16, 19, 35, 236–7; domain 4, 7, 9–11, 13–14, 16–17, 19, 73, 99, 236
Chōshū Five 11–12, 14
chōzen shugi see transcendental policy
Christianity 30–1, 166, 196
civilization policy 190, 209
civilized: country 31, 79, 91–3, 160, 191; government 18, 21, 32, 91–4, 107, 162, 190; people 77, 93–4, 98, 124, 190–1, 195
class system 97, 218
coinage legislation 20
colonial parliament 213
colonization 180, 184
Confucian 95, 190–1, 193–4, 200–1, 214–15, 219; conservatism 67, 169; scholars 193–5, 200–1, 209
Confucianism 166–7, 171, 193–6, 215
constitutional: campaign (stumping) tours 81, 86–7, 93–4, 98–9, 102, 106, 108, 118, 120, 153, 158, 165–6, 173, 175, 191, 220, 241; government 3, 6, 37, 39–42, 47, 50–1, 56–7, 60–1, 64, 66, 69–72, 76–81, 88, 92–6, 99, 102–3, 106–10, 121–2, 124, 127, 141, 143–4, 150, 153, 158–60, 162, 179–80, 186; reforms 127, 135, 137–8, 140, 142–3, 146, 152, 154–5, 178, 183–4, 190, 201, 206–7, 210, 214; school 142–3; state 5, 48–9, 53, 58, 61–2, 70, 78, 88, 92, 102, 107, 115, 134, 144, 153, 179, 183; study 46–8, 57, 74, 239
constitutionalism 43, 60, 71, 75, 78, 81, 103, 107–8, 110, 138, 140, 143–4, 152–4, 160, 167–8, 173, 178–80, 192, 209, 240–1, 244
Constitutional party 82, 103, 115, 125, 158, 240; *see also* Kenseitō

Constitutional Reform party 54, 78, 158; *see also* Rikken Kaishintō (Kaishintō)
continental expansion 176
Council for Korean Administration Reform 190, 192, 200

Daye iron mine 172–3, 177, 182
Diet: members 1, 65, 121; session 5–6, 81, 131, 240
diplomatic affairs 185–6
direct election system 108
Disraeli, Benjamin 120
dual legal order (system) 136–8, 154

eastern barbarians 160
educational reform 59, 192, 195–6
egalitarian society 219
1898 coup 161–3, 181; *see also* Hundred Day's Reform
elder statesmen *see genrō*
electoral campaign 103
Emperor Gojong 159, 183–6, 189, 191, 193, 195, 209, 241
emperor-granted constitution 62
Emperor Guangxu 160, 164, 241, 244
Emperor Meiji 4, 52, 210, 237
empiricism 96–7
Empress Dowager Cixi 158, 161, 163, 241, 244
Endō Kinsuke 11–12, 15, 236
expel the barbarians 9–10, 16, 67

finance ministry 12, 16, 22, 73
freedom: of expression 17, 91; of religion 31, 196–7; of speech 75, 78, 243–4
Friends of Constitutional Government *see* Rikken Seiyūkai (Seiyūkai)
Fukuzawa Yukichi 54, 78, 114, 218–19, 221

Gabo Reform 186
Gando 207–8, 211–12, 243–4
garrison 187–9, 202–3, 206–8, 210, 243–4
general-affairs official 135, 138, 140; *see also goyōgakari*
General Plan for Korea 185, 191, 196, 242
genrō 13, 132, 162, 187, 195
Genrōin 41–2, 56, 71, 238
German connection 30
Gneist, Rudolf von 33, 48–9, 51, 71, 73
gold standard 19–21
Gotō Shinpei 189

government: -military relationship 207, 210; officials 24, 32, 36, 62, 75, 78–9, 111, 156, 162, 166, 168, 183, 186, 191, 193, 200, 215, 244
goyōgakari 138, 242; *see also* general-affairs official
gradualism 20–3, 33, 35, 37, 40–3, 71, 164, 177, 191–2, 195, 197, 209
gradual reform 24, 41
Gu Hongming 172
gunrei 137, 146–7, 152, 156–7, 202, 204, 206, 243; *see also* military ordinances
Gunrei ni Kansuru Ken *see* "On Military Ordinances"
gunsei see military administrative regulations

habutae silk 87, 177
Hague Secret Emissary Affair 183, 243
haihan chiken 22
Hanawa Jirō Tadatomi 8, 236
hanbatsu 4
hanseki hōkan 18, 237
Hanyang Steel Mill 168, 172
Hara Takashi 82, 128–34, 149, 185–7, 202
Hasegawa Yoshimichi 188, 193, 207, 214, 244
Hayashi Gonsuke 161, 167, 214
hinomaru enzetsu see rising sun speech
Hisho ruisan 168
Hokkaido Colonization Office 46, 238–9
Hokuriku 86–7, 104, 106, 115, 120, 177–8, 241
Hoshi Tōru 4, 84, 101, 104–6, 115–16, 121, 128
House of Councilors 1
House of Peers 1, 114, 131, 155
House of Representatives 5, 84, 93, 110, 112, 115, 118, 121, 131, 155, 240
Hozumi Yatsuka 135, 143, 178, 242
Huang Zunxian 166–7
Hubei economic zone 175
Hundred Days' Reform 158, 174; *see also* 1898 coup
Hyōgo Proposal *see* "Kokuze kōmoku"

iaku jōsō 137, 146–8, 150, 154, 202, 204–6
Iino Kichisaburō 194–5
imperial: court 4, 10, 18, 35, 52, 135, 137, 140–3, 152, 186, 193, 197, 209, 215, 239, 243; household ordinances *see kōshitsurei*; household system 135–8, 140, 147, 183; ordinances 144–5, 149–50, 206; sovereignty 62

Imperial Diet 65, 81, 110, 218, 240
Imperial Household Law 53, 136–8, 140–1, 145, 152, 154, 243
Imperial Household Research Committee 135–8, 140–2, 144, 146–7, 152–4, 178, 183–4, 190, 201, 218, 220, 241–2
imperialist 2, 175, 178
Imperial University 35, 52–3, 156, 178, 198, 218–19, 239
Inner Mongolia 210
Inoue Kaoru 11–14, 32–3, 44, 47, 51, 56, 58–9, 71–4, 77, 98–9, 114, 128–33, 155, 168–9, 181, 186, 236, 238–9
Inoue Kowashi 2–3, 44–5, 52, 56–7, 72, 101, 238
Inukai Tsuyoshi 46, 54, 167
investigating constitutional government 39–41, 71
Itagaki Taisuke 1, 37, 43, 72, 82–4, 103–5, 115, 123, 125, 155, 158, 162, 168, 200, 238, 241
Itō Miyoji 66, 78–80, 99, 101, 106, 115, 117, 121, 128, 131, 135–6, 138, 140, 146–7, 150, 154–6, 179, 241–2
Iwakura Mission 14–15, 23–4, 32, 37–9, 43, 71–2, 159, 237–8
Iwakura paper on constitution 45, 238
Iwakura Tomomi 14, 23–5, 27–8, 30, 34, 37–9, 44–6, 52, 56–7, 72–3, 238
Iwasaki Yanosuke 113–14

Jakō-no-ma 41, 72
Japan-Korea Treaty: First 184–5, 242; Second 186–7, 209, 242–3; Third 183, 208–9, 243
Japan Overseas Education Society (Dai Nippon Kaigai Kyōiku Kai) 176, 189
jiyū minken undō 43; *see also* people's rights movement
Jiyū Minshutō *see* Liberal Democratic Party
Jiyūtō 82–3, 115, 125, 129, 155, 158, 240; *see also* Liberal party
Joseon dynasty 159, 186

Kaiser Wilhelm I 49, 71, 238
Kang Youwei 158, 160–1, 163, 165–8, 170–1, 174, 181, 241
Katō Takaaki 82, 129, 131
Katsura Tarō 131–4, 179, 187, 189, 211, 213, 241, 243–4
Kazoku Dōhō Kai 66, 74, 240
Kazoku Kaikan 41
Keiō Gijuku 54

Kenpō gikai 3, 240
Kensei Hontō 103–4, 114, 125
Kenseikai (Constitutional Association) 82
"Kensei kōgi" 140–1, 156, 179; *see also* Lectures on Constitutionalism
kensei no jōdō 82
Kenseitō 82–4, 87, 101, 103–4, 110, 115–16, 120, 125, 158, 240; *see also* Constitutional party
Kido Takayoshi 2, 4, 7–8, 16–17, 19–20, 22–3, 28–34, 36–42, 71–2, 238
Kishida Ginkō 169, 182
knowledge-based state 6
Kokka Gakkai 53, 156, 219, 239
Kokugaku (National Learning) 75, 219
Kokumin Kyōkai (Nationalist Association) 104
kokutai 62, 67, 81, 96; *see also* national polity
"Kokuze kōmoku" 18, 55, 237
Komura Jutarō 189, 211, 244
"Korea expedition" policy *see seikanron*
Korean: annexation 184, 189, 211–13; -Chinese border issue 208; empire 159; independence movement 184; intellectuals 197, 199–201
Kōshikirei Order 136–7, 144–6, 149–50, 152, 154, 190, 202–3, 205–6, 243
kōshitsurei 136, 145
Kōshitsu Tenpan *see* Imperial Household Law
kunmin kyōchi 40
Kuroda Kiyotaka 8, 46, 62–3, 77
Kuruhara Ryōzō 7–8, 10–11, 14, 97, 236
Kusaka Genzui 8, 35
Kyōiku-gi 55, 197, 238

late-Qing New Policy (*Qin mo xinzheng*) 178
Lectures on Constitutionalism 140, 179, 244; *see also* "Kensei kōgi"
Left Chamber 22, 238
Letters of Credence Incident 26, 28
Liang Qichao 161, 163, 167–8, 173, 189, 241
Liberal Democratic Party xiv, 76, 101
Liberal party 3–4, 82, 84, 106, 115, 125, 129, 159, 240; *see also* Jiyūtō
Li Hongzhang 161, 163, 168, 239

Maebara Issei 8
Maejima Hisoka 54
Manchuria and Mongolia issue 210–12, 242

248 Index

Man'en monetary reforms 21
Meiji: regime 17, 28, 42, 76; state 6, 34, 76, 135–6, 172
Meiji Constitution xiii, 2–3, 6, 43, 46–7, 51, 53, 61–2, 64, 66, 70, 72–3, 75–7, 81–4, 88–9, 93, 99, 101, 106–7, 125, 131, 135–8, 141–2, 144–6, 152–4, 158, 162, 177, 179, 188, 209, 217–8, 220, 240, 243
Meiji Restoration 2, 7, 19, 25, 90
Meiji 6-nen Seihen 38
military: administrative regulations 146–7; conscription 192; expedition to Taiwan 41; independence of 152; ordinances 146–52, 154, 156–7, 204– 6 (*see also gunrei*); reforms 164, 201
"On Military Ordinances" 137, 151
mixed residence *see naichi zakkyo*
monarchical constitution 3
Mori Arinori 200
Mosse, Albert 48–50
movement for constitutional monarchy 158
Mutsu Munemitsu 4, 89, 200

Nagai Uta 8, 10, 35
naichi zakkyo 89
Naikaku Kansei *see* Cabinet Organization Order
National Bank Regulation (Kokuritsu Ginkō Jōrei) 21
National Diet 1, 46
nationalist movement 197, 215, 219
national polity 42, 62, 64, 67–8, 80–1, 84, 96, 186; *see also kokutai*
nationwide prefectural assembly elections 108
New Currency Regulation 19–21, 35, 237
Nitobe Inazō 190
Nomura Yakichi (Masaru) 11–12, 15, 236
non-party cabinet 3
normal course of constitutional government *see kensei no jōdō*
North China Incident *see* Boxer Rebellion

Odagiri Masunosuke 168–70, 181–2
Ōkubo Toshimichi 2–3, 23, 26–7, 29–30, 33, 36, 42–9, 71–2, 238
Ōkuma-Itagaki cabinet 82–3, 99, 103, 123, 158, 162, 168, 241
Ōkuma-Ono line 57
Ōkuma paper 44–6, 71
Ōkuma Shigenobu 1, 3–4, 31–2, 43–6, 51–8, 72, 77, 82–4, 99, 103–4, 114, 123, 125, 158, 162, 167–8, 200, 238–9, 241

Ono Azusa 46, 54–7
Osaka Conference 41–2, 71–2, 238
Ōyama Iwao 148, 188, 243
Ozaki Yukio 54, 134

Pacific War 101
parliamentarianism 143
parliamentary: democracy xiii, 106; system 2, 5, 22–3, 32–3, 43, 50, 71, 75, 80, 82, 88, 91–2, 107, 192, 213, 218–19
party: cabinet 51, 66, 81–2, 84, 89, 106, 118, 123, 129, 131, 162; -led government 79, 81, 106; politics 4, 101, 103, 106, 109, 111, 118, 120, 122, 127–8, 178
patriotism 90, 96, 176
Peace Conference in The Hague 183
Peers Club *see* Kazoku Kaikan
Peers Research Association *see* Kazoku Dōhō Kai
people's rights movement 43, 46, 219; *see also jiyū minken undō*
Perry, Commodore 11
policy think-tank 53
Political Crisis of 1881 43, 46–8, 51, 53, 56, 71, 239
Political Crisis of 1873 *see* Meiji 6-nen Seihen
popular: government 5, 61, 66, 70–1, 76, 81, 84, 93, 98, 131, 134, 177, 191, 217–18, 220; participation 40, 43, 50, 64, 70–1, 76–7, 81, 88, 93, 106–7, 110, 153, 180, 213
Portsmouth Peace Conference (Treaty) 186, 242
post-annexation plan 213
pragmatism 97
Prince Itō Memorial Park 1–2
Prince Shunpo 1, 204
Principles of National Policy *see* "Kokuze kōmoku"
private school 54–5, 197–9, 244
Private School Act 199, 244
Privy Council 4, 53, 77, 134, 139, 187, 240, 242
Progressive party 82, 104, 106, 110, 114, 125, 240; *see also* Shinpotō
pro-Korea expedition 38–9
Prussian Constitution 46, 48–9, 51, 56
Prussian model (style) 3, 45, 51, 56, 238

Qing dynasty 160
Quota of Army Personnel (Rikugun Tei'in Rei) 148

Index 249

radicalism 65, 168
residency-general 187, 189–90, 207, 218, 242
Residency-General Organization Ordinance 187, 206, 210
resident-general 2, 16, 111, 149, 155, 159, 177, 179–80, 183–5, 187–93, 197–8, 201, 203, 206–10, 212–13, 215, 217, 219–20, 242, 244
Right Chamber (U-in) 22
righteous armies (ŭibyŏng) 197, 215
Rikken Kaishintō (Kaishintō) 54, 78–9, 115; *see also* Constitutional Reform Party
Rikken Seiyūkai (Seiyūkai) xiii–xiv, 4, 70, 76, 81–2, 86–7, 98, 100–3, 109–10, 112, 114–17, 120–9, 131–6, 153–4, 158, 162, 177–8, 218–20, 241–2
rising sun speech 26, 237
Roesler, Hermann 60, 73
Royal Household 62
rule of law 91–2, 168, 191–2, 207
Russo-Japanese entente 132, 242
Russo-Japanese War 61, 136, 178, 184, 189, 194, 242

Saigō Takamori 2, 4, 37–9, 42, 238
Sa-in *see* Left Chamber
Saionji Kinmochi 129, 185, 200, 202–3, 242
San Francisco 14, 23, 25, 237
Sanjō Sanetomi 27, 38, 41, 52, 54, 72–4
Satsuma-Chōshū: alliance 237; oligarchy 82–3, 162
Satsuma domain 4, 13, 73
Satsuma Rebellion 3, 42, 238
Sei-in *see* Central Chamber
seikanron 37, 72
seitai torishirabe see investigating constitutional government
sham constitutionalism (*Scheinkonstitutionalismus*) 51
Shibusawa Eiichi 112–13, 126, 177
Shinagawa Yajirō 4–5, 28, 214
Shinka Jōrei *see* New Currency Regulation
Shinpotō 82–3, 125, 240; *see also* Progressive party
shishi 8
shizoku 7
Shōka Sonjuku 7–8, 236
shūsenka 9
Sino-Japanese War 83, 111, 139, 240
the Society for *Staatswissenschaft see* Kokka Gakkai
Soejima Taneomi 28, 31–2, 238

sōmō kukki 9
sonnō jōi 9
Staatswissenschaft 49, 53
statesman: of institutions 33, 38–9, 50, 53, 61, 217; (-advocate) of knowledge (*chi no seijika*) 6, 18, 53, 61, 217
steel industry 168, 172–3
Stein, Lorenz von 49–53, 57–61, 65, 71, 74, 139, 221
Sufu Masanosuke 10–11

Taikan Shisetsu Kōryō *see* General Plan for Korea
Takasugi Shinsaku 8, 16, 236–7
Terashima Munenori 27, 39, 41
Terauchi Masatake 150, 157, 188, 203–5, 207, 216, 243
Tocqueville, Alexis de 15, 218
Tokugawa period 67
Tokugawa shogunate 6, 8, 19, 35, 73, 77, 89, 97, 217
Tokugawa Yoshinobu 18
Tokutomi Sohō 15, 127, 214
Tōkyō Senmon Gakkō (Waseda University) 54–6, 198
transcendental policy 62, 65
treaty revision 24, 27, 77, 89, 239
True Constitutional party *see* Kensei Hontō
Tsuda Umeko 15, 218
Twenty-one Demands on China 173
two-party system 51, 70

unbroken line of emperors 67
unequal treaties 5, 24, 77, 89, 98, 239
upper legislative assembly 42
Uraga 11
utilitarianism 97

Verfassung see constitutional government

Wada Tsunashirō 172–3
Watanabe Kunitake 129, 131–2
way of the king (king's way; *wangdao*) 191, 214
Western-affairs (*yangwu*) 90, 165–6
Williamson, Alexander 14–15

Yahata Steel Works 168–9, 172–3, 175, 177, 221
Yamagata Aritomo 8, 72, 74, 83–4, 87, 99, 105, 126–8, 131–2, 134, 137–8, 150–1, 155, 157–8, 162, 167, 181, 188, 195, 202–6, 212, 215–16, 240–1, 243

Yamaguchi Naoyoshi 23
Yan Fu 160
Yano Fumio 46, 54
Yikuang (Prince Qing) 160–1, 164–5, 170, 241
Yi Un (Korean Crown Prince) 212, 243–4

Yoshida Shōin 7–9, 11, 14, 16, 97, 236
Yuan Shikai 163, 178

Zhang Yinhuan 161, 166
Zhang Zhidong 162–3, 166, 168–73, 175, 182, 189, 221, 241
Zhongti-xiyong 166